Migration Law in Germany

Migration Law in Germany

Second Edition

Gerhard Robbers

This book was originally published as a monograph in the International
Encyclopaedia of Laws/Migration Law.

Founding Editor: Roger Blanpain
General Editor: Frank Hendrickx
Volume Editor: Helen Oosterom-Staples

 Wolters Kluwer

Published by:
Kluwer Law International B.V.
PO Box 316
2400 AH Alphen aan den Rijn
The Netherlands
E-mail: international-sales@wolterskluwer.com
Website: lrus.wolterskluwer.com

Sold and distributed by:
Wolters Kluwer Legal & Regulatory U.S.
7201 McKinney Circle
Frederick, MD 21704
United States of America
Email: customer.service@wolterskluwer.com

DISCLAIMER: The material in this volume is in the nature of general comment only. It is not offered as advice on any particular matter and should not be taken as such. The editor and the contributing authors expressly disclaim all liability to any person with regard to anything done or omitted to be done, and with respect to the consequences of anything done or omitted to be done wholly or partly in reliance upon the whole or any part of the contents of this volume. No reader should act or refrain from acting on the basis of any matter contained in this volume without first obtaining professional advice regarding the particular facts and circumstances at issue. Any and all opinions expressed herein are those of the particular author and are not necessarily those of the editor or publisher of this volume.

Printed on acid-free paper

ISBN 978-94-035-3472-5

e-Book: ISBN 978-94-035-3473-2
web-PDF: ISBN 978-94-035-3474-9

Printed and bound by CPI Group (UK) Ltd, Croydon, CR0 4YY

The Author

Gerhard Robbers is an emeritus Professor of Public Law at the University of Trier, Germany. For many years, he was also a judge at the Administrative Appeals Court of Rhineland-Palatinate as a member of a senate in charge of foreigners and asylum law. He has served as a judge at the Constitutional Court of Rhineland-Palatinate. From 2014 to 2016, Gerhard Robbers was Minister of Justice and for Consumer Protection of Rhineland-Palatinate.

Born in Bonn, Germany, in 1950, he received his doctoral degree in Law in 1978 and his final Law degree in 1980 in Freiburg. From 1982 to 1984, he has served as law clerk to the president of the German Federal Constitutional Court. In 1986, he obtained his *habilitation* in Law. From 1988 to 1989, he was a professor of Law at the University of Heidelberg, Germany. Professor Robbers has taught as a guest professor in many universities around the world.

A selection of the author's publications includes: *Constitutional Law in Germany*, Alphen aan den Rijn 2017, *Encyclopedia of World Constitutions* (ed.) 3 volumes, New York 2006; *An Introduction to German Law*, 7th edition, Baden-Baden 2019 (also in German: 7th edition, Baden-Baden 2019); *Encyclopedia of Law and Religion* (ed. together with Cole Durham), 5 volumes, Leiden 2016; *State and Church in the European Union* (ed.), 3rd edition, Baden-Baden 2019 (previous eds. also in German, French, Greek, Italian, Spanish, Czech, Hungarian, Polish, Russian, Georgian, Serbian, and Chinese); *Religion and Law in Germany*, 2nd edition, Alphen aan den Rijn 2013. Further publications cover public law, European Union law, constitutional history, ecclesiastical law, and legal philosophy.

The Author

Table of Contents

Table of Contents

Table of Contents

Table of Contents

Table of Contents

Table of Contents

Table of Contents

Foreign skilled workers who have an employment contract and a recognised qualification have access to all occupations they are qualified for. The previous limitation to shortage occupations has ceased to exist. Also, entry into Germany to seek employment by skilled workers has been facilitated as has been the determination of equivalence of a foreigner's occupational and vocational certificates.

Access to an economic activity has been, as a matter of principle, simplified for all foreigners. Foreigners holding a residence title may now pursue an economic activity unless there is a law prohibiting such activity. Such laws, however, remain numerous. The economic activity may be restricted by law. The pursuit of an economic activity going beyond a ban or restriction requires permission. Every residence title must indicate whether the pursuit of an economic activity is permitted or not.

3. Political Asylum

7. The fundamental right of political asylum has been guaranteed by the German Basic Law in its Article 16(2) since its entry into force in 1949. It was substantially amended by introducing the concept of safe third countries and safe countries of origin, as well as tightening procedural rules in 1993, relocating it to Article 16a of the Basic Law. Initially, the asylum procedure was regulated by the Asylum Ordinance of 1953, since 1965 by sections 28 et seq. of the Foreigners Act, and since 1982 by the Asylum Procedure Act (*Asylverfahrensgesetz*), which was substantially amended in 1992 to comply with the new rules of the Basic Law. It was renamed into Asylum Act (*Asylgesetz*, AsylG) in 2015.

B. *German Democratic Republic*

8. In the former Democratic Republic of Germany, the Foreigners Act of 28 June 1979 together with the Ordinance on Foreigners regulated entry and stay of foreigners. Rules on foreign workers were provided by intergovernmental agreements and guidelines. The Constitution of the German Democratic Republic of 1949 did contain a right of political asylum in Article 10(2). In the new 1968 Constitution it was replaced by a mere provision of discretion, in Article 23(3). These rules were abolished by the accession of the German Democratic Republic to the Federal Republic of Germany in 1990.

II. Current Applicable Legislation

A. *Federal Laws*

1. General Legal Structure

9. German migration law is somewhat complex and heterogeneous, not the least because Germany is a federation of sixteen individual federal states (*Länder*). The

most important issues of migration law lie within the competence of the Federal Republic. However, there are many areas of this field of law which belong to the competence of the federal States. Each '*Land*' is a (partly) sovereign State in its own right with the power to legislate and organise within the limits set by the federal constitution, the Basic Law (*Grundgesetz*). While the most important legislation on migration law lies in the hands of the Federal Republic, the *Länder* administer most of migration law issues, and their courts decide in the case of legal disputes with only the highest courts being those of the Federal Republic.

10. To quite an extent, migration law in Germany is also made up by EU law. EU regulations are directly applicable without any need for a further act of implementation, while EU directives are implemented through German legislation.

11. A multitude of international covenants and agreements relevant to the law on foreigners have been implemented into German law.

12. The following overview of constitutional law, laws, ordinances, regulations, and other legal documents governing migration law is a list of the most important and significant legal sources. There are also a multitude of General Administrative Rules (*Allgemeine Verwaltungsvorschrift*, AVV) which provide internal rules for the administrative authorities ensuring a uniform application of the law. The Federal Office for Migration and Refugees as well as the Federal Foreign Office present valuable information on their websites in English as well as in some other languages.[5]

2. The Basic Law

13. The constitution of the Federal Republic of Germany provides fundamental rights of foreigners, guaranteeing human rights for everyone as well as the fundamental right of political asylum. The federal constitution also determines the basic structures for legislating and administrating in the field of migration law, as well as for the competences of the courts.

3. The Residence Act

14. The most important law regulating migration and the status of migrants in Germany for persons who are not citizens of the EU is the AufenthG.[6] According to its section 1(1) the AufenthG is meant to control and restrict the influx of foreigners

---

5. http://www.bamf.de/EN/Startseite/startseite-node.html; https://www.auswaertiges-amt.de/en/einreise undaufenthalt/visabestimmungen-node.
6. Gesetz über den Aufenthalt, die Erwerbstätigkeit und die Integration von Ausländern im Bundesgebiet (Aufenthaltsgesetz – AufenthG) – Act on the Residence, Economic Activity and Integration of Foreigners in the Federal Territory (Residence Act), full citation: Residence Act in the version promulgated on 25 Feb. 2008 (BGBl. I p. 162), last amended by Art. 10 of the Act of 9 Dec. 2020

into Germany. It aims to enable and organise immigration with due regard to the capacities for admission and integration and the interests of Germany in terms of its economy and labour market. At the same time, the AufenthG aims at serving to fulfil Germany's humanitarian obligations. To this end, it regulates the entry, stay, economic activity and integration of foreigners. This is already indicated by the full title of the Act, namely: 'Act on the Residence, Economic Activity and Integration of Foreigners in the Federal Territory'. The numerous provisions contained in other Acts, such as the AsylG, remain unaffected by the AufenthG.

15. A foreigner is anyone who is not German within the meaning of Article 116(1) of the Basic Law (section 2(1) AufenthG). A German within the meaning of the Basic Law is a person who possesses German citizenship or is a so-called German by status. A German by status is a person who was admitted to the territory of the German *Reich*, within the boundaries of 31 December 1937, as a refugee or expellee of German ethnic origin or as the spouse or descendant of such person. Former German citizens, who, between 30 January 1933 and 8 May 1945, were deprived of their German citizenship on political, racial or religious grounds, as well as their descendants, have, on application, their German citizenship restored. They are deemed never to have been deprived of their German citizenship if they have established their domicile in Germany after 8 May 1945 and have not expressed a contrary intention. The Federal Law on Refugees and Exiles[7] specifies in more detail who is a German by status.

16. The AufenthG does not apply to foreigners whose legal status is regulated by the Act on the FreizügG/EU,[8] in the absence of any legal provision to the contrary. Such a provision to the contrary is, e.g., section 11 Act on the General Freedom of Movement for EU Citizens which extends a multitude of provisions of the AufenthG to persons whose legal status is regulated by the Act on the General Freedom of Movement for EU Citizens. Thus, whenever the AufenthG applies, this does not entail citizens of the other EU Member States and their dependants, nor those of the other States to which the Act on the General Freedom of Movement for EU Citizens applies (e.g., section 12 Act on the General Freedom of Movement for EU Citizens), unless indicated otherwise.

(BGBl. I p. 2855) . This volume uses and is based on the translation provided by the Language Service of the Federal Ministry of the Interior (https://www.gesetze-im-internet.de/englisch_aufenthg/englisch_aufenthg.html); the translation includes the amendment(s) to the Act by Art. 4b of the Act of 17 Feb. 2020 (BGBl. I p. 166).

7. For detailed provisions cf. Gesetz über die Angelegenheiten der Vertriebenen und Flüchtlinge (Bundesvertriebenengesetz – BVFG) – Federal Law on Refugees and Exiles, full citation: Federal Law on Refugees and Exiles in the version promulgated on 10 Aug. 2007 (BGBl. I p. 1902), last amended by Art. 162 of the Ordinance of 19 June 2020 (BGBl. I p. 1328).

8. Gesetz über die allgemeine Freizügigkeit von Unionsbürgern (Freizügigkeitsgesetz/EU – FreizügG/EU) – Act on the General Freedom of Movement for EU Citizens Freedom of Movement Act/EU, full citation: Freedom of Movement Act/EU of 30 Jul. 2004 (BGBl. I pp. 1950, 1986), last amended by Art. 1 of the Act of 12 Nov. 2020 (BGBl. I p. 2416).

17. The AufenthG also does not apply to persons who are not subject to German jurisdiction according to the Courts Constitution Act.[9] Those are the members of diplomatic missions established in Germany, the members of their families and their private servants, the members of the consular posts established in Germany, including the honorary consular officers; special international agreements concerning the exemption of these persons from German jurisdiction remain unaffected. German jurisdiction also does not apply to representatives of other States and persons accompanying them who are staying in Germany on the official invitation of the Federal Republic of Germany. Moreover, the AufenthG does not apply to persons insofar as they are exempted from German jurisdiction pursuant to the general rules of international law or on the basis of international agreements or other legislation. Furthermore, the AufenthG does not apply to certain categories of persons. This applies to those who, by virtue of treaties on diplomatic and consular communication and on the activities of international organisations and institutions, are exempted from immigration restrictions, from the obligation to notify the foreigners authority of their stay and from the requirement to have a residence title, and when reciprocity applies, insofar as this may constitute a prerequisite for such exemptions.

18. A great number of ordinances regulate further details: the Residence Ordinance (*Aufenthaltsverordnung,* AufenthV) is perhaps the most important for general issues. Further, there are, e.g., the Integration Course Ordinance (*Integrationskurs-Verordnung*), Integration Course Test Ordinance (*Integrationskurstest-Verordnung*), Ordinance on Vocational German Language Promotion (job-related language training courses) (*Verordnung über die berufsbezogene Deutschsprachförderung (Deutschsprachförderverordnung,* DeuFöV)). Collecting and processing of data on foreigners is regulated by the Central Register of Foreigners Act (*AusländerzentralregisterG*) and the Central Register of Foreigners Act's Implementing Regulations (*AZRG-DurchführungsVO*), the Law on the Establishment of a Visa Warning File (*Gesetz zur Errichtung einer Visa-Warndatei (Visa-Warndateigesetz,* VWDG)) and the Law on the Establishment of a Visa Warning File-Implementing Regulations (*Verordnung zur Durchführung des Visa-Warndateigesetzes (VWDG-Durchführungsverordnung,* VWDG-DV)).

19. A legal act with a major practical impact is the Employment Ordinance (*Beschäftigungsverordnung,* BeschV). It provides detailed rules on the employment of foreigners.

---

9. Sections 18–20 Gerichtsverfassungsgesetz (GVG) – ss 18–20 of the Courts Constitution Act, full citation: Courts Constitution Act in the version promulgated on 9 May 1975 (BGBl. I p. 1077), last amended by Art. 4 of the Act of 9 March 2021 (BGBl. I p. 327).

4. The Asylum Act

20. The AsylG[10] contains rules that apply to foreigners applying for protection against political persecution under Article 16a(1) of the Basic Law. It also applies to foreigners seeking international protection under Directive 2011/95/EU. Provisions on financial assistance to asylum seekers are found in the Asylum Seekers Benefits Act (*Asylbewerberleistungsgesetz*, AsylbLG).[11] The Ordinance on Determination of Competencies Concerning Asylum (*Asylzuständigkeitsbestimmungs-Verordnung*), the Proof of Arrival Ordinance (*Ankunftsnachweis-Verordnung*), and the Guideline on Integration Measures for Refugees (*Richtlinie Arbeitsmarktprogramm Flüchtlingsintegrationsmaßnahmen*) provide detailed rules that apply to asylum seekers.

5. The Freedom of Movement Act/EU

21. A special regime applies to citizens of the EU. The Act on the General Freedom of Movement for EU Citizens (Freedom of Movement Act/EU)[12] regulates entry into and residence in Germany by nationals of other EU Member States (EU citizens) and their dependants.

6. Other Laws and Rules

22. There are a great number of further laws and ordinances which are specifically relevant to foreigners as such. Furthermore, AVV govern the equal application of the law; these are internal rules of the German administration.

23. The Criminal Code[13] establishes punishment for crimes such as human trafficking. The Administrative Offences Act[14] governs the prosecution of administrative offences. Labour law, such as the Act to Combat Clandestine Employment (*Schwarzarbeitsbekämpfungsgesetz*, SchwarzArbG), the Act on Temporary Employment Businesses (*Arbeitnehmerüberlassungsgesetz*, AÜG), or the Posted Workers Act (*Arbeitnehmer-Entsendegesetz*, AEntG), and social law, in particular

---

10. Asylum Act – Asylgesetz (AsylG), full citation: Asylum Act in the version promulgated on 2 Sep. 2008 (BGBl. I p. 1798), last amended by Art. 3 section 1 of the Act of 9 Oct. 2020 (BGBl. I p. 2075).
11. Asylum Seekers Benefits Act – Asylbewerberleistungsgesetz (AsylbLG), full citation: Asylum Seekers Benefits Act in the version promulgated on 5 Aug. 1997 (BGBl. I p. 2022), last amended by Art. 5 of the Act of 10 March 2021 (BGBl. I p. 335).
12. Act on the General Freedom of Movement for EU Citizens (Freedom of Movement Act/EU) – Gesetz über die allgemeine Freizügigkeit von Unionsbürgern (Freizügigkeitsgesetz/EU – FreizügG/EU), full citation: Freedom of Movement Act/EU of 30 Jul. 2004 (BGBl. I pp. 1950, 1986), last amended by Art. 1 of the Act of 12 Nov. 2020 (BGBl. I p. 2416).
13. Criminal Code – Strafgesetzbuch (StGB), full citation: Criminal Code in the version promulgated on 13 Nov. 1998 (BGBl. I p. 3322), last amended by Art. 1 of the Act of 10 March 2021 (BGBl. I p. 333).
14. Administrative Offences Act – Ordnungswidrigkeitengesetz.

Book Three of the Social Code (*Sozialgesetzbuch*, SGB, *Drittes Buch (III) – Arbeitsförderung*, SGB III), also contains provisions on foreigners.

B. EU Law

24. EU law forms and influences German migration law significantly. There is a multitude of regulations, directly applicable in the EU Member States, as well as directives which have been implemented into the national legal system. In particular, there is the European Visa Code on visa requirements,[15] the VIS Regulation. The Schengen Borders Code[16] that contains rules governing the movement of persons across borders. The Dublin III Regulation (No. 604/2013),[17] which provides the principle that the first EU Member State where fingerprints are stored, an asylum claim is lodged or where the EU external border has been crossed is responsible for processing an asylum claim. The basic EU treaties, i.e., the Treaty on EU, the Treaty on the Functioning of the EU, and the Charter of Fundamental Rights of the EU contain general provisions also applicable or relating to foreigners.

C. Laws of the Länder

25. There is a multitude of legal instruments which regulate immigration issues that have been adopted by the German *Länder*. These are often *ordinances* by which the *Länder* put federal law into more detailed terms within their scope of competencies. There are also special laws on integration of foreigners, such as the Integration Act of the Free State of Bavaria[18] or the Participation and Integration Act of Baden-Wuerttemberg.[19]

D. Transitional Rules

26. The current AufenthG regulates in detail the position of foreigners who have been granted residence permission by the German authorities prior to its coming into force on 1 January 2005. There are also transitional rules applicable to those

---

15. Regulation (EC) No. 810/2009 of the European Parliament and of the Council of 13 Jul. 2009 establishing a Community Code on Visas (Visa Code), OJ 2009, L 243.
16. Regulation (EU) No 2016/399 of the European Parliament and of the Council of 9 Mar. 2016 on a Union Code on the rules governing the movement of persons across borders (Schengen Borders Code), OJ 2016, L 77/1.
17. Regulation (EU) No 604/2013 of the European Parliament and of the Council of 26 Jun. 2013 establishing the criteria and mechanisms for determining the Member State responsible for examining an application for international protection lodged in one of the Member States by a third-country national or a stateless person (recast), OJ 2013, L 180/31.
18. Bayerisches Integrationsgesetz (BayIntG) of 13 Dec. 2016, GVBl. p. 335.
19. Partizipations- und Integrationsgesetz für Baden-Württemberg (PartIntG BW) of 1 Dec. 2015, GBl. pp. 1047–1048.

affected by amendments which have been passed since then. Some of these provisions have lost much of their practical relevance. Others still have a considerable impact.

27. The continued validity of previous rights of residence, as provided for in section 101 AufenthG, is, perhaps, one of the most relevant, although little surprising rules. Further, specific rules are provided by sections 102–105c AufenthG.

III. Administrative and Judicial Authorities

A. *Foreigners Authorities*

28. The basic features of distribution of competencies in matters relating to foreigners are set out in section 71 AufenthG. The authorities that deal with foreigners as a day-to-day matter are the foreigners authorities. These are the authorities the foreigners are usually in touch with while they stay in Germany. The foreigner authorities are for the most part authorities of the *Länder*. Article 83 of the German Basic Law stipulates that the *Länder* execute federal laws in their own right. They provide for the establishment of the requisite authorities and regulate the administrative procedures. The federal government adopts AVV in order to ensure uniform practice in all of the *Länder*. This distribution of competencies also applies to the AufenthG which determines the specific competencies of the foreigners authorities, such as deciding on the granting of residence titles. Section 71(1) AufenthG stipulates that the foreigners authorities are competent for residence- and passport-related measures and rulings in accordance with the AufenthG and in accordance with provisions relating to foreigners in other Acts, such as the AsylG. A *Land* may determine that only one or several specific foreigners authorities are competent. The foreigners authorities are, e.g., also in charge of granting or refusing permission to remain pending the asylum decision (*Aufenthaltsgestattung*), whereas the asylum procedure as such is an exclusive competence of the Federal Office for Migration and Refugees.

B. *The Federal Foreign Office*

29. Foreigners abroad mostly have to contact the German diplomatic mission in their country of residence for entry and residence issues. Outside Germany, the diplomatic missions, authorised by the Federal Foreign Office, are responsible for matters relating to German passports and visa for non-nationals.

C. *The Authorities Charged with Policing Cross-Border Traffic*

30. The authorities charged with policing cross-border traffic are responsible for a variety of issues which sometimes, in extreme cases, even entail the use of bodily force. The most visible of these authorities is the Federal Police (*Bundespolizei*).

31. The authorities charged with policing cross-border traffic are responsible for removal from and refusal of entry at the border, including the transfer of third-country nationals on the basis of Regulation (EU) No 604/2013 (Dublin III Regulation) if the foreigner is apprehended by the border authority in the vicinity of the border and in close chronological proximity to an unlawful entry into Germany. They are also responsible for deportations at the border, insofar as the foreigner has been apprehended during or following unlawful entry into Germany across a border within the meaning of Article 2(1) of Regulation (European Community (EC)) No. 562/2006 (Schengen Borders Code); this is the so-called internal border, i.e., the national border of a Member State of the EU with another Member State of the EU. Furthermore, they conduct deportations at the border, insofar as the foreigner has already entered Germany unlawfully, has subsequently proceeded to another border area or to an airport, airfield, landing site or maritime or inland port, whether approved or not as a border-crossing point, where he or she has then been apprehended. They impose time limits on the effects of deportations and removals which they carry out (section 11 AufenthG). They are also responsible for the return of foreigners from and to other States and for taking foreigners into custody and effectuating an arrest where necessary to prepare and take such measures. Furthermore the authorities charged with policing cross-border traffic are responsible for granting a visa and issuing a passport substitute (section 14(2) AufenthG), and suspending deportation measures (section 60a(2a) AufenthG). They are also responsible for the withdrawal and revocation of a national visa, as well as decisions pursuant to Article 34 of Regulation (EC) No. 810/2009 (Visa Code) in the situations listed in that provision. This is the case for a refusal to grant entry permission, a removal or deportation decision, insofar as the foreigner has been apprehended during or following unlawful entry into Germany across an internal border or insofar as the foreigner has already entered Germany unlawfully, has subsequently proceeded to another border area or to an airport, airfield, landing site or maritime or inland port, whether approved or not as a border-crossing point, where the foreigner has then been apprehended. This is also the case if such a request is made by the diplomatic mission abroad which has issued a visa or at the request of the foreigners authority which has approved issuing the visa, insofar as this approval was required for that visa to be issued. The authorities charged with policing cross-border traffic are moreover competent for departure bans and the measures (section 66(5) AufenthG) that are adopted at the border, to verify, at the border, whether transport carriers and other third parties have observed the rules in the AufenthG and the ordinances and orders enacted on the basis of the AufenthG as well as for other measures and rulings adopted in accordance with the law on foreigners which prove necessary at the border and for which those authorities have been granted authorisation by the Federal Ministry of the Interior or for which they have been authorised by that Ministry in an individual case, as appropriate. Finally, these border authorities are charged with procuring return travel documents for foreigners by way of official assistance, and with the issuing of notes and certificates, as provided for by EU legislation, confirming the date and place of entry via the external border of a Member State which applies the Schengen *acquis* in full.

32. There is also the Federal Customs Service (*Bundeszollverwaltung*), which is an executive and fiscal administrative unit of the federal government and part of the Federal Ministry of Finance. One of its many tasks, such as administering federal taxes and monitoring cross-border movements of goods with regard to compliance with bans and restrictions, is the prevention of illicit work.

33. In the Free and Hansestadt Hamburg and in the Free State of Bavaria, the *Land* police authorities are also charged with policing cross-border traffic, on the basis of federal laws and administrative agreements with these *Länder*.

D. Police Forces of the Länder

34. The general police forces of the *Länder* also bear responsibility in matters concerning foreigners. This applies to matters such as: establishing a person's identity, the enforcement of allocation obligations, the execution of expulsion, detention, and custody measures.

E. Federal Office for Migration and Refugees

35. One of the publicly most visible authorities in the context of migration is the Federal Office for Migration and Refugees. It acts under the authority of the Federal Ministry of the Interior and is based on section 75 AufenthG.

36. The Federal Office for Migration and Refugees is in charge of coordinating the information on residence for the purpose of pursuing an economic activity between the foreigners authorities, the Federal Employment Agency and the German diplomatic missions abroad that are authorised by the Federal Foreign Office to deal with matters concerning passports and visas. It has to develop the basic structure and content of the integration courses (section 43(3) AufenthG) and job-related language training (section 45a AufenthG) and to implement them. It provides expert support for the Federal Government in the field of the promotion of integration and the production of information material on integration programmes offered by the Federal Government, *Land* governments and local government authorities for foreigners and ethnic German resettles. The Federal Office for Migration and Refugees conducts scientific research on migration issues as accompanying research with the aim of obtaining analytical conclusions for use in controlling immigration. It also conducts scientific research on integration issues.

37. Furthermore, the Federal Office for Migration and Refugees cooperates with the administrative authorities of the other EU Member States as the National Contact Point and competent authority (Article 27 of Directive 2001/55/EC, Article 25 of Directive 2003/109/EC, Article 22(1) of Directive 2009/50/EC, Article 26 of Directive 2014/66/EU and Article 37 of Directive (EU) 2016/801), and communicates with the other Schengen States pursuant to section 51(8a) AufenthG. It is also the registrar for the Temporary Protection Register (section 91a AufenthG).

38. The Federal Office for Migration and Refugees is in charge of examining notifications submitted in the context of mobility of students (section 16c(1) AufenthG), short-term mobility for researchers (section 18e(1) AufenthG) and short-term mobility for Intra-Corporate Transferees (ICT) (section 19a(1) AufenthG). It also is in charge of issuing certain certificates allowing entry and residence in these contexts or denying entry and residence permission for one of these purposes.

39. Further tasks of the Federal Office for Migration and Refugees are: coordinating the programmes and taking part in projects to promote the voluntary return of foreigners and paying out funds approved under those schemes; conducting the admission procedure for foreigners from specific States or certain categories of foreigners to be granted approval for admission in order to safeguard special political interests of Germany and for the resettlement refugees (section 23(2) and (4) AufenthG) and the allocation of foreigners admitted on such grounds or to protect Germany's political interests (section 23 and section 22, sentence 2 AufenthG) to the *Länder*. It further provides migration advisory services pursuant to section 45, sentence 1 AufenthG, unless such services are provided by other bodies; it may enlist the services of private or public institutions to this end and recognise research establishments in order to conclude admission agreements for researchers with those establishments (section 18d AufenthG). In the latter case, the Federal Office for Migration and Refugees is supported by a consultative council on research migration. The Office also coordinates the transfer of information and evaluates information received from the federal authorities, in particular of the Federal Criminal Police Office and the Federal Office for the Protection of the Constitution, on foreigners for whom a measure under the law on foreigners, asylum or nationality must be considered owing to a risk to public security. It is competent to impose time limits on an entry and residence ban (section 11(2) AufenthG) in the case of a deportation warning issued pursuant to sections 34, 35 AsylG, a deportation order issued pursuant to section 34a AsylG or on the order and imposition of an accompanying time frame (section 11(7) AufenthG).

F. *Commissioner for Migration, Refugees and Integration*

40. A more political institution is the Commissioner for Migration, Refugees and Integration who is appointed by the Federal Government according to section 92 AufenthG.

41. The Commissioner's office is established at one of the supreme federal authorities, currently the Federal Chancellor's Office, and may be held by a Member of the German Bundestag. The Commissioner has the status of a Parliamentary State Secretary (section 5(2), sentence 2 of the Act Governing Federal Ministers, section 7 of the Act Governing the Legal Status of Parliamentary State Secretaries). Discharge of the Commissioner's duties remains unaffected by this legal status, who is, thus not subject to orders by superiors.

42. The staff and material resources required to perform the duties of the office are provided. The budget allocation is a separate section of the individual plan of the Federal Chancellor's Office.

43. Except in the case of dismissal, the period of office of the Commissioner for Migration, Refugees and Integration ends when a new Bundestag is convened.

44. The Commissioner's duties as set out in section 93 AufenthG, are to promote the integration of migrants who are permanently resident in Germany and, in particular, to support the Federal Government in developing its integration policy, certain aspects of its employment and social policy, and to provide ideas for the further development of integration policies in the European context. The Commissioner also develops the necessary conditions for the most harmonious co-existence possible between foreigners and Germans and between different groups of foreigners; promotes mutual understanding; counteracts xenophobia and unequal treatment of foreigners; helps ensure that the interests of the foreigners resident in Germany receive due consideration, and provides information on the legal possibilities for naturalisation. In addition, the Commissioner safeguards the rights of freedom of movement of EU citizens and submits proposals for supplementary legislation to safeguard such rights. The Commission also encourages and supports initiatives to integrate migrants who are permanently resident in Germany, including such initiatives at the level of the *Länder* and local authorities as well as among social groups. Furthermore, the Commissioner has to monitor immigration to Germany and to the EU and the development of immigration to other States; to cooperate with the local authorities, *Länder*, other EU Member State authorities and the EU in those areas for which she or he is competent, and inform the public of developments in the areas of all the duties listed.

45. The Commissioner has to be involved at the earliest possible juncture in law-making projects of the Federal Government or individual federal ministries and in other matters within the scope of the Commissioner's competence. The Commissioner may submit proposals and forward opinions to the Federal Government and has to submit a report to the German Bundestag at least every two years. The federal ministries have to support the Commissioner in discharging his or her duties.

46. If the Commissioner possesses adequate information indicating that federal public bodies are guilty of unequal treatment of foreigners (section 93, No. 3 AufenthG) or fail to protect the rights of foreigners in any other way, he or she may require a statement from that body. The Commissioner may attach an own assessment to this statement and forward the statement to the public body and the latter's superior authority. The federal bodies are obliged to provide information to and to answer questions of the Commissioner. The public bodies may only transfer personal data if the data subject him- or herself has approached the Commissioner and requested her or him to take action in relation to a public body on the data subject's behalf, or if the foreigner's consent is established by any other means.

G. The Federal Employment Agency

47. A federal authority important for foreigners who want to perform economic activities is the Federal Employment Agency (*Bundesagentur für Arbeit*). It is competent for matters relating to economic activities, such as granting permission to take up employment where this is needed by law.

H. Parallel Competencies

48. In a number of issues, several authorities are competent. The foreigners authorities, the authorities charged with policing cross-border traffic and the police forces of the *Länder* are responsible for the measures that have to be taken pursuant to sections 48, 48a and 49(2)–(9) AufenthG. Measures included are examining and verifying identification papers, establishing a foreigner's identity, nationality and/or personal circumstances. If the foreigner's identity is verified by means of identification measures when allocation is ordered for a foreigner who has entered Germany unlawfully (section 15a and section 49(4) AufenthG), the authorities initiating allocation are also responsible for the execution of this measure. However, it is the diplomatic missions abroad, authorised by the Federal Foreign Office, that are competent to establish and document a foreigner's identity when he or she applies for a national visa (section 49(5), No. 5 AufenthG).

49. The police forces of the *Länder* are also responsible for removal, following an order for enforcing the obligation to leave Germany (section 12(3) AufenthG), for deportation, and, where necessary to prepare and safeguard these measures, for arrests and for applying for custody, as appropriate.

50. The Federal Ministry of the Interior decides, in consultation with the Federal Foreign Office, on the recognition of passports and passport substitutes (section 3(1) AufenthG). These decisions are general orders and may be published in the Federal Gazette (section 71(6) AufenthG).

I. Head Judicial Authorities

51. Of the utmost importance for foreigners are the courts. Measures taken by the administrative authorities in Germany can, as a rule and depending on the specific procedural provisions, be taken to court by those affected by the act. In most cases relating to foreigners as such, the administrative courts are competent. The first instance courts are the Administrative Courts. The second instance courts are the Administrative Courts of Appeal. Both instances are courts of the *Länder*. The Federal Administrative Court (*Bundesverwaltungsgericht*, BVerwG) is the highest and final instance, which is a court of the Federation. Furthermore, there is a possibility of filing a constitutional complaint to the Federal Constitutional Court or, in some cases, also to the constitutional courts of the *Länder* against administrative measures, court decisions, and laws.

§3. Overview of Applicable International Legal Instruments

52. Of the many international treaties which Germany has signed relating to the status of foreigners, the United Nations (UN) Convention Relating to the Status of Refugees of 1951 and its 1967 Additional Protocol[20] is probably the most visible. This agreement generally referred to as the Geneva Convention is complemented by the Convention Relating to the Status of Stateless Persons of 1954.[21] The European Convention on Human Rights of 1950, formally called the Convention for the Protection of Human Rights and Fundamental Freedoms,[22] is a most important reference point for many provisions of German migration law. There are a great many, predominantly, bilateral international treaties relating to the status of the respective citizens.

§4. Legal Position of Foreigners in General

I. Cooperation with Authorities

A. Presentation of Documents

53. The law obliges foreigners to cooperate in specific and manifold ways with the German authorities.

54. Foreigners are required, pursuant to section 47a AufenthG, and when requested by the authority entrusted with the task of checking a person's identity, such as police officers, the border police, or welfare authorities, to present their passport, passport substitute or substitute identity document and enable the authority to check their faces against the photograph in the document. This also obliges persons who want to cover their faces for religious reasons. The same obligations apply to the certificate confirming permission to remain pending an asylum decision (section 63(1), sentence 1 AsylG). Foreigners holding an arrival certificate (section 63a(1), sentence 1 AsylG), a residence title or a document confirming suspension of deportation (section 48(1), No. 2 AufenthG) are required to present, upon request, their arrival certificate or document to the authority entrusted with the task of checking the information stated therein and enable that authority to check their faces against the photograph on the document.

55. Similar obligations are stipulated in section 48 AufenthG. On request, a foreigner is obliged to present and surrender his or her passport, passport substitute or substitute identity document and residence title or a document confirming suspension of a deportation order to the authorities entrusted with enforcing the law on foreigners and to leave such documents with these authorities for a temporary period, where necessary in order to implement or ensure that measures can be taken in

---

20. BGBl. 1953 II p. 559.
21. BGBl. 1976 II p. 473.
22. BGBl. 1954 II p. 14.

accordance with the AufenthG. The obligation to present and surrender one's pass-port, passport substitute or substitute identity document also applies if a German national who also holds a foreign nationality, has been prohibited from leaving the country (section 10(1) of the Passport Act), and presenting, handing over and tem-porarily leaving the foreign passport or passport substitute with the German authori-ties is necessary to carry out or ensure the execution of a departure ban.

56. In the case of a foreigner who neither possesses a passport or passport sub-stitute nor can reasonably be expected to obtain one, it is sufficient for the purpose of complying with the obligation to have and present identification papers, to carry the certificate confirming a residence title or the suspension of deportation, pro-vided that such document contains the foreigner's personal details and a photo-graph and contains an indication that it is a substitute identity document.

57. If the foreigner does not possess a valid passport or passport substitute, he or she is obliged to cooperate with the authorities to obtain the necessary identity paper and to present, surrender to and leave with the authorities entrusted with enforcing the AufenthG all such documents, other papers and data carriers as may be of importance to establish a foreigner's identity and nationality and to establish and enforce a decision to return the foreigner to another State. If a foreigner fails to meet this obligation and if there is reason to believe that the foreigner is in posses-sion of such documents or data carriers, that foreigner and the objects he or she is carrying may be searched. The foreigner is required to tolerate this measure.

B. Furnishing of Information

58. Special provisions obliging a foreigner to cooperate with the German authorities are found in section 82 AufenthG. These obligations apply when a for-eigner applies for a residence title as well as in rejection procedure, where appro-priate.

59. When applying for a residence title, a foreigner is obliged to express his or her interests and any circumstances in that foreigner's favour which are not evident or known. The circumstances specified need to be verifiable. The foreigner also has to produce the necessary evidence relating to his or her personal situation, other cer-tificates, permits and documents where required, which the foreigner is able to fur-nish.

60. The foreigners authority may impose a reasonable deadline for this purpose. It has to set such a deadline when postponing the processing of an application for a residence title if the information provided is insufficient or incomplete and must specify the information still to be furnished. Circumstances put forward and docu-ments furnished after that deadline has expired may be set aside. Foreigners who have applied for an ICT Card pursuant to section 19b AufenthG are obliged to inform the competent foreigners authority of any changes that occur during the application procedure which affect the conditions for granting an ICT Card.

61. A foreigner should be notified of these obligations as well as his or her essential rights and duties under the AufenthG by the foreigners authority. This relates, in particular though not exclusively, to the duties arising from the obligation to take an integration course and the obligations relating to present or surrender identification papers. It also relates to such obligations as to furnish the authorities entrusted with enforcing the law on foreigners with information concerning ones age, identity and nationality and to submit such declarations in connection with the procurement of return travel documents. If a time limit is set, the foreigner must be informed of the consequences of a failure to observe it.

C. Personal Appearance

62. Where necessary to prepare and implement measures under the AufenthG and in accordance with provisions relating to foreigners in other Acts, an order may be issued requiring a foreigner to report personally to the competent authority and to the diplomatic missions or authorised officials of the State whose nationality the foreigner putatively possesses. It is also permitted to require a medical examination to determine whether the foreigner is fit to travel. If a foreigner fails to comply with such orders, the order may be enforced using direct force. The guarantees on treatment of persons in custody, such as a court decision, humane treatment, or limited duration of custody (section 40(1) and (2), sections 41, 42(1), sentences 1 and 3 of the Act on the Federal Police) apply accordingly.

D. Identification Measures

63. On request, the foreigner for whom a document has to be issued in accordance with the AufenthG, the AsylG or the provisions enacted to implement these Acts has to submit a current photograph or to cooperate in the taking of such a photograph and cooperate in the taking of his or her fingerprints in accordance with a statutory instrument enacted on this matter (section 99(1), No. 13 and 13a AufenthG). The photograph and the fingerprints may be incorporated into documents and processed and used by the competent authorities to document and subsequently establish a foreigner's identity.

E. Notification Requirements

64. Foreigners holding a temporary residence permit for educational purposes or for the purpose of an economic activity (Chapter 2, Part 3 or 4 AufenthG) must notify the competent foreigners authority should the employment for which the residence title was granted be terminated earlier than envisaged (section 82(6) AufenthG). Notification must be performed within two weeks from the date on which the foreigner becomes aware of the fact of early termination of the employment. The foreigner has to be informed of this obligation when the residence title is issued.

F. Data Collection

1. Data Carriers

65. Analysis of data carriers, such as smartphones, tablets or laptops, is permissible, pursuant to section 48(3a) AufenthG, only in as far as is necessary to establish a foreigner's identity and nationality and to establish and enforce a foreigner's return to another State if the purpose of the measure cannot be achieved by less restrictive means.

66. Where there is reason to believe that analysing data carriers would only provide insight into the core area of private life, the measure is not permitted. The core area of private life is the area of a strictly personal nature which the person concerned does not want to reveal to third persons. It includes emotions, thoughts, and ideas as well as sexual practices. It also applies to highly confidential communication with persons in a position of trust, such as close family members, clergy, or defence lawyers.

67. The foreigner must provide the access data required for the permissible analysis to obtain access to information on data carriers. Data carriers may only be analysed by employees who are qualified to hold judicial office. That is those persons who have passed the Second State Examination in law.

68. Insights into the core area of private life which are acquired in the course of analysing data carriers may not be used. Records thereof have to be deleted immediately. A written record has to be made of the fact that they have been acquired and subsequently deleted. Where personal data acquired in the course of analysing data carriers are no longer necessary for the purpose to establish the foreigner's identity and nationality and to establish and enforce the return of a foreigner to another State, they have to be deleted immediately.

2. Data Collection at Third Persons

69. Details on data collection beyond the foreigner's cooperation are regulated by section 48a AufenthG. Where the foreigner does not provide the access data needed to access and analyse data on devices used for telecommunication purposes, the commercial providers of telecommunication services or those involved in the provision of such services may be required, where the statutory conditions for the use of the data are met, to provide information about the data used to protect access to devices or to storage devices located in these devices or separate from them (section 113(1), sentence 2, of the Telecommunications Act (*Telekommunikationsgesetz*)). The foreigner must first be informed about a request for information. On the basis of a request for such information, the commercial providers of telecommunication services or those involved in the provision of such services must immediately transmit the data necessary to provide the information. Section 23(1) of the

Judicial Remuneration and Compensation Act (*Justizvergütungs- und -entschädigungsgesetz*) applies accordingly to compensation paid to service providers.

3. Data Collection in Specific Circumstances

70. The AufenthG enumerates permitted measures regarding a foreigner's personal data to be collected in specific circumstances. A foreigner has to tolerate all such measures.

71. In order to implement or ensure measures in accordance with the AufenthG, the authorities entrusted with the enforcement of the AufenthG may, pursuant to section 49(1) AufenthG, read out biometric and other data stored on the electronic storage and processing medium of a passport, passport substitute or substitute identity document, residence title or a document confirming suspension of a deportation order. They may obtain the necessary biometric data from the holder of one of these documents and compare the biometric data stored on them. The same applies to these documents issued to German nationals who also hold a foreign nationality, if they have been prohibited from leaving the country (section 10(1) of the Passport Act), where this is necessary to carry out or ensure compliance with a departure ban. All other authorities to whom data is transmitted from the Central Register of Foreigners (sections 15–20 of the Act on the Central Register of Foreigners (*Ausländerzentralregister-Gesetz*)) and the registration authorities are also authorised to take such measures, insofar as they are permitted to verify the authenticity of the document or the holder's identity. Biometric data comprise only the fingerprints and the photograph of a person.

G. *Establishing Identity*

72. On request, every foreigner is obliged to furnish the authorities entrusted with enforcing the law on foreigners with information on his or her age, identity and nationality and to submit such statements in connection with the procurement of return travel documents as are required by the diplomatic mission of the State whose nationality the foreigner possesses or putatively possesses and are in line with German law.

73. In case of doubt regarding the foreigner's identity, age or nationality, the measures necessary in order to establish his or her identity, age or nationality are taken if the foreigner is to be granted entry permission or a residence title or where the foreigner's deportation is to be suspended or if this is necessary in order to implement other measures in accordance with the AufenthG.

74. The foreigner's identity is verified by means of identification measures when allocation is carried out in accordance with section 15a AufenthG. This provision regulates the allocation of foreigners who have entered Germany unlawfully and do not apply for asylum and who, when their unlawful entry has been detected, cannot be placed in custody pending deportation and deported or expelled directly from custody. The correct procedure is to allocate them to the *Länder* before deciding on the suspension of a deportation or to issue a residence title.

75.   The necessary measures should be taken in order to establish and document the foreigner's identity if the foreigner intends to enter or has entered Germany with a forged or falsified passport or passport substitute or if there are other reasons to believe that the foreigner is intending to re-enter Germany unlawfully, following a refusal of entry or the termination of stay in Germany. The same applies in the case of foreigners who are enforceably required to leave Germany, insofar as removal or deportation is considered, and if that foreigner is refused entry and returned to a safe third country (section 26a(2) AsylG). The necessary measures in relation to the foreigner's identity should also be taken when the foreigner applies for a national visa or when temporary protection is granted on the basis of a decision by the Council of the EU pursuant to Directive 2001/55/EC[23] and the foreigner declares his or her willingness to be admitted into Germany (section 24 AufenthG). The same applies to a foreigner who is granted temporary protection as a foreigner from a specific third State or who belongs to a certain group, in accordance with international law, on humanitarian grounds or in order to protect the political interests of Germany, where there are special political interests or in the case of resettling persons seeking international protection. All situations are covered by section 23 AufenthG. The same measures can be adopted in the case of subsequent immigration of dependants who wish to join a foreigner (section 29(3) AufenthG). This is also the case if a public interest that justifies denying a residence title and subsequent expulsion of a foreigner (section 5(4) AufenthG) has been established. Permitted measures to establish a foreigner's identity, age or nationality in all cases with the exception of granting a national visa are: the taking of photographs and fingerprints, the taking of a person's measurements and similar measures, including bodily intrusions by a physician if in accordance with prevailing medical standards in order to establish a foreigner's age and provided that no ill effect on the latter's health is to be feared. These measures are only permitted if a foreigner is aged 14 or over. Any doubts as to whether the foreigner has reached the age of 14 are to the detriment of the foreigner. These measures are only permitted for the purpose of establishing a foreigner's identity if the identity cannot be established by other means, in particular via inquiries made to other authorities, or if the identity cannot be established in time by such other means or if such other means would involve substantial difficulties. Measures permitted in the context of granting a national visa are the taking of photographs and fingerprints.

---

23. Council Directive 2001/55/EC of 20 Jul. 2001 on minimum standards for giving temporary protection in the event of a mass influx of displaced persons and on measures promoting a balance of efforts between Member States in receiving such persons and bearing the consequences thereof, OJ 2001, L 212/12.

76. In order to determine the foreigner's country or region of origin, a foreigner's spoken word may be recorded on audio and data media. Such recordings may only be made if the foreigner is informed in advance.

77. The identity of a foreigner, who is apprehended for unlawful entry and is not refused entry, must be documented by means of identification measures. The same applies in the case of a foreigner who is residing in Germany without the required residence title. Only photographs and prints of all ten fingers may be taken. If a foreigner is younger than 14, his or her identity may only be documented by taking a photograph.

II. Decision on Residence

78. Decisions on the residence of foreigners are taken in accordance with section 79 AufenthG. They are based on the circumstances which are known in Germany and other accessible information. However, the foreigners authority decides whether the conditions apply under which deportation is inadmissible under the terms of the 1950 European Convention on Human Rights,[24] as specified in section 60(5) AufenthG, or if the foreigner should not be deported to another State as the foreigner will face a substantial and specific danger to his or her life and limb or liberty if sent there, as is specified in section 60(7) AufenthG, on the basis of the knowledge in its possession and the knowledge accessible in Germany and, where necessary in individual cases, the knowledge accessible to the federal authorities located outside Germany, such as German embassies.

III. Legal Capacity

79. Special provisions apply to the legal capacity of foreigners according to section 80 AufenthG. As a general rule, when applying the AufenthG, the provisions of the Civil Code determine whether a foreigner is regarded as a minor or an adult. Usually, minority ends at the age of 18. If a foreigner is of age according to the law of the foreigner's home country, the legal capacity and capacity to contract, however, remain unaffected.

80. A foreigner who is of age is capable of performing procedural actions pursuant to the AufenthG, provided that he or she would not be legally incapacitated according to the Civil Code or would not require supervision and prior approval in this matter.

81. A minor's lack of legal capacity does not protect him or her from being refused entry or removed. The same applies to the notice of an intention to deport

---

24. BGBl. 1952 II p. 685.

and the subsequent deportation to the country of origin, if the minor's legal representative is not resident in Germany or the latter's whereabouts in Germany are unknown.

82. The legal representatives of a minor foreigner and any other person acting on his or her behalf in Germany other than the legal representative is obliged to file the necessary applications on behalf of the minor foreigner for the issuing and extending of the residence title of that minor and the issuing and extending of a passport, passport substitute and substitute identity document.

83. Where the foreigner is under 18 years of age, any planned stay in accordance with Chapter 2 Parts 3 and 4 of the AufenthG requires the consent of the persons entitled to the foreigner's care and custody. This requirement relates to stays for educational purposes and those for the purpose of economic activity.

IV. Data Protection

84. In the context of data protection, the AufenthG provides for detailed and complex rules, especially in Part IV. These provisions aim at balancing the interests of foreigners, protecting their data, and the public interest in administrating migration legally and efficiently.

85. The authorities charged with implementing the AufenthG may collect personal data in accordance with section 86 AufenthG for the purpose of implementing the AufenthG and provisions relating to foreigners in other Acts, where this is necessary for them to discharge of their duties under the AufenthG and in accordance with the rules on foreigners in other Acts.

86. On request, public bodies with the exception of schools and other educational and care establishments for young people, inform these authorities of circumstances of which they become aware, as far as necessary as provided for in section 87 AufenthG.

87. Details of data transmission to other authorities, such as the registration authorities, the Federal Foreign Office or intra-Community data transmission and other data transmission based on EU directives are provided primarily by section 91–91g AufenthG.

88. The Federal Office of Administration (*Bundesverwaltungsamt*) keeps a database pursuant to section 49a AufenthG in which information is stored on identity documents issued by foreign public bodies and belonging to nationals of the States specified in Annex I to Regulation (EC) No. 539/2001[25] which are found in Germany. This is the Database for Found Documents. The purpose of storing this data is to establish a foreigner's identity or nationality and to enable the subsequent

---

25. OJ 2001, L 81/1.

return of foreigners. The Federal Office of Administration is a federal office that falls under the responsibility of the Federal Ministry of the Interior and that administers a large variety of matters, including some issues relating to migration.

V. Political Activities

89. Foreigners are subject to some restrictions as to their political activities. These restrictions are stipulated in section 47 AufenthG and in provisions throughout the legal system. The basic approach is that foreigners may pursue political activities within the boundaries set out in the general statutory provisions. There are several statutory provisions which entail special, mostly restricting rules on political activities of foreigners. For example, certain fundamental rights guaranteed in the Basic Law only apply to Germans, Examples are: the right to freely assemble or to found or participate in associations. On the other hand, the right to assemble also applies to foreigners as provided for in the Assembly Act. This right can, however, be more easily restricted than that of Germans. Similar rights exist at the level of ordinary law for the right to found or participate in associations. Foreigners face restrictions in the law on political parties. On the other hand, the fundamental right of free speech or freedom of the press applies to foreigners in the same way as to Germans. These rights have to be fully respected when a restriction or prohibition of a foreigner's political activities is being considered on the grounds of ordinary law.

90. A foreigner's political activities may be restricted or prohibited if they impair or endanger the development of informed political opinion in Germany, the peaceful co-existence of Germans and foreigners or of different groups of foreigners in Germany, public safety and order or any other substantial interests of Germany. The same applies if the activities may be counter to Germany's foreign policy interests or to its obligations under international law. The former can be the case, e.g., if demonstrations on foreign national memorial days could endanger Germany's foreign policy interests, and a restriction or prohibition is compellingly necessary to achieve that aim. Political activities of foreigners may also be restricted or prohibited if a foreigner's political activities contravene German laws, particularly in connection with the use of violence. If a foreigner's political activities are intended to promote parties, other organisations, establishments or activities outside Germany whose aims or means are incompatible with the fundamental values of a system of government which respects human dignity, they may also be restricted or prohibited.

91. If a foreigner's political activities endanger the free and democratic constitutional system or the security of Germany or contravene the codified standards of international law, they are to be prohibited. This has been assumed for the public endorsement of the 'State of the Kalifat' (*Kalifatstaat*) which has been prohibited as

endangering the free and democratic order of Germany.[26] Political activities of foreigners are also to be prohibited if they publicly support, advocate or incite the use of violence as a means of enforcing political, religious or other interests or are capable of inciting such violence. Political activities of foreigner's are also to be prohibited if they support organisations, political movements or groups within or outside Germany which have initiated, advocated or threatened attacks on persons or objects in Germany or attacks on Germans or German establishments outside Germany.

VI. Economic Activity

A. *General Definition*

92. The right of a foreigner to pursue an economic activity in Germany is specified on the residence title on the basis of statutory law.

93. Economic activity is defined in section 2(2) AufenthG as being self-employment, work as a civil servant, and employment within the meaning of section 7 of Book Four of the Social Code, which is any non-self-employed work, especially in an employment relationship.[27]

B. *Exceptions*

94. There are a number of exceptions from this somewhat broad definition which apply only to foreigners. These exceptions are stipulated in section 30 of the BeschV and relate mostly, although not exclusively, to short-term activities performed in Germany.

95. The law does not treat activities pursuant to sections 3 and 16 BeschV which last up to 90 days within a period of 180 days as economic activities if they are performed by certain executive employees such as members of the board of governors, or a representative of foreign companies who negotiates contracts in Germany for that company. Also not regarded as an economic activity within the meaning of the AufenthG are activities pursuant to sections 5, 14, 15, 17, 18, 19(1), 20, 22, and 23 BeschV which are performed for a period of up to ninety days within a period of twelve months by foreigners, such as visiting scholars or language teachers at a university, foreigners who are employed predominantly for charitable or religious purpose, interns or journalists. This also applies to artists, athletes or models, driving

---

26. Hörich/Hruschka, in: BeckOK AuslR, Kluth/Heusch, 21. ed., 1 Feb. 2019, §47 Aufenthaltsgesetz, 19.
27. Social Code Book Four – Sozialgesetzbuch (SGB) Viertes Buch (IV) – Gemeinsame Vorschriften für die Sozialversicherung – (Artikel I des Gesetzes vom 23 Dec. 1976, BGBl. I S. 3845).

personnel or interpreters. Furthermore, the work of those foreigners does not constitute an economic activity if they are exempted from the requirement of a residence title by sections 23–30 of the AufenthV. Examples are aircrew members, sailors, members of diplomatic missions and their dependants and employees of diplomatic missions, or rescue staff on a rescue mission.

C. Documents

96. Permission to engage in an economic activity is closely linked to the foreigner's residence title, by section 4a AufenthG.

97. Foreigners holding a residence title may pursue an economic activity unless there is a law prohibiting such activity. The economic activity may be restricted by law. The pursuit of an economic activity going beyond a ban or restriction requires permission.

98. Every residence title must indicate whether the pursuit of an economic activity is permitted and whether it is subject to any restrictions. Furthermore, residence titles must indicate any restrictions on the pursuit of employment imposed by the Federal Employment Agency.

VII. Illegally Staying Foreigners

99. Foreigners who are unlawfully staying in Germany find themselves in a difficult and precarious situation. They usually face criminal prosecution, and they can be victims of criminal exploitation. This makes life for them and their families extremely difficult. On the other hand, there is some humanitarian effort to ease their situation.

100. Private persons are in no case obliged to report foreigners who unlawfully stay in Germany to the authorities.

101. While, as a rule, public bodies have to inform the competent authorities of illegal activities of foreigners which they become aware of (section 87 AufenthG), this does not apply to all public bodies under all situations. Schools and other educational and care establishments for young people, such as kindergartens, are exempted from this obligation. This is, in particular, to protect children and young people by enabling them to be educated and live a life in human dignity. Also, medical care is available to all foreigners. Physicians, care staff, and administrative staff of hospitals do not have to report unlawfully staying foreigners to the authorities, because otherwise they would violate their obligation to observe professional secrecy; this also applies to public hospitals.

§5. BASIC PRINCIPLES OF GERMAN MIGRATION LAW

I. Open-Mindedness and Well-Functioning of the System

102. German migration law can be characterised by a number of basic principles which have developed and are developing during the course of time.

103. Germany being a country that has caused and experienced the devastating effects of xenophobia in its history has pledged itself, in its Basic Law, to be open-minded to foreigners, friendly and helpful to refugees. The German constitution guarantees human rights to everybody. Not to forget, but on a secondary level, open-mindedness to foreigners is a key precondition to the economic success of the country in international trade.

104. On the other hand, German migration law is also coined by the need to organise and to restrict immigration in order to ensure the well-functioning of the labour market and the social security systems. It has to be prudent in fostering the coherence and development of society and culture.

II. Integration

105. In doing so, German migration law has underlined the aim of integrating foreigners into German society. Integration does not mean assimilation; foreigners are not expected to cut their ties with their culture of origin. Rather, the aim of integration efforts is to assist foreigners in becoming acquainted with the way of life in Germany. A foreigner is regarded to be integrated in Germany if he or she is able to act independently in all aspects of daily life, without the assistance or mediation of third parties. In order to achieve this goal, requirements concerning language proficiency, housing conditions secure subsistence and integration courses feature throughout German migration law where the legislator believes this to be appropriate.

106. The AufenthG defines some of these requirements in detail. They are part of many individual provisions of the AufenthG.

III. Secure Subsistence

107. One of the basic requirements is that the subsistence of the foreigner is secure as a matter of principle. This general requirement is meant to protect human dignity and the health of the foreigner and also to ensure the well-functioning of the social security system in Germany. A foreigner's subsistence is secure pursuant to section 2(3) AufenthG when the foreigner is able to earn a living, including sufficient health insurance coverage, without having to take recourse to public funds. Drawing certain defined benefits, however, does not constitute recourse to public funds. These are child benefits, children's allowances, child-raising benefits, parental allowances, and educational as well as training assistance which is provided for by Book Three of the Social Code, the Federal Education and Trainings Assistance Act (*Bundesausbildungsförderungsgesetz*) or the Upgrading Training Assistance Act (*Aufstiegsfortbildungsförderungsgesetz*). Also, drawing public funds based on own contributions or granted in order to enable residence in Germany and payments made in accordance with the Act on Advance Maintenance Payments (*Unterhaltsvorschussgesetz*) do not constitute recourse to public funds in this meaning.

108. Other family members' contributions to the household income are taken into account when issuing or renewing a temporary residence permit allowing the subsequent immigration of dependants.

IV. Health Insurance

109. The requirement of sufficient health insurance coverage is met if the foreigner is enrolled in a statutory health insurance fund.

V. Sufficient Living Space

110. In the context of many residence titles, sufficient living space is required. This condition is defined in section 2(4) AufenthG. The space which is required to accommodate a person in need of accommodation in State-subsidised welfare housing constitutes sufficient living space. The law seeks to prevent discrimination against foreigners. Thus, living space which does not comply with the statutory provisions for Germans with regard to living conditions and occupancy is also not adequate for foreigners. Children up to the age of 2 are not counted when calculating 'sufficient living space' for the accommodation of families.

111. In practice, this means that for each family member above 6 years of age there must be 12 square meters living space available, and for each family member between 2 and 6 years of age 10 square meters, always in connection with adequate use of additional rooms such as kitchen and bath. These amounts may be undercut by about 10%.[28]

VI. Language Proficiency

112. Specific requirements are also defined for German language proficiency which is a prerequisite for granting many residence titles. The law distinguishes different levels of proficiency in section 2(9)–(12) AufenthG. These language levels constitute prerequisites for several entitlements to stay in Germany which are used throughout the law. The different language levels are: basic knowledge, elementary

---

28. Eichenhofer, in: BeckOK AuslR, Kluth/Heusch, 21. ed., 1 Feb. 2019, §2, 12; AVV 2.4.2.

knowledge, sufficient command, and good command of the German language. Basic knowledge of the German language corresponds to Level A 1 of the Common European Framework of Reference for Languages.[29] Elementary knowledge of the German language corresponds to Level A 2 of the Common European Framework of Reference for Languages. Sufficient command of the German language corresponds to Level B 1 of the Common European Framework of Reference for Languages. A foreigner has a good command of the German language if his or her knowledge of the German language corresponds to Level B 2 of the Common European Framework of Reference for Languages. Foreigners whose knowledge of the language corresponds to Level C 1 of the Common European Framework of Reference for Languages have an advanced command of the German language.

VII. Integration Measures

113. One of the key objects of migration law in Germany is the integration of those foreigners into the German society who live in Germany on a permanent basis. Integration being the ability to act independently in all aspects of daily life in Germany, the aim of integration is not assimilation where the foreigner would lose his or her own cultural identity if this is different from the German way of life. However, the general policy is to avoid ghettos and parallel societies. Definitions in this field are complicated and often misleading.

114. Integration efforts by the foreigners themselves are supported by a basic package of measures provided by the German State and society and designed to promote integration. An important part of these measures are the integration courses. The aim of these integration courses is to successfully impart the German language, legal system, culture and history to foreigners. In this way, foreigners are supposed to become acquainted with the way of life in Germany to such an extent as to enable them to act independently in all aspects of daily life, without the assistance or mediation of third parties.

115. A great many of German individuals and associations are engaged in schemes to assist migrants with their integration. This is a way of counteracting existing xenophobia. These initiatives in which Germans assist foreigners receive ample support from the side of the State.

---

29. Recommendation No. R(98)6 of 17 Mar. 1998 of the Committee of Ministers of the Council of Europe to Member States concerning the Common European Framework of Reference for Languages – CEFR.

Part I. Border Control and Entrance

Chapter 1. Organisation of Border Control

§1. AUTHORITIES

116. Border control is primarily the task of the Federal Police. Pursuant to section 2 of the Federal Police Act[30] (*Bundespolizeigesetz*, BpolG) it is the duty of the Federal Police to perform the protection of the German border. This applies to all German borders be they land borders, sea borders or the border at airports.

117. Border protection entails the policing of the border, police control of trans-border traffic which includes examining the documents authorising the crossing of the border and the entitlement to cross the border, searches conducted at the border, and danger prevention. The Federal Police also has to avert dangers to the security of the border within the land border area of up to a distance of 30 kilometres from the border and the coastal border, up to a distance of 50 kilometres into the land.

118. A *Land* may also take on the task of border control for the part of the German border in its territory in mutual agreement with the Federation. Such agreements stipulate, e.g., that the police forces of the respective *Land* performs policing cross-border traffic at certain smaller airports.[31]

119. The customs authorities also take care of border control at specifically identified border-crossing points pursuant sections 66 and 68 of the BpolG. In doing so, their activities are regarded as activities of the Federal Police. This does not affect their own responsibilities in controlling the traffic of goods and combatting illicit labour.

---

30. Federal Police Act – Gesetz über die Bundespolizei (Bundespolizeigesetz – BpolG).
31. Cf., e.g., s. 1 of the Administrative Agreement between the Federal Ministry of the Interior and the Bavarian State Chancellery on the Performance of Tasks of Individual Services of Border Policing of 18 Apr. 2008 (Verwaltungsabkommen zwischen dem Bundesministerium des Innern und der Bayerischen Staatsregierung über die Wahrnehmung von Aufgaben des grenzpolizeilichen Einzeldienstes in Bayern vom 17 Apr. 2008), Bekanntmachung vom 17 Apr. 2008 (Bundesanzeiger Allgemeiner Teil No. 61 p. 1448), http://www.gesetze-bayern.de/Content/Document/BayGrenzVwA bk/true?AspxAutoDetectCookieSupport=1.

120. The water police forces are forces of the individual *Länder*. They also perform border control tasks. In the harbour area of Hamburg, the water police of Hamburg is competent for the border control.[32] There is no special federal coast guard in legal terms. What is generally called 'coast guard' is a joint force of Federal Police, Customs, the Federal Waterways and Shipping Administration, and the Federal Agency for Agriculture and Food. The coast guard, as it sometimes calls itself in a colloquial manner, also performs border control tasks.

121. At the German border with EU Member States and Switzerland there is, as a matter of principle, no general policing of cross-border traffic. This applies to the borders with Belgium, the Netherlands, Luxembourg, France, Austria, the Czech Republic, Poland, and Switzerland. However, policing cross-border traffic can be reintroduced for certain periods of time for security reasons. This was, for instance, the case for the borders with Austria in order to address the influx of refugees in the summer of 2015. Since 2015 there have been border controls at the German border with Austria in national responsibility; such activities are performed on the basis of Articles 25–35 of the Schengen Borders Code[33] for cases requiring urgent action.

122. While there is no border control of persons crossing the German border into Switzerland, customs controls remain in force, since the Schengen Borders Code does not abolish such customs measures and Switzerland is not a member of the EU Customs Union.

123. The police forces of the German *Land* Free State of Bavaria have rendered support to the Federal Police in policing cross-border traffic at Germany's border with Austria. In 2018, Bavaria founded the special Bavarian Border Police for policing that border and for controlling the cross-border traffic.[34]

§2. Cooperation and Information

124. Cooperation and information requirements of public authorities are regulated in section 71a AufenthG. These provisions are important for data protection, as well as for the effective implementation of rights and duties in general.

125. There are numerous consultation requirements between various authorities listed in section 72 AufenthG, as well as rules on how to deal with such requirements. They are not easily visible for the foreigner concerned, but none the less important for being granted the necessary administrative acts.

---

32. Cf. 225 Jahre Wasserschutzpolizei Hamburg, p. 84, https://www.dpolg-hh.de/wp-content/uploads/WSP-HH-Festschrift.pdf.
33. Regulation (EU) No 2016/399 of the European Parliament and of the Council of 9 Mar. 2016 on a Union Code on the rules governing the movement of persons across borders (Schengen Borders Code), repealing Regulation EC 562/2006.
34. Act on Establishing the Bavarian Border Police – Gesetz zur Errichtung der Bayerischen Grenzpolizei vom 24 Jul. 2018, p. 607, Bayerisches Gesetz- und Verordnungsblatt No. 14/20.

Chapter 2. Right to Enter the Country

§1. CONDITIONS FOR THE RIGHT TO ENTER

I. Passport Requirement

126. There are, in general, two basic requirements which a foreigner must meet to lawfully enter Germany. These two requirements are, as a matter of principle, having a passport and a residence title.

127. Foreigners may enter or stay in Germany only if they possess a recognised and valid passport or passport substitute (section 3 AufenthG). Statutory instruments can exempt them from the passport requirement, and, thus, exemptions are found in the AufenthV. For the purpose of residence in Germany, possession of a substitute identity document (*Ausweisersatz*) is sufficient to comply with the passport requirement (section 48(2) AufenthG).

128. Minor foreigners who have not yet reached the age of 16 also satisfy the passport requirement if they are included in the passport or passport substitute of their legal representative. This only applies to a foreigner who has reached the age of 10 if his or her own photograph is included in the document of the legal representative (section 2 AufenthV).

129. There are several documents that are recognised as passport substitutes listed in sections 3 and 4 AufenthV. These are, in particular, a refugee travel document, the travel document for stateless persons, a laissez passer issued to members and servants of the institutions of the EU, travel documents issued to the members of the Parliamentary Assembly of the Council of Europe, the official ID cards of the EU Member States, the other signatory States of the Agreement of the European Economic Area (EEA) and Switzerland for their nationals, the list of travellers of school trips, a crew identification card, the inland navigation card, the travel document for foreigners, an emergency travel document, the certificate of change of residence, and the EU travel document for the return of irregularly staying third-country nationals.

130. The border-crossing certificate for foreigners, which entitles them to enter, reside and work or study in Germany is not a passport substitute. It may be granted to a foreigner who lawfully resides in a neighbouring State and returns to that State at least once a week.

131. Foreigners are exempted from the passport requirement if they enter Germany from a neighbouring State, by sea or air rescue flights from other States and provide or want to receive help in cases of accidents or catastrophes (section 14 AufenthV). The same applies to foreigners who are crew members of rescue flights.

132. In justified individual cases, the Federal Ministry of the Interior or the body designated by it (this is the Federal Office for Migration and Refugees), may also permit exemptions from the passport requirement before the foreigner enters Germany. This is possible for the purpose of crossing the border and for a subsequent stay of up to six months.

II. Residence Title Requirement

A. *General Requirement*

133. In addition to the passport requirement, foreigners need a residence title in order to enter and stay in Germany (section 4 AufenthG). Exceptions from this requirement can follow from EU law, such as the mobility rules that apply in the Schengen area. Exceptions can also result from a statutory instrument such as section 19c AufenthG by which a foreigner is not required to have a residence title for stays for ICT not exceeding 90 days within a 180-day period. Another exception is provided for stays up to 360 days within a student mobility scheme (section 16a AufenthG). There is also an exception when a right of residence exists as a result of the agreement of 12 September 1963 establishing an association between the then European Economic Community and Turkey (EEC/Turkey Association Agreement).[35]

134. The granting of a residence title presupposes, in general, according to section 5(1) AufenthG that the foreigner's subsistence is secure, that the foreigner's identity is established, as well as the foreigner's nationality, if the foreigner is not entitled to return to another State. It also presupposes, in general, that there is no public interest in expelling the foreigner. It is also, in general, required that, if the foreigner is not entitled to a residence title, the foreigner's residence does not compromise or jeopardise the interests of Germany for any other reason. Furthermore, in general, the passport requirement pursuant to section 3 AufenthG must be met.

B. *Forms of Residence Titles*

135. The residence titles provided by German migration law do not distinguish between short stay, residence, and long-term stay. Rather, these categories implicitly follow from the distinction in German migration law between the different kinds of visas, temporary residence and permanent settlement.

136. The residence titles are granted in various forms (section 4 AufenthG).

137. There is the visa (*Visum*), which is issued either as a Schengen visa for short stays, an airport transit visa (*Flughafentransitvisum*),[36] a national visa (also called visa for the federal territory, *Nationales Visum*) required for longer stays, or

---

35. EEC/Turkey Association Agreement, BGBl. 1964 II p. 509.
36. Cf. https://www.auswaertiges-amt.de/de/newsroom/buergerservice-faq-kontakt/faq/33-airporttransit visum/606472.

it can be granted as an exceptional visa which is issued by the authorities charged with policing cross-border traffic, such as the Federal Police (sections 6 and 14(2) AufenthG).

138. There is also: the temporary residence permit (*Aufenthaltserlaubnis*, section 7 AufenthG), the EU Blue Card for highly educated third-country nationals (*Blaue Karte EU*, section 19a AufenthG), the ICT Card (*ICT-Karte*, section 19b AufenthG), the Mobile ICT Card (*Mobiler-ICT-Karte*, section 19d AufenthG), the permanent settlement permit (*Niederlassungserlaubnis*, section 9 AufenthG), and the EU long-term residence permit (*Erlaubnis zum Daueraufenthalt – EU*, section 9a AufenthG).

139. A foreigner who enjoys a right of residence in accordance with the EEC/Turkey Association Agreement is obliged to provide evidence of the existence of this right of residence through the possession of a temporary residence permit. This residence permit is issued on application. This temporary residence permit is not required, however, if the foreigner is in possession of a permanent settlement permit or an EU long-term residence permit.

140. The legal provisions governing temporary residence permits also apply to the EU Blue Card, the ICT Card and the Mobile ICT Card in the absence of any law or statutory instrument to the contrary.

141. Asylum seekers receive permission to remain pending the asylum decision (*Aufenthaltsgestattung*) for the time of their asylum procedure. This permission to remain pending the asylum decision is not a residence title.

C. Residence Purposes

142. The AufenthG provides for five different purposes of stay in Germany. These are education, in particular for study purposes; economic activity; international law, humanitarian or political grounds; family reasons, in particular subsequent immigration of dependants; and special reasons for stay, e.g., of former Germans. However, other purposes are also possible.

D. Conditions

143. It is of major importance that a visa and a temporary residence permit may be issued and extended subject to conditions (section 12(2) AufenthG). Conditions, in particular geographic restrictions, may also be imposed subsequently on visa and temporary residence permit holders. Conditions, therefore, are not possible for permanent settlement permits and EU long-term permits; these are valid without conditions other than those especially provided for by law. The stay of a foreigner who does not require a residence title may be made subject to time limits, geographic restrictions, conditions and requirements.

144. A foreigner must immediately leave any part of Germany if there is no permission of the foreigners authority for him or her to stay there, Residence in that area is in breach of a geographic restriction.

145. The foreigners authority may permit a foreigner to leave the area to which the foreigner's residence is restricted on the basis of the AufenthG. This permission is granted if an urgent public interest applies, if it is necessary for compelling reasons or if denying permission would constitute undue hardship. Typical examples for such permission are the need of special medical treatment, or a birth, wedding, or death within the family. The foreigner, however, does not need a permission to attend appointments with authorities or court hearings where the foreigner's personal appearance is necessary.

§2. ADMINISTRATIVE PROCEDURES AND DOCUMENTS

I. Residence Title Application

146. There are some formal requirements for granting a residence title stipulated in section 81 AufenthG. A residence title is issued to a foreigner only upon application by the foreigner, unless otherwise specified. Such an exception is the birth of a child in Germany (section 33 AufenthG). In general, the authorities do not issue a residence title ex officio.

147. A residence title which may be obtained after entering Germany must be applied for immediately after entry or within the period stipulated in the applicable statutory instrument. The AufenthV provides for several of such situations, e.g., applications by foreigners who are already staying lawfully in Germany (sections 39–41 AufenthV). A residence title application for a child born in Germany who is not to be granted a residence title ex officio must be filed within six months of its birth. This is the case, e.g., when the parents or the parent having the sole right of custody only hold(s) a visa.

148. Residence is made somewhat easier if a foreigner who applies for a residence title is already legally resident in Germany and does not possess a residence title. This applies, e.g., to foreigners from countries whose nationals are exempted from the visa obligation. In such a case, a foreigner's residence is deemed to be permitted up to the time of the decision on the residence application by the foreigners authority. If the application is filed too late, deportation is deemed to be suspended from the time of application up to the time of the decision by the foreigners authority. If a foreigner applies for an extension of the residence title or for a different residence title before the current residence title expires, the current residence title is deemed to remain in force from the time it expires until the time of the decision of the foreigners authority. This does not, however, apply to Schengen visas and airport transit visas (section 6(1) AufenthG). If the application to issue or extend a residence title is filed too late, the foreigners authority may order that the previous residence title remains valid in order to avoid undue hardship.

149. For the period between application and decision by the authorities, the foreigner is issued a certificate confirming the effect of the application. This is called a provisional residence document.

150. If the application for a temporary residence permit allowing the subsequent immigration of dependants wishing to join the holder of an ICT Card or a Mobile ICT Card is filed at the same time as the application for an ICT Card or a Mobile ICT Card, then a decision on the application for the temporary residence permit allowing the subsequent immigration of dependants is adopted at the same time as the decision on the application for an ICT Card or Mobile ICT Card.

II. Entry Procedure

151. As a rule, pursuant to section 13(1) AufenthG, entry into and exit from Germany is permitted only at the approved border-crossing points and within the stipulated traffic hours. There can be exceptions on the basis of statutory provisions or intergovernmental agreements. These exceptions, as far as entry and exit at land borders are concerned, today constitute the rule. According to Article 1(1) and (22) of the Schengen Borders Code[37] internal borders may be crossed at any point without a border check on persons, irrespective of their nationality, being carried out. This applies to all common borders, including river and lake borders, with Germany's neighbouring countries, which are all EU Member States that apply the Schengen *acquis*, Germany's airports as far as flights to and from other EU Member States are concerned, and its sea, river and lake ports with regular internal ferry connections. The other borders are external borders. Thus, e.g., German airports are external borders as far as flights to and from countries to which the Schengen Borders Code does not apply are concerned.

152. Foreigners are obliged to carry a recognised and valid passport or passport substitute when entering or leaving Germany and to submit it to the police control of cross-border traffic as far as such exceptions do not apply. A foreigner is deemed to have entered Germany only after having crossed the border and passed through the border checkpoint. Should the authorities charged with policing cross-border traffic allow a foreigner to pass the border checkpoint for a specific temporary purpose prior to a decision on the refusal of entry (section 15 AufenthG, section 18, 18a AsylG) or when this decision is being prepared, safeguarded and implemented, border crossing does not constitute entry as long as the authorities remain able to monitor the foreigner's stay. The foreigner is otherwise deemed to have entered Germany when crossing the border.

---

37. Regulation (EU) No 2016/399 of the European Parliament and of the Council of 9 Mar. 2016 on a Union Code on the rules governing the movement of persons across borders (Schengen Borders Code), OJ 2016, L 77/1.

III. Costs, Accommodation and Transport Obligations

153. The law regulates in detail the costs arising from administering the specific affairs of foreigners in sections 66–70 AufenthG. Costs arising in connection with the enforcement of a geographic restriction, a refusal of entry, removal or deportation have to be borne by the foreigner pursuant to section 66 AufenthG. In addition to the foreigner, parties who have provided the foreigners authority or the diplomatic mission abroad with a guarantor statement that they will bear the costs of the foreigner's departure are also liable for those costs.

154. The party liable for costs may be required to furnish security. The order for security, to be furnished by the foreigner or the party liable for costs of a deportation or removal (section 66(4), sentences 1 and 2 AufenthG), may be enforced by the authority that has issued the order without a prior writ of execution and without allowing a period for payment, if recovery of the costs would otherwise be at risk. By way of security for the costs relating to the foreigner's departure from Germany, return air tickets and other travel vouchers in the possession of a foreigner who is to be refused entry, removed, expelled or deported or who is permitted to enter and stay in Germany solely for the purpose of filing an application for asylum may be confiscated.

155. The AufenthG provides for a number of foreigner related obligations, which are imposed on third persons, such as transport carriers or persons who have assumed special responsibilities for foreigners.

156. In the case of a return transport obligation on the part of a transport carrier (section 64(1) and (2) AufenthG), the carrier is, in addition to the foreigner, liable for any costs for return transportation of the foreigner and for the costs which occur from the time of the foreigner's arrival at the border-crossing point until the enforcement of the decision on admission. A carrier who culpably contravenes an order prohibiting the transporting of foreigners into Germany (section 63(2) AufenthG) is, in addition to the foreigner, liable for any other costs arising from a refused entry (section 64(1) AufenthG) or from deportation (section 64(2) AufenthG).

157. In section 63 AufenthG the obligations of transport carriers are enumerated. Transport carriers are predominantly airline and shipping companies, railway companies, and bus companies. A transport carrier may only transport foreigners into Germany if they possess a valid passport and a residence title, as required.

158. The Federal Ministry of the Interior or an authority designated by it may, in agreement with the Federal Ministry of Transport and Digital Infrastructure, prohibit a transport carrier from transporting foreigners into Germany who do not possess a passport or a residence title, as required under the threat of a fine if violated. The authority designated by the Federal Ministry of the Interior for this purpose is the Federal Police National Headquarters. Any objections or legal actions do not have suspensory effect; this also applies with regard to the imposition of a fine. The fine that the transport carrier risks is no less than EUR 1,000 and no more than EUR

5,000 for each foreigner whom the transport carrier transports in contravention of such order. The fine may be set and enforced by the Federal Police National Headquarters.

159. The Federal Police National Headquarters may make special arrangements for the implementation of this obligation with transport carriers.

160. If a foreigner is refused entry, the carrier who transported the foreigner to the border is required to remove the foreigner from Germany without delay, as section 64 AufenthG stipulates.

161. This obligation applies for a period of three years with regard to foreigners who have been transported into Germany without a passport, passport substitute or a residence title, as required, and who are not refused entry because they claim political persecution, persecution within the meaning of section 3(1) AsylG or the risk of suffering serious harm within the meaning of section 4(1) AsylG, or the circumstances justifying a temporary suspension of deportation referred to in section 60(2), (3), (5) or (7) AufenthG. The obligation expires if the foreigner is granted a residence title under the terms of the AufenthG. On request of the authorities charged with policing cross-border traffic, the carrier is required to transport the foreigner to the State which issued the travel document or from which the foreigner was transported, or to another State where the foreigner's admission is ensured.

162. The operator of a commercial airport is obliged, pursuant to section 65 AufenthG, to provide suitable accommodation on the airport premises for foreigners who do not possess a passport or visa as required until the decision on admission is enforced by the border police.

IV. Letter of Commitment by Third Persons

163. Liability for living expenses is usually based on a declaration of commitment provided by a host in Germany. The resulting costs can be significant. Rules on the liability are stipulated in section 68 AufenthG. Anyone who has provided the foreigners authority or a diplomatic mission abroad with a declaration of commitment to bear a foreigner's living expenses is required, during a period of five years, to reimburse all public funds used to cover the foreigner's living expenses, including providing accommodation, medical care in case of illness and nursing care, including any expenses which are based on a legal entitlement of the foreigner. Expenses that are based on the payment of contributions, such as benefits from social insurance systems financed by contributions, however, do not have to be reimbursed. The period of five years (section 68(1), sentence 1 AufenthG) begins with the foreigner's entry which was possible, due to the declaration of commitment. The declaration of commitment does not expire before the period of five years from the foreigner's entry has elapsed, if a residence title is granted on grounds of international law, humanitarian or political reasons (Part 5 of Chapter 2 AufenthG) or if that foreigner is granted refugee or subsidiary protection status (section 3 or section 4 AsylG).

164. The declaration of commitment must be furnished in writing. The public authority, which has made expenses funded by public funds, is entitled to the reimbursement.

165. The diplomatic mission abroad has to immediately notify the foreigners authority of the existence of a declaration of commitment.

166. When it becomes aware that public funds have been used by a public authority that is entitled to reimbursement of these costs, the foreigners authority has to immediately notify the public body concerned of the fact that there is a declaration of commitment. It provides that authority with all the information necessary to assert and enforce the reimbursement claim. The public authority may only use the data thus provided for the purpose of reimbursing the costs which were made using public funds and may refuse to provide the foreigner with any further benefits.

167. These rules on reimbursement on the basis of a declaration of commitment also apply to declarations of commitment made before 6 August 2016, subject to the proviso that the period of five years becomes a period of three years (section 68a AufenthG). If this three-year period had already expired on 6 August 2016, the commitment to reimburse public funds is considered to have ended on 31 August 2016.

Chapter 3. Refusal of Entry

§1. REASONS FOR REFUSAL

168. There are several reasons to refuse entry of a foreigner into Germany (section 15(1) AufenthG). The AufenthG provides a list of reasons for unlawful entry in section 14(1) AufenthG. Entry is unlawful if the foreigner does not possess a passport or passport substitute or a residence title, as required. The entry is also unlawful if the foreigner does possess the necessary visa upon entry, but obtained it by threat, bribery or collusion or by providing incorrect or incomplete information. In these situations, a visa is revoked or annulled retrospectively. Entry is also unlawful, if a foreigner is not permitted to enter Germany because of a ban on entry and residence (section 11(1), (6) or (7) AufenthG).

169. As appropriate, the authorities charged with policing cross-border traffic may issue exceptional visas and passport substitutes (section 14(2) AufenthG). This is the case if a foreigner was not able to apply for a visa in advance due to lack of time, e.g., because of a sudden, serious illness of a close relative.

170. Exceptional visas are issued either as a Schengen visa with a maximum duration of fifteen days (Article 35(3) Regulation (EC) No. 810/2009) or as a national visa if a longer period of validity, i.e., more than ninety days, is required.

171. In a number of cases, entry may be refused at the border: if there is a public interest to expel a foreigner or if there is a well-founded suspicion that the foreigner does not intend to stay in Germany for the stated purpose. Entry may also be refused if a foreigner only possesses a Schengen visa or is exempted from the visa requirement for a short-term stay during which he or she intends to pursue an economic activity. Moreover, entry may be refused if the foreigner does not fulfil the conditions for entering and short stays in Article 6 of the Schengen Borders Code (section 15(3), section 3(1), and section 5(1) AufenthG).

172. A foreigner who is exempted from the requirement of a residence title for a temporary stay in Germany may be refused entry if the foreigner does not possess a recognised and valid passport, passport substitute or a substitute identity document, if the foreigner's subsistence is not secure, the foreigner's identity is not established, as is the foreigner's nationality, if the foreigner is not entitled to return to another State. Entry may also be refused if there is a public interest in expelling the foreigner, and, if the foreigner has no entitlement to a residence title, the foreigner's residence does compromise or jeopardise the interests of Germany for any other reason (section 15(3), section 3(1), and section 5(1) AufenthG).

§2. BAN ON ENTRY AND RESIDENCE

173. A ban on entry and residence may apply. A foreigner who has been expelled, removed or deported from Germany may not be permitted to re-enter or to stay in Germany. This foreigner is also not entitled to be granted a residence title, even if he or she is entitled thereto under the AufenthG (section 11(1) AufenthG).

174. However, by way of exception the foreigner may, before the ban on entry and residence expires, be allowed to enter Germany for a short period if the foreigner's presence is required for compelling reasons or if the denial of entry permission would constitute undue hardship (section 11(8) AufenthG). A compelling reason can be a request to appear in court. Undue hardship may be based on serious illness of a relative. Entry permission is not possible, however, if the foreigner has been deported from Germany on account of a crime against peace, a war crime or a crime against humanity, or on the basis of a deportation order to avert a special danger to the security of Germany or a terrorist threat (section 58a AufenthG), unless the supreme *Land* authority has granted an exception in an individual case.

175. However, according to section 15(4) AufenthG, section 60(1)–(3), (5) and (7)–(9) AufenthG apply accordingly. Thus, a foreigner may not be refused entry if the conditions for the 'small asylum' are met. This is, *inter alia*, the case if a danger of imposition or enforcement of the death penalty exists or if the foreigner faces a substantial and real danger to life and limb or liberty. A foreigner who has filed an application for asylum may not be refused entry if that foreigner is permitted to stay in Germany in accordance with the provisions of the AsylG.

176. According to section 11(2) AufenthG, a ban on entry and residence is subject to a time limit imposed ex officio. The period begins to run when the foreigner leaves the country. In the event of expulsion, the period is set when the expulsion order is issued. In other cases, the period starts when the deportation warning is issued, at the latest, if the foreigner is deported or removed. In addition to imposing a time limit, a condition may also be imposed in order to prevent a threat to public safety and order, in particular requiring the foreigner to provide proof of not being subject to punishment or not using illegal drugs. If this condition is not satisfied before the time limit expires, the time limit is extended ex officio when the time limit starts to run.

177. A discretionary decision is adopted regarding the length of the time limit. It may only exceed five years if the foreigner is expelled on of the ground of a criminal conviction or if the foreigner presents a serious threat to public safety and order. This period should not exceed ten years (section 11(3) AufenthG).

178. If it is no longer required for the purpose of the ban on entry and residence, the ban on entry and residence may be revoked in order to protect the legitimate interests of the foreigner, or the period of the ban may be shortened. The ban on entry and residence should be revoked if the conditions for issuing a residence title for reasons under international law or on humanitarian or political grounds (Chapter 2, Part 5 AufenthG) are met. The period of the ban may be extended on the grounds of public safety and order. Again, the decision is a discretionary one, and

the period of up to five years, in cases of criminal conviction or a serious threat to public safety and order up to ten years, apply accordingly (section 11(4) and (3) AufenthG).

179. Pursuant to section 11(5a) AufenthG, the time limit shall be twenty years if a foreigner has been deported from Germany on account of a crime against peace, a war crime or a crime against humanity, or to avert a danger to the security of Germany. No time limit applies if the foreigner has been deported on the basis of a deportation order to avert a special danger to the security of Germany or a terrorist threat (sections 11(5b), 58a AufenthG). The supreme *Land* authority may permit exceptions in individual cases.

180. A ban on entry and residence may be imposed against a foreigner pursuant to section 11(6) AufenthG who has not fulfilled the obligation to leave the country within the period allowed for departure, unless the foreigner was prevented from leaving through no fault of his or her own, or has exceeded the period allowed for departure by an insignificant amount of time. If the foreigner has been expelled, removed or deported, the ban on entry and residence must be imposed. The rules on compelling or discretionary time limits apply accordingly (section 11(1)–(6) AufenthG). The ban on entry and residence must be subject to a time limit when it is ordered because the foreigner has not fulfilled the obligation to leave the country within the period allowed for departure. The first time a ban on entry and residence is ordered for this reason, the period should not exceed one year. Otherwise, the period should not exceed three years. A ban on entry and residence is not ordered where there are grounds for temporarily suspending deportation (section 60a AufenthG) for which the foreigner was not responsible; this can be a serious illness of the foreigner.

181. Furthermore, as stated in section 11(7) AufenthG, the Federal Office for Migration and Refugees may impose a ban on entry and residence against a foreigner whose asylum application was rejected as manifestly unfounded because the foreigner comes from a safe country of origin (section 29a(1) AsylG), and who was not granted subsidiary protection, for whom the existence of the conditions for imposing a ban on deportation for reasons justified by the European Convention on Human Rights or because the foreigner faces a substantial and real danger to life and limb or liberty in the State to which the foreigner would be deported (section 60(5) or (7) AufenthG) was not established and who does not possess a residence title or whose follow-up or secondary application (section 71 or section 71a AsylG) repeatedly did not lead to a follow-up asylum procedure. The ban on entry and residence takes effect when the decision on the application for asylum assumes legal validity. If the foreigner has been expelled, removed or deported, a ban on entry and residence must be imposed. The rules on compelling or discretionary time limits apply accordingly (section 11(1)–(6) AufenthG). The ban on entry and residence must be subject to a time limit when it is ordered because the foreigner has not fulfilled the obligation to leave the country within the period allowed for departure. The first time a ban on entry and residence is ordered for this reason, the period should not exceed one year. Otherwise, the period should not exceed three years.

182. Section 11(9) AufenthG provides that if a foreigner enters Germany in contravention of a ban on entry and residence, the period during which the entry and residence ban applies will be suspended during the foreigner's stay in Germany. The period may be extended in such cases, at the most, however, with the length of the original time limit imposed. The foreigner must be informed of this possibility when a time limit is imposed for the first time. A discretionary decision is taken regarding the length of the extension. It may only exceed a period of five years if the foreigner was expelled on the ground of a criminal conviction or if the foreigner presents a serious threat to public safety and order. If the ban on entry and residence is no longer required for the purpose it was issued for, it may be revoked in order to protect the legitimate interests of the foreigner. In the alternative the period may be shortened (section 11(3) and (4), sentence 1 AufenthG).

Part II. Right of Residence: General Provisions

Chapter 1. Short Stay

§1. CONDITIONS FOR SHORT STAY

I. Schengen Visa

A. General Requirement

183. For a short stay in Germany, foreigners, in general, need a so-called Schengen visa or an airport transit visa.

184. There are numerous exceptions from these requirements, such as the short-term mobility for ICT (section 19c AufenthG). A Schengen visa, an airport transit visa or a visa exemption does not entitle the foreigner to enter the Schengen area; it only allows the foreigner to seek entry at the external border. For several states the visa requirement has been waived.[38]

185. Residence titles other than the Schengen visa, such as a temporary residence permit or a permanent settlement permit, also allow for short stays, because they entitle their holder for longer or permanent stays, anyway.

B. Scope of Entitlement

186. A Schengen visa is a visa for intended stays on the territory of the Schengen States or for the purpose of transit through this territory of up to 90 days within a period of 180 days. The basic rules are in section 6 AufenthG which refers to Regulation (EC) No. 810/2009 establishing a Community Code on Visas (Visa Code). As a Regulation, the Visa Code is directly applicable to EU law.

---

38. For a list of States cf. https://www.auswaertiges-amt.de/en/einreiseundaufenthalt/visabestimmungen -node/staatenlistevisumpflicht-node.

187. Depending on the reasons for visiting the Schengen States and the frequency of those visits, a Schengen visa can be issued as a single-entry visa, double-entry visa, or a multiple-entry visa. The period of validity must not exceed five years.[39]

188. Schengen States are, pursuant to section 2(5) AufenthG, those States in which the following legal acts apply in their entirety. These legal acts are the Convention implementing the Schengen Agreement of 14 June 1985 between the Governments of the States of the Benelux Economic Union, the Federal Republic of Germany and the French Republic on the Gradual Abolition of Checks at Their Common Borders,[40] Regulation (EU) No 2016/399 of the European Parliament and of the Council of 9 March 2016 on a Union Code on the Rules Governing the Movement of Persons across Borders,[41] and Regulation (EC) No. 810/2009 of the European Parliament and of the Council of 13 July 2009 establishing a Community Code on Visas.[42]

189. The Schengen States are most of the EU Member States; only Bulgaria, Croatia, Cyprus, Ireland, and Romania are not Schengen States. The United Kingdom is also not a Schengen State. A number of European States that are not an EU Member State are part of the Schengen area. Thus, the Schengen visa is valid for the following States: Austria, Belgium, the Czech Republic, Denmark, Estonia, Finland, France, Germany, Greece, Hungary, Italy, Latvia, Lithuania, Luxembourg, Malta, the Netherlands, Poland, Portugal, Slovakia, Slovenia, Spain, Sweden, and the non-EU States: Iceland, Norway, Switzerland, and Liechtenstein. Monaco, San Marino, and the Vatican City State are considered to be de facto part of the Schengen area, since they share open borders with their neighbouring States that are part of the Schengen area. At present, the EU Member States Bulgaria, Romania, and Croatia only apply some of the Schengen provisions; until these three countries apply what is referred to as the Schengen *acquis* in full, passport controls will remain in place at internal borders with these Member States. Andorra remains outside the Schengen Agreement; it maintains border controls with the EU Member States. In practice, as Andorra does not issue visas, and as travellers to Andorra have to travel through the Schengen area, entry requirements for that State are the same as in the Schengen area. A visitor to Andorra who needs a visa to enter the Schengen area needs a Schengen visa allowing multiple entries, a so-called multiple-entry Schengen visa, because in order to leave Andorra the visitor must re-enter the Schengen area.[43]

190. Quite a number of other States, although not or not in full part of the Schengen area, allow entry of foreigners holding only a Schengen visa, subject to some restrictions which vary according to the State concerned. These States are: Albania,

---

39. Article 24(1) of Regulation (EC) No. 810/2009/EC.
40. OJ 2000, L 239/19.
41. Schengen Borders Code, OJ 2016, L 77/1.
42. OJ 2009, L 243/1.
43. Cf. https://visitandorra.com/en/the-country/before-you-arrive/passport-visas-customs/.

Antigua and Barbuda, Belarus, Bosnia and Herzegovina, Colombia, Georgia, Gibraltar, Kosovo, Macedonia, Mexico, Montenegro, Sao Tome and Principe, Serbia, and Turkey.[44] This list of countries is subject to changes in the course of time.

191. A Schengen visa is issued as a category 'C' visa which allows its holder to enter all Schengen States. If it is issued as a category 'A' visa, it is an airport transit visa. The category 'C' visa can be issued as a single-entry visa, a double-entry visa, or as a multiple-entry visa. A single-entry visa allows its holder to enter one Schengen country; it expires when leaving that specific country. The double-entry visa allows its holder to enter, exit, and re-entry a Schengen country; it expires by leaving a country for the second time. The multiple-entry visa allows for multiple entries into a Schengen country and entry into any other Schengen country within the period of its validity.

C. Extension

192. While a Schengen visa can be issued for a period of up to 90 days within a 180-day period, it may be extended in accordance with Regulation (EC) No. 810/2009 up to a total stay of 90 days within a 180-day period if it was initially issued for a shorter period than 90 days.

193. According to Article 33 of Regulation (EC) No. 810/2009 the reasons justifying an extension are: force majeure or humanitarian reasons preventing the foreigner from leaving the territory of the EU Member States before the expiry of the period of validity of a Schengen visa or the duration of stay authorised by that visa. A visa extension is granted free of charge. The period of validity as well as the duration of stay of a visa may also be extended if the visa holder provides proof of serious personal reasons justifying the extension of the period of validity or the duration of stay. A fee of EUR 30 is charged for such an extension.

194. A Schengen visa may be extended by a further 90 days within the 180-day period concerned as provided for by Article 33 of Regulation (EC) No. 810/2009/EC, to safeguard Germany's interests or if required by international law. A Schengen visa then becomes a national visa.

195. A Schengen visa that has expired cannot be extended.

D. Discretion

196. The authority in charge of issuing the visa enjoys discretionary powers to decide on whether or not to issue a visa. There is no automatic entitlement to a

---

44. https://www.schengenvisainfo.com/non-eu-countries-where-you-can-go-with-schengen-visa/ (last updated: 28 Sep. 2018).

Schengen visa. However, any discretion used must comply with strict legal standards; it must always be dutiful discretion. The competent visa authority has to take into account all the circumstances in any given individual case.

197. When issuing a Schengen visa, the competent authorities have to establish whether the conditions for entry pursuant to Article 6(a), (c), (d), and (e) of the Visa Code (Regulation (EU) No 2016/399)[45] are met. These conditions are, in particular, that the applicant is in possession of a valid travel document entitling the holder to cross the border which has been issued within the past ten years and which is valid for at least three months after the intended departure from the Schengen area. The latter may be waived in a justified case of emergency. Furthermore, the authorities have to establish that the foreigner is not considered to be a threat to public policy, internal security, public health or the international relations of any of the EU Member States, and that the foreigner justifies the purpose and meets the conditions of the intended stay. The visa applicant also has to have sufficient means of subsistence, both for the duration of the intended stay and for the return to the foreigner's country of origin or transit to a third country into which the foreigner is certain to be admitted, or is in a position to acquire such means lawfully.

II. Airport Transit Visa

198. An airport transit visa is, as a matter of principle, required for the purpose of passing through the international transit area of German airports for the nationals of a number of States among which: Afghanistan, Sudan, India, and Somalia. Nationals from the great majority of States are exempted from this requirement. The airport transit visa is not a residence title. It is a special Schengen visa in the sense that it is regulated by the Schengen rules.

199. Pursuant to section 99(3a) AufenthG and in accordance with Article 3(2) of Regulation (EC) No. 810/2009, the Federal Ministry of the Interior has, by way of the Ordinance on Residence,[46] drawn up a list of States whose nationals must be in possession of an airport transit visa. It has also provided a multitude of exceptions to this requirement.

200. Currently, there are six airports in Germany which have transit areas where transit visas are required. These airports are: Frankfurt and Munich, which are open day and night, Hamburg, Düsseldorf, Cologne-Bonn, and Berlin-Tegel, which are closed during night hours.

201. Persons who do not need an airport transit visa enjoy the so-called transit privilege. This applies to the vast majority of passengers passing through airports in

---

45. https://eur-lex.europa.eu/legal-content/EN/TXT/HTML/?uri=CELEX:32016R0399&from=DE.
46. Cf. s. 26 AufenthV.

Germany. They do not need a visa for a stop over in Germany if they do not leave the transit area and their final destination is in a State which does not form part of the Schengen area.[47]

III. Short-Term Mobility Schemes

202. There are a number of special short-term mobility schemes, which allow for short stays within the context of broader residence programmes, designed for a specific residence purpose, such as working in trans-border corporations, study or for research purposes. These schemes are open to foreigners who hold a suitable residence permit issued by the authorities of another Member State of the EU for a specified purpose. These short-term mobility schemes are dealt with in more detail within the context of these broader residence programmes.

203. Short-term stays are facilitated within the scope of ICT by the short-term mobility scheme pursuant to section 19a AufenthG. Within this scheme, foreigners are not required to have a residence title if they wish to stay in Germany as an ICT. These stays may not exceed 90 days within a 180-day period.

204. Studying in Germany is facilitated by the rules on student mobility in section 16c AufenthG. According to this scheme a foreigner holding a residence title for study purposes in another EU Member State does not need a German residence title for a stay for the purpose of study that does not exceed 360 days.

205. The rules facilitating short-term mobility for researchers are found in section 18e AufenthG. Within this scheme, a foreigner is not required to have a residence title for a stay in Germany for research purposes if that stay does not exceed 180 days within a 360-day period.

IV. Transit

206. Foreign States may return foreigners to another State from their territory via Germany or readmit foreigners into their territory from another State via Germany pursuant to section 74a AufenthG and section 30 AufenthV. Such operations are called transit operations (*Durchbeförderung*).

207. Transit operations are carried out on the basis of several intergovernmental agreements concluded by the German government and EU legislation, in particular the Directive 2003/110/EC On Assistance in Cases of Transit for the Purposes of Removal. The foreign government needs the permission of the competent German authorities prior to the execution of a transit operation. The competent central authority to which the necessary request for transit must be directed (Article 4(5) of

---

47. Article 3 and Annex IV Regulation (EC) No. 810/2009 of 13 Jul. 2009 (Visa Code); s. 26 and Annex C AufenthV.

Directive 2003/110/EC) is the Federal Police Authority (*Bun-despolizeipräsidium*), as specified in the statutory instrument adopted pursuant to section 58(1) of the Act on the Federal Police.

208. A foreigner in transit must tolerate the interventions by the German authorities, which are necessary in connection with his or her transit journey. The rules on transit operations do not provide an individual right for the foreigner concerned.

§2. ADMINISTRATIVE PROCEDURES AND DOCUMENTS FOR SHORT STAY

209. As a matter of principle, visas have to be applied for at the German diplomatic or consular missions abroad.

210. The documents, which have to be presented when applying for a Schengen visa are: an application form that has been completely filled out; two photographs on which the whole face is visible; any Schengen visa that has previously been issued; a passport that is valid for at least three months after the end of the intended stay and with at least two empty pages proof of medical insurance with a coverage of at least EUR 30,000; an indication of the purpose of travel and the travel schedule, flight schedules; proof of accommodation, family status, and proof of means of subsistence of at least EUR 45 for each day of the intended stay.[48] There are additional requirements depending on the specific purpose of the intended stay, such as an employment contract for working purposes, an enrolment certificate for study purposes, or invitation letters.

211. An additional condition that applies for transit visas is a visa for the next transit country, if applicable, and a visa for the final destination, if applicable.

§3. LEGAL POSITION IN THE EVENT OF A SHORT STAY

212. Holders of a Schengen visa may travel through and stay in any part of the Schengen area, unless this is stipulated otherwise on the visa itself. The same applies to foreigners in a short-term mobility scheme. Airport transit visas allow stays only within the transit area of an airport. The conditions of stay during a transit operation are stipulated in the authorisation to perform the transit operation.

213. A Schengen visa does not, as a matter of principle, entitle its holder to engage in an economic activity while in Germany. This does not apply, however, if the visa that has been issued stipulates otherwise. Airport transit visas as well as transit operations do not entitle a foreigner to engage in an economic activity while in Germany.

---

48. https://www.schengenvisainfo.com/de/visum-deutschland/.

214. Many short-term activities, which theoretically do amount to paid work often do not constitute an economic activity within the meaning of the law, as stipulated in section 30 BeschV. Examples are negotiating contracts by company representatives, the work of mechanics, athletes and coaches, or artists if they do not exceed a period of ninety days. The period of time during which these activities are not to be regarded as an economic activity by the law matches, in many cases, the period of time for which the Schengen visa can be granted.

215. Most of the short-term mobility schemes are meant to facilitate economic activity and thus entitle the participant using that scheme to act accordingly.

§4. POSITION OF FAMILY MEMBERS

216. Neither a Schengen visa, nor airport transit visas, nor transit operations have any effect as such on family members. Each family member needs his or her own Schengen visa. The same applies to airport transit visas and transit operations.

Chapter 2. Residence

§1. Conditions for Residence

I. Temporary Residence Permit

217. A temporary residence permit (*Aufenthaltserlaubnis*), according to section 7 AufenthG, is a residence title which is limited in time. It is issued for the purposes of residence in the AufenthG. This Act covers quite a variety of purposes and reasons, among which economic activity, study, subsequent immigration of dependants or humanitarian reasons. In justified cases, a temporary residence permit may also be issued for a purpose of residence which is not provided for in the AufenthG. This could be, e.g., that the foreign father of the unborn child wants to be present at the birth of the child or a wealthy foreign widow wants to spend her remaining years in Germany.

218. A temporary residence permit is issued subject to a time limit which must reflect the intended purpose of residence. Should a condition that was vital to the issuance, extension or the duration of validity of a temporary residence permit cease to apply, then it is possible to reduce the length of validity of that permit.

219. A temporary residence permit may be extended as provided for in section 8 AufenthG. The same rules apply to an extension as those that apply when issuing a temporary residence permit. As a general rule, a temporary residence permit may not be extended if the competent authority has prohibited an extension in the case of a stay which is temporary by nature according to the purpose of residence or when the temporary residence permit was last extended.

220. Before a temporary residence permit is extended, it must be ascertained whether the foreigner has met his or her obligation to duly attend an integration course. If a foreigner does not comply with the obligation to duly attend an integration course pursuant to section 44a (1), sentence 1 AufenthG, this is taken into account in the decision on extending the period of validity of a temporary residence permit. Where there is no right to be issued a temporary residence permit in the first place, an application for an extension of that permit has to be refused in the case of a repeated and gross breach of the obligations to attend the integration course. Where an entitlement to an extension of a temporary residence permit only follows from the AufenthG, an extension may be refused, unless the foreigner provides evidence that he or she has achieved integration into the community and society by other means than attendance of a compulsory integration course. When deciding on this matter, due consideration must be given to the duration of lawful stay, the foreigner's legitimate ties to Germany and the consequences of a termination of the right of residence for the dependants of the foreigner who are lawfully resident in Germany. If a foreigner was or is obliged to attend an integration course because his or her command of the German language is insufficient (section 44a(1), sentence 1 AufenthG), a temporary residence permit should be extended for at the longest one year, if that foreigner has not successfully completed the integration course or has failed to provide evidence that his or her integration into the community and society has been achieved by other means.

221. These limitations do not apply to the extension of a temporary residence permit issued to a foreigner who has been granted asylum, refugee status or if a deportation ban applies (section 25(1), (2) or (3) AufenthG).

II. EU Blue Card

222. The EU Blue Card was introduced in order to simplify and promote the migration of highly qualified persons. It is based primarily on section 18b AufenthG and Council Directive 2009/50/EC.[49] The legal provisions governing temporary residence permits also apply to the EU Blue Card in the absence of any law or statutory instrument to the contrary.

III. ICT Card

223. ICT are facilitated by the ICT Card pursuant to section 19 AufenthG and Directive 2014/66/EU.[50] The legal provisions governing temporary residence permits also apply to the ICT Card if no law or statutory instrument provide otherwise.

IV. Mobile ICT Card

224. Foreigners who already have a residence title in another EU Member State and are planning to stay in Germany within the scope of ICT for more than ninety days may apply for a Mobile ICT Card pursuant to section 19b AufenthG. As long as no law or statutory instrument provides otherwise, the legal provisions governing temporary residence permits also apply to the Mobile ICT Card.

§2. ADMINISTRATIVE PROCEDURES AND DOCUMENTS FOR RESIDENCE

225. Applications for residence permission require a variety of documents as evidence that residence conditions are satisfied and trigger multiple administrative procedures depending on the specific residence permit to be issued. Procedures also vary depending on the time and place of an application. As there are various different temporary residence titles, the administrative procedures that apply and the documents that are required are dealt with when dealing with the specific temporary residence title.

---

49. OJ 2009, L 155/17.
50. OJ EU 2014, L 157/1.

§3. LEGAL POSITION OF RESIDENTS

I. Scope and Conditions

226. As a matter of principle, residence titles are issued for the whole of Germany; the holder may thus travel and stay anywhere in Germany (section 12(1) AufenthG). This does not affect the validity of a residence title pursuant to the Convention Implementing the Schengen Agreement; the German residence title can, therefore, also be valid in other Schengen States which is the case, e.g., for a Schengen visa.

227. A temporary residence permit may be issued and extended subject to the conditions in section 12(2) AufenthG. The temporary residence permit may, e.g., state that that permit becomes invalid if the employment for which the title was granted is terminated. Of immense practical importance are geographical restrictions which require a foreigner to reside and stay in a certain part of Germany. The right to remain of a foreigner who does not require a residence title may be made subject to time limits, geographic restrictions, conditions, and requirements. Such foreigners can be tourists from countries exempted from the general visa requirement.

228. Conditions, in particular geographic restrictions, may also be imposed after a visa or temporary residence permit has been issued. When this happens, a foreigner must leave the part of Germany if he or she is staying there without the permission of the foreigners authority immediately, if he or she stays there, residence is in breach of a geographic restriction (section 12(3) AufenthG).

229. The foreigners authority may permit a foreigner, whose residence is restricted to a specified part of Germany, to leave the defined residence area. This permission has to be granted if there is an urgent public interest if this is necessary for compelling reasons, such as medical treatment, or if denying permission would constitute undue hardship, e.g., to attend a family or religious ceremony. A foreigner needs no permission to attend appointments with authorities or court hearings where his or her personal appearance is necessary.

230. The right to pursue an economic activity is determined by the foreigner's specific residence title.

II. Integration Courses

A. Structure

231. A major element of German migration law is to strive for integration of foreigners into the German society. Foreigners living lawfully in Germany on a permanent basis are provided with support to help them integrate into the economic, cultural and social life of Germany and are expected to undertake commensurate integration efforts in return.

232. German migration law attempts to promote integration primarily by way of integration courses. They are provided for in sections 43 et seq. AufenthG where the premises of the German integration policy are set out. Certain foreigners are entitled to attend integration courses, and certain foreigners are obliged to do so.

233. The integration courses are coordinated and given by the Federal Office for Migration and Refugees. It has enlisted the services of a multitude of private and public organisations for this purpose, such as adult education centres and education institutions run by religious communities.

234. The integration course consists of two different parts.[51] It comprises a basic and advanced language course of identical duration to provide sufficient command of German and an orientation course on the legal system, culture and history in Germany. These courses are offered as full-time courses and as part-time courses. The latter are designed for foreigners who are in employment. The courses are completed by taking final examinations.

235. A language course and an orientation course together amount in general to 660 lessons. Each lesson lasts 45 minutes. Depending on the focus of the course which is attended by an individual foreigner, the course can be longer than the 660 lessons mentioned. The language course comprises in general a total of 600 lessons as a general integration course. In addition there are special courses of 1000 lessons which include literacy skills or helping children with their school homework.

236. The language course covers aspects of everyday life including work and career, bringing up and raising children, leisure time and social interaction, health, and housing. Topics vary depending on the different types of courses. There are, e.g., youth integration courses that deal with topics which are estimated to be of particular interest to young people, for instance applying for an apprenticeship.

237. The orientation course in general is attended after the language course and consists of sixty lessons in total. It provides information on a number of topics, such as the German legal system, history and culture, rights and obligations in Germany,

---

51. http://www.bamf.de/EN/Willkommen/DeutschLernen/Integrationskurse/InhaltAblauf/inhaltablauf-n
    ode.html.

77

ways of co-existing in society, and important values in German society such as freedom of religion, tolerance and equal rights.

238.   A foreigner has to contribute towards the costs of these integration courses. However, there is a possibility that a foreigner is partly or fully exempted from bearing these costs if there are special circumstances, in particular related to social needs. Costs differ according to the duration of a course and amount, in general, to EUR 1.95 per lesson. The total costs for integration courses thus ranges between EUR 1,365 and EUR 1,950.

B. Entitlement to Attend an Integration Course

239.   Qualified foreigners are entitled to attend an integration course, and for others there is an obligation to do so. Section 44 AufenthG stipulates when there is an entitlement, while section 44a AufenthG sets out when it is mandatory to attend an integration course.

240.   Certain foreigners residing in Germany on a permanent basis are entitled to one-time enrolment in an integration course. Permanent residence is generally assumed if a foreigner is issued a temporary residence permit valid for at least one year or has held a temporary residence permit for more than eighteen months, unless the stay is of a temporary nature; the latter is the case, e.g., if an extension of temporary residence permits has been excluded.

241.   If the requirement of residence on a permanent basis is met by the foreigner, further conditions have to be fulfilled. A foreigner is entitled to enrolment in the integration course upon receiving a temporary residence permit for the first time for employment purposes, be it employment or self-employment (sections 18, 21 AufenthG). The foreigner is also entitled to enrolment if the temporary residence permit has been granted for the purpose of subsequent immigration by dependants (sections 28, 29, 30, 32, 36, 36a AufenthG). The same applies to holders of a temporary residence permit on humanitarian grounds because of asylum, refugee or subsidiary protection status or because a temporary residence permit has been granted to the victim of human trafficking after conclusion of the criminal proceedings (section 25(1), (2), (4a), sentence 3 AufenthG). It also applies to holders of a temporary residence permit because of lasting integration (section 25b AufenthG). Also entitled is a foreigner who is a long-term resident in another Member State of the EU (section 38a AufenthG). A foreigner upon receiving a residence title as being from a specific State or belonging to a certain category of foreigners in order to safeguard special political interests of Germany is equally entitled as is a resettlement refugee (section 23(2) and (4) AufenthG).

242.   This entitlement lapses one year after the residence title establishing the entitlement was issued or when that title expires. This does not apply if the foreigner was unable to register for an integration course within that period for reasons beyond his control, such as illness.

243. The entitlement to attend an integration course, however, does not apply to children, juveniles and young adults who attend school education in Germany. It also does not apply to foreigners for whom there is no if their need for integration is discernibly minimal, e.g., because they are already well integrated. There is also no entitlement if the foreigner has a sufficient command of the German language. In this case, the entitlement to attend an orientation course remains unaffected.

244. A foreigner who is not entitled to attend an integration course may be allowed to do so if there is a place available in the course of his or her choice (section 25(5) AufenthG). This provision applies accordingly to German nationals who do not have a sufficient command of the German language and have special integration needs. The same applies to foreigners who have permission to remain pending their asylum decision and who are expected to be permitted to remain lawfully and permanently in Germany. It furthermore applies to a foreigner whose deportation has been suspended because his or her continued presence in Germany is necessary for urgent humanitarian or personal reasons or due to a substantial public interest (section 60a(2), sentence 3 AufenthG). It equally applies to a foreigner who possesses a temporary residence permit because his or her departure is impossible in fact or in law and the obstacle to deportation is not likely to disappear in the foreseeable future.

245. It is assumed that asylum applicants from a safe country of origin (section 29a AsylG) will not be permitted to remain lawfully and permanently in Germany; they are therefore not allowed to attend an integration course.

C. Obligation to Attend an Integration Course

246. As a matter of principle, integration courses are voluntary. However, as an equivalent to the entitlement to attend an integration course, certain foreigners are expected by law to integrate and for this purpose attend an integration course. The specific and detailed circumstances are set out in section 44a AufenthG.

247. All foreigners who are entitled to attend an integration course, as is stipulated in section 44 AufenthG, and who meet at least one of the following additional conditions are obliged to attend an integration course.

248. One of these alternative conditions is that the foreigner is unable to communicate at least at a basic level in the German language.

249. Foreigners entitled to take an integration course are also obliged to do so if they have been granted a residence title in order to safeguard special political interests of Germany. For instance, because they are a national of a specific State or belong to a certain category of foreigners, such as Jewish immigrants from the former Union of Soviet Socialist Republics (USSR) (section 23(2) AufenthG), and do not have a sufficient command of the German language at the time the temporary residence title was issued.

250. The same applies to the foreign spouse of a German who does not have a sufficient command of the German language when the temporary residence title was issued. Foreign spouses are also obliged to attend an integration course if their command of the German language is insufficient when they are issued a temporary residence title for the purpose of subsequent immigration of spouses, either under the general rules on subsequent immigration of spouses or in the context of subsidiary protection.

251. The additional condition is also fulfilled if the foreigner receives basic support for job seekers (Book Two of the Social Code) and a labour market integration agreement provides for participation in an integration course.

252. Furthermore, a foreigner is obliged to attend an integration course if he or she has special integration needs and the foreigners authority has requested the foreigner to participate in an integration course. This, in practice, concerns immigrants who have resided in Germany for a longer time when the integration obligation is imposed on them.

253. The same applies if the foreigner receives benefits under the AsylbLG, is asked by the competent benefit authority to participate in an integration course and who belongs to the group of persons referred to in section 44(4), sentence 2, Nos 1–3 AufenthG. This group of persons is made up of foreigners who have permission to remain pending the asylum decision and who are expected to be permitted to remain lawfully and permanently in Germany. Furthermore, it is made up of foreigners whose deportation has been suspended because their continued presence in Germany is necessary on urgent humanitarian or personal grounds or due to substantial public interests (section 60a(2), sentence 3 AufenthG). The same applies to foreigners who possess a temporary residence permit because their departure is impossible in fact or in law and the obstacle to their deportation is not likely to be removed in the foreseeable future (section 25(5) AufenthG).

254. The foreigners authority determines, when issuing a residence title, whether a foreigner is obliged to participate in an integration course (section 44a(1), sentence 1, No. 1 AufenthG). It does so if the foreigner is entitled to attend such a course (section 44 AufenthG) and is unable to communicate at least at a basic level in German. If the residence title is issued either in order to safeguard special political interests of Germany to a foreigner from a specific State or of a certain category of foreigners (section 23(2) AufenthG) or is issued to the foreign spouse of a German (section 28(1), sentence 1, No. 1 AufenthG) or for the purpose of subsequent immigration of spouses (sections 30 and 36a(1), sentence 1, first alternative AufenthG), this also applies if the foreigner does not have a sufficient command of the German language.

255. If a foreigner receives basic support for job seekers and the integration agreement (section 15 Book Two of the Social Code) specifies participation in an integration course, the foreigner is obliged to participate if the institution providing basic security for job seekers, a so-called Jobcentre, requires him or her to do so. A

'Jobcentre' is a joint office composed of the Federal Employment Agency and the local districts and district free cities that provides employment services. An integration agreement is an agreement concluded between the Federal Employment Agency and a job seeker regardless of whether the job seeker is a foreigner or a German. These integration agreements are meant to facilitate the finding of a job and often require the job seeker to take steps to improve his or her chances on the labour market.

256. In certain cases in which the foreigner receives benefits on the basis of an integration agreement, the institution providing basic security for job seekers should, as a general rule, follow the obligation imposed by the foreigners authority. These cases are determined by section 44a(1), sentence 1, Nos 1 and 3 AufenthG. They are those in which the foreigners authority has ascertained whether the foreigner is obliged to participate in an integration course because the foreigner is entitled to take such a course and is unable to communicate at least at a basic level in German. The same applies to a foreigner who is entitled to attend an integration course and does not have a sufficient command of the German language at the time a residence title is issued either in order to safeguard special political interests of Germany to a foreigner from a specific state or belonging to a certain category of foreigners (section 23(2) AufenthG). It furthermore applies if the residence title is issued to the foreign spouse of a German or for the purpose of subsequent immigration of spouses if the foreign spouse is entitled to attend an integration course and does not have a sufficient command of the German language (section 28(1), sentence 1, No. 1 AufenthG, sections 30 and 36a(1), sentence 1, first alternative AufenthG). It is also the case if the foreigner has special integration needs and the foreigners authority has required him or her to participate in an integration course.

257. If, in an individual case, the institution providing basic security for job seekers decides otherwise, it must notify the foreigners authority accordingly, which then has to revoke the obligation to attend an integration course. The obligation is revoked if it is unreasonable to expect a foreigner to attend a part-time course in addition to pursuing an economic activity.

258. When issuing a temporary residence permit to a foreigner recognised as being entitled to asylum or enjoying refugee or subsidiary protection status (section 25(1) and (2) AufenthG), the foreigners authorities may oblige the foreigner to take an integration course if he or she only has a basic command of the German language.

D. *Cessation of the Obligation to Attend an Integration Course*

259. If the obligation to duly participate in an integration course because a foreigner is unable to communicate at least at a basic level in the German language is not withdrawn or revoked, it can only expire if the foreigner has in fact duly participated in an integration course. Due participation means that the foreigner has

taken the final test and has regularly attended the lessons in such a way that successful completion of the course is possible and success is, in particular, not endangered by dropping out of the course or by frequently not attending lessons (section 14(6), sentence 2, of the Ordinance on Integration Courses).

260. The obligation to attend an integration course does not apply to foreigners who attend vocational training or any other form of training or education in Germany or who provide evidence of participation in comparable education measures in Germany. A foreigner is also not obliged to attend an integration course if attendance on a sustained basis is infeasible or unreasonable; this may be the case if the foreigner is nursing a family member, e.g., his or her mother.

261. Foreigners having a temporary residence permit for long-term residents in another EU Member State are exempted from the obligation to take an orientation course if they provide evidence that they have already participated in integration measures in another EU Member State in order to attain their legal status as a long-term resident. This does not, however, affect an obligation to attend a German language course if they lack required German language skills.

E. *Failure to Duly Attend an Integration Course*

262. If a foreigner fails to comply with the obligation to attend an integration course for reasons for which he or she is responsible or fails to pass the final integration test before his or her temporary residence permit is extended, the competent foreigners authority informs the foreigner of the possible consequences of this failure.

263. The failure has bearings on the decision to extend a temporary residence permit. Where there is no right to be issued a temporary residence permit, an application for an extension of a temporary residence permit will be refused if there is a repeated and gross breach of the obligation to duly attend an integration course.

264. In other cases, an extension may be refused, unless the foreigner provides evidence that he or she has integrated into the community and society by other means. The temporary residence permit of a foreigner who was or is obliged to attend an integration course (section 44a(1), sentence 1 AufenthG), is extended for at the most one year if that foreigner has not successfully completed an integration course or has not yet provided evidence of realising his or her integration into the community and society by other means (section 8(3) AufenthG).

265. Another consequence of a failure to duly attend an integration course or pass an integration test is that a permanent settlement permit will, in general, only be issued if a foreigner has sufficient command of the German language and possesses a basic knowledge of the legal and social system and the way of life in Germany (section 9(2), sentence 1, Nos 7 and 8, sentences 2–6 AufenthG). The same

applies in view of granting an EU long-term residence permit (Article 2(b) of Directive 2003/109/EC, section 9a(2), sentence 1, Nos 3 and 4 AufenthG), and the possibility that the waiting period for acquiring German citizenship is reduced (section 10(3) of the Nationality Act). The foreigners authority may take administrative enforcement measures, such as imposing penalty payments, in order to enjoin the foreigner to comply with the obligation to attend an integration course. Furthermore, non-compliance with the obligation to attend an integration course means that a prospective charge to cover integration costs may be levied in advance in the form of a single sum by issuing an official notice of fees.

III. Other Integration Measures

A. *Integration Programme*

266. In addition to integration courses, there is a far more extensive integration programme, which is meant to foster integration of foreigners. This integration programme is set out in section 45 AufenthG.

267. According to this provision, an integration course is supplemented by additional integration measures that are organised by the Federation and the *Länder* in cooperation with private entities and religious communities. The additional integration measures entail, in particular, socio-educational assistance and advice, as well as migration-specific advising services, for instance for young female migrants.

B. *Job-Related Language Training*

268. Another additional integration measure that is designed to promote integration is the job-related language training set out in section 45a AufenthG.

269. Integration into the labour market is promoted by means of job-related German language courses. As a rule, these courses build on the general language training provided in the integration courses. Job-related language training is coordinated and conducted by the Federal Office for Migration and Refugees. The Federal Office for Migration and Refugees commissions private and public institutions to run these job-related language training courses.

270. Foreigners are obliged to take a job-related language training course if they are drawing benefits within the scope of basic security for job seekers (Book Two of the Social Code). Participation in this language course is included in an integration agreement (section 15 of Book Two of the Social Code). Labour market integration benefits which are provided for by Book Two of the Social Code and active job promotion benefits as set out in Book Three of the Social Code remain unaffected.

271. Participation in job-related language training is not open to foreigners who have permission to remain pending their asylum decision pursuant to the AsylG and who are not expected to have been given permission to remain lawfully and permanently in Germany. It is assumed that asylum applicants from a safe country of origin (section 29a AsylG) are not permitted to remain lawfully and permanently in Germany.

§4. POSITION OF FAMILY MEMBERS OF RESIDENTS

I. Subsequent Immigration of Dependants (Family Reunion)

A. General Principles

272. The position of family members is governed by principles pertaining to the subsequent immigration of dependants. These principles primarily build on the protection of marriage and the family as a human right guaranteed by Article 6 of the Basic Law. In German migration law context, the term 'subsequent immigration of dependants' is used as the more comprehensive expression to include family reunion as well as reunion of persons who do not belong to the family in a strict, family law sense.

273. The AufenthG regulates the position of family members in sections 27–36a. Some of these provisions contain general rules which apply to a variety of situations. Others only apply to individual groups of foreigners such as section 36a AufenthG which relates to subsequent immigration to foreigners with a subsidiary protection status.

274. The AufenthG provides for a special type of temporary residence permit for the purpose of family reunion. This residence title is described as a temporary residence permit to enable foreigners to be joined by foreign dependants so that they can live together as a family. It is granted and extended to protect marriage and the family in accordance with Article 6 of the Basic Law. This is outlined in section 27 AufenthG which describes the situation as subsequent immigration of dependants, as family reunion is referred to in German law.

275. Living together as a family requires, as a general rule, a centre of family life in the form of shared accommodation. If there is no shared accommodation, family cohabitation, again as a general rule, is only assumed if a relationship of mutual assistance or care exists in some other form, e.g., if accommodation in a nursing home is necessary. In these cases, there needs to be regular contact between the family members, which is more than just visits from time to time.

276. The technical rules on subsequent immigration regarding marriage and spouses apply accordingly to enable the establishment and maintenance of a registered partnership in Germany (section 27(1a) and (3), section 9(3), section 9c, sentence 2, sections 28–31, section 51(2) and (10), sentence 2 AufenthG). Since marriage has been opened for same-sex couples in several countries of the world, and in Germany in 2017, these provisions only apply to a smaller number of such couples (section 20a of the Civil Partnerships Act).

277. The period of validity of a temporary residence permit for the purpose of subsequent immigration of dependants must not exceed the period of validity of the temporary residence permit held by the foreigner whom the dependants concerned are joining in Germany. It must be issued for this period if the foreigner who is to be joined in Germany holds a temporary residence permit for research purposes, a temporary residence permit for mobile researchers, a temporary residence permit for long-term resident third country nationals in another EU Member State (sections 18d, 18f or 38a AufenthG), an EU Blue Card, an ICT Card or a Mobile ICT Card, or is entitled to stay in Germany within the scheme of short-term mobility for researchers (section 18e AufenthG). The period of validity of this temporary residence permit must, however, not exceed that of the dependant's passport or passport substitute. In all other cases, a temporary residence permit is issued for an initial period of at least one year.

278. The subsequent immigration of dependants is not permitted if it is established that the marriage has been entered into or kinship has been established solely for the purpose of enabling the persons immigrating subsequently to enter and stay in Germany. In order to combat forced marriages, the AufenthG also prohibits subsequent immigration of the respective dependant if there are specific indications that one of the spouses has been forced into marriage.

279. A temporary residence permit for the subsequent immigration of dependants may be denied if the person to be joined is dependent on basic security for job seekers or general social assistance benefits (Book Two or Book Twelve of the Social Code) for the maintenance of other dependants or members of his or her household.

280. The general condition that there is no public interest in expelling a foreigner may be waived (section 5(1), No. 2 AufenthG). However, a temporary residence permit for the subsequent immigration of dependants is denied if the person to be joined poses a threat to Germany's free democratic order or national security (section 27(3a) AufenthG). Such a threat is assumed to exist if there is reason to believe that the person to be joined is or has been a member of an organisation which supports terrorism or the foreigner supports or has supported such an organisation or is preparing or has prepared a serious violent offence endangering the state (section 89a(1) and (2) of the Criminal Code).

281. A temporary residence permit for the subsequent immigration of dependants is also denied if the person to be joined was one of the leaders of an organisation which has been banned because its purposes or activities contravene criminal law or it opposes the German constitutional order or the concept of international understanding. The same applies if the person to be joined engages in violent activities to achieve his or her political or religious objectives or calls publicly for the use

of violence or threatens to use violence to achieve those objectives. Furthermore, it also applies if the person to be joined incites others to hatred against segments of the population. Incitement is assumed where the person to be joined exerts a targeted and permanent influence on other persons in order to incite or increase hatred against members of certain ethnic groups or religions. It is also assumed if the person to be joined publicly, either in a meeting or by disseminating documents in such a manner that this could disturb public safety and law and order, incites others to undertake arbitrary measures against segments of the population, maliciously disparages segments of the population and in doing so affects the human dignity of others or endorses or promotes crimes against peace, against humanity, war crimes or acts of terrorism of a comparable severity.

B. Subsequent Immigration of Dependants to a Foreigner

282. Subsequent immigration of dependants to join a foreigner is premised on the protection of marriage and the family as a human right in Article 6 of the Basic Law. However, it is assumed that the protection of marriage and the family does not, as a general rule, constitute a human right to live as a family in Germany. Also, colliding constitutional rights, interests, and principles such as the well-functioning of the social system or the labour market apply and can limit family rights. In its details this is regulated by sections 29 et seq. AufenthG.

283. However, previous rules in force until 31 July 2018 will be applied to the subsequent immigration of foreigners who have been granted a temporary residence permit until 17 March 2016 if the application for initial granting of a residence title for subsequent immigration of dependants has been filed until 31 July 2018 (section 104(13) AufenthG).

284. For the purpose of subsequent immigration of dependants to join a foreigner, the foreigner to be joined must hold a specific residence title. This must be either a permanent settlement permit or an EU long-term residence permit, a temporary residence permit, an EU Blue Card, an ICT Card or a Mobile ICT Card, or the foreigner to be joined must be entitled to stay in Germany under the terms of short-term mobility of researchers (section 18e AufenthG).

285. The general requirement for granting a residence title that the foreigner's subsistence is secure (section 5(1), No. 1 AufenthG) and that sufficient living space must be available (section 29(1), No. 2 AufenthG) may be waived in certain cases of subsequent immigration to join a foreigner. This is the case for the spouse and the minor, unmarried child of a recognised refugee. The possible privilege applies if the foreigner to be joined possesses a temporary residence permit either as a resettlement refugee (section 23(4) AufenthG) or as a foreigner recognised as being entitled to asylum, having been granted refugee status or subsidiary protection status (section 25(1) or (2) AufenthG). The same applies if the foreigner to be joined holds a permanent settlement permit as a foreigner recognised as being entitled to

asylum, having been granted refugee status (section 26(3) AufenthG) or subsidiary protection status (section 26(4) and section 25(2), sentence 1, second alternative AufenthG).

286. In these cases, the conditions of secure means of subsistence and adequate accommodation must be waived if the application for a residence title required for subsequent immigration of dependants is filed within three months of the final decision recognising that the foreigner is entitled to asylum or the final granting of refugee or subsidiary protection status or after a temporary residence permit for resettlement refugees has been issued (section 23(4) AufenthG). This exception only applies, however, if it is not possible for a foreigner and the dependants to live as a family unit in a State which is not an EU Member State with which the foreigner or the dependants have special ties.

287. The deadline of three months (section 29(2), sentence 2, No. 1 AufenthG) is considered to be satisfied if the foreigner to be joined files the application on time, as it is often difficult or impossible for dependants to file an application from abroad.

288. In certain cases, the temporary residence permit for subsequent immigration of a spouse or a minor child may only be granted, if this is for reasons of international law, on humanitarian grounds or in order to safeguard political interests of Germany. Humanitarian grounds exist, as a rule, if the family community can only be achieved in Germany within a reasonable time. These conditions apply, if the foreigner to be joined possesses a temporary residence permit for the purpose of admission from abroad (section 22 AufenthG) or a temporary residence permit ordered by the supreme *Land* authority or the Federal Ministry of the Interior to be granted to foreigners from specific states or to certain groups of foreigners (section 23(1) and (2) AufenthG). It is also the case if a deportation ban applies because deportation is inadmissible under the terms of the European Convention on Human Rights such as the prohibition of torture, is inadmissible to another state in which the foreigner faces a substantial concrete danger to his or her life and limb or liberty, or because the foreigner has been the victim of human trafficking (section 25(3) or (4a), sentence 1 AufenthG). The conditions also applies if the foreigner holds a temporary residence title for a juvenile or adolescent foreigner whose deportation has been suspended (section 25a(1) AufenthG) or for a foreigner whose deportation has been suspended because he or she has become lastingly integrated into the way of life in Germany (section 25b(1) AufenthG).

289. Humanitarian grounds exist if, e.g., the family unit can only be established in Germany.

290. In regard to a permanent residence title, section 26(4) AufenthG applies accordingly. This means that a foreigner who possesses a temporary residence permit for family reasons (Part 6 AufenthG) may be granted a permanent settlement permit if the conditions stipulated in section 9(2) AufenthG are met. Thus, the general requirements for granting a permanent settlement permit apply such as: having

held a temporary residence permit for five years, secure subsistence, sufficient command of the German language, and sufficient living space. Residence during the asylum procedure preceding granting of the temporary residence permit does count towards the qualifying period. Also, section 35 AufenthG providing for children's independent, permanent right of residence may be applied accordingly to children who entered Germany before reaching the age of 18.

291. Under certain circumstances, the temporary residence permit will also be granted to the spouse and the minor, unmarried child of a foreigner or the minor, unmarried child of the foreigner's spouse if the foreigner has been granted temporary protection on the basis of a decision by the Council of the EU pursuant to Directive 2001/55/EC on minimum standards for giving temporary protection in the event of a mass influx of displaced persons.[52] The foreigner must have declared willingness to be admitted into Germany (section 24(1) AufenthG) and the family unit in the country of origin has been broken up as a result of the foreigner having fled the country of origin and the dependant is admitted from another Member State of the EU or is located outside of the EU and is in need of protection. In this case, sections 5(1) and 27(3) AufenthG are derogated. Thus, it is not required that the foreigner's subsistence is secure; also, the temporary residence permit for the subsequent immigration of dependants may not be denied because the person to be joined by the dependants relies on basic security for job seekers or general social welfare benefits for the maintenance of other dependants or other members of the household.

292. However, subsequent immigration of dependants will not be granted to a foreigner who has been granted a temporary residence permit for a temporary stay because his or her continued presence in Germany is necessary on urgent humanitarian or personal grounds or due to substantial public interests (section 25(4) AufenthG). The same applies to intended immigration to join a foreigner who has been granted a temporary residence permit for a temporary stay because he or she has been a victim of a criminal offence of labour exploitation (section 25(4b) AufenthG). It also applies to cases of a foreigner who is enforceably required to leave Germany but has been granted a temporary residence permit because departure is impossible in fact or in law (section 25(5) AufenthG).

293. The subsequent immigration of dependants will also not be granted in certain cases where deportation has or had been suspended (section 29(3), sentence 3 AufenthG). This applies to subsequent immigration to foreigners holding a temporary residence permit as a parent possessing the right of care and custody of a foreign minor whose deportation had been suspended and who holds now a temporary residence permit for well-integrated juveniles (section 25a(1) and (2) AufenthG). It

---

52. Council Directive 2001/55/EC of 20 Jul. 2001 on minimum standards for giving temporary protection in the event of a mass influx of displaced persons and on measures promoting a balance of efforts between Member States in receiving such persons and bearing the consequences thereof, OJ EU L 2012, 7 Aug. 2012.

also applies to subsequent immigration to a foreigner whose deportation had been suspended and who now holds a temporary residence because of lasting integration (section 25b(4) AufenthG).

294. The subsequent immigration of dependants will furthermore not be granted in some old cases under transitional provisions; this applies to subsequent immigration to a foreigner whose deportation had been suspended and who has been granted a temporary residence permit as an old case continuously residing in Germany before 1 July 2007 (section 104a(1), sentence 1 AufenthG). It also applies in the case of a child who has reached the age of 14 before the year 2007 and has been granted the right of residence for integrated children of foreigners whose deportation has been suspended (section 104b AufenthG).

295. In all of these cases the reason for the decision is that the residence of the foreigner to be joined is of only a temporary nature.

C. *Subsequent Immigration of Spouses*

1. Conditions

296. Further special rules apply to subsequent immigration of spouses to foreigners pursuant to section 30 AufenthG.

297. A foreigner's spouse is granted a temporary residence permit if both spouses are at least 18 years of age and the spouse who intends to subsequently immigrate is able to communicate in the German language at least on a basic level. In addition to these basic requirements, the foreigner to be joined in Germany has to meet one out of a number of special requirements.

298. If the basic requirements are met, the spouse may subsequently immigrate to a foreigner who either holds a permanent settlement permit or an EU long-term residence permit.

299. The additional requirement is also met if the foreigner possesses a temporary residence permit for research purposes or a temporary residence permit for mobile researchers.

300. Given the basic requirements, subsequent immigration of a spouse is also possible to a foreigner holding a temporary residence permit as being entitled to asylum or having been granted refugee status (section 25(1) or (2), sentence 1, first alternative AufenthG).

301. The same applies if the foreigner has held a temporary residence permit for two years and the temporary residence permit is not subject to the subsidiary provision that an extension is prohibited because the stay is of only a temporary nature (section 8(2) AufenthG) or the subsequent issuance of a permanent settlement permit has not been ruled out by virtue of a law; however, this does not apply to a temporary residence permit for subsidiary protection (section 25(2), sentence 1, second alternative AufenthG).

302. Given the basic requirements, subsequent immigration of a spouse is furthermore possible if the foreigner holds a temporary residence permit (section 7(1), sentence 3, or sections 3–5 or 6, or section 37 or 38), if the marriage existed at the time when that permit was granted and the duration of the foreigner's stay in Germany is expected to exceed one year; this, however, does not apply to a temporary residence permit for subsidiary protection (section 25(2), sentence 1, second alternative AufenthG).

303. Furthermore, the additional requirement is met if the foreigner possesses a temporary residence permit for persons having the status of long-term residents in another EU Member State (section 38a AufenthG) and the marriage already existed in the EU Member State in which the foreigner has the status of a long-term resident.

304. Given the basic requirements, subsequent immigration of a spouse is furthermore possible to a foreigner who holds an EU Blue Card, an ICT Card or a Mobile ICT Card.

2. Exceptions to Conditions

305. There are some exceptions to the basic requirements of age and language skills. Thus, it is not required for subsequent immigration of spouses that both spouses are at least 18 years of age and the spouse is able to communicate in the German language at least on a basic level if the foreigner possesses a temporary residence permit for persons having the status of long-term residents in other EU Member States (section 38a AufenthG) and the marriage already existed in the EU Member State in which the foreigner has the status of a long-term resident (section 30(1), sentence 1, Nos 1 and 2, section 30(1), sentence 1, No. 3(f) AufenthG).

306. Language skills are not required in certain circumstances. The general language requirement stipulated in section 30(1), sentence 1, No. 2 AufenthG has no bearing on issuance of the temporary residence permit, and thus the spouse who intends to subsequently immigrate is not required to be able to communicate in the German language at least on a basic level, where one of the following conditions is met.

307. The foreigner holds a residence title as a resettlement refugee, as being entitled to asylum, having refugee status or subsidiary protection status, and the marriage already existed at the time when the foreigner established the main ordinary residence in Germany (sections 23(4), 25(1) and (2), 26(3) and (4), 30(1), sentence 3, No. 1 AufenthG).

308. It also applies if the spouse is unable to provide evidence of basic German language skills on account of a physical or mental illness or disability.

309. It is also met if the spouse's need for integration is discernibly minimal (section 43(4) AufenthG) or the spouse would, for other reasons, not be eligible for an integration course (section 44 AufenthG) after entering Germany.

310. Section 30(1), sentence 1, No. 2 AufenthG has also no bearing if by virtue of his or her nationality, the foreigner may enter and stay in Germany without requiring a visa for a period of residence which does not constitute a short stay.

311. Language skills are also not required if the foreigner to be joined holds an EU Blue Card, an ICT Card, a Mobile ICT Card or a temporary residence permit for research reasons or for mobile researchers (section 18d or 18f AufenthG).

312. The same applies if the particular circumstances of the case mean that the spouse is unable to or it is unreasonable to expect the spouse to undertake efforts before entering the country to acquire basic German language skills. This can be the case, e.g., if there is no German language course available in the region.

313. It also applies if the foreigner possesses a residence title pursuant to sections 18c(3) and 21 AufenthG and the marriage already existed at the time when the foreigner established main ordinary residence in Germany. The foreigner thus, in this case, must hold a permanent settlement permit for highly skilled workers on the assumption that integration into the way of life in Germany and the foreigner's subsistence without state assistance are assured, or a temporary residence permit for the purpose of self-employment.

314. Language skills of the spouse are also not required if the foreigner held a temporary residence permit for research purposes (section 18d AufenthG) immediately before a permanent settlement permit or an EU long-term residence permit was issued.

3. Particular Hardship

315. A temporary residence permit may be issued to avoid particular hardship even if one or both of the spouses are not yet 18 years of age (section 30(1), sentence 1, No. 1, and (2), sentence 1 AufenthG). If the foreigner already resident in Germany has been issued a temporary residence permit, a temporary residence permit may also be granted to that foreigner's spouse even though the marriage did not exist at the time when the foreigner's permit was granted or if the duration of the foreigner's stay in Germany is not expected to exceed one year (section 30(1), sentence 1, No. 3(e) and (2), sentence 2 AufenthG).

4. Extension

316. A temporary residence permit issued to the spouse joining a foreigner already resident in Germany may be extended for as long as the marital cohabitation continues. It is not required that the foreigner's means of subsistence are secure or that there is sufficient accommodation to be granted an extension of a temporary residence permit (section 5(1), No. 1, section 29(1), No. 2, and 30(3) AufenthG).

5. Polygamous Marriage

317. In the case of polygamous marriage, the law prohibits admission of more than one spouse. Where a foreigner is simultaneously married to several spouses and lives with one spouse in Germany, no other spouse is granted a temporary residence permit in the scope of subsequent immigration of spouses (section 30(1), (3), and (4) AufenthG).

6. Short-Term Mobility for Researchers

318. If the foreigner to be joined is entitled to stay in Germany within the scheme of short-term mobility for researchers, his or her spouse does not need a residence title if the spouse has stayed in the other EU Member State lawfully as the foreigner's dependant. This requires evidence that the foreigner possesses a valid residence title for research purposes issued by another EU Member State, and a copy of the spouse's recognised and valid passport or passport substitute as well as evidence of the fact that the spouse's subsistence is secured. The grounds for rejection pursuant to section 19f AufenthG, such as insolvency of the research entity, falsification of documents or a public interest in expelling the foreigner, also apply accordingly to the spouse (section 18e(1), sentence 1, Nos 1, 3 and 4, and section 30(5) AufenthG, Directive (EU) 2016/801).

D. *Independent Right of Residence of Spouses*

1. Termination of Marital Cohabitation

319. Special rules govern the situation in which the marital cohabitation has ended. In such cases, there may be an independent right of residence of the spouse who has subsequently immigrated. These rules are enumerated in section 31 AufenthG.

320. In the event of termination of marital cohabitation, the spouse's temporary residence permit is extended by one year as an independent right of residence unrelated to the purpose of the subsequent immigration of dependants if marital cohabitation has lawfully existed in Germany for at least three years or the foreigner who had been joined has died while marital cohabitation existed in Germany. In both cases, it is required that the foreigner possessed a temporary residence permit, permanent settlement permit or EU long-term residence permit up to this point in time, unless the foreigner was unable to apply for an extension in time for reasons beyond his or her control. The spouse's temporary residence permit must not be extended if no ex-tension of the foreigner's temporary residence permit is permissible. The spouse's temporary residence permit must also not be extended if it is not permissible to issue the foreigner a permanent settlement permit or an EU long-term residence permit because this is precluded by a rule of law on account of the purpose of residence or by a subsidiary provision attached to the temporary residence permit by which the competent authority has prohibited an extension in the case of a stay which is of only a temporary nature in accordance with the purpose of residence (section 8(2), and section 31(1), sentence 2 AufenthG). Such a preclusion by a rule of law exists, e.g., if the temporary residence permit has been granted for employment as a speciality cook for four years (section 11(2) BeschV).

2. Particular Hardship

321. Provision is made to avoid particular hardship. The requirement for an independent right of residence of the spouse that marital cohabitation must have existed lawfully for three years in Germany is waived if necessary to enable the spouse to continue his or her residence in order to avoid particular hardship, unless an extension of the foreigner's temporary residence permit is not permitted. This is stipulated in section 31(1), sentence 1, No. 1, AufenthG. Particular hardship is deemed to apply especially if the marriage is not valid or has been suspended under German law owing to the spouse's minority. Particular hardship is also deemed to apply if the obligation to return to the country of origin resulting from the termination of marital cohabitation threatens to substantially harm the foreigner's legitimate interests, or if continuing the marital cohabitation is unreasonable due to the harm to the foreigner's legitimate interests; in particular, this is to be assumed where the spouse is the victim of domestic violence. Such legitimate interests also include the well-being of a child living with the spouse as part of a family unit. In order to avoid abuse, extension of the temporary residence permit may be denied if the spouse relies on basic security for job seekers or social welfare benefits (Book Two or Book Twelve of the Social Code) for reasons for which he or she is responsible.

3. Extension

322. Claiming basic security for job seekers or general social welfare benefits (Book Two or Book Twelve of the Social Code) by the spouse does not preclude extension of the temporary residence permit. The temporary residence permit may thus be extended as long as the conditions for granting the permanent settlement permit or EU long-term residence permit have not been met. This does not apply, however, if the spouse relies on such benefits for reasons for which he or she is responsible and this constitutes a misuse of public funds (section 31(2), sentence 4, and (4) AufenthG).

4. Permanent Settlement Permit

323. The spouse is also issued a permanent settlement permit if his or her means of subsistence are ensured after the termination of marital cohabitation by maintenance payments paid from the foreigner's own funds and the foreigner possesses a permanent settlement permit or an EU long-term residence permit. Thus, it is not required that the spouse has paid compulsory or voluntary contributions into the statutory pension scheme for at least sixty months or provides evidence of an entitlement to comparable benefits from an insurance or pension scheme or from an insurance company. It is also not required that the spouse is permitted to be in employment, if he or she is in employment, or that the spouse possesses one of the other permits required for the purpose of the permanent pursuit of an economic activity (section 31(3), and section 9(2), sentence 1, Nos 3, 5, and 6 AufenthG).

E. Subsequent Immigration of Children

324. Further special rules apply for the subsequent immigration of children of foreigners pursuant to sections 32 et seq. AufenthG.

325. The minor, unmarried child of a foreigner is granted a temporary residence permit if the parents or the parent having the sole right of care and custody hold an EU Blue Card, an ICT Card, a Mobile ICT Card, a permanent settlement permit or an EU long-term residence permit, or a temporary residence permit (section 32(1), 7(1), sentence 3 AufenthG, Part 3 or 4 AufenthG, section 25(1) or (2) first alternative AufenthG, sections 28, 30, 31, 36, or 36a AufenthG). However, if the foreigner holds a temporary residence permit for subsidiary protection, only the special rules on subsequent immigration to foreigners under subsidiary protection apply (section 32(1), No. 4, section 25(2), sentence 1, second alternative, and section 36a AufenthG).

326. There is, however, an additional impediment for older children. If the minor, unmarried child is aged 16 or over and if it does not relocate its main ordinary residence to Germany together with its parents or the parent possessing the sole right of care and custody, subsequent immigration of dependants is possible only if the child speaks German and appears, on the basis of its education and way of life to date, that it will be able to integrate into the way of life in Germany. However, this exceptional impediment does not apply if the foreigner to be joined possesses a temporary residence permit as a resettlement refugee (section 23(4) AufenthG), or as a foreigner recognised as being entitled to asylum, having refugee status or subsidiary protection status (section 25(1) or (2) AufenthG). The same applies if the foreigner to be joined holds a permanent settlement permit as a foreigner recognised as being entitled to asylum, having been granted refugee status (section 26(3) AufenthG) or subsidiary protection status (section 26(4) and section 25(2), sentence 1, second alternative AufenthG). The exception does also not apply if the foreigner or his or her spouse living together as a family possesses a permanent settlement permit for highly qualified foreigners, an EU Blue Card, an ICT Card or a Mobile ICT Card or a temporary residence permit for research purposes or for mobile researchers (sections 19, 20 and 20b AufenthG).

327. Where parents share the right of care and custody, such a temporary residence permit should also be granted for the purpose of joining just one parent, if the other parent has agreed to the child's stay in Germany or if the relevant legally binding decision has been supplied by a competent authority such as a family court (section 32(1) or (2) AufenthG).

328. A minor, unmarried child of a foreigner may otherwise be granted a temporary residence permit if necessary to prevent special hardship on account of the circumstances pertaining to the individual case concerned. The child's well-being and the family situation have to be taken into consideration. These rules do not apply to minor, unmarried children of foreigners holding a temporary residence permit for subsidiary protection. In such cases, only the special provision on subsequent immigration of dependants to foreigners under subsidiary protection applies (section 32(4), sentence 3, and section 36a AufenthG).

329. If the foreigner is entitled to stay in Germany within the scheme of short-term mobility for researchers, the minor unmarried child does not need a residence title if it has been established that the child stayed lawfully in the other EU Member State as the foreigner's dependant. Evidence has to be submitted that the foreigner possesses a valid residence title for research purposes issued by another Member State, a copy of the child's recognised and valid passport or passport substitute has to be submitted as well as evidence of the fact that the child's subsistence is secure. Moreover, the grounds for rejection such as insolvency of the host entity or a public interest in expelling the foreigner apply accordingly to the minor child (section 32(4), 20a(1), sentence 1, Nos 1, 3 and 4, section 20c AufenthG, and Directive (EU) 2016/801).

F. Children Born in Germany

330. If the foreign child is born in Germany, further special facilitating rules apply pursuant to section 33 AufenthG. A foreign child who is born in Germany may be granted a temporary residence permit ex officio if one parent possesses a temporary residence permit, permanent settlement permit or EU long-term residence permit. Where both parents or the parent possessing sole right of care and custody hold a temporary residence permit, a permanent settlement permit or an EU long-term residence permit at the time of birth, the child born in Germany has to be granted a temporary residence permit ex officio. A child born in Germany whose mother or father possesses a visa or is permitted to stay in Germany without a visa at the time of the birth is permitted to stay in Germany until the visa or the lawful period of stay without a visa expires. The general prerequisites for granting a residence title which are stipulated by section 5 AufenthG do not apply such as that the foreigner's subsistence is secure. Also, section 29(1), No. 2 AufenthG does not apply and thus it is not required that sufficient living space is available.

331.   Where the passport requirement is waived pursuant to section 33 AufenthG, a substitute identity document is issued to the child if the cooperation obligations are met, such as presenting, handing over or ceding relevant documents (section 48(3) and (4) AufenthG).

332.   It should be noted that the provision only applies to children who are not German nationals. Children of foreigners can, however, obtain German citizenship by birth on the basis of section 4(3) of the Citizenship Act. In Germany born children of foreigners obtain the German citizenship upon birth if at least one of the parents has been lawfully ordinarily resident in Germany for eight years and holds a permanent residence title or holds, as a Swiss national or as a family member of a Swiss national, a residence permit on the basis of the Swiss-EU-Agreement on the free movement of persons.[53]

G. Right of Residence of Children

1. Extension

333.   Similar principles, found in section 34 AufenthG, govern a child's right of residence.

334.   A temporary residence permit issued to a child is extended as long as the parent invested with the right of care and custody holds a temporary residence permit, a permanent settlement permit or an EU long-term residence permit and the child is a member of that parent's household.

335.   A temporary residence permit issued to a child is also extended if that child enjoys a right of return (section 37 AufenthG) if it left Germany. In this case, it is not required that the parent invested with the right of care and custody holds a residence title. The right of return presupposes that a child has habitually resided in Germany as a minor for eight years and meets the other requirements in section 37 AufenthG.

---

53. Agreement of 21 Jun. 1999 between the European Community and its Member States on the one hand and the Swiss Confederation on the other hand on the free movement of persons, BGBl. 2001 II p. 810, https://eur-lex.europa.eu/resource.html?uri=cellar:29b7e319-1314-4fbd-b1df-c0c0be226fe b.0004.02/DOC_1&format=PDF.

336. In both cases, the extension of a temporary residence permit does not require that the foreigner's subsistence is secure, or that there is sufficient living space available, as neither section 5(1), No. 1 AufenthG nor section 29(1), No. 2 AufenthG apply to these cases. It is also not required that the child is a minor or unmarried.[54]

337. When a child comes of age, a temporary residence permit issued to a child becomes an independent right of residence which is unrelated to the purpose for which residence permission was initially granted, i.e., subsequent immigration of dependants. The same applies to the issuing of a permanent settlement permit and an EU long-term residence permit and when a temporary residence permit is extended because the child has a right of return (sections 34(2), and 37 AufenthG).

338. A temporary residence permit may be extended as long as the conditions for issuing a permanent settlement permit and an EU long-term residence permit are not met.

2.   Permanent Residence Permit

339. A child who has been issued a temporary residence permit can become entitled to an independent permanent settlement permit when the conditions in section 35 AufenthG are satisfied.

340. A minor foreigner who has been issued a temporary residence permit in accordance with the rules on family reunion (Chapter 2, Part 6 AufenthG) is granted a permanent settlement permit if he or she has been in possession of a temporary residence permit for five years when reaching the age of 16. The general requirements to issue a permanent settlement permit, such as secure subsistence or sufficient command of the German language (section 9(2) AufenthG), do not apply.

341. Similar, yet somewhat stricter rules apply when the child is of age. A temporary residence permit can be replaced by a permanent settlement permit if a child is of age, has held a temporary residence permit for five years, has sufficient command of the German language and secure means of subsistence. The same applies to a child who is attending education or a training which leads to a recognised school, vocational or higher education qualification. These requirements are, however, waived if the foreigner is unable to fulfil them on account of a physical or mental illness or disability (section 35(4) AufenthG).

342. Periods in which the child attended school outside Germany are normally not taken into account when the five-year period of a temporary residence permit is calculated.

---

54. Tewocht, AufenthG §34, in: BeckOK AuslR, Kluth/Heusch, 20. ed., 1 Nov. 2018.

343. There is no entitlement to a permanent settlement permit, if there is a public interest in expelling the child which is based on that child's personal conduct (section 35(3) AufenthG). This is also the case if a child has been sentenced to a term of youth custody of at least six months or a prison term of at least three months or a fine of at least ninety daily rates in the past three years due to an intentionally committed offence, or if a youth prison sentence has been suspended. Suspension of a youth prison sentence is possible if a young offender has been sentenced, but the punishment has yet to be determined. Moreover, there is no entitlement to a permanent settlement permit, if the foreigner's subsistence cannot be assured without claiming basic security for job seekers, general welfare benefits, or youth welfare (Book Two, Twelve, or Eight of the Social Code), the exception being that the foreigner is in education or training which leads to a recognised school or vocational qualification. The requirement that the child's means of subsistence are assured without claiming benefits is waived, if the foreigner is unable to fulfil them on account of a physical or mental illness or disability (section 35(4) AufenthG).

344. A permanent settlement permit may be issued and a temporary residence permit may be extended in the aforementioned cases. The child then has a right to due exercise of discretion which is not the same as a right to a positive decision. If a foreigner is placed on probation or the term of youth custody is suspended, a temporary residence permit will usually be extended until the end of the probationary period. This covers cases in which a child has been sentenced to a term of youth custody of at least six months, a prison term of at least three months or a fine of at least ninety daily rates in the past three years due to an intentionally committed offence, or if a youth prison sentence has been suspended (section 35(3), sentences 2 and 3 AufenthG).

H. Subsequent Immigration of Parents

345. The AufenthG also allows for the subsequent immigration of parents. The rules governing this are found in section 36 AufenthG.

346. A temporary residence permit is issued to the parents of a minor foreigner who has been issued a temporary residence permit as a resettlement refugee (section 23(4) AufenthG); as a foreigner recognised as being entitled to asylum (section 25(1) AufenthG); or who has been granted refugee status (section 25(2), sentence 1, first alternative AufenthG). It is also granted to the parents of a minor foreigner who has been issued a permanent residence permit as being entitled to asylum (section 25(1) AufenthG), refugee status or subsidiary protection status (section 26(3), section 25(2), sentence 1, second alternative AufenthG). A further requirement that applies in all of these cases is that there is no parent with the right of care and custody resident in Germany. In these cases, the general conditions for granting a residence title, namely that the foreigner's means of subsistence are secure and that there is sufficient accommodation, do not apply.

I. Subsequent Immigration of Other Dependants

1. Particular Hardship

347. Dependants who are not the spouse, children or the parents of a foreigner, e.g., grandparents, aunts, uncles and siblings, may be issued a temporary residence permit for the purpose of subsequent immigration to join a foreigner if this is necessary in order to avoid particular hardship (section 36(2) AufenthG). For these extended family members subsequent immigration is rather difficult and only possible in exceptional cases for instance if appropriate care of elderly people cannot be provided in any other way. The rules governing an extension of a temporary residence permit that apply in cases of marital cohabitation (section 30(3) AufenthG) apply accordingly to these dependants if they are adults. This is also the case for the provision of an independent right of residence of the spouse (section 31 AufenthG). If these other dependants are still minors, the rules on a child's right of residence (section 34 AufenthG) apply accordingly.

348. A temporary residence permit may be extended for as long as these family members cohabit with the foreigner.

2. Temporary Protection

349. In cases of temporary protection, these rules on subsequent immigration of parents and other dependants also apply to dependants who are not the foreigner's spouse, the foreigner's child or the child of the foreigner's spouse. Such dependants of a foreigner who has been granted temporary protection on the basis of a decision by the European Council may be issued a temporary residence permit for subsequent immigration of dependants to avoid particular hardship. The rules on the granting of residence for temporary protection including the provisions on allocation and employment in such cases apply to those other dependants (Directive 2001/55/EC, and sections 24, 36, and 29(4), sentence 2 AufenthG).

J. Subsequent Immigration to Persons with Subsidiary Protection Status

350. Subsequent immigration of dependants to persons granted subsidiary protection status has been limited pursuant to section 36a AufenthG. No more than one thousand national visas per month may be issued for a temporary residence permit to this end.

351. The spouse or the minor unmarried child of a foreigner who holds a temporary residence permit for subsidiary protection (section 25(2), sentence 1, second alternative AufenthG) may be granted a temporary residence permit for humanitarian reasons. The same applies to parents of a minor foreigner who holds a temporary residence permit for subsidiary protection if no parent possessing the right of care and custody resides in Germany. There is no need for the subsistence to be secure or sufficient living space be available, section 5(1), No. 1 and section 29(1), No. 2 AufenthG do not apply.

352. There is no entitlement of these persons to subsequent immigration of dependants. Sections 22, 23 remain unaffected; thus, beyond this subsequent immigration of dependants, a foreigner may be granted a temporary residence permit for the purpose of admission from abroad in accordance with international law or on urgent humanitarian grounds, and a Land as well as the Federal Ministry of the Interior may order a temporary residence permit to be granted to foreigners from specific states or to certain groups of foreigners, in accordance with international law, on humanitarian grounds or in order to uphold the political interests of Germany.

353. Humanitarian reasons in the meaning of this provision exist in particular if establishing the family unit has not been possible for a long time or a minor unmarried child is affected. The same applies if life and limb or liberty of the spouse, the minor unmarried child or of the parents of a minor foreigner are seriously threatened in the country of residence, and if the foreigner, the spouse or the minor unmarried child or a parent of a minor foreigner are seriously ill or in need of care in the meaning of a serious impairment of the independence or the abilities or has a serious handicap. The illness, the need for care or the handicap have to be made plausible by a qualified certificate, unless there is other evidence connected with the dependant abroad indicating the existence of the illness, need of care or the handicap.

354. While only 1,000 national visas for such a temporary residence permit may be issued per month, the welfare of the child has to be taken into account in particular. If there are 'existing humanitarian reasons' related to integration these have to be taken into account in particular. Examples of 'existing humanitarian reasons' related to integration are, e.g., German language skills, social engagement, an intensive endeavour to take up employment or independent securing of subsistence or adequate accommodation.

355. Such a temporary residence permit may, as a rule, not be granted if, in the case of a temporary residence permit for a spouse, the marriage was not concluded before absconding. It may also as a rule not be granted if the foreigner to be joined has been sentenced for serious crimes. This is the case if the foreigner to be joined has been non-appealably sentenced to imprisonment of at least one year because of one or several intentional crimes or has been non-appealably sentenced to imprisonment or youth custody because of one or several intentional crimes against life, bodily integrity, sexual self-determination, property or of resisting enforcement officers if the crime has been committed by force, by use of threat of danger for limb or life or by guile or is a crime of sexual assault by use of force or threats or is rape (section 177 of the Criminal Code); this applies in the case of serial commission of crimes against property also if the offender has not used force, threat or guile. The same applies if the foreigner to be joined has been non-appealably sentenced to youth custody of at least one year and the execution of the sentence has not been suspended, or has been non-appealably sentenced because of one or several intentional crimes of unlawfully supplying narcotics (section 29(1), sentence 1, No. 1, of the Narcotic Drugs Act).

356. Such a temporary residence permit for the purpose of subsequent immigration of dependants may also, as a rule, not be issued if the extension of a temporary residence permit and the granting of a different residence title with regard to the foreigner to be joined are not to be expected. The same applies if the foreigner to be joined has applied for a border-crossing certificate, which means that the foreigner is about to leave Germany.

357. Also in the case of subsequent immigration of dependants of persons who have been granted subsidiary protection status, both spouses must be at least 18 years of age unless particular hardship is to be avoided. Only one spouse is permitted into Germany in the case of polygamous marriages (sections 36a(4) and 30(1), sentence 1, No. 1, (2), sentence 1, and (4) AufenthG).

358. Where parents share the right of care and custody, a temporary residence permit under this scheme should also be granted for the purpose of joining just one parent, if the other parent has agreed to the child's stay in Germany or if the relevant legally binding decision has been supplied by a competent authority such as a family court (sections 36a(4) and 32(3) AufenthG).

K. Subsequent Immigration to a German National

1. Conditions

359. Special rules apply if the dependant is to join a German national. In such cases, subsequent immigration of dependants is facilitated. This is regulated in section 28 AufenthG. In the case of subsequent immigration of dependants to join a German national, the temporary residence permit is granted to the foreign spouse of a German, the minor, unmarried child of a German, and to the parent of a minor, unmarried German for the purpose of care and custody, if the German's habitual residence is in Germany.

360. In several circumstances, the general condition of secure subsistence for granting a residence title does not apply (section 5(1), No. 1, section 28(1), sentence 2 AufenthG). The temporary residence title for subsequent immigration of dependants must be granted to a minor, unmarried child of a German as well as to a parent of a minor, unmarried German for the purpose of care and custody, even if the foreigner's subsistence is not secure. Also, even if the foreigner's subsistence is not secure, the temporary residence permit should be granted as a general rule if the foreigner is the spouse of a German. The temporary residence permit may be granted to the parent of a minor, unmarried German who does not possess the right of care and custody of that child, if the family unit already exists in Germany.

361. In view of a foreign spouse of a German, a number of further special rules apply pertaining to age of the spouses and language skills (section 28(1), sentence 1, No. 1, and sentence 5, section 30(1), sentence 1, Nos 1 and 2, sentence 3, and (2), sentence 1 AufenthG).

362. The foreign spouse of a German will be granted a temporary residence permit if both spouses are at least 18 years of age, unless this requirement would cause particular hardship. Particular hardship only exists if there are exceptional circumstances, and the matrimonial cohabitation must be the proper and necessary condition to overcome such exceptional circumstances.

363. The second requirement is that the foreigner's spouse is able to communicate in the German language at least on a basic level. This language requirement, however, has no bearing on granting the temporary residence permit in a number of special circumstances. The language requirement does not apply if the spouse is unable to provide evidence of basic German language skills on account of a physical or mental illness or disability, the spouse's need for integration is discernibly minimal (section 43(4) AufenthG) or the spouse would, for other reasons, not be eligible for an integration course (section 44 AufenthG) after entering Germany. The language requirement also does not apply if the particular circumstances of the case mean that the spouse is unable to or it is unreasonable to expect the spouse to undertake efforts before entering the country to acquire basic German language skills. This can be the case if German courses are unavailable in the region. However, even if such exemptions cannot be granted because of the circumstances of the individual case, subsequent immigration of the foreign spouse to join the German in Germany can be possible because of the protection of marriage afforded by the German Basic Law in Article 6(1). In balancing the interests and values at stake, protection of marriage on the one side and integration efforts on the other, protection of marriage can lead to waiving the language requirement.[55]

2. Permanent Settlement Permit

364. Granting a permanent settlement permit is also facilitated in case of subsequent immigration to a German national. As a rule, the foreigner must be granted a permanent settlement permit if he or she has held a temporary residence permit for three years instead of the normal five years, the family unit with the German continues to exist in Germany, and there is no public interest in expelling the foreigner. The foreigner must also have a sufficient command of the German language; this requirement, however, can be waived to avoid hardship. They are deemed to be fulfilled if the foreigner has successfully completed an integration course and they are waived if the foreigner is unable to fulfil them on account of a physical or mental illness or disability. The same applies if the foreigner is able to communicate verbally in the German language at a basic level and has not been entitled or obliged to participate in an integration course (section 9(2), sentences 2–5 AufenthG).

---

55. BVerwG NVwZ 2013, 515.

365. The temporary residence permit will otherwise be extended as long as the family unit continues to exist.

366. The rules on an independent right of residence of spouses and on children's right of residence (sections 31 and 34 AufenthG) apply subject to the proviso that the foreigner's residence title will be replaced by the ordinary residence of the German in Germany. This means that the spouse and children subsequently immigrating to join a German can acquire an own right of residence independent of the continued existence of the family unit under the same conditions as can the foreign spouse and children joining a foreigner in Germany if the German's ordinary residence is in Germany.

367. The situation of parents subsequently immigrating for the purpose of care and custody is less comfortable. They cannot, as a matter of principle, acquire their own right of residence under this scheme of subsequent immigration of dependants. However, the temporary residence permit granted to a parent of a minor and unmarried German national for the purpose of care and custody must be extended after the child has come of age as long as the child lives with him in a family household and is in education or training which leads to a recognised school, vocational or higher education qualification.

368. Other foreign dependants of the German may be granted a temporary residence permit only to avoid exceptional hardship (sections 36 and 28(4) AufenthG). This applies, *inter alia*, to stepchildren, adult children, parents, and parents in law.

II. Other Residence Rights for Family Reasons

369. Residence titles issued for the purpose of family reunion pursuant to Part 6 of the AufenthG entitle their holders to pursue an economic activity in Germany (section 27(5) AufenthG).

Chapter 3. Long-Term Residence

§1. CONDITIONS FOR LONG-TERM RESIDENCE

I. Permanent Settlement Permit

370. According to the terminology and system of German migration law, long-term residence is referred to as permanent settlement. Section 9 AufenthG describes the nature of this status. A permanent settlement permit (*Niederlassungserlaubnis*) is a residence title which is not limited in time.

371. There are several special provisions which determine when a permanent settlement permit can be issued due to specific circumstances. Within their scope of application, they take precedence over the general provision, section 9 AufenthG. Special rules apply to the following foreigners: graduates of German universities (section 18b AufenthG); skilled and highly skilled workers (section 18c(1) and (3) AufenthG); holders of an EU Blue Card (section 18c(2) AufenthG); civil servants (section 19c(4) AufenthG); self-employed foreigners (section 21(4) AufenthG); foreigners admitted to protect Germany's special political interests (section 23(2) AufenthG); foreigners with an asylum or a refugee status (section 26(3) AufenthG); subsequently immigrated dependants (section 28(2) AufenthG); spouses with an independent right of residence for family reasons (section 31(3) AufenthG); children with an independent right of residence for family reasons (section 35 AufenthG); and former Germans (section 38(1) AufenthG). The specific conditions to be met in order to be entitled to a permanent settlement permit are dealt with in the respective sections of this monograph.

372. If these special provisions do not apply, a permanent settlement permit will be granted if the following requirements are met (section 9 AufenthG).

373. The foreigner must have held a temporary residence permit for five years.

374. Furthermore, secure subsistence is required and the foreigner must have paid compulsory or voluntary contributions into the statutory pension scheme for at least sixty months or furnish evidence of an entitlement to comparable benefits from an insurance or pension scheme or from an insurance company; time off for the purposes of child care or nursing at home is duly taken into account. These requirements related to subsistence and pension fees are waived if the foreigner is unable to fulfil them on account of a physical or mental illness or disability.

375. A further condition for granting the permanent settlement permit is that the foreigner is permitted to be in employment, if he or she is in employment, and that the foreigner possesses the other permits required for the purpose of the permanent pursuit of the economic activity.

376. Also, the foreigner must possess sufficient living space for the whole family forming part of his or her household.

377. Moreover, the foreigner must have sufficient command of the German language and possess a basic knowledge of the legal and social system and the way of life in Germany. These requirements are deemed to be fulfilled if the foreigner has successfully completed an integration course, but evidence may also be given in any other way. They are waived if the foreigner is unable to fulfil them on account of a physical or mental illness or disability. They may also be waived in order to avoid hardship. These requirements are further waived if the foreigner is able to communicate verbally in the German language at a basic level and has not been entitled to participate in an integration course or has not been obliged to participate in an integration course (section 44(3), No. 2, and section 44a(2), No. 3 AufenthG).

378. In the case of cohabiting spouses, it suffices if the requirements as to pension fees, employment permit and permits related to economic activities are fulfilled by one spouse (section 9(2), sentence 1, Nos 3, 5, and 6 AufenthG). This also applies in cases of granting a permanent residence permit for reasons of international law, or on humanitarian or political grounds (section 9(3), sentence 3, and sections 22–26 AufenthG). The requirement as to pension fees will be waived, if the foreigner is undergoing education or training which leads to a recognised school, vocational or higher education qualification (section 9(2), sentence 1, No. 3 AufenthG).

379. Certain periods are taken into account with regard to the periods of possession of a temporary residence permit which are necessary in order to qualify for issuance of a permanent settlement permit. These periods are: the duration of former possession of a temporary residence permit or permanent settlement permit, if the foreigner was in possession of a permanent settlement permit at the time of leaving Germany, minus the duration of intermediate stays outside of Germany which led to expiry of the permanent settlement permit; a maximum of four years is taken into account. Also is taken into account a maximum of six months for each stay outside of Germany which did not lead to expiry of the temporary residence permit. Finally is taken into account half of the period of lawful stay for the purposes of study or vocational training in Germany.

380. Granting a permanent settlement permit can be precluded by reasons of public safety or order, according to due consideration to the severity or the nature of the breach of public safety or order or the danger emanating from the foreigner, with due regard to the duration of the foreigner's stay to date and the existence of ties in Germany.

II. EU Long-Term Residence Permit

381. An EU long-term residence permit is a permanent residence title pursuant to section 9a(1) AufenthG. It is largely, though not entirely, equivalent to the German permanent settlement permit.

382.   A foreigner is issued an EU long-term residence permit pursuant to Article 2(b) of Directive 2003/109/EC upon application if he or she has resided lawfully in Germany for five consecutive years. There are some differences compared with the German permanent residence title that apply when calculating this period. How the five-year period is calculated is set out in section 9b of the AufenthG.

383.   To be eligible for the EU long-term residence permit, the foreigner's means of subsistence for himself or herself and of dependants whom he or she is required to support are to be ensured by a fixed and regular income. This condition is deemed to be satisfied if the foreigner has met his or her tax obligations and the foreigner or his or her cohabiting spouse has paid the old-age pension contributions due or made adequate provision for an old-age pension in Germany or abroad. There is an exemption for those who cannot satisfy this condition due to a physical or mental illness or disability. No higher contributions or provisions are required than are required for a permanent settlement permit (sections 9c and 9(2), sentence 1, No. 3 AufenthG). In order to meet the income requirement, the foreigner must provide evidence that he or she has a statutory health insurance or an essentially equivalent form of insurance coverage which applies for an indefinite period or is extended automatically that covers the costs of illness and nursing care for him or herself and his or her dependants. Furthermore, a foreigner who generates a regular income from an economic activity must have been issued the required permit to be entitled to perform the economic activity concerned. In the case of cohabiting spouses, it suffices if one of the spouses has been issued the necessary work permits.

384.   A foreigner must also provide evidence of adequate accommodation for all the family members who are a member of his or her household. Furthermore, a foreigner must have sufficient command of the German language and a basic knowledge of German legal and social system and the way of life in Germany. The latter requirements are deemed to be fulfilled if the foreigner has successfully completed an integration course. They are waived if the foreigner is unable to fulfil them on account of a physical or mental illness or disability. They may be waived in order to avoid hardship. These requirements re further waived if the foreigner is able to communicate verbally in German language at a basic level and was not entitled or obliged to participate in an integration course (section 44(3), No. 2, and section 44a(2), No. 3 AufenthG).

385.   A refusal to issue an EU long-term residence permit is permitted if justified by reasons of public safety or order. When determining whether a foreigner poses such a risk, the authorities have to pay due consideration to the severity or the nature of the breach of public safety or order, the danger emanating from the foreigner and the duration of the foreigner's residence in and ties with Germany at the time that the decision to refuse to issue an EU long-term residence permit is adopted.

386.   The AufenthG lists a number of situations when an application for an EU long-term residence permit can be turned down (section 9a(2) AufenthG). No EU long-term residence permit is issued to a foreigner who has been issued a residence title for humanitarian reasons (Part 5 AufenthG) or whose application for this residence title is still pending, unless the foreigner has been granted approval to be admitted in order to safeguard Germany's special political interests (section 23(2) AufenthG). Foreigners who have applied for international or temporary protection are also not eligible for an EU long-term residence permit as long as their application is pending (section 24 AufenthG). Excluded are furthermore diplomats and persons with an equivalent status. Also excluded are students, persons in vocational training or persons who stay for another purpose of an inherently temporary nature in Germany. The latter is in particular the case by virtue of a temporary residence permit related to a maximum term of employment (sections 18, 42(1) AufenthG) or if an extension to the temporary residence permit has been prohibited because of the only temporary nature of the purpose of residence (section 8(2) AufenthG). The same applies if the foreigner's temporary residence permit serves to live together as a family with a foreigner who is only resident in Germany for a purpose of an inherently temporary nature, where no independent right of residence would arise if the family unity ends.

§2. ADMINISTRATIVE PROCEDURES AND DOCUMENTS FOR LONG-TERM RESIDENCE

387. Permanent settlement permits and EU long-term residence permits are issued by the foreigners authorities. An applicant has to submit a fully filled out application form, an up-to-date biometrical photograph, valid passport, evidence of sufficient means of subsidence depending on status, i.e., employee, self-employed person or pensioner, a health insurance, as well as evidence of adequate accommodation, successful completion of an integration course, and a pension scheme.

§3. LEGAL POSITION OF LONG-TERM RESIDENTS

388. A permanent settlement permit entitles the holder to pursue any economic activity in Germany. It may only be issued subject to a subsidiary provision if this is expressly provided for by the AufenthG. An example of a subsidiary provision is the restrictions on political activities of foreigners in section 47 AufenthG.

389. Like the permanent settlement permit, the EU long-term residence permit entitles the holder to pursue an economic activity and may only be supplemented with a subsidiary provision if this expressly provided for by the AufenthG (section 9(1), sentences 2 and 3 AufenthG). There are some privileges which holders of an EU long-term residence permit do and holders of a German permanent settlement permit do not enjoy. Thus, an EU long-term residence title is not lost due to residence outside Germany for a period of six months or more (section 51(1), No. 7 AufenthG). A particular advantage is the right to mobility within the EU that comes with the EU long-term residence status (section 38a AufenthG).

§4. POSITION OF FAMILY MEMBERS OF LONG-TERM RESIDENTS

390. The rules on family reunion that apply to foreigners who have been issued a permanent settlement permit or an EU long-term residence permit are similar to those that apply to foreigners who have been issued a temporary residence permit (*see* §3 of the Chapter on residence). The relevant provisions in the AufenthG are: section 29(1), No. 1, and (2), sentence 1, section 30(1), sentence 1, No. 3, and sentence 3, No. 1, section 31(1) and (3), section 32(1)–(2), Nos 1 and 2, section 33, sentences 1 and 2, section 34(1)–(2), as well as section 36(1) AufenthG.

391. Residence titles issued for family reasons (Part 6 AufenthG) entitle their holders to pursue an economic activity, anyway (section 27(5) AufenthG).

Part III. Right of Residence for Specific Categories of Persons

Chapter 1. Nationals with Preferential Treatment

§1. EU CITIZENS

I. Freedom of Movement

392. The status of EU citizens is regulated by the Act on the FreizügG/EU.[56] This Act regulates entry into and residence in Germany by nationals of the other EU Member States and their dependants. The basic features of entry and residence in Germany are set out in section 2 of the Act.

393. EU citizens and their dependants who are entitled to the right to freedom of movement enjoy a right to enter and reside in Germany as stipulated in the Freedom of Movement Act/EU.

394. The right of freedom of movement under EU law applies to EU citizens who wish to reside in Germany to pursue an economic activity (section 2(2) of the Freedom of Movement Act/EU). This refers to employment, self-employment, cross-border service providers and recipients of cross-border services and to vocational training. EU citizens seeking work also enjoy a right to free movement, albeit it is one that is restricted to a period of six months. This period can be extended if the job seeker can prove that he or she is still seeking work and has a justified reason to believe that he or she will find employment. The conditions governing the right to free movement accorded to recipients of services and economically inactive EU citizens are found in section 4 of the Freedom of Movement Act/EU. Inactive EU citizens need to provide evidence that they have adequate health insurance coverage and adequate means of subsistence.

---

56. Freedom of Movement Act/EU (– Freizügigkeitsgesetz/EU) of 30 Jul. 2004 (BGBl. I pp. 1950, 1986), last amended by Art. 6 of the Act of 20 Jul. 2017 (BGBl. I p. 2780).

395. Dependants of the aforementioned EU citizens share in the right to free movement, subject to the requirements in sections 3 and 4 of the Freedom of Movement Act/EU. These requirements entail, i.e., that the dependant joins or accompanies the EU citizen to Germany and that there are adequate health insurance coverage and adequate means of subsistence.

396. The right of free movement under EU law also applies to EU citizens and their dependants who have acquired a right of permanent residence.

397. The right to enter and reside in Germany, as stipulated in the Freedom of Movement Act/EU, remains unaffected for employees and self-employed persons in the event of a temporary reduction in earning capacity as a result of illness or an accident, as well as in the event of involuntary unemployment confirmed by the competent employment agency. After more than one year of pursuing a self-employed activity, this right also remains unaffected if a self-employed activity can no longer be pursued due to circumstances beyond the control of the self-employed person (section 2(3) of the Freedom of Movement Act/EU). The same applies if a self-employed person starts a vocational training, if there is a connection between the training and the former economic activity. This connection is not necessary if the EU citizen has lost his or her job involuntarily.

398. In the case of involuntary unemployment confirmed by an employment agency after a period of employment of less than one year, the right to enter and reside in Germany as provided for in the Freedom of Movement Act/EU remains unaffected for a period of six months.

399. EU citizens do not need a short-stay visa to enter Germany, nor a residence title to stay in Germany according to section 2(4) of the Freedom of Movement Act/EU. Dependants who are not EU citizens may need a short-stay visa to enter Germany. Short-stay visas are issued to dependants of an EU citizen as provided for in the AufenthG. Holders of a valid residence card issued by the competent authorities of Germany or another EU Member State are exempted from the visa obligation according to Article 5(2) of Directive 2004/38/EC.

400. The possession of a valid identity card or passport is sufficient for an EU citizen to stay in Germany for a period of up to three months. Dependants who are not EU citizens themselves enjoy the same right if they are in possession of a recognised or otherwise approved of passport or passport substitute if they accompany or join the EU citizen in Germany (section 2(5) of the Freedom of Movement Act/EU).

401. Short-stay visas are issued free of charge (section 2(6) of the Freedom of Movement Act/EU).

402. If the competent authorities have established that the EU citizen or one of his or her dependants has used forged or falsified documents or presented false information to mislead them into believing that one of the entry and residence requirements has been met, they may determine that there is no right to enter and reside in Germany. If it has been established that an EU citizen's dependant who is not an EU citizen him or herself does not accompany or join the EU citizen in Germany so that they can live together as a family, the competent authorities may determine that there is no right to enter and reside in Germany. In such cases, dependants who are not EU citizens themselves may be denied a residence card or short-stay visa. In the alternative, a residence card that has been issued may be withdrawn. A decision to withhold or withdraw a right to enter or reside has to be made in writing (section 2(6) of the Freedom of Movement Act/EU).

II. Dependants of EU Citizens

403. The status and rights of an EU citizen's dependant are set out in section 3(1) of the Freedom of Movement Act/EU. Both the residence status and rights differ from status and rights of dependants in the meaning of the AufenthG.

404. Dependants of the EU citizens, as defined in section 2(2), Nos 1–5 of the Freedom of Movement Act/EU – employees, self-employed persons and recipients of services – are entitled to enter and reside in Germany if they accompany or join an EU citizen in Germany. Dependants of so-called inactive EU citizens (i.e., EU citizens who are not in gainful employment) enjoy a right to reside in Germany subject to the condition that there are adequate means of subsistence to cover their stay without having recourse to the German social benefits system (sections 4 and 2(2), No. 5 of the Freedom of Movement Act/EU).

405. Dependants of EU citizens enjoy their right of residence pursuant to EU law as implemented in the Freedom of Movement Act/EU. The requirements in the AufenthG that apply to subsequent immigration of dependants in general, such as language requirements, do not apply to them. Only where the AufenthG provides more favourable rights than the Freedom of movement Act /EU, do these more favourable provisions apply to dependants of an EU citizen (section 11(1), sentence 11 Freedom of Movement Act/EU).[57]

406. As, in general, the Freedom of Movement Act/EU does not apply to German nationals, the AufenthG governs the status of dependants of German nationals. However, the Freedom of Movement Act/EU does apply if a German national has used his or her right to freedom of movement under the Freedom of Movement Act/EU. These are the cases in which German nationals return to Germany after having stayed in another EU Member State, so-called return cases.

407. Who is a dependant of an EU citizen for the purpose of the Freedom of Movement Act is determined in section 3(2) of that Act? Dependants within the meaning of the Freedom of Movement Act/EU are: the spouse, the partner with whom the EU citizens has entered a registered partnership, family members under

---

57. AVV 3.0.2.

21 years of age in the direct descending line of both the aforementioned partners; as well as their dependants in the direct ascending and direct descending line who depend on the EU citizen or his or her registered partner for their means of subsistence.

408. Dependants who are not EU citizens themselves retain their right of residence upon the death of the EU citizen, if they are in employment or self-employment or attending a vocational training and have resided in Germany as a dependant of an EU citizen for at least one year prior to his or her death (section 3(3), sentence 1, and section 2(2), Nos 1–3 or No. 5 of the Freedom of Movement Act/EU). However, the rules on subsequent immigration of dependants and the protection against loss of the right of residence for reasons of public order, security or health do not apply to them. Instead, the relevant provisions in the AufenthG apply in such cases (section 3(3), sentence 2, section 3(1), and sections 6 and 7 of the Freedom of Movement Act/EU).

409. The children of an EU citizen who is entitled to the right to freedom of movement and the parent who actually enjoys parental custody over the children retain their right of residence following the death of an EU citizen or if the EU citizen leaves Germany until the children have completed their education, provided that the children reside and are in education in Germany (section 3(4) of the Freedom of Movement Act/EU).

410. Spouses or registered partners who are not EU citizens retain their right of residence following divorce or the annulment of their marriage or partnership if they meet the work-related conditions that apply to EU citizens (section 2(2), Nos 1–3 or 5 of the Freedom of Movement Act/EU) and if the marriage or registered partnership existed for at least three years prior to divorce or annulment proceedings being started of which the couple resided at least one year in Germany. The same applies if a court ruling based on an agreement between the spouses or registered partners specifies that the spouse or registered partner has parental custody of their children. If retention of the right to reside is necessary in order to avoid special hardship, in particular, because the spouse or registered partner cannot be expected to continue the marriage or partnership due to the infringement of his or her legitimate interests, or if there is a court order specifying that the spouse or registered partner only has access to a minor child in Germany, that spouse or registered partner is entitled to continue residence in Germany. Section 3(1)–(2), sections 6 and 7 of the Freedom of Movement Act/EU do not apply; in these cases. Rather, the rules in the AufenthG apply (section 3(5) of the Freedom of Movement Act/EU).

411. The law restricts the right to freedom of movement of a certain category of EU citizens and their dependants in section 4 of the Freedom of Movement Act/EU.

412. Economically inactive EU citizens and their dependants who accompany or join the EU citizen in Germany are only entitled to enter and reside in Germany for more than three months if they have adequate health insurance coverage and adequate means of subsistence (section 2(1) of the Freedom of Movement Act/EU).

Stays of less than three months are governed by section 2(5), section 2(1) of the Freedom of Movement Act/EU exclusively. If an EU citizen resides in Germany as a student, this right only extends to his or her spouse, registered partner and children for whom maintenance is provided.

III. Permanent Residence

413. The Freedom of Movement Act/EU provides EU citizens and their dependants with a far-reaching right of permanent residence in its section 4a.

414. EU citizens who have resided lawfully and continuously in Germany for five years are entitled to enter and reside in Germany, irrespective of whether the other requirements that apply to persons for enjoying the freedom of movement under EU law such as residing as employee, carrying out vocational training or seeking work (section 2(2) of the Freedom of Movement Act/EU) continue to be fulfilled. This is called the right of permanent residence. Their dependants who are not EU citizens enjoy the same right if they have resided lawfully and continuously in Germany with an EU citizen for five years. In such cases, the rules in the AufenthG regulating the right to subsequent immigration of dependants joining a holder of an EU long-term residence permit apply.

415. Special rules apply to EU citizens within the meaning of section 2(2), Nos 1–3 of the Freedom of Movement Act/EU, i.e., employees, job seekers and self-employed persons. These EU citizens enjoy a right of permanent residence if they have resided in Germany continuously for at least three years and have pursued an economic activity in Germany or another EU Member State during the last twelve months at least (section 4a(2) of the Freedom of Movement Act/EU) if they are 65 years or older at the time that they retire from gainful employment or end their employment under an early retirement scheme. The same applies if they have to give up their gainful employment because they are permanently incapable of working, as a result of an occupational accident or an occupational disease which gives rise to an entitlement to a pension paid by an institution providing pension benefits in Germany, or after having resided continuously in Germany for a minimum of two years. If the spouse or the registered partner of an EU citizen is a German within the meaning of Article 116 of the Basic Law or has lost his or her German nationality as a result of marrying the EU citizen before 31 March 1953, the conditions concerning the duration of residence and employment do not apply (section 4a(2), sentence 2, of the Freedom of Movement Act/EU).

416. Permanent residence is facilitated for commuters. EU citizens within the meaning of section 2(2), Nos 1–3 of the Freedom of Movement Act/EU enjoy a right of permanent residence before the period of five years expires if, after having pursued an economic activity in Germany for three years, following which they are gainfully employed in another EU Member State, they retain their place of residence in Germany and return to that residence at least once a week.

417. Dependants of a deceased EU citizen within the meaning of section 2(2), Nos 1–3 of the Freedom of Movement Act/EU who resided permanently at the address of the deceased at the time of his or her death enjoy a right of permanent residence if the EU citizen had resided continuously in Germany for at least two years at the time of his or her death. The same applies if the EU citizen has died as a result of an occupational accident or an occupational disease. It also applies if the surviving spouse or the registered partner of the EU citizen is a German within the meaning of Article 116 of the Basic Law or has lost his or her German nationality as a result of marrying an EU citizen before 31 March 1953 (section 4a(3) of the Freedom of Movement Act/EU).

418. The dependants of an EU citizen who acquire a right of permanent residence in this indirect way also enjoy a right of permanent residence if they have resided permanently at the EU citizen's address (section 4a(4) of the Freedom of Movement Act/EU).

419. Dependants who are not EU citizens (section 3(3)–(5) of the Freedom of Movement Act/EU) acquire a right of permanent residence if they have resided lawfully and continuously in Germany for five years (section 4a(5) of the Freedom of Movement Act/EU).

420. The period of continuous residence is not affected by periods of absence totalling up to six months per year or absence for the purpose of military service or community service. The same applies in the case of a single absence of up to twelve consecutive months for compelling reasons, such as pregnancy and childbirth, a serious illness, study, vocational training or a posting to another country in connection with work (section 4a(6) of the Freedom of Movement Act/EU).

421. An absence for a reason which is not temporary by nature for more than two consecutive years, however, results in loss of the right of permanent residence (section 4a(7) of the Freedom of Movement Act/EU).

IV. Documents and Data Protection

422. There are special residence documents for EU citizens and their dependants who are not EU citizens. These are provided for in section 5 Freedom of Movement Act/EU.

423. Dependants entitled to freedom of movement who are not EU citizens are issued with a residence card for dependants of EU citizens that is valid for five years and issued ex officio within six months after the competent authorities have received the necessary information. On receipt of the necessary information, the dependants are informed in writing by the competent authorities that they have received the necessary information.

V. Loss of the Right to Freedom of Movement

424. The reasons which result in the loss of an EU citizen and his or her dependants' right to entry and residence are limited. They are enumerated in section 6 of the Freedom of Movement Act/EU.

425. The right to enter and reside in Germany is lost if the documents used to acquire those rights were forged or falsified or if they were acquired by presenting incorrect information (section 2(7) of the Freedom of Movement Act/EU). These rights are also lost if the requirements for such rights are no longer satisfied in the initial period of five years residence in Germany (section 5(4) of the Freedom of Movement Act/EU). These rights and the certificate confirming the right of residence under EU law can only be withdrawn (the EU residence permit) for reasons of public order, security or health (Article 45(3) and Article 52(1) TFEU). Public health reasons can only be invoked in the case of an illness with an epidemic potential, as defined by the International Health Regulations of the World Health Organisation, or an infectious or contagious parasitic disease, provided that Germany has adopted protection measures and the illness is detected within the first three months after entering Germany.

426. A criminal conviction alone does not constitute sufficient grounds to lose the right to enter and reside in Germany, or for withdrawal of the registration certificate. The criminal conviction must still be registered in the Federal Central Criminal Register, in which particular criminal convictions are registered. In addition, the circumstances in which an offence was committed must indicate personal behaviour which constitutes a current threat to the German public order and there must be a real and sufficiently serious threat to the public order, affecting the basic interest of society (section 6(2) of the Freedom of Movement Act/EU). Special consideration must be accorded to the duration of the foreigner's residence in Germany, his or her age, state of health, family and economic situation, social and cultural integration in Germany and the extent of the EU citizen or the dependant's ties with his or her country of origin.

427. More stringent conditions apply to the loss of the right to permanent residence. The appropriate test is serious grounds (section 6(4) and (5) Freedom of Movement Act/EU). In the case of EU citizens and their dependants who have been resident in Germany for the past ten years and in the case of minors, a loss of their right of residence requires compelling grounds of public security. This does not apply to minors if loss of the right of residence is necessary to protect the child's well-being. Compelling grounds of public security can only be invoked if the person concerned has been sentenced to a prison term or a term of youth custody of at least five years for one or more intentionally committed offences and this decision cannot be appealed, or if preventive detention has been ordered in connection with the most recent conviction that cannot be appealed, if the security of Germany is affected or if the person concerned poses a terrorist threat.

428. Economic reasons do not justify the loss of the right of residence or of the right of permanent residence. A passport, identification card or passport substitute that has become invalid cannot constitute a justification to terminate the holder's residence.

429. The person concerned should be heard prior to a decision to withdraw the right to enter and reside in Germany and to withdraw the documents attesting that right. Any decision must be issued in writing.

430. The law provides a limited number of reasons that justify an obligation for EU citizens and their dependants to leave Germany in section 7 of the Freedom of Movement Act/EU.

431. EU citizens and their dependants are required to leave Germany if the foreigners authority has established that there is no right to entry and residence. The decision requesting an EU citizen or his or her dependants to leave Germany must include a deportation notice and set a time limit for departure. Except in urgent cases, the time limit is at least one month. If an application is filed to grant suspensive effect to the decision (section 80(5) of the Code of Administrative Court Procedure), deportation must not take place before a decision is reached on that application.

432. EU citizens and their dependants who have lost their right to freedom of movement for reasons of public order, security or health are not permitted to re-enter and stay in Germany. They may also be denied the right to re-enter and stay in Germany if they have submitted forged or falsified documents or presented false information to obtain a right to enter and reside in Germany. In particularly serious cases, they should be denied the right to re-enter and stay in Germany, especially if they have repeatedly misled the authorities into believing that they meet the requirements for entry and residence or if their stay severely harms the public order and security of Germany. Where such a decision is taken because of the person having submitted forged or falsified documents or presented false information, special consideration is accorded to the duration of the foreigner's residence in Germany, his or her age, state of health, family and economic situation, social and cultural integration in Germany and the extent of the foreigner's ties to the country of origin. Decisions or measures must not be undertaken for economic purposes. The person concerned should be heard prior to the decision and the decision must be issued in writing. The bans are temporary ex officio. The time limit is determined in view of the circumstances of the individual case and may exceed five years only in the cases of decisions and measures taken for reasons of public order, security or health. The time limit begins when the person concerned leaves Germany. An application for the ban to be lifted or reduced which is filed after a reasonable period or after three years has to be decided upon within six months.

VI. Sanctions

433. Penal provisions and provisions on fines in the Freedom of Movement Act/EU are found in section 9 of that Act.

434. Anyone who uses or presents false or incomplete information to procure, either for him or for herself or someone else, a residence card, permanent residence card or a certificate confirming the right of permanent residence, or who knowingly uses a document obtained in this manner for the purpose of deceit in legal matters is liable to be convicted to a term of imprisonment of up to three years or a fine. Objects related to such an offence may be confiscated.

435. EU citizens and their dependants who enter or stay in Germany although they have lost their right to freedom of movement for reasons of public order, security or health risk being sentenced to up to one year of imprisonment or a fine (section 7(2), first sentence, and section 9(2) Freedom of Movement Act/EU).

436. Administrative fines are dealt with in section 10 of the Freedom of Movement Act/EU.

437. A failure to submit the required identification documents is an administrative offence. The same holds true for an obstruction to verify a photograph on a document or to comply with these obligations in due time. The fine can be up to EUR 3,000 (section 10(1) and (4), and section 8(1), No. 1, letter b, and No. 3, and (1a) Freedom of Movement Act/EU).

438. It is also an administrative offence to either intentionally or through negligence enter or leave Germany without carrying a passport or passport substitute. The fine can be up to EUR 3,000 (section 8(1), No. 1, letter a, and section 10(3) and (4) of the Freedom of Movement Act/EU).

439. Furthermore, EU citizens and their dependants who, intentionally or through negligence, do not possess a passport or passport substitute while they are staying in Germany also commit an administrative offence. The fine for this offence can be up to EUR 1,000 (section 8(1), No. 2, and section 10(2) and (4) of the Freedom of Movement Act/EU).

VII. Relation to the AufenthG

440. A considerable number of the provisions in the AufenthG also apply to EU citizens and their dependants who are entitled to enter and stay in Germany (section 2(1) Freedom of Movement Act/EU) by operation of section 11 Freedom of Movement Act/EU. These provisions are divers and cover exemptions to the passport requirements, on entry and residence bans, border crossing, exceptional visa and passport substitutes, subsequent immigration of parents and other dependants, integration courses, job-related language training, prohibitions and obligations to leave

Germany, deportation warning, fees, consultation requirements, individual instructions by federal government, form requirements, legal capacity, cooperation obligations that apply to foreigners, the calculation of residence periods, proceedings for specific indications of wrongful acknowledgement of paternity, the collection of personal data, the transfer of data and information to the foreigners authorities, the transmission of data and information, the transmission of information by foreigners authorities, storage and erasure of personal data, and authorisation to adopt statutory instruments (sections 3(2), 11(8), 13, 14(2), 36, 44(4), 45a, 46(2), 50(3)–(6), 59(1), sixth and seventh sentences, 69, 73, 74(2), 77(1), 80, 82(5), 85–88, 90, 91, and 99 AufenthG).

441. In addition, certain provisions concerning criminal and administrative offences in the AufenthG also apply to EU citizens and their dependants. These provisions are section 95(1), Nos 4 and 8, (2), No. 2, (4), sections 96, 97, 98(2), No. 2, (2a), (3), No. 3, (4), (5) AufenthG.

VIII. Political Rights of EU Citizens

442.   Special rules apply to EU citizens regarding their participation in elections. As specified in Article 28(1), sentence 3 of the Basic Law, nationals of an EU Member State, are eligible to vote and to be elected in accordance with EU law in the county and municipal elections.

§2. EEA STATES AND SWITZERLAND

443.   The Freedom of Movement Act/EU also applies to nationals of countries belonging to the EEA and their dependants within the meaning of the Freedom of Movement Act/EU as is stipulated in section 12 Freedom of Movement Act/EU. The EEA includes the EU Member States, on the one hand, and the non-EU Member States Iceland, Liechtenstein and Norway, on the other.

444.   While Switzerland is neither an EU nor an EEA Member State, it is part of the single market. Swiss nationals, in practice, enjoy a similar status as nationals of EEA states. Although the AufenthG applies to them as a matter of principle, the Freedom of Movement Agreement between Switzerland and the EU and its Member States provides detailed provisions on their right to freedom of movement.[58] The rules on freedom of movement, including the pursuit of an economic activity, in this Agreement are supplemented by rules on the mutual recognition of diplomas, the right to acquire real estate and the coordination of the social welfare systems.

---

58. Agreement of 21 Jun. 1999 between the European Community and its Member States, of the one part, and the Swiss Confederation, of the other, on the free movement of persons, OJ EC 2002, L 114.

§3. TURKISH CITIZENS

445. In principle, as they are third-country nationals, the immigration rights of Turkish citizens are those in the AufenthG. However, Turkish citizens enjoy a privileged status pursuant to the Agreement Creating an Association between the Republic of Turkey and the EEC,[59] commonly known as the Ankara Agreement, of 12 September 1963. Their immigration status is developed by the Additional Protocol of 23 November 1970,[60] Decision No. 2/76 of the Association Council of 20 December 1976 on the Development of the Association,[61] and Decision No. 1/80 of the Association Council of 19 September 1980 on the Development of the Association,[62] which are, in practice, particularly important legal instruments. These legal instruments are an integral part of EU law.

446. While there is no initial right for Turkish citizens to enter Germany and the German labour market, Decision No. 1/80 provides them with a right of residence and access to the labour market once the conditions, as developed by the Court of Justice of the EU, to acquire those rights are satisfied.

447. A Turkish worker duly registered as belonging to the German labour force enjoys privileged access to Germany's labour market after one year's legal employment (Article 6 of Decision No. 1/80). The Turkish worker is entitled, to the renewal of his or her permit to work for the same employer, if a job is available. Subject to the priority to be given to workers of EU Member States, a duly registered Turkish worker is entitled and, to respond to another offer of employment, with an employer of his or her choice, made under normal conditions and registered with the employment services of that State, for the same occupation after three years. After four years of legal employment, a Turkish worker enjoys free access in that Member State to any paid employment of his or her choice in Germany.

448. This right of access to the labour market entails a right to have one's residence title extended, to ensure that the right of access to the labour market would be ineffective.

449. These rights are only enjoyed by workers. Turkish citizens who are self-employed remain subject to the usual provisions in the AufenthG, subject to the operation of the so-called standstill provision, Article 41(1) of the Additional Protocol. According to this standstill provision, signed in 1970, the Contracting Parties

---

59. Agreement Creating an Association between the Republic of Turkey and the EEC of 12 Sep. 1963, OJ EEC 1973, C 113/2.
60. Additional Protocol of 23 Nov. 1970, OJ EEC 1973, C 113/18.
61. Decision No. 2/76 of the Association Council of 20 Dec. 1976 on the Development of the Association, EEC – Turkey Association Agreement and Protocols and other Basic Texts, Office for Official Publications of the European Communities, Brussels – Luxembourg 1992, ISBN 92-824-0905-8.
62. Decision No. 1/80 of the Association Council of 19 Sep. 1980 on the Development of the Association, EEC – Turkey Association Agreement and Protocols and other Basic Texts, Office for Official Publications of the European Communities, Brussels – Luxembourg 1992, ISBN 92-824-0905-8.

refrain from introducing between themselves any new restrictions on the freedom of establishment and the freedom to provide services.[63]

450. Turkish workers can only lose their special rights under Decision No. 1/80 on grounds of public policy, public security or public health (Article 14 of the Decision No. 1/80) and if they leave Germany for a longer period of time, which would mean, in any event, for six months.[64]

451. The family members of a Turkish worker who is duly registered as belonging to the German labour force, who have been authorised to join him or her, enjoy similar rights (Article 7 of Decision No. 1/80). They are entitled, subject to the priority to be given to workers of EU Member States, to respond to any offer of employment after they have been legally resident in Germany for at least three years with the Turkish worker. They enjoy free access to any paid employment of their choice provided after five years of residence. Children of Turkish workers who have completed a course of vocational training in Germany may respond to any offer of employment in this country, irrespective of the length of time they have been resident in Germany, provided one of their parents has been legally employed in Germany for at least three years in the past.

§4. OTHER NATIONALS

452. A great many of friendship and trade treaties provide the nationals of the contracting parties with special privileges which they can invoke when they are in the other contracting party's territory. An example is the 1954 German-US Friendship Treaty.[65]

---

63. OJ EEC 1977, L 361/59.
64. Cf. Kay Hailbronner, Asyl- und Ausländerrecht, 4th ed. 2017, p. 522.
65. Treaty of Friendship, Commerce and Navigation between the Federal Republic of Germany and the United States of America of 29 Oct. 1954, BGBl. II 1956 p. 487.

Chapter 2. Students

§1. BASIC PRINCIPLES

453. The AufenthG provides some basic principles pertaining to residence for reasons of education or training in section 16. According to the legislator, the access of foreigners to education or training serves the general education and international understanding as well as covering the need of the German labour market for skilled workers. In addition to strengthening Germany's international relations in the field of science, it also contributes to international development. The way it is shaped in detail aims at ensuring public safety.

The AufenthG reduces the requirement of secure subsistence for issuing a temporary residence permit to foreign students in section 2(3) AufenthG. For the purpose of issuing a temporary residence permit in accordance with section 16a–16c, 16e and 16f AufenthG, with the exception of participants in language courses not preparing for a course of study, the subsistence of foreigners is deemed to be secure if they have funds in the amount of the monthly requirement, as determined pursuant to section 13 and 13a(1) of the Federal Education Assistance Act. For the purpose of issuing a temporary residence permit in accordance with section 16d AufenthG and section 16f(1) AufenthG for participants in language courses not preparing for a course of study, and in accordance with section 17 AufenthG, the subsistence of foreigners is deemed to be secure if they have such funds plus an additional 10% of those funds.

§2. VOCATIONAL TRAINING AND ADVANCED VOCATIONAL TRAINING

454. German migration law pays special attention to vocational training. Vocational training and advanced vocational training are regulated in section 16a AufenthG.

A temporary residence permit may be issued for the purpose of company-based basic and advanced vocational training if the Federal Employment Agency has granted approval or it has been determined by the Employment Ordinance or by intergovernmental agreement that such basic and advanced vocational training is permissible without such approval. During a stay for the purpose of company-based basic and advanced vocational training, a temporary residence permit for another purpose of residence may be granted only for some specified purposes.

These specified purposes are training which serves to acquire a vocational qualification, the pursuit of an employment as a skilled worker, and the pursuit of employment to acquire distinct professional skills pursuant to section 19c(2) AufenthG. The latter means that a foreigner with distinct professional skills may be granted a temporary residence permit to pursue qualified employment if the

Employment Ordinance stipulates that the foreigner may be admitted to this employment; this is the case for employment in professions of information and communications technology.[66]

A special purpose is not needed if there is a legal entitlement to a temporary residence permit for another purpose of residence, for instance, when an entitlement on the basis of subsequent immigration of dependants exists. The purpose of residence of company-based qualified vocational training also entails attending a German language course to prepare for a vocational training, in particular attending a job-related German language training course in accordance with the Ordinance on Job-related Language Training Courses.

A temporary residence permit may be granted for the purpose of vocational training in a school which leads, pursuant to federal or *Land* regulations, to a State-recognised vocational qualification if the course does not primarily aim at nationals of a specific State. Bilateral or multilateral agreements of the *Lands* with public bodies of another State on attending a German school by foreign students remain unaffected. Temporary residence permits for the purpose of school attendance pursuant to such agreements may only be granted if the supreme *Land* authority responsible for residence matters has approved the agreement.

Where such training serves to acquire a vocational qualification, the temporary residence permit authorises its holder to work up to 10 hours per week in jobs which need not be related to such vocational training. In the case of training which serves to acquire a vocational qualification, a certificate on sufficient command of the German language is required if the language skills needed for the specific vocational training have not been tested by the educational institution nor are to be acquired in a preparatory German language course.

Before the temporary residence permit for the purpose of training which serves to acquire a vocational qualification is withdrawn, revoked or limited retrospectively because a prerequisite for issuance, extension or the duration of validity ceases to apply (section 7(2), sentence 2 AufenthG), the foreigner must be given, for the period of up to six months, the opportunity to seek another training place.

§3. FURTHER EDUCATION

I. Scope

455. Special residence rules apply to foreign university students. For the purpose of full-time studies at a State or State-recognised university or at a comparable educational institution, a foreigner will be granted a temporary residence permit pursuant to section 16b AufenthG. To be eligible for a temporary residence permit, a student has to have been accepted by the educational institution. Residence for study purpose also extends to measures to prepare for a study or compulsory training. Examples of such preparation measures are: attending a language course, if the foreigner has been accepted provisionally for a full-time study and acceptance

---

66. Cf. Bundestagsdrucksache (Bundestag document) 19/8285, p. 102.

depends on attending a preparatory language course as well as the attendance of a preparatory or comparable course prior to studying.

Proof of knowledge of the language in which a study is taught is required if the foreigner's knowledge of that language was not a condition to be accepted as a student for that study programme and acquiring language skills is not the objective of the preparatory measures.

A temporary residence permit issued for the purpose of attending a study is initially issued for one year. It can be extended for the same period and its validity should not exceed two years. The period of validity will be at least two years if the foreigner takes part in an EU or multilateral mobility programme or if the student is a beneficiary of an agreement between two or more higher education institutions. Where a study programme is shorter than two years, a temporary residence permit is granted for the duration of the course of study. A temporary residence permit is extended if the purpose of residence has not been achieved and can be achieved within a reasonable period of time. The host educational institution may be consulted to establish whether the purpose of residence is still achievable.

A temporary residence permit for study purpose entitles the holder to take up employment totalling no more than 120 days or 240 half-days per year, and to take up spare-time student employment. This does not apply in the first year of residence if residence permission has been granted for the purpose of preparatory measures to become enrolled in a study programme. Holidays are exempted.

During a stay for the purpose of full-time studies or preparatory measures, a temporary residence permit may be granted or extended for another purpose only for specific, limited purposes. This is the purpose of training which leads to a vocational qualification or the pursuit of employment as a skilled worker. A qualifying specific purpose is also the pursuit of employment for reasons of distinct professional skills pursuant to section 19c(2)AufenthG. This refers to qualified employments in regard of which the Employment Ordinance has stipulated that the foreigner may be admitted to this employment; this is the case for employment in professions of information and communications technology.[67] The temporary residence permit for another reason has to be granted if there is a legal entitlement to it.

A student may be issued a temporary residence permit if he or she has been accepted by a State, State-recognised or comparable educational institution for full-time study and acceptance is subject to a condition that does not qualify as a measure to prepare for a study programme. The aforementioned conditions and modalities for granting the temporary residence permit also apply in this case.

Issuing a temporary residence permit is also possible if a student has been accepted by an institution for a full-time study programme and the acceptance is subject to the condition that a preparatory or comparable course is attended and the foreigner is unable to provide proof of being accepted for that preparatory or comparable course. Here too, the aforementioned conditions and modalities for granting the temporary residence permit apply.

---

67. Cf. Bundestagsdrucksache (In particular to Section 19c, Bundestag document) 19/8285, p. 102.

A temporary residence permit may also be issued if a student has been accepted by an institution for a part-time study programme. Furthermore, the aforementioned conditions and modalities for granting the temporary residence permit apply in this case, too.

Furthermore, a temporary residence permit may be issued if a student is enrolled in a preparatory language course, without having been accepted for a study programme by a State or State-recognised university or a comparable educational institution, This is also the case if he or she has been accepted for a preparatory company traineeship. In these cases, permission to work is limited to holidays or as a trainee. The conditions and modalities as to duration of validity and extension as well as to granting a temporary residence permit for other reasons, as mentioned above, also apply.

II. Withdrawal, Revocation, and Retroactive Limitation

456. Before a temporary residence permit for further education (section 16b(1) and (5) AufenthG) can be withdrawn, revoked or limited retrospectively because an essential prerequisite for its issuance, extension or duration of validity has lapsed for which the student cannot be held responsible, the student must be given the opportunity, for a period up to nine months, to apply to be admitted to another educational institution.

III. International Protection Status

457. A foreigner who has been granted international protection by the authorities of another EU Member State may be granted a temporary residence permit for the purpose of study if he or she has studied in another EU Member State for at least two years,[68] This is subject to the condition that the foreigner has been accepted by the German host educational institution. Furthermore, evidence must have been provided that the foreigner wishes to carry out part of his or her studies at an educational institution in Germany, because he or she is taking part in an EU or multilateral programme that comprises mobility measures or because an agreement between two or more higher education institutions applies to the foreigner. The temporary residence permit is granted for the duration of the part of the study programme that is to be carried out in Germany. Here too, the temporary residence permit for the purpose of study entitles the holder to take up employment totalling no more than 120 days or 240 half-days per year, and to take up spare-time student

---

68. Cf. also Directive (EU) 2016/801 of the European Parliament and of the Council of 11 May 2016 on the conditions of entry and residence of third-country nationals for the purposes of research, studies, training, voluntary service, pupil exchange schemes or educational projects and au pairing (OJ L 132, 21 May 2016, p. 21).

employment. There is no right to take up employment during the first year of residence if the purpose of residence is to complete preparatory measures, except during holidays (section 16b(7) and 16c(1), sentences 2 and 3 AufenthG). Again, the general rules on a permanent settlement permit do not apply (sections 9 and 16b(7), sentence 4 AufenthG).

§4. STUDENT MOBILITY

458. Studying in Germany is further facilitated by the rules on student mobility in section 16c AufenthG, which implements Directive (EU) 2016/801.[69] A student does not need a residence title to stay in Germany for the purpose of study if that stay does not exceed 360 days and the following conditions are satisfied.

The first condition is that the host educational institution in Germany has notified the Federal Office for Migration and Refugees that the foreign student intends to carry out part of his or her studies in Germany. The second is that following this notification the host educational institution has to submit evidence that the foreign student has been issued a residence title for the purpose of study by the authorities of the other EU Member State which is valid for the duration of the intended stay. The residence permit has to be issued in accordance with the conditions in Directive (EU) 2016/801. Third, the host institution in Germany has to provide evidence that the foreign student, who wishes to carry out part of his or her study at an educational institution in Germany, is participating in an EU or multilateral programme that comprises mobility measures or is covered by an agreement between two or more higher education institutions. Fourth, there needs to be evidence that the foreign student has been accepted by the host education institution in Germany. Fifth, a copy of the foreign student's recognised and valid passport or passport substitute needs to be submitted, as well as evidence that the foreign student has secure means of subsistence.

The host educational institution must notify the German authorities when a foreign student applies for a residence title within the meaning of Directive (EU) 2016/801 in another EU Member State. If that has been done and if the foreigner is not denied entry and residence as provided for in section 19f(5) AufenthG because, e.g., insolvency proceedings have been instigated against the host entity or there is a public interest in expelling the foreign student, that student may enter Germany at any time during the period of validity of the residence title issued by another Member State and stay in Germany for the purpose of study.

If, at the time that the application is made, the host educational institution is not yet aware of a foreign student's intention to carry out part of his or her studies in Germany, it must notify the competent authorities as soon as it is aware that this is the case. If this is the case and if the foreigner is not denied entry and residence as provided for in section 19f(5) AufenthG because, e.g., insolvency proceedings have

---

69. Directive (EU) 2016/801 of the European Parliament and of the Council of 11 May 2016 on the conditions of entry and residence of third-country nationals for the purposes of research, studies, training, voluntary service, pupil exchange schemes or educational projects and au pairing, OJ EU 2016, L 132/21.

been instigated against the host entity or there is a public interest to expel the foreign student, that student may enter and reside in Germany for the purpose of study.

Within this scheme, a foreign student is entitled to take up employment totalling no more than one-third of the period of residence, and to take up spare-time student employment.

A foreigner must cease his or her study immediately if he or she is denied entry and residence pursuant to section 19f(5) AufenthG, because, e.g., the host entity and its business have been wound up in insolvency proceedings or there is a public interest in expelling the foreigner. The exemption from the obligation to hold a residence title, which previously applied for study purposes, ceases to exist in this situation.

If, within thirty days of receipt of the notification for mobility for the purpose of study, a student has not been denied entry and residence in line with section 19f(5) AufenthG, the Federal Office for Migration and Refugees must issue a certificate confirming the right to enter and stay in Germany to study as part of a short-term mobility programme.

After the foreigner has been denied entry and residence in accordance with section 19f(5) AufenthG or has been issued a certificate confirming the right to enter and stay in Germany to study as part of a short-term mobility programme, the foreigners authority is responsible for further measures and decisions regarding the right of residence. The foreigner and the receiving education institution are obliged to inform the foreigners authority of any changes of the conditions for entry and stay in the student's mobility scheme (section 16c(1) and (5) AufenthG).

§5. RECOGNITION OF FOREIGN PROFESSIONAL QUALIFICATIONS

459. Special facilitating rules apply if a foreigner intends to prepare for recognition of his or her foreign professional qualifications (section 16d AufenthG). For this purpose, a foreigner may be granted a temporary residence permit to complete a training course and sit a subsequent examination. This is possible if the authority responsible according to federal or *Länder* law on the recognition of professional qualifications has determined that adaptation measures or further qualifications are necessary to establish the equivalence of a foreign professional qualification with a German professional qualification or to grant authorisation to practise a regulated profession in Germany. The details for recognition are specified in the Professional Qualifications Assessment Act and a multitude of special laws of the *Länder.*

Granting a temporary residence permit requires that the foreigner has a command of the German language corresponding to the qualification measure, usually at least elementary knowledge of the German language. Supplementary training must be suited to enable recognition of a foreigner's professional qualification or to practice the profession. If the majority of the supplementary training is carried out as a trainee in a business, issuing a temporary residence permit also presupposes that the Federal Employment Agency has granted approval for that foreigner to take up employment (section 39 AufenthG) or it is determined, pursuant to the Employment Ordinance or intergovernmental agreement, that participation in the qualification measure is permissible without such approval.

The temporary residence permit is granted for up to eighteen months and extended for six months at the most up to a maximum length of stay of two years. This temporary residence permit entitles its holder to pursue an economic activity for up to ten hours per week which is independent of the qualification measure.

A temporary residence permit for the purpose of recognizing a professional qualification entitles the holder to pursue an economic activity which is not restricted in terms of work hours, if there is an offer to employ the holder of that permit in a profession for which recognition has been requested or which is covered by the application for authorisation to practise a specific profession. The specifications for that activity must be closely related to the specialist skills needed for the envisaged later economic activity. In addition, the Federal Employment Agency has to have granted its approval (section 39 AufenthG) unless the Employment Ordinance specifies that the employment is permitted without such approval. Pursuit of an economic activity also presupposes that any legally prescribed professional licence has been granted or promised (sections 16d(2), 18(2), No. 3 AufenthG).

More rules facilitating employment by foreigners who wish to have their foreign professional qualifications recognised are found in section 16d(3) AufenthG. For the purpose of recognizing the professional qualifications which a foreigner has acquired abroad, the foreigner should be granted a temporary residence permit for two years, and the pursuit of qualified employment should be permitted in a profession which is not regulated in Germany if a foreigner has the necessary qualifications. To be eligible for this opportunity, the foreigner needs to have a command of the German language corresponding to the activity, as a matter of principle at least elementary knowledge of the German language. It must also have been determined by a body, which according to federal or *Länder* regulations is responsible for the recognition of professional qualifications, that the foreigner lacks specific skills, knowledge, and abilities in operational practice. Furthermore, there must be a job-offer and the employer must have committed him- or herself to make possible, within this period of time, the compensation of the differences which the competent body has determined. Also, the Federal Employment Agency must have granted approval (section 39 AufenthG) unless it is set out in the Employment Ordinance or an intergovernmental agreement that the employment is permitted without such approval.

For the purpose of recognizing professional qualifications which a foreigner has acquired abroad, a foreigner may be granted a temporary residence permit if he or she is employed on the basis of an agreement between the Federal Employment Agency and the labour administration of the country of origin. This temporary residence permit may be granted for a period of one year and may be extended for one year in each case up to a maximum period of stay of three years. The agreement must regulate the procedure, selection, commission and application of the procedure used to determine equivalence of foreign professional qualifications and the granting of the professional licence in professions which are regulated by federal or *Land* law in the field of health and care. This is also required for other selected professional qualifications, but the granting of the professional licence only needs to be regulated as far as necessary, having regard to the adequacy of the training structures in the country of origin.

Furthermore, the Federal Employment Agency must have granted approval (section 39 AufenthG) unless it is determined in the Employment Ordinance or by intergovernmental agreement that granting a temporary residence permit is permitted without such approval. It is also required that a foreigner has a command of the German language as specified in the agreement, which is, as a matter of principle, at least elementary knowledge of the German language. This type of temporary residence permit authorises the holder to pursue an economic activity which is independent of the training for up to ten hours per week.

For the purpose of taking exams for the recognition of his or her foreign professional qualifications, a foreigner may be granted a temporary residence permit. This requires the foreigner to have a command of the German language commensurate with the exam to be taken. As a matter of principle, the command of the German language must be at least elementary knowledge of the German language, unless this is not to be established by the exam. The foreigner, however, does not have the right to pursue an economic activity.

After the maximum period of validity of a temporary residence permit for the purpose of recognizing a professional qualification has expired, a temporary residence permit may be only granted for a limited number of residence purposes. This is stipulated in sections 16d, 16a, 16b, 18a, 18b, and 19c AufenthG. Issuing a temporary residence permit is possible for the purpose of vocational training and advanced vocational training, and for studies, as well as to skilled workers and skilled workers with an academic education. Other employment purposes also qualify if the Employment Ordinance or an intergovernmental agreement stipulates that a foreigner may be admitted for the purpose of this employment. A further possibility is that a foreigner with distinct professional skills may be granted a temporary residence permit for pursuing qualified employment if the Employment Ordinance stipulates that a foreigner may be admitted to pursue this kind of employment. Also, a foreigner may be granted a temporary residence permit in well-founded individual cases in which a public, in particular a regional or economic interest or an interest of labour market policy, exists in employing the foreigner. Foreigners in a civil servant relationship with a German employer are granted a temporary residence permit without approval by the Federal Employment Agency to discharge their official duties in Germany. As usual, a temporary residence permit will be granted in other cases if a legal right exists.

For the purpose of seeking a job that suits the qualification of a foreigner, he or she may be granted a temporary residence permit for up to twelve months after establishing the equivalence of his or her professional qualification or after a professional German licence has been granted. Residence falls in the framework of stay for the purpose of recognition of foreign professional qualifications if a job vacancy may be filled by foreigners (sections 20(3), No. 4, 16d, 18a, 18b, 18d, 19c, and 21 AufenthG).

§6. STUDY-RELATED TRAINING PROGRAMME EU

460. There are special rules in section 16e AufenthG that apply to an application for a temporary residence permit for the purpose of a Study-related training programme EU. A temporary residence permit for a Study-related training programme EU (Directive (EU) 2016/801) is issued if a training programme is designed to enable a foreigner to gain knowledge, practice and experience in a professional environment. Approval by the Federal Employment Agency is not required. The foreigner must present the following documents: a training agreement, which provides for theoretical and practical training with a host entity; a description of the training programme, including the educational objective or learning components; the duration of the training programme; the conditions under which the trainee will work and be supervised; the working hours; and the legal relationship between the trainee and the host entity. Furthermore, the applicant has to provide evidence of having obtained a higher education degree in the two years preceding the date of application or that he or she is pursuing a course of study that will lead to a higher education degree. The training has to be equivalent to the higher education degree or study programme, both in terms of its content and level. Further requirements to obtain this temporary residence permit are that the host establishment has undertaken in writing to bear any costs incurred by public authorities up to six months after termination of the admission agreement for the foreigner's subsistence during an unlawful stay in Germany, and whilst executing a deportation measure.

A temporary residence permit for the purpose of a Study-related training programme EU is issued for the agreed duration of training, but does not exceed a period of six months.

§7. LANGUAGE COURSES AND SCHOOL ATTENDANCE

461. Temporary residence permits for the purpose of attending language courses and school may be granted according to section 16f AufenthG.

A foreigner may be granted a temporary residence permit to attend a language course, not in preparation for a course of study, or to take part in a pupil exchange scheme. A temporary residence permit for participation in a pupil exchange scheme may also be granted if there is no direct exchange scheme.

Furthermore, a foreigner may be granted a temporary residence permit for the purpose of attending school from, as a matter of principle, the ninth grade onwards if it is guaranteed that the school class is composed of pupils of different nationalities. The school must either be a public or State-recognised school of international orientation or a school that is not or not predominantly financed by public funds and prepares the pupils to obtain international school qualifications, school qualifications of another State or State-recognised school qualifications.

During a stay to attend a language course or school, a temporary residence permit for another purpose should, as a matter of principle, be granted only in the case of a legal entitlement. After the completion of a stay to participate in a pupil exchange scheme, a temporary residence permit for another purpose may only be granted if there is a legal entitlement. The general rules on granting a permanent residence permit in section 9 AufenthG do not apply.

The temporary residence permit for the purpose of attending a language course and school does not entitle the holder of that document to pursue an economic activity.

Bilateral and multilateral agreements of the *Länder* with public bodies in another State about attending domestic schools by foreign pupils remain unaffected. Temporary residence permits issue to attend school may only be granted on the basis of such agreements, if the supreme *Land* authority competent for residence matters has granted approval to the agreement.

§8. SEEKING TRAINING OR STUDY PLACES

462. Granting temporary residence permits for the purpose of seeking a place to train or study is regulated in section 17 AufenthG. A foreigner may be granted a temporary residence permit for the purpose of seeking a place to pursue a training to acquire a vocational qualification if the foreigner is less than 25 years old and the subsistence of the foreigner is secured. Furthermore, the foreigner must hold a certificate of a German school abroad or must hold a school certificate which entitles the holder to attend a university in Germany or in the State in which the certificate was obtained. The foreigner must also have a good command of the German language (level B 1 of the Common European Framework of Reference for Languages).

The temporary residence permit is granted for a period of up to six months. It may only be granted again if the foreigner has stayed abroad after leaving Germany for at least as long as he or she has stayed in Germany on the basis of a temporary residence permit for the purpose of seeking a place to train or study.

During a stay for the purpose of seeking a place to train or study, a temporary residence permit for another purpose should, as a matter of principle, only be granted for the purpose of pursuing a qualified employment as a skilled worker with a vocational qualification or an academic education (section 18a or 18b AufenthG). It is also granted if there is a legal entitlement.

For the purpose of applying for a place to study, a foreigner may also be granted a temporary residence permit. In this case, the foreigner must meet the school and language requirements to start the study programme or must intend to acquire them within the duration of the stay for the purpose of applying for a place to study. The foreigner's subsistence must be secure.

This temporary residence permit is granted for a period of up to nine months.

During a stay for the purpose of applying for a place to study, a temporary residence permit for another purpose should, as a matter of principle, only be granted for the purpose of vocational training, vocational continued training, further education, or to pursue qualified employment as a skilled worker with a vocational qualification or an academic education (sections 16a, 16b, 18a or 18b AufenthG). It is also granted if there is a legal entitlement.

A temporary residence permit for the purpose of seeking a place to train or study or to apply for a place to study does not entitle its holder to pursue an economic activity or to take up a student job.

§9. DENIAL

463. The AufenthG has concentrated the rules on denial of residence titles concerning students, researchers, and EU voluntary service in section 19f AufenthG. This provision regulates the rejection of residence titles, as far as students are concerned, when one of the following purposes of entry and stay is at stake: further education, student's mobility, study-related training programmes EU, language courses and schools, and seeking a place to train or study (sections 16b, 16c, 16e, 16f, 17 AufenthG). However, not all of these rules apply to all of these matters; the AufenthG differentiates between certain applications. In order to provide a more transparent description of residence conditions, the relevant rules are, where appropriate, set out in the context of the respective purpose of residence.

According to section 19f AufenthG, foreigners will not be granted a residence title for the purpose of full- or part-time studies, a preparatory language course or company traineeship, a study-related training programme EU, or to apply for a place to study (section 16b(1) and (5), sections 16e, 17(2) AufenthG) if the following reasons apply. It is not granted to a foreigner who is resident in an EU Member State because he or she has filed an application for refugee status, subsidiary protection (Directive 2004/83/EC), or international protection status (Directive 2011/95/EU), or if the foreigner enjoys international protection (Directive 2011/95/EU) in an EU Member State. The application will also be rejected, if the foreigner resides in an EU Member State under the terms of an arrangement to provide temporary protection or has filed an application for recognition of temporary protection in an EU Member State. Furthermore, the residence title will not be granted to a foreigner whose deportation has been suspended in an EU Member State on grounds of fact or law. Foreigners also do not qualify for such residence titles if they hold an EU long-term residence permit or a residence title issued by another EU Member State (Directive 2003/109/EC of 25 November 2003 concerning the status of third-country nationals who are long-term residents). The same applies to foreigners who enjoy rights of free movement equivalent to those of EU citizens on the basis of treaties between the EU and its Member States on the one hand and third countries on the other.

All these reasons for denial apply to a residence title for the purpose of full-time studies at a State or State-recognised university or a comparable education institution (section 16b(1) AufenthG). They also apply to applications for a residence title for the purpose of full-time study, with acceptance dependent on a condition other than attending measures to prepare for studies, as well as for full-time study, with acceptance dependent on attending a preparatory or comparable course, where the foreigner is unable to furnish proof of being accepted for a preparatory or comparable course (section 16b(1), sentence 3, No. 2, section 16b(5) AufenthG). It furthermore applies to applications for a part-time study, and if the foreigner has been enrolled in a preparatory language course, without having been accepted for a course of study by a State or State-recognised university or a comparable educational institution, or if the foreigner has been accepted for a preparatory company traineeship (section 16b(5) AufenthG). The same reasons to deny a residence title also apply to Study-related training programmes EU (section 16e AufenthG) and applications for a place to study (section 17(2) AufenthG).

Denial of a temporary residence permit for the purpose of further education, study-related training programmes EU, or an application for a place to study (sections 16b, 16e, 17(2) AufenthG) is regulated in section 19f(3) AufenthG. The grounds for denial set out in section 19f(1) AufenthG apply as set out above.

The application to grant a temporary residence permit for the purpose of further education, study-related training programmes EU, a language course and school, or to seek a place to train or study (sections 16b, 16e, 16f, 17 AufenthG) may be rejected according to section 19f(4) AufenthG if one of the following reasons apply. The application may be rejected if the host entity was established for the main purpose of facilitating the entry and residence of foreigners for the purposes mentioned in the provisions. It may also be rejected if insolvency proceedings have been instituted against the host entity's assets aiming to wind up the entity and its business. The same applies if the host entity and its business have been wound up in insolvency proceedings or the institution of insolvency proceedings against the entity's assets has been refused for lack of assets, and its business has been wound up. The application may also be rejected if the host entity does not pursue any economic activity or if there is proof or there are concrete indications that the purpose of residence of a foreigner would not be the one for which he or she has applied for a temporary residence permit.

The Federal Office for Migration and Refugees denies the foreigner entry and residence within the scheme of student's mobility if the requirements stipulated for participation in that scheme are not met (section 19f(5), section 16c(1) AufenthG). It will also deny entry and stay if the necessary documents presented, for instance the residence title in the other EU Member State, were fraudulently acquired, falsified, or tampered with (section 19f(5), section 16c(1) AufenthG), In these cases, the decision to deny has to be made no later than thirty days after the Federal Office for Migration and Refugees has received the complete notification (section 19f(5), sentence 2, section 16c(1), sentence 1 AufenthG). The Federal Office for Migration and Refugees also denies the foreigner entry and residence if the host entity was established for the main purpose of facilitating the entry and residence of foreigners for the purpose mentioned in one of the provisions. Entry and residence will also be denied if insolvency proceedings have been instituted against the host entity's assets aiming to wind up the entity and its business. The same applies if the host entity and its business have been wound up in insolvency proceedings or the institution of insolvency proceedings against the entity's assets has been refused for lack of assets, and its business has been wound up. The Federal Office for Migration and Refugees will also deny the foreigner entry and stay, if the host entity does not pursue an economic activity or if there is proof or there are concrete indications that the foreigner would reside for any other purpose than those for which he or she applies for the temporary residence permit. Denial also takes place if there is a public interest in expelling the foreigner. In this latter case, a decision to deny residence may be made at any time during the foreigner's stay. In all cases of denial, the foreigner and the competent authority of the other EU Member State as well as the notifying entity must be informed of the denial in writing.

Chapter 3. Researchers

§1. BASIC RESIDENCE STATUS OF RESEARCHERS

I. General Principles

464. Foreign researchers are foreigners who enter Germany for the purpose of conducting research. In the AufenthG, they are included in the Chapter on residence for the purpose of economic activity. As a rule, the provisions on residence for the purpose of economic activity also apply to researchers. Therefore, the principles of immigration of skilled workers as well as the general provisions on residence for the purpose of economic activity as set out in sections 4a and 18 AufenthG also govern the status of foreign researchers in Germany.

The admission of foreign researchers is thus geared to the requirements of the German economy and Germany as a science location. Due consideration must be accorded to the labour market situation. The specific opportunities for researchers in German migration law also serve to secure skilled labour and to strengthen the system of social security. They are oriented to the sustainable integration of researchers into the labour market and society. Furthermore, due attention must be accorded to the interests of public safety.

Foreign researchers benefit from a number of special provisions in migration law. The rules on granting a temporary residence permit for the purpose of conducting research also apply to those researchers who do not engage in an employment relationship, such as researchers who come on the basis of grants or scholarships.

II. Temporary Residence Permit for Researchers

465. According to section 18d AufenthG and Directive (EU) 2016/801, a foreigner is granted a temporary residence permit for the purpose of conducting research if a number of special conditions are fulfilled. If this is the case, the temporary residence permit does not require approval of the Federal Employment Agency.

A temporary residence permit is granted if the foreigner has concluded an admission agreement or an equivalent contract to carry out a research project with a research establishment which has been recognised for the implementation of the special admission procedure for researchers in Germany. The rules governing this procedure are set out in the Ordinance on Residence (section 38a and 38f AufenthV). A temporary residence permit to conduct research with a recognised research establishment is granted within sixty days of making the application. The contract requirement is also satisfied if there is an admission agreement or an equivalent contract with a research establishment that conducts research.

In both cases, the research establishment must have undertaken, in writing, to bear all costs incurred by public bodies relating to the foreigner's means of subsistence and deportation for a period of up to six months after the admission agreement has expired if that foreigner remains unlawfully in an EU Member State. This requirement should be waived if the activities of a research establishment are financed primarily from public funds. The requirement may be waived if the research project serves a special public interest. The rules on providing security, on charging costs, as well as on enforceability and reimbursement, apply accordingly to the declaration by which the research establishment has undertaken to reimburse any costs incurred by public bodies caused by unlawful stay of a foreigner (sections 18d(2), 66(5), 67(3), 68(2), sentences 2 and 3, and (4) AufenthG).

The research establishment may also provide the body that is responsible for the recognition of research institutions with a general declaration for all foreigners to whom a temporary residence permit is issued based on an admission agreement concluded with that research establishment.

Some general requirements on granting a temporary residence permit to pursue an economic activity as specified in section 18(2) AufenthG also apply to researchers. Any legally prescribed professional licence must have been granted or promised, and the equivalence of the professional qualification must have been established or a recognised foreign higher education degree or a foreign higher education degree that is comparable to a German higher education degree must exist if this is a condition to grant the residence title. The general requirement of a specific job-offer, however, is met if there is an admission agreement or an equivalent contract to carry out a research project.

A temporary residence permit for the purpose of research is issued for at least one year. If the foreign researcher takes part in an EU or multilateral programme that includes mobility measures, a temporary residence permit is issued for at least two years. If the research project is completed in a shorter period, the validity of the temporary residence permit is limited to the duration of the research project. In the case of an EU or multilateral programme that includes mobility measures, this shorter period is at least one year.

A temporary residence permit for the purpose of research entitles its holder to take up a research position at the research establishment specified in the admission agreement and includes teaching activities. Changes to the research project during the period of validity of the temporary residence permit do not affect its validity.

A foreigner who enjoys international protection within the meaning of Directive 2011/95/EU in an EU Member State may be granted a temporary residence permit for research purposes if the requirements to grant a temporary residence permit, as set out in the above, are met and he has stayed in that Member State for at least two years after having been granted protection (section 18d(1) and (6) AufenthG). Also, in this case, the temporary residence permit entitles its holder to take up a research position at the research establishment specified in the admission agreement and includes teaching activities. Changes to the research project during the period of validity of the temporary residence permit also do not affect its validity.

Usually, researchers will be a skilled worker within the meaning of the AufenthG. They would be skilled workers with a vocational qualification (section 18a AufenthG) or, even more likely, those with an academic education (section 18b AufenthG). Accordingly, researchers enjoy the same privileges as do skilled workers with a vocational qualification or an academic education, if this is the case.

III. Permanent Settlement Permit for Researchers

A. *General Rules*

466. A researcher will be granted a permanent settlement permit without approval of the Federal Employment Agency if the following requirements, set out in section 18c(1) AufenthG, are met. The foreign researcher must have held a residence title for the purpose of research purpose or as a skilled worker with a vocational qualification or an academic education for four years. This period is reduced to two years if the skilled worker has successfully completed a vocational training or a study programme in Germany. Furthermore, the foreigner must have had a job which he or she is permitted to hold as a skilled worker with a vocational qualification or an academic education or as a researcher. Also, the researcher must have paid the compulsory or voluntary contributions into the statutory pension scheme for at least forty-eight months or furnish evidence of an entitlement to comparable benefits from an insurance or pension scheme or from an insurance company. The period is reduced to twenty-four months if the skilled worker has successfully completed a vocational training or a study programme in Germany. The researcher must, moreover, have sufficient command of the German language. Furthermore, a number of the general requirements to grant a permanent residence permit must be met. The foreign researcher's subsistence must be secure. Granting a temporary residence permit must not be precluded by reasons of public safety or order. When determining whether there are public safety concerns due consideration must be given to the severity or the nature of the breach of public safety or order or the danger emanating from the foreigner, the duration of the foreigner's stay to the date of issuance of the permanent residence permit, as well as the existence of ties in Germany. If employed, the foreign researcher must have been granted permission to be in employment and possess all permits that are required for the permanent pursuit of his or her economic activity. A further requirement is that the foreign researcher has sufficient living space for him- or herself and the family members that are part of his or her household. Granting such permanent residence permit also requires that the foreign researcher possesses a basic knowledge of the legal and social system and the way of life in Germany. The latter requirement, as well as that of having sufficient command of the German language, is deemed to be fulfilled if the foreigner has successfully completed an integration course. They are waived if the foreigner is unable to fulfil them on account of a physical or mental illness or disability, and they may be waived in order to avoid hardship. The requirements of secure subsistence and contributions to the statutory pension scheme are also waived if the foreigner is unable to fulfil them on account of a physical or mental illness or disability.

B. *EU Blue Card Holders*

467. Somewhat reduced requirements to grant a permanent residence permit apply, pursuant to section 18c(2) AufenthG, to holders of an EU Blue Card.

EU Blue Card holders are entitled to a permanent settlement permit if a number of conditions are met. A holder of an EU Blue Card must be issued a permanent settlement permit according to section 9 AufenthG, if he or she has held a position of employment in accordance with section 18b(2) AufenthG for at least thirty-three months. This means that the employment must be equivalent to the foreigner's qualification and the foreigner must receive a salary of at least two-thirds of the annual assessment threshold for the statutory pension insurance. For science and engineering professions, medical doctors, and information and communications technology professions,[70] a salary of least 52% of the annual assessment threshold for the statutory pension insurance suffices. None of the reasons for refusal set out must exist (section 19f(1) and (2) AufenthG).The permission of the foreigners authority is only necessary in the case of a job change within the first two years of employment; it is granted if the conditions to grant a Blue Card EU are fulfilled.

Furthermore, the foreigner must have made all mandatory or voluntary contributions to the statutory pension insurance scheme for that period, or provide evidence of an entitlement to comparable benefits from an insurance or pension scheme or from an insurance company. The foreigner also has to satisfy the requirements in section 9(2), sentence 2, Nos 2, 4–6, 8 and 9 AufenthG. These requirements are: the foreigner's subsistence is secure and there are no reasons of public safety or order or any other danger emanating from the foreigner that justify a refusal to issue a temporary residence permit. It is furthermore required that the foreigner concerned is allowed to be in employment, and if he or she is in employment that all permits which are required for the purpose of the permanent pursuit of the economic activity have been issued to the foreigner. Furthermore, the foreigner has to provide evidence that he or she possesses a basic knowledge of the legal and social system and the way of life in Germany. Moreover, the foreigner must have accommodation that is sufficient for him- or herself and the family members who are part of the foreigner's household. The foreigner must also have acquired basic German language skills. The period of thirty-three months will be reduced to twenty-one months if the foreigner provides evidence of a sufficient command of the German language.

Section 9(2), sentences 2–4 and 6 AufenthG applies accordingly. This means that the requirements of basic German language skills and of basic knowledge of the legal and social system and the way of life in Germany are deemed to be satisfied if the foreigner has successfully completed an integration course. These requirements are waived if the foreigner is unable to fulfil them on account of a physical or mental illness or disability. They may also be waived in order to avoid hardship. The requirements that the foreigner's subsistence is secure and that he or she has paid the compulsory or voluntary contributions into the statutory pension scheme for a period of at least sixty months or has provided evidence of an entitlement to comparable benefits from an insurance or pension scheme or an insurance company (section 9(2), sentence 1, Nos 2 and 3 AufenthG) will also be waived if the foreigner is unable to fulfil them on account of a physical or mental illness or disability.

---

70. Group 21, 221, or 25 pursuant to Commission Recommendation of 29 Oct. 2009 on the use of the International Standard Classification of Occupations (ISCO-08) (OJ L 292, 10 Nov. 2009, p. 31).

C. *Highly Qualified Persons*

468. There are further privileges for highly qualified skilled workers with an academic education, as stipulated in section 18c(3) AufenthG. Such highly qualified persons are, in particular, researchers with special technical knowledge as well as teachers in prominent positions and scientific personnel in prominent positions with several years of professional experience.

A highly qualified skilled worker with an academic education may be granted a permanent settlement permit in special cases without approval of the Federal Employment Agency, if there is reason to assume that integration into the way of life in Germany and the foreigner's secure subsistence without State assistance are assured. The requirements, set out in section 9(2), sentence 1, No. 4 AufenthG, must be met, meaning that granting such a permanent residence permit is not precluded by reasons of public safety or order, according to due consideration to the severity or the nature of the breach of public safety or order or the danger emanating from the foreigner, with due regard to the duration of the foreigner's stay to date and the existence of ties in Germany. The *Land* government may stipulate that the issuance of a permanent settlement permit requires the approval of the supreme *Land* authority or a body designated by it.

§2. SHORT-TERM MOBILITY FOR RESEARCHERS

469. There are more favourable rules for short-term mobility of researchers in section 18e AufenthG that apply by way of derogation from the usual requirements for legal residence set out in section 4(1) AufenthG. A foreign researcher does not need a residence title if the duration of his or her stay for the purpose of research does not exceed 180 days within a 360-day period. Stays for the purpose of research that do not exceed this period have to be notified by the German host research establishment to the Federal Office for Migration and Refugees, informing those authorities that the foreign researcher intends to carry out part of his or her research activities in Germany. It also has to submit all relevant information when making this notification. The required information includes: evidence that the foreign researcher possesses a valid residence title for the purpose of conducting research issued by another EU Member State (Directive (EU) 2016/801); an admission agreement or an equivalent contract concluded with the host research establishment in Germany; a copy of the foreign researcher's recognised and valid passport or passport substitute; and evidence of secure means of subsistence.

This notification has to be made by the host research establishment when the foreigner applies for a residence title for the purpose of conducting research in another EU Member State. In this case, the foreign researcher may enter Germany at any time during the period of validity of the residence title and stay there for that purpose, unless the foreigner has been denied entry and residence in line with section 19f(5) AufenthG. This could, e.g., be the case because the host entity has been declared insolvent and its business activities have stopped or because there is a public interest in expelling the foreign researcher.

If, at the time of the application, the host research establishment is not yet aware of a foreigner's intention to carry out part of his or her research activities in Germany, this notification must be made as soon as it becomes aware of this intention. In this case, a foreign researcher may enter Germany at any time during the validity period of the residence title that has been issued by another EU Member State and stay there to conduct research.

Foreign researchers who satisfy the requirements for short-term mobility for the purpose of conducting research are entitled to develop research activities in the host research establishment and to assume teaching activities for that establishment.

If a residence title has been issued by a non-Schengen State and the foreign researcher enters Germany via a non-Schengen State, he or she must carry a copy of the notification and present it to the responsible authorities at their request.

The foreign researcher and the host research establishment have to inform the competent foreigners authority of any changes which were relevant to grant permission to a foreign researcher under the rules on short-term mobility for researchers.

If a foreign researcher is denied entry and residence pursuant to section 19f(5) AufenthG, he or she must immediately cease his or her research activities and any exemption derived from the rules on research short-term mobility to hold a residence title ceases to exist. If a foreign researcher is not denied entry and residence, then the Federal Office for Migration and Refugees issues the foreign researcher a certificate confirming the right to enter and stay in Germany for the purpose of conducting research under the rules on short-term mobility.

If entry and residence have been denied pursuant to section 19f(5) by the Federal Office for Migration and Refugees, the foreigners authority is responsible for further measures and decisions of residence law (section 71(1) AufenthG). The same applies if the certificate confirming the right to enter and stay in Germany to conduct research under the rules on short-term mobility has been issued. The foreigner as well as the host research establishment are required to inform the competent foreigners authority of any changes related to the requirements of granting short-term mobility for researchers.

§3. TEMPORARY RESIDENCE OF MOBILE RESEARCHERS

470. For stays that exceed those permitted under the short-term mobility rules for mobile researchers in Germany section 18f AufenthG provides special rules on the issuing of temporary residence permits. A foreign researcher is issued a temporary residence permit for a stay for the purpose of conducting research in excess of 180 days, but shorter than one year. To be eligible for this temporary residence permit, a foreign researcher must have been issued a residence title for the purpose of conducting research by another EU Member State (Directive (EU) 2016/801) for the duration of the research project and submit a copy of his or her recognised and valid passport or passport substitute, as well as the admission agreement or an equivalent contract, concluded with the host research establishment in Germany.

If the application for a temporary residence permit is filed at least 30 days prior to the beginning of the intended stay in Germany and if the residence title issued by the other EU Member State is still valid, a foreign researcher is permitted to work and reside in Germany for up to 180 days in a 360-day period until the foreigners authority decides on the application.

A temporary residence permit for the purpose of research as a mobile researcher entitles its holder to take up a research position at the research establishment specified in the admission agreement and includes teaching activities (section 18f(3), 18d(5) AufenthG). Changes to the research project during the period of validity of the temporary residence permit do not affect its validity.

The foreigner as well as the host research establishment are required to inform the competent foreigners authority of any changes related to the requirements of granting the temporary residence permit for mobile researchers.

The application for a temporary residence permit for mobile researchers is rejected if it was filed at the same time as the notification of short-term mobility of researchers was made (section 18f(5), 18e(1), sentence 1 AufenthG). Applications which were filed during the stay as a mobile researcher, but not in their entirety at least thirty days prior to the end of this stay, are also rejected.

§4. DENIAL

471. Reasons to deny a residence title in the field of research are enumerated in section 19f AufenthG. This applies to residence for the purpose of research, short-term mobility for researchers and temporary residence permits for mobile researchers (section 18b(2), 18d, 18e, 18f AufenthG).

These residence titles are denied, as are residence titles for the purpose of study, as outlined above, for the following reasons. They are not granted to foreigners who are resident in a Member State of the EU because they have filed an application for recognition of refugee status or subsidiary protection within the meaning of Directive 2004/83/EC or for recognition of international protection status within the meaning of Directive 2011/95/EU, or who enjoy international protection within the meaning of Directive 2011/95/EU in a Member State. They are also not issued to foreigners who reside in a Member State of the EU under the terms of an arrangement to provide temporary protection or who have filed an application for temporary protection status in another Member State. Denial also the case if deportation has been suspended in a Member State of the EU on grounds of fact or law, or who hold an EU long-term residence permit or a residence title issued by another Member State of the EU on the basis of Directive 2003/109/EC concerning the status of third-country nationals who are long-term residents. Finally, the following reasons to deny a residence title apply to foreigners who, owing to treaties between the EU and its Member States, on the one hand, and third countries, on the other, enjoy free movement rights equivalent to those of Union citizens.

Denial of a temporary residence permit for the purpose of research (section 18d AufenthG) is further regulated in section 19f(3) AufenthG. The grounds for denial set out in section 19f(1) AufenthG also apply, as outlined above. In addition to these grounds, a temporary residence permit is not granted to foreigners who hold an EU Blue Card (section 18b(2) AufenthG) or a residence title issued by another EU Member State on the basis of Council Directive 2009/50/EC of 25 May 2009 on the conditions of entry and residence of third-country nationals for the purpose of highly qualified employment (Official Journal EU Legislation (OJ L) 155, 18 June 2009, p. 17). Furthermore, a temporary residence permit for the purpose of research (section 18d AufenthG) is not granted if the research activities constitute part of a doctoral study in a full time study programme. In this case, a residence permit is issued for the purpose of further education pursuant to section 16b AufenthG.

An application for a temporary residence permit for the purpose of research and for mobile researchers (section 18d and 18f AufenthG) may be rejected if one of the following reasons apply. The application may be rejected if the host entity was established for the main purpose of facilitating the entry and residence of foreigners for one of the purposes mentioned in the provisions. It may also be rejected if insolvency proceedings have been instituted against the host entity's assets aiming to wind up the entity and its business. The same applies if the host entity and its business have been wound up in insolvency proceedings or the institution of insolvency proceedings against the entity's assets has been refused for lack of assets, and its business has been wound up. The application will also be rejected, if the host entity does not pursue an economic activity or if there is proof or there are specific indications that the foreigner actually wishes to reside for another purpose than that for which he or she has applied for a temporary residence permit.

The Federal Office for Migration and Refugees denies the foreigner entry and residence within the scheme of short-term mobility for researchers if the requirements stipulated for participation in that scheme are not met (section 19f(5), section 18e(1) AufenthG). It will also deny entry and stay, if the necessary documents presented, such as the residence title issued by another EU Member State, were fraudulently acquired, or falsified, or tampered with (section 19f(5), section 18e(1) AufenthG). In these cases, the denial decision has to be adopted no later than thirty days after the Federal Office for Migration and Refugees has received the complete notification (section 19f(5), sentence 2, section 18e(1), sentence 1 AufenthG). The Federal Office for Migration and Refugees also denies a foreigner entry and residence, if the host entity was established for the main purpose of facilitating the entry and residence of foreigners for one of the purposes mentioned in the provisions. Entry and residence will also be denied, if insolvency proceedings have been instituted against the host entity's assets aiming to wind up the entity and its business. The same applies if the host entity and its business have been wound up in insolvency proceedings or the institution of insolvency proceedings against the entity's assets has been refused for lack of assets, and its business has been wound up. The Federal Office for Migration and Refugees will also deny the foreigner entry and stay if the host entity does not pursue any economic activity or if there is proof or there are specific indications that a foreigner wishes to reside for another purpose than that for which he or she has applied for a temporary residence permit. Denial also takes place if there is a public interest to expel a foreigner. In this case, the decision to deny may be made at any time during the foreigner's stay. In all these cases, the foreigner and the competent authority of the other EU Member State, as well as the notifying entity must be informed of the denial in writing.

Chapter 4. Labour and Economic Migration

§1. Labour Employment

I. General Principles of Residence for the Purpose of Economic Activity

472. Foreigners holding a residence title may pursue an economic activity unless there is a law prohibiting such activity. This principle is set out in section 4a(1) AufenthG. An economic activity may be restricted by law. The pursuit of an economic activity going beyond a ban or restriction requires permission.

Every residence title must indicate whether the pursuit of an economic activity is permitted and whether it is subject to any restrictions (section 4a(3) AufenthG).

If pursuing an employment is banned or restricted by law, pursuing an economic activity or an economic activity going beyond the restriction requires permission. Such permission may be subject to the approval by the Federal Employment Agency under section 39 AufenthG. The Federal Employment Agency may restrict its approval. If permission does not require approval by the Federal Employment Agency, the general provisions stating grounds under which permission may be denied apply accordingly. These are set out in section 40(2) and (3) AufenthG. Thus, permission may be denied if, e. g., important personal grounds relating to the foreigner exist or the employer or the host entity has failed to meet its legal obligations regarding social security, taxation, labour rights or working conditions.

Residence titles must indicate any restrictions on the pursuit of employment imposed by the Federal Employment Agency (section 4a(3), sentence 1 AufenthG). Permission is required to change a restriction on a residence title. If a residence title was granted for the purpose of a specific employment, pursuing another economic activity is prohibited as long as and to the extent that the competent authority has not given its permission. These requirements do not apply if there is a change in ownership owing to a transfer of business, as defined in section 613a of the Civil Code, or if there is a change in the legal form of the business.

Foreigners not holding a residence title may only carry out seasonal work if they hold a seasonal work permit and they may only pursue another economic activity if an intergovernmental agreement, a law or a statutory instrument entitles them to do so without a residence title or if the competent authority has given its permission (section 4a(4) AufenthG).

Foreigners may, according to section 4a(5) AufenthG, only be employed or commissioned to perform other paid work or services if they possess a residence title and if there is no relevant ban or restriction. Foreigners not holding a residence title may only be employed if an intergovernmental agreement, a law or a statutory instrument entitles them to do so or if the competent authority has given its permission.

Anyone employing a foreigner in Germany must verify whether the aforementioned requirements on employment are met. They must also keep a copy of the residence title, the seasonal work permit or the certificate confirming permission to remain pending the asylum decision or confirming suspension of deportation, in electronic or paper form for the duration of the employment. Furthermore, they must inform the competent foreigners authority within four weeks of having learnt of the fact that the employment for which a residence title was granted for the purpose of economic activity (Chapter 2, Part 4 AufenthG) was terminated earlier than envisaged.

Those commissioning a foreigner on a sustained basis to perform paid work or services for gain must verify whether the foreigner possesses a residence title and whether there is no relevant ban or restriction. They may only commission the foreigner who does not hold a residence title if an intergovernmental agreement, a law or a statutory instrument entitles them to do so or if the competent authority has given its permission.

Granting a residence title to pursue employment presupposes, as section 18(2) AufenthG stipulates, that there is a specific job offer and the Federal Employment Agency has granted approval (section 39 AufenthG). An approval is not needed in several cases. Namely if this has been determined by law, by intergovernmental agreement or by the Employment Ordinance that the pursuit of that employment is permitted without such approval. In this case a temporary residence permit may also be refused if there are specific grounds for denial, e.g., the employer has failed to meet its obligations under social security or taxation law, labour rights or working conditions (section 40(2), (3) AufenthG). An example of cases in which an approval of the Federal Employment Agency is not needed, is granting a temporary residence permit to foreigners who are employed for predominantly charitable purposes. Further conditions to grant a residence title to pursue an employment are that the foreigner has been granted or promised any legally prescribed professional licence. The equivalence of the qualification must also have been established or a recognised foreign higher education degree or a foreign higher education degree, which is comparable to a German higher education degree exists as far as this is a condition for granting the residence title.

When a residence title for the purpose of employment is issued to a skilled worker with vocational qualification or academic education(section 18a, 18b(1) AufenthG) who is older than 45 years for the first time, the salary must be at least 55% of the annual assessment threshold for the statutory pension insurance, unless the foreigner can provide evidence of an adequate old-age pension. The Federal Ministry of the Interior, Building and Community announces the minimum wage for each calendar year until 31 December of the prior year in the Federal Gazette.

These requirements may only be waived in well-founded exceptional cases in which a public, in particular a regional or economic interest or a labour market policy exists in employing the foreigner.

II. Approval by the Federal Employment Agency

473. The general requirements for access to the labour market are set out in section 39 AufenthG. These requirements and the conditions for denial are dealt with in more detail below in the Part on access to the labour market and in the respective contexts.

A residence title, which permits a foreigner to take up employment may only be issued with the approval of the Federal Employment Agency, unless pursuant to a law, either in the Employment Ordinance or an international instrument, it is provided that such approval is not necessary. Approval to work may be granted if provided for by a law, either in the Employment Ordinance, or in an intergovernmental agreement.

III. Skilled Workers

A. General Approach

474. German migration policy works towards attracting skilled workers. The law underscores this objective by outlining general principles of immigration while also providing some general rules on labour migration in section 18 AufenthG.

According to these general principles, the admission of foreign employees is determined by the requirements of the German economy and Germany as a science location; due consideration is given to the labour market situation. The specific opportunities for foreign skilled workers serve to secure skilled labour and to strengthen the system of social security. The objective of these general principles is the sustainable integration of skilled workers into the labour market and society, according to due attention to the interests of public safety.

B. Definition

475. Section 18(3) AufenthG defines the term skilled worker as it applies in this Act. The AufenthG distinguishes between 'skilled worker with vocational training qualification' and 'skilled workers holding a university degree'. There are different rules on labour immigration that apply to the two kinds of skilled workers.

A skilled worker within the meaning of the Resident Act is a foreigner who has successfully completed quality vocational training in Germany or has a foreign quality vocational qualification, which is equivalent to one acquired in Germany. This is a skilled worker with vocational training qualification.

Skilled workers with an academic education are persons who have a German, a recognised foreign or a foreign higher education qualification which is equivalent to a German higher education qualification. These are skilled workers holding a university degree.

The AufenthG defines what quality vocational training is in section 2(12a) AufenthG. Vocational qualification in a State-recognised or similarly regulated occupation for at least two years, as determined by federal or State provisions, constitutes quality vocational training within the meaning of this Act.

Work requiring skills, knowledge and competences acquired in a course of study or in quality vocational training constitutes skilled employment (section 2(12b) AufenthG).

C. Temporary Residence Permit for Skilled Workers

476. A skilled worker with vocational qualification may be issued a temporary residence permit to pursue qualified employment for which he or she is qualified according to his or her qualification (section 18a AufenthG).

A skilled worker with academic education may be issued a temporary residence permit to pursue qualified employment for which he or she is qualified according to his or her qualification (section 18b(1) AufenthG).

Residence titles for skilled workers in both meanings are issued with a duration of four years or, if the employment or the approval by the Federal Employment Agency is limited to a shorter period of time, for this shorter period (section 18(4), sentence 1 AufenthG).

The Federal Employment Agency may grant permission to take up employment as a skilled worker if a number of requirements such as equal terms of employment are met. Approval for employment as a skilled worker is given without an examination of priority – the labour market test – unless the Employment Ordinance stipulates otherwise. This means that there is no consideration whether there are German workers available or not for the type of employment concerned. It is also not considered whether or not there are foreigners available for the job who already have the same legal status as German workers with regard to the right to take up employment or other foreigners who are entitled to preferential access to the labour market under EU law.

A skilled worker may not be employed on terms less favourable than those that apply to comparable German workers. It must be qualified employment for which the skilled worker is qualified according to his or her qualification. In the case of professions in science and engineering, medical doctors, as well as information and communications technology professionals must pursue employment that matches to the skilled worker's qualification. Furthermore, it must be national employment and the specific requirements in the Employment Ordinance, if any, that apply to the kind of employment pursued must be met.

D. EU Blue Card

1. Conditions

477. The general conditions to issue an EU Blue Card are set out in section 18c(3) AufenthG. A skilled worker with academic education is issued an EU Blue Card for the purpose of employment equivalent to his or her qualification without approval of the Federal Employment Agency if he or she receives a salary of at least two-thirds of the annual assessment threshold for the statutory pension insurance. It is refused if one of the reasons for refusal set out in section 19f(1) and (2) AufenthG apply, for instance if the foreigner's deportation has been suspended in an EU Member State on grounds of fact or law.

In certain defined professions, the salary threshold is lower, but then the approval of the Federal Employment Agency is required. This applies to professions in science and engineering, medical doctors, and information and communications technology professionals.[71] In these cases, the minimum salary required amounts to 52% of the annual assessment threshold for the statutory pension insurance. The Federal Ministry of the Interior communicates the minimum wages for each calendar year until each 31 December of the prior year in the Federal Gazette.

The permission of the foreigners authority is only necessary if a holder of an EU Blue Card changes job within the first two years of employment. Approval for a job change is given if the preconditions for issuing an EU Blue Card are met.

The EU Blue Card is issued for a period of four years. It is issued or extended for the duration of the employment contract plus three months if the duration of the employment contract is less than four years (section 18(4) AufenthG).

2.   Denial

478.   A refusal to issue an EU Blue Card is regulated in section 19f(1) and (2) AufenthG. Skilled workers holding a university degree will not be issued an EU Blue Card (section 18b(2) AufenthG), if the following reasons apply. It is not granted to a foreigner who is resident in an EU Member State because he or she has filed an application for recognition of refugee status, subsidiary protection (Directive 2004/83/EC), or international protection status (Directive 2011/95/EU), or if the foreigner enjoys international protection (Directive 2011/95/EU) in an EU Member State. The application is also rejected if the foreigner resides in an EU Member State under the terms of an arrangement to provide temporary protection or has filed an application for temporary protection in an EU Member State. Furthermore, the residence title is not issued to a foreigner whose deportation has been suspended in an EU Member State on grounds of fact or law. Foreigners do also not qualify for an EU Blue card if they hold an EU long-term residence permit or a residence title issued by another EU Member State (Directive 2003/109/EC of 25 November 2003 concerning the status of third-country nationals who are long-term residents). The same applies to foreigners who enjoy rights of free movement equivalent to those of EU citizens on the basis of treaties concluded between the EU and its Member States, on the one hand, and one or more third countries, on the other.

In addition to the grounds set out in section 19f(1) AufenthG, an EU Blue Card for skilled workers holding a university degree is not issued in one of the situations set out in section 19f(2) AufenthG. It is not issued to foreigners who hold a residence title for reasons of international law or on humanitarian or political grounds, unless they have been admitted to Germany in order to safeguard one of Germany's special political interests or as resettlement refugees or who hold a comparable legal position in another EU Member State (section 19f(2), Part 5, and section 23(2) and (4) AufenthG). This also applies to foreigners who have applied for such a title or such a legal position and the application has not yet been finally decided upon. An

---

71. Group 21, 221, and 25 of the Commission Recommendation of 29 Oct. 2009 on the Use of the International Standard Classification of Occupations (ISCO-08) (OJ L 292, 10 Nov. 2009, p. 31).

EU Blue Card is also not granted to foreigners whose entry into an EU Member State is subject to obligations arising from an international treaty to facilitate entry and temporary residence of specific categories of natural persons engaged in trade- or investment-related activities, or who have been admitted as seasonal workers by an EU Member State. The same applies to foreigners who have come to Germany as posted workers for the duration of their posting to Germany (Directive 96/71/EC of the European Parliament and of the Council of 16 December 1996 concerning the posting of workers in the framework of the provision of services (OJ L 18, 21 January 1997, p. 1), in the version of Directive 2018/957 of the European Parliament and of the Council of 28 June 2018 amending Directive 96/71/EC concerning the posting of workers in the framework of the provision of services (OJ L 173, 9 July 2018, p. 16)).

E. Permanent Settlement Permit for Skilled Workers

1.   General Rules

479.   Skilled workers are issued a permanent settlement permit under favourable conditions, which are set out in section 18c(1) AufenthG.

A skilled worker is issued a permanent settlement permit without approval of the Federal Employment Agency if the following requirements are met. The foreign skilled worker must have held a residence title for the purpose of research or as a skilled worker with a vocational qualification or academic education for four years. This period is reduced to two years if the skilled worker has successfully completed a vocational training or a study programme in Germany. Furthermore, the foreigner must have a job, which he or she is permitted to hold as a skilled worker with a vocational qualification, an academic education or as a researcher. Also, the foreigner must have paid the compulsory or voluntary contributions into the statutory pension scheme for at least forty-eight months or furnish evidence of an entitlement to comparable benefits from an insurance or pension scheme or from an insurance company. The period is reduced to twenty-four months if the skilled worker has successfully completed a vocational training or a study programme in Germany. A researcher, moreover, must have sufficient command of the German language. Furthermore, a number of the general requirements to issue a permanent residence permit must be met. The foreign researcher's subsistence must be secure. Issuing a temporary residence permit must not be precluded by reasons of public safety or order, paying due consideration to the severity or the nature of the breach of public safety or order or the danger emanating from the foreigner and due regard must be given to the duration of the foreigner's stay to the date of issuance of the permanent residence permit as well as the existence of ties in Germany. The foreign skilled worker must be permitted to be in employment and if in employment, must possess all the permits required for the permanent pursuit of his or her economic activity. A further requirement is that the foreigner possesses sufficient living space for him- or herself and the family members who belong to his or her household. To be issued a permanent residence permit the foreign researcher must possess a basic knowledge of the legal and social system and the way of life in Germany. The latter requirement, as well as that of having sufficient command of the German language is deemed to be fulfilled if the foreigner has successfully completed an integration course. They are waived if the foreigner is unable to satisfy them due to a physical or mental illness or disability, and they may be waived in order to avoid hardship. The requirements of secure subsistence and contributions paid into the statutory pension scheme are also waived if the foreigner is unable to satisfy them due to a physical or mental illness or disability.

2.   EU Blue Card Holders

480.   Somewhat more lenient requirements to issue a permanent residence permit apply, pursuant to section 18c(2) AufenthG, to holders of an EU Blue Card.

EU Blue Card holders are entitled to a permanent settlement permit if they satisfy the following conditions. A holder of an EU Blue Card must be issued a permanent settlement permit if he or she has been employed in accordance with section 18b(2) AufenthG for at least thirty-three months. This means that the employment must match the foreigner's qualification and the foreigner must receive a salary of at least two-thirds of the annual assessment threshold for the statutory pension insurance. For the following professions, science and engineering, medical doctors, and information and communications technology,[72] a salary of least 52% of the annual assessment threshold for the statutory pension insurance suffices. None of the reasons for refusal set out in section 19f(1) and (2) AufenthG must exist. The permission of the foreigners authority is only necessary if there is a job change within the first two years of employment. It is given if the preconditions for granting a Blue Card EU are fulfilled.

Furthermore, the foreigner must have made all mandatory or voluntary contributions to the statutory pension insurance scheme for that period, or provide evidence of an entitlement to comparable benefits from an insurance or pension scheme or from an insurance company. Furthermore, the foreigner has to satisfy the requirements in section 9(2), sentence 2, Nos 2, 4–6, 8 and 9 AufenthG. These requirements are that the foreigner's subsistence is secure and there are no reasons of public safety or order or other danger emanating from the foreigner that justify a refusal to issue a temporary residence permit. It is furthermore required that the foreigner concerned is allowed to be in employment, and if he or she is in employment that all permits which are required for the purpose of the permanent pursuit of the economic activity have been issued to the foreigner. Furthermore, the foreigner has to provide evidence that he or she possesses a basic knowledge of the legal and social system and the way of life in Germany. Moreover, the foreigner must have accommodation that is sufficient for him- or herself and the family members who belong to the foreigner's household. The foreigner must also have acquired basic German language skills. The period of thirty-three months is reduced to twenty-one months if the foreigner provides evidence of sufficient command of the German language.

---

72. Group 21, 221, or 25 pursuant to Commission Recommendation of 29 Oct. 2009 on the use of the International Standard Classification of Occupations (ISCO-08) (OJ L 292, 10 Nov. 2009, p. 31).

Section 9(2), sentences 2–6 AufenthG applies accordingly. This means that the requirements of basic German language skills and basic knowledge of the legal and social system and the way of life in Germany are deemed to be satisfied if the foreigner has successfully completed an integration course. These requirements are waived if the foreigner is unable to satisfy them on account of a physical or mental illness or disability. They may also be waived in order to avoid hardship. The integration obligation is also waived if the foreigner is able to communicate verbally in German at a basic level and was not entitled to participate in an integration course because the need for integration is discernibly minimal (section 44(3), No. 2 AufenthG) or if the foreigner was not obliged to participate in an integration course because attendance on a sustained basis is unfeasible or unreasonable (section 44a(2), No. 3 AufenthG). Some requirements will be waived if the foreigner is unable to fulfil them on account of a physical or mental illness or disability. These requirements are: the foreigner's subsistence is secure and he or she has paid the compulsory or voluntary contributions into the statutory pension scheme for a period of at least sixty months or has provided evidence of an entitlement to comparable benefits from an insurance or pension scheme or an insurance company (section 9(2), sentence 1, Nos 2 and 3 AufenthG).

F. Highly Qualified Persons

481. There are further privileges for highly qualified skilled workers with an academic education, as stipulated in section 18c(3) AufenthG. Highly qualified persons have several years of professional experience and are, in particular, researchers with special technical knowledge as well as teaching personnel with a prominent position and scientific personnel with a prominent position.

In special cases, a highly qualified skilled worker with an academic education may be granted a permanent settlement permit without the approval of the Federal Employment Agency if there is reason to assume that there is no problem with their integration into the way of life in Germany and the foreigner's subsistence is secure, i.e., State assistance is not presumed. The requirements set out in section 9(2), sentence 1, No. 4 AufenthG must be met. This means that issuing a permanent residence permit is not precluded by reasons of public safety or order, paying due consideration to the severity or the nature of the breach of public safety or order or the danger emanating from the foreigner, and with due regard to the duration of the foreigner's stay to date and the existence of ties in Germany. The *Land* government may stipulate that the issuing of a permanent settlement permit requires the approval of the supreme *Land* authority or a body designated by it.

IV. Intra-Corporate Transfers

A. ICT Card

482. ICT are facilitated by the ICT Card pursuant to section 19 AufenthG, implementing Directive 2014/66/EU.[73]

The ICT scheme aims at addressing the challenges resulting from the globalisation of business – increased trade and an increasing number of multinational groups with locations across the globe – which has triggered movement of managers, specialists and trainee employees of branches and subsidiaries of multinationals, who are temporarily relocated for short assignments to other entities of the company. The rules aim at advancing a knowledge-based economy and fostering investment flows across the EU by facilitating ICT of key personnel and thus promoting new skills and knowledge, innovation and enhanced economic opportunities for the host entities.

An ICT is the temporary secondment of a foreigner to a national entity belonging to the undertaking by which the foreigner is employed, if the undertaking is located outside the EU. The same applies to a national entity of another undertaking of the group of undertakings to which the undertaking located outside the EU belongs and that employs the foreigner.

An ICT Card is issued for the duration of the transfer, but no more than three years for managers and specialists and for the duration of the transfer, but no more than one year for trainee employees. These maximum periods must not be exceeded by an extension of the ICT Card.

A foreigner will be granted an ICT Card if a number of special conditions are met. The foreigner has to work as a manager, specialist or as a trainee employee in the host entity. Furthermore, the foreigner must have been employed by the undertaking or group of undertakings for at least six months immediately prior to the transfer. Further conditions are: the foreigner has been employed without interruption by the undertaking or group of undertakings during the transfer period; and the ICT exceeds ninety days.

In addition, the foreigner must provide a work contract valid for the duration of the ICT and, if necessary, an assignment letter providing specific information regarding the place and kind of work and remuneration, as well as the other terms and conditions of employment that apply during the ICT. There must also be evidence that, after completion of the ICT, the foreigner will be able to return to an entity belonging to the same undertaking or group of undertakings established outside the EU. In addition, the foreigner must provide evidence of his or her professional qualifications, unless the application concerns trainee employees.

A manager within the meaning of the AufenthG is a person holding a senior position, who primarily directs the management of the host entity, receives general supervision or guidance principally from the board of directors or shareholders of the business or their equivalent. This position includes directing the host entity or a department or subdivision of the host entity and supervising and controlling the

---

73. OJ EU 2014, L 157/1.

work of the other supervisory, professional or managerial employees. It furthermore includes having the authority to recommend hiring, dismissing staff or other actions concerning staff.

A specialist within the meaning of the AufenthG is a person who possesses specialised knowledge, which is essential to the host entity's areas of activity, techniques or management, has obtained a high level qualification, as well as adequate professional experience.

A trainee employee within the meaning of the AufenthG is a person with a university degree who is completing a traineeship for career development purposes or in order to obtain training in business techniques or methods, and is paid during the transfer.

An ICT Card is not issued to a foreigner who enjoys the right to free movement equivalent to that of EU citizens pursuant to a treaty concluded between the EU and its Member States, on the one hand, and the third country of which the foreigner is a national, on the other, or who is employed by an undertaking located in one of those third countries. This applies to Iceland, Liechtenstein, Norway, and Switzerland. In addition, an ICT Card is not issued if the foreigner is employed by an undertaking located in one of those third countries. An ICT Card is also not issued to a foreigner who is completing a training programme as part of his or her studies. Furthermore, it will not be issued if the receiving undertaking has been founded primarily for the purpose of facilitating the entry of ICT. It will also not be granted to a foreigner, who, in the context of entry and stay in several EU Member States, will spend more time in another Member State than in Germany in the context of the transfer. In this case, the foreigner will have to apply for an ICT Card in that other Member State. Finally, an ICT Card cannot be issued if an application is filed within six months of the end of the foreigner's last stay in Germany for the purpose of an ICT; this is the so-called cooling-down period.

B. *Short-Term Mobility for ICT*

483. Short-term stays are facilitated within the scope of ICT by the Short-term Mobility scheme (section 19a AufenthG). To qualify as a short stay, the stay must not exceed 90 days within a 180-day period. Within the context of the Short-term Mobility scheme, a foreigner is not required to have a residence title for a stay as an ICT.

The host entity in the other EU Member State must notify the Federal Office for Migration and Refugees that the foreigner intends to take up employment in Germany. In doing so, the host entity has to submit evidence that the foreigner possesses a valid residence title issued by another EU Member State (Directive 2014/66/EU), evidence that the national host entity belongs to the same undertaking or group of undertakings as the undertaking established outside the EU that employs the foreigner. It must also submit a work contract and, if necessary, an assignment letter specifying the place, kind of work and remuneration as well as the other terms and conditions of employment that will apply during the ICT. An assignment letter is necessary if the work contract does not already contain detailed information on the terms and conditions of employment. These documents also have to provide evidence that, after completion of the ICT, the foreigner will be able to return to an entity belonging to the same undertaking or group of undertakings established outside the EU (section 19(2), sentence 1, No. 3 AufenthG). These documents must have been presented to the competent authorities of the other Member State prior to making an application with the German authorities. The host entity, furthermore, has to submit a copy of the foreigner's recognised and valid passport or passport substitute when lodging the application. It also has to submit evidence that any legally prescribed professional licence has been issued or promised.

The host entity must notify the German authorities when the foreigner applies for a residence title (Directive 2014/66/EU) in another EU Member State. In this case and if the foreigner has not been denied entry and residence, that foreigner may enter Germany at any time during the period of validity of the residence title issued by the other Member State and stay in Germany for the purpose of an ICT.

If, at the time of an application, the host entity in the other Member State is not yet aware of the foreigner's intention to be transferred to an entity in Germany, it must notify the German authorities as soon as it becomes aware of this intention. The foreigner may then enter Germany at any time during the period of validity of the residence title issued by the other Member State, and stay in Germany for the purpose of an ICT.

If a residence title has been issued by a non-Schengen State, and if the foreigner enters Germany via a non-Schengen State, the foreigner must carry a copy of the notification and present it to the competent authorities at their request.

The foreigner must also inform the German foreigners authority without delay if the other Member State extends that residence title.

The following conditions justify a refusal by the foreigners authority to grant a foreigner entry and/or residence. This is the case if the remuneration that the foreigner will receive during the ICT period is less favourable than that paid to German employees in comparable positions. This is also the case, if the foreigner has stayed in the EU for more than three years (managers and specialists), or, in the case of a trainee employee, for more than one year. Entry and residence permission is also denied if there is no evidence of a valid residence title issued by another EU Member State and the host entity's affiliation to the foreign employer is absent, or if the passport requirement is not met. Furthermore, entry and stay will be denied under the Short-term Mobility scheme if the documents presented as evidence were fraudulently acquired, falsified, or tampered with. The same applies if there is no evidence of the required professional licences. Entry and residence will also be denied if there is a public interest justifying an expulsion measure. For this purpose the rules on verification and security measures, such as transmitting data and consulting security authorities (section 73(2) and (3) AufenthG), apply.

Unless there is a public interest justifying an expulsion measure, a rejection must be made no later than twenty days after the Federal Office for Migration and Refugees receives all information required to process a notification of a short-term transfer. If a public interest justifies an expulsion measure, the application for a short-term transfer may be rejected any time during the foreigner's stay in Germany.

The foreigner and the competent authority of the other Member State as well as the host entity in the other Member State must be informed that an application has been rejected. When a rejection is made within the allotted time of the short-term transfer, the foreigner must cease his or her employment without delay; the exemption from obtaining a residence title ceases to exist.

If, within twenty days of receiving a notification, the foreigner has not been denied entry and residence, the Federal Office for Migration and Refugees must issue the foreigner a certificate confirming the right to enter and stay in Germany for the purpose of an ICT in the context of short-term mobility.

After denying entry or residence, as well as after the certificate confirming the right to enter and stay in Germany has been issued, the foreigners authority is responsible for further measures and decisions concerning residence law.

C. Mobile ICT Card

484. Foreigners, with a residence title in another EU Member State and are planning to stay in Germany within the scope of ICT for more than ninety days, may apply for a Mobile ICT Card.

The Mobile ICT Card is a residence title pursuant to section 19b AufenthG and Directive 2014/66/EU for the purpose of an ICT. To apply for this card, a foreigner must have been issued a residence title which is valid for the duration of the application procedure by another Member State (Directive 2014/66/EU).

The Mobile ICT Card is issued to a foreigner who will work as a manager, specialist or trainee employee in the host entity if the ICT exceeds a period of ninety days. The Mobile ICT Card applicant has to provide a work contract, valid for the duration of the transfer and, if necessary, an assignment letter with detailed information regarding the place and kind of work and remuneration, as well as the other terms and conditions of employment that apply during the transfer. An assignment letter is only necessary if the work contract does not contain detailed information on the terms and conditions of employment, as required. In addition, evidence has to be provided that the foreigner will be able to return to an entity belonging to the same undertaking or group of undertakings, established outside the EU when the transfer period ends.

If the application for a Mobile ICT Card is filed at least 20 days prior to the beginning of the intended stay in Germany and the residence title issued by the other Member State is still valid, a foreigner is permitted to reside and take up employment in Germany for a period of maximum 90 days in an 180-day period until the foreigners authority decides on the application. This facilitates the speedy begin of an ICT.

An application is rejected if it was filed at the same time as the notification for a short-term mobility transfer (section 19a(1), sentence 1 AufenthG). Applications which are filed during a stay in the context of a short-term mobility transfer, but not in their entirety at least twenty days prior to the end of this stay, are also rejected.

The Mobile ICT Card is also not issued if, in the context of the ICT, the foreigner intends to stay longer in Germany than in another Member State.

An application may be rejected if the maximum duration of the ICT (section 19(4) AufenthG) has been reached, or if the application is filed within six months of the end of the foreigner's last stay in Germany for the purpose of an ICT (section 19(6), No. 3 AufenthG). Thus, like with the ICT Card, there is a cooling-down period.

The national host entity is required to inform the competent foreigners authority without delay, as a rule within one week, of any changes in the conditions subject to which the Mobile ICT Card was issued.

V. Other Employment Purposes

485. Foreigners may be granted entry and residence for the purpose of employment other than that of skilled workers in special cases according to section 19c AufenthG.

A foreigner may be granted a temporary residence permit for the purpose of employment, regardless of his or her qualification as a skilled worker, if the Employment Ordinance or an intergovernmental agreement stipulates that the foreigner may be admitted to take on this employment. Intergovernmental agreements, which permit the issuing of a residence permit for the purpose of unskilled labour are currently in place with Turkey, Serbia, Bosnia-Herzegovina, and Macedonia (section 29 BeschV).[74] Examples regulated in the Employment Ordinance are: seasonal workers and au-pair activity.

If the foreigner has distinct professional skills, he or she may be granted a temporary residence permit to pursue qualified employment, if the Employment Ordinance stipulates that the foreigner may be admitted to pursue this employment. Distinct professional skills are special skills which are not certified as a professional qualification. This is the case for professions in the field of information and communication technology (section 6 BeschV).The provision aims at covering the need for such skilled personnel on the labour market.

Foreigners who are employed as civil servants in Germany are issued a temporary residence permit to discharge of their official duties. This temporary residence permit is issued for a period of three years, unless the employment relationship is for a shorter period. After three years, a permanent settlement permit is issued.

VI. Foreigners Whose Deportation Has Been Suspended

486. Special rules apply according to section 19d AufenthG to foreigners whose deportation has been suspended. Such a foreigner may be issued a temporary residence permit for the purpose of taking up employment that matches his or her vocational qualification. The issuing of such a temporary residence permit requires that the foreigner has either completed a vocational training in a State-recognised establishment for higher education or a training programme for a regulated occupation in Germany. This additional requirement is also met if a foreigner has been employed continuously for two years in Germany in a job for which a higher education qualification is required and the foreigner has a foreign higher education qualification

---

74. BeckOK AuslR/Breidenbach, 20. ed. 1 May 2018, AufenthG §18 Rn. 23, 23.1.

which is recognised or otherwise comparable to a German higher education qualification. It is also met if a foreigner has been employed continuously in Germany as
a skilled worker for a period of three years in a job which requires a vocational
qualification and has not relied on public funds for his or her means of subsistence,
including dependants or other members of the foreigner's household, in the year
preceding the application for a temporary residence permit. Reliance on public
funds to cover the necessary costs for accommodation and heating are not classed
as 'not having sufficient means of subsistence'. The foreigner must also provide evidence that he or she has: adequate accommodation; sufficient command of the German language; not wilfully provided the foreigners authority with incorrect
information on the circumstances which are relevant to his or her immigration
rights; and has not wilfully delayed or obstructed the execution of official measures
to end his or her right of residence. In addition, a foreigner must not have any links
with extremist or terrorist organisations or support such organisations and may not
have been convicted of an offence, wilfully committed in Germany. Fines totalling
up to fifty daily rates or up to ninety daily rates in the case of offences which, in
accordance with the AufenthG or the AsylG, can only be committed by foreigners,
such as unlawful entry or stay in Germany (section 95 AufenthG), are not taken into
consideration as a matter of general principle.

When the execution of a deportation has been suspended for urgent personal reasons, because a foreigner has started or intends to start a vocational training at a
State-recognised institute for higher education or a similarly regulated training programme for an occupation which requires formal training in Germany, a temporary
residence permit is issued. The temporary residence permit is valid for a period of
two years after the foreigner has successfully concluded the vocational training programme. It entitles the foreigner to take up employment that matches the professional qualification acquired if the conditions in section 19d(1), Nos 2, 3, 6, 7
AufenthG are satisfied. These conditions include: adequate accommodation, sufficient command of the German language, no links with extremist or terrorist organisations or support such organisations and no conviction of an offence wilfully
committed in Germany. Again, fines totalling up to fifty daily rates or up to ninety
daily rates in the case of offences which, in accordance with the AufenthG or the
AsylG, can only be committed by foreigners, such as unlawful entry or stay in Germany (section 95 AufenthG), are not taken into consideration as a matter of general
principle.

This temporary residence permit is revoked if the employment relationship,
which is the reason why the temporary residence permit was issued, is terminated
for reasons relating to the person of the foreigner or if the foreigner has been convicted for an offence committed intentionally in Germany. In the latter case, again,
fines totalling up to fifty daily rates or up to ninety daily rates in the case of offences
which, in accordance with the AufenthG or the AsylG, can only be committed by
foreigners, are not taken into account as a general principle.

This temporary residence permit entitles the holder to take up any employment
after having been employed in a position that matches his or her vocational qualification for a period of two years.

According to section 19d(3) AufenthG, a temporary residence permit may be
issued by derogation from section 5(2) and section 10(3), sentence 1 AufenthG

when the execution of a deportation order has been suspended or an asylum application has been rejected. Thus, a temporary residence permit that has been issued for the purpose of employment to a highly qualified foreigner whose deportation has been suspended does not presuppose that that foreigner has entered Germany with the necessary visa, nor that he or she has already provided the necessary information to be issued the residence title for which the visa application is made. A foreigner whose asylum application has been incontestably rejected or who has withdrawn his or her asylum application may, under these circumstances, be granted a residence title prior to leaving Germany even if the residence conditions which follow from international law or apply according to humanitarian or political grounds, as stipulated in Part 5 AufenthG, are not satisfied.

VII. European Voluntary Service

487. A special labour employment scheme is the Participation in a European Voluntary Service Scheme in section 19e AufenthG, which is the implementation provision of Article 14 of Directive (EU) 2016/801. There are numerous volunteer services, which are organised by just as many organisations that provide a large variety of services, for instance assisting people with a handicap, health care services, and cultural activities.

A temporary residence permit that allows a foreigner to participate in a European Voluntary Service scheme is issued on submission of an agreement with a host entity specifying the voluntary service scheme. This information must indicate the duration of the voluntary service and the volunteering hours, where the voluntary services will be provided and who will supervise the activities, the financial resources available to cover the foreigner's cost of living, accommodation and pocket money. It also has to state, where applicable, any training that the foreigner will receive to help him or her perform the voluntary service as agreed. Approval of the Federal Employment Agency is not necessary (section 14(1), No. 1 BeschV).

The residence title is issued for the agreed duration of the foreigner's participation in the European Voluntary Service scheme, with a maximum of one year.

Foreigners will not be granted a residence title for the purpose an EU voluntary service (section 19e, 19f(1) AufenthG) if the following reasons apply. The residence title is not granted to a foreigner who is resident in an EU Member State because he or she has filed an application for refugee status, subsidiary protection (Directive 2004/83/EC), or international protection status (Directive 2011/95/EU), or if the foreigner enjoys international protection (Directive 2011/95/EU) in an EU Member State. The application will also be rejected if the foreigner resides in an EU Member State under the terms of an arrangement to provide temporary protection or has filed an application for temporary protection in an EU Member State. Furthermore, the residence title will not be issued to a foreigner whose deportation has been suspended in an EU Member State on grounds of fact or law. Foreigners also do not qualify for such a residence title if they hold an EU long-term residence permit or a residence title issued by another EU Member State (Directive 2003/109/EC of 25 November 2003 concerning the status of third-country nationals who are long-term residents). The same applies to foreigners who enjoy rights of free movement equivalent to those of EU citizens on the basis of a treaty concluded between the EU and its Member States, on the one hand, and one or more third countries, on the other.

Denial of a temporary residence permit for the purpose of an EU voluntary service is regulated in section 19f(3) AufenthG. In addition to the grounds set out in section 19f(1) AufenthG, a temporary residence permit is not granted to foreigners who hold an EU Blue Card (section 18b(2) AufenthG) or a residence title issued by another EU Member State on the basis of Council Directive 2009/50/EC of 25 May 2009 on the conditions of entry and residence of third-country nationals for the purpose of highly qualified employment (OJ L 155, 18 June 2009, p. 17).

An application to be granted a temporary residence for the purpose of an EU voluntary service may be rejected if one of the following reasons apply. The application may be rejected if the host entity was established for the main purpose of facilitating the entry and residence of foreigners for the purpose mentioned in the individual provisions. It may also be rejected if insolvency proceedings have been instituted against the host entity's assets aiming to wind up the entity and its business. The same applies if the host entity and its business have been wound up in insolvency proceedings or the institution of insolvency proceedings against the entity's assets has been refused for lack of assets, and its business has been wound up. The application will also be rejected if the host entity does not pursue any economic activity or if there is proof or there are specific indications that the foreigner would reside for a purpose other than that for which he or she has applied for a temporary residence permit.

VIII. Seeking Employment

488. Seeking employment is facilitated according to section 20 AufenthG. Again, the law distinguishes between skilled workers with a vocational qualification and skilled workers with and academic education, on the one hand, and other (qualified) foreigners, on the other.

A skilled worker with a vocational qualification may be granted a temporary residence permit for up to six months for the purpose of seeking a job that his or her qualification enables him or her to pursue. The skilled worker must have a command of the German language commensurate to the desired activity. Foreigners already residing in Germany must have possessed a residence title for the purpose of employment or a study-related training programme EU immediately before they are issued a temporary residence permit that allows them to seek employment. The Federal Ministry of Labour and Social Affairs may, by means of statutory instruments, with the approval of the *Bundesrat*, determine professions in which skilled workers may not be issued a temporary residence permit that allows them to seek employment. A temporary residence permit for the purpose of seeking employment only entitles a skilled worker to pursue probationary periods that his or her qualification enables him or her to pursue and only for up to ten hours per week. This possibility is to enable the employer to assess the skills of the foreign job-seeker in order to decide about future full employment.

A skilled worker with an academic education may be issued a temporary residence permit for up to six months for the purpose of seeking a job that his or her qualification enables him or her to pursue. Again, foreigners already residing in Germany must have possessed a residence title for the purpose of employment or a study-related training programme EU immediately before they are issued a temporary residence permit for the purpose of seeking employment. The temporary residence permit for the purpose of seeking employment only entitles a skilled worker to pursue probationary periods that his or her qualification enables him or her to pursue and only for up to ten hours per week. In the case of skilled workers with an academic education, the Federal Ministry of Labour and Social Affairs may not determine professions in which skilled workers may not be issued a temporary residence permit for the purpose of seeking employment.

If certain requirements are met, foreigners are or may be issued a temporary residence permit for the purpose of seeking a job that his or her qualification enables him or her to pursue.

A foreigner is issued a temporary residence permit for up to eighteen months after successful completion of a study programme in Germany within the framework of a stay for the purpose of further education or student mobility (sections 20, 16b, and 16c AufenthG).

A foreigner is issued a temporary residence permit for up to nine months after completing his or her research activities within the framework of a stay as a researcher or as a mobile researcher (sections 20, 18d and 18f AufenthG).

A foreigner may be issued a temporary residence permit for up to twelve months after successful completion of a vocational training in Germany in the framework of a stay for vocational or continued vocational training (sections 20, 16a AufenthG).

A foreigner may be granted a temporary residence permit for up to twelve months after establishing the equivalence of the professional qualification or issuing a professional licence in Germany in the framework of a stay for the purpose of recognition of foreign professional qualifications (sections 20, 16d AufenthG). This presupposes that the vacancy may be filled by foreigners in accordance with the rules on skilled workers with a vocational qualification or an academic education, researchers, other employment purposes, or self-employment (sections 20, 18a, 18b, 18d, 19c, and 21 AufenthG).

Issuing a temporary residence permit for the purpose of seeking employment according to these rules requires secure subsistence of the foreigner. An extension of the temporary residence permit may not exceed the maximum periods for which the temporary residence permit may be issued. A temporary residence permit for the purpose of seeking employment for skilled workers with a vocational qualification or with an academic education may only be issued anew if the foreigner, after leaving Germany, has stayed abroad for at least as long as he or she has stayed in Germany on the basis of a residence title for the same purpose. The general rules on granting a permanent settlement permit as stipulated in section 9 AufenthG do not apply.

IX. Denial of Specific Residence Titles

489. Special rules apply to the denial of an EU Blue Card for skilled workers holding a university degree and a residence title for the purpose of participation in a European voluntary service (sections 18b(2), 19e AufenthG) according to section 19f AufenthG.

Foreigners will not be issued an EU Blue Card for skilled workers with an academic education and will not be granted a residence title for the purpose of participation in an EU voluntary service (sections 18b(2), 19e, 19f(1) AufenthG) if the following reasons apply. The residence title is not granted to a foreigner who is resident in an EU Member State because he or she has filed an application for refugee status, subsidiary protection (Directive 2004/83/EC), or international protection status (Directive 2011/95/EU), or if the foreigner enjoys international protection (Directive 2011/95/EU) in an EU Member State. The application will also be rejected if the foreigner resides in an EU Member State under the terms of an arrangement to provide temporary protection or has filed an application for temporary protection in an EU Member State. Furthermore, the residence title will not be issued to a foreigner whose deportation has been suspended in an EU Member State on grounds of fact or law. Foreigners also do not qualify for such residence titles if they hold an EU long-term residence permit or a residence title issued by another EU Member State (Directive 2003/109/EC of 25 November 2003 concerning the status of third-country nationals who are long-term residents). The same applies to foreigners who enjoy free movement rights equivalent to those of EU citizens on the basis of a treaty concluded between the EU and its Member States, on the one hand, and one or more third countries on the other.

The rules on refusing an EU Blue Card are set out in section 19f(2) AufenthG. In addition to the grounds set out in section 19f(1) AufenthG, section 19f(2) AufenthG provides that an EU Blue Card is not issued in one of the following situations. It is not issued to foreigners who hold a residence title for reasons of international law or on humanitarian or political grounds, unless they have been admitted to Germany in order to safeguard Germany's special political interests or as resettlement refugees or who hold a comparable legal position in another EU Member State (section 19f(2), Part 5, and section 23(2) and (4) AufenthG). This also applies to foreigners who have applied for such a title or such a legal position and the application has not yet been finally decided upon. A Blue Card is also not issued to foreigners whose entry into an EU Member State is subject to obligations arising from international treaties to facilitate the entry and temporary residence of specific categories of natural persons engaged in trade- or investment-related activities, or who have been admitted as seasonal workers by an EU Member State. The same applies to foreigners who have come to Germany as posted workers for the duration of their posting to Germany (Directive 96/71/EC of the European Parliament and of the Council of 16 December 1996 concerning the posting of workers in the framework of the provision of services (OJ L 18, 21 January 1997, p. 1), in the version of Directive 2018/957 of the European Parliament and of the Council of 28 June 2018 amending Directive 96/71/EC concerning the posting of workers in the framework of the provision of services (OJ L 173, 9 July 2018, p. 16)).

Denial of a temporary residence permit for the purpose of participation in an EU voluntary service (section 19e AufenthG) is regulated in section 19f(3) AufenthG. To these refusals the grounds for denial set out in section 19f(1) AufenthG, as described above, also apply. In addition to these grounds, a temporary residence permit is not granted to foreigners who hold an EU Blue Card (section 18b(2) AufenthG) or a residence title issued by another EU Member State on the basis of Council Directive 2009/50/EC of 25 May 2009 on the conditions of entry and residence of third-country nationals for the purpose of highly qualified employment (OJ L 155, 18 June 2009, p. 17). Furthermore, a temporary residence permit for the purpose of research (section 18d AufenthG) is not issued if the research activities constitute part of a doctoral study in a full time study programme. In this case, a residence permit is issued for the purpose of further education pursuant to section 16b AufenthG.

An application for a temporary residence for the purpose of participation in an EU voluntary service (section 19e AufenthG) may be rejected if one of the following reasons apply. The application may be rejected if the host entity was established for the main purpose of facilitating the entry and residence of foreigners for the purposes mentioned in the individual provisions. It may also be rejected if insolvency proceedings have been instituted against the host entity's assets, aiming to wind up the entity and its business. The same applies if the host entity and its business have been wound up in insolvency proceedings or the institution of insolvency proceedings against the entity's assets has been refused for lack of assets, and its business has been wound up. The application will also be rejected if the host entity does not pursue any economic activity or if there is proof or there are specific indications that the foreigner would reside for purposes other than those for which he or she applies for a temporary residence permit.

X. Fast-Track Procedure for Skilled Workers

490. In order to speed up employment of skilled workers there is a fast-track procedure pursuant to section 81a AufenthG.

This fast-track procedure applies to stays for the purpose of vocational and continued vocational training, the recognition of foreign professional qualifications, employment of skilled workers with a vocational qualification or with an academic education, as well as for highly qualified skilled workers with an academic education. It is also available for other qualified employees (section 81a(1) and (5), sections 16a, 16d, 18a, 18b, and 18c(3) AufenthG).

The law facilitates entry and residence for these persons. Employers may apply for a fast-track procedure at the competent foreigners authority. The employer and the competent foreigners authority conclude an agreement. This agreement has to include, in particular, contact data of the foreigner, the employer, and the authority and the authorisation of the employer by the foreigner. It must also cover the authorisation of the competent foreigners authority by the employer to start and conduct the procedure to establish the equivalence of the vocational qualification acquired abroad, and any evidence to be supplied. The agreement must further specify the employer's obligation to work towards fulfilling the obligations to cooperate pursuant to section 82(1), sentence 1 AufenthG by the foreigner. These obligations are: to put forward his or her interests and any circumstances in his or her favour which are not evident or known, to specify verifiable circumstances, and to produce forthwith the necessary evidence relating to his or her personal situation, other required certificates and permits and other required documents which the foreigner is able to furnish. The agreement must also contain a description of the processes, including participants and completion periods and the employer's cooperation obligation to notify the competent foreigners authority within a period of four weeks if the employment has been terminated prematurely. The consequences in the case of non-compliance with the agreement must also be indicated in the agreement.

Within the framework of the fast-track procedure for skilled workers the competent foreigners authority has to ensure a speedy decision procedure. It has to provide advice to the employer on the procedure and the evidence to be supplied. It has to start, as far as necessary, the procedure to establish the equivalence of vocational qualifications which have been acquired abroad or of the assessment of certificates of the foreign higher education qualification at the respective body referring to the fast-track procedure; if the foreigner is to be employed in a profession which is regulated in Germany, the professional licence must be obtained. The foreigners authority must also forward without delay confirmations of receipt and completeness provided by the competent bodies to the employer for information, if a procedure to establish the equivalence of vocational qualifications and certificates has been initiated. If the competent body requires further evidence and on receipt of findings made by the competent body, the employer has to be invited within three working days after receipt for delivery and discussing further proceedings. The competent foreigners authority is obliged to obtain, as far as necessary and by referring to the fast-track procedure, approval by the Federal Employment Agency. It also has to notify the competent mission abroad of the forthcoming visa application by the foreigner, and to approve, without delay and in advance, to the granting of the visa if the requirements are met, including the establishment of equivalence or the comparability of the vocational qualification as well as the approval of the Federal Employment Agency. If the competent body decides, by way of official decision, that the vocational qualification, which has been acquired abroad is not equivalent, equivalence, however, can be obtained by way of a qualification measure. The fast-track procedure, aiming at entry for the purpose of for the recognition of foreign professional qualifications, may be continued (section 16d AufenthG).

The fast-track procedure also includes subsequent immigration of the spouse and minor unmarried children whose visa applications have been filed in close temporal connection.

§2. Seasonal Workers and Temporary Workers

I. Seasonal Workers

A. Conditions

491. Special rules on seasonal workers are provided for in section 39(6), (2), and (4) AufenthG and section 15a of the Employment Ordinance, which implements Directive 2014/36/EU.[75]

492. Foreigners not holding a residence title may only carry out seasonal work if they hold a seasonal work permit (section 4a(4) AufenthG).

493. The requirements set out in section 19, 19b, 19c(3) or section 19d(1), No. 1 AufenthG and in the Employment Ordinance for approval regarding the pursuit of employment must be met if seasonal work is to be pursued in one of these contexts, This means, that the requirements that apply to ICT Cards for ICT, mobile ICT Cards, and justified individual cases must be met, as well as employment relevant requirements for taking up employment by foreigners whose deportation has been suspended. Also, requirements set out in the Employment Ordinance must be met. These specific requirements are dealt with in more detail in the respective context.

494. The Federal Employment Agency may issue a seasonal work permit if there is no labour available on the German labour market to do the work (priority examination). It may thus issue a permit if employing a foreign seasonal worker does not have an adverse effect for the German labour market, in particular with regard to the employment structure, the regions and the branches of the economy. The priority test essentially means that there are no German workers, foreigners having the same legal status as German workers with regard to the right to take up employment or other foreigners who are entitled to preferential access to the labour market under EU law available for the type of employment concerned or that it has been established that filling the vacancies with foreign applicants is justifiable in terms of labour market policy and integration. Foreign seasonal workers may not be employed on terms less favourable than those that apply to comparable German workers. The future or present employer of a foreigner who requires or has obtained approval for seasonal employment must provide the Federal Employment Agency with information on pay, working hours and the other terms and conditions of employment.

495. When approving an application for seasonal work, the Federal Employment Agency may stipulate the duration and form of the occupational activity and may also restrict employment to specific locations or regions.

---

75. Directive 2014/36/EU of the European Parliament and of the Council of 26 Feb. 2014 on the conditions of entry and stay of third-country nationals for the purpose of employment as seasonal workers, OJ EU 2014, L 94/375.

496. In the absence of any law or statutory instrument to the contrary, the legal rules governing approval by the Federal Employment Agency apply to the issuing of a work permit.

497. The Federal Employment Agency may set demand-oriented admission figures with regard to the number of residence titles for seasonal work and the number of seasonal work permits that can be issued. A work permit is issued and approval is granted without a priority examination if the Federal Employment Agency has set a demand-oriented admission figure (section 15(6) BeschV).

498. Foreigners who intend to perform seasonal work may be granted entry and a right to stay in Germany on the basis of an agreement of the Federal Employment Agency with the employment administration of their country of origin. This can be the case for foreigners who perform seasonal work regularly for at least thirty hours per week in agriculture, forestry and horticulture, in the hotel and catering industry, in the fruit and vegetable sector, and in sawmills.

499. In the case of foreigners who are exempted from the short-stay visa requirement, the Federal Employment Agency may issue a work permit for the purpose of seasonal work for the duration of up to 90 days per period of 180 days. The States whose nationals are exempted from the short-stay visa requirement are listed in Annex II of Regulation (EC) No. 539/2001.[76]

500. A temporary residence title is required for stays for the purpose of seasonal work longer than 90 days. In this case, the Federal Employment Agency may approve of a stay in excess of 90 days per period of 180 days. The Federal Employment Agency may also issue a temporary residence title for the purpose of taking up seasonal employment if a foreigner is a national of one of the States listed in Annex I of Regulation (EC) No. 539/2001. The nationals of the States on this list are foreigners who need a visa to enter and stay in Germany.

501. Seasonal employment of a foreigner may not exceed a period of six months within a twelve-month period. Under no circumstance may the duration of seasonal employment exceed the period of validity of a foreigner's travel document.

502. If a foreigner who holds a seasonal work permit applies for a residence title for the purpose of seasonal work before the seasonal work permit expires, approval is deemed to have been granted until the application has been decided on (section 39, No. 11, of the Ordinance on Residence). Foreigners who have been active as seasonal workers in Germany at least once within the last five years are considered with preference if the Federal Employment Agency has set a quorum for the number of work permits and approvals. The period of employment of seasonal workers

---

76. Council Regulation (EC) No. 539/2001 of 15 Mar. 2001 listing the third countries whose nationals must be in possession of visas when crossing the external borders and those whose nationals are exempt from that requirement, OJ EC 2001, L 81/1.

by one enterprise may not exceed eight months within a period of twelve months. This does not apply for fruit, vegetable, vine, hop, tobacco and agricultural enterprises.

503. Issuing a work permit or granting approval to issue a residence title requires submission of a number of documents attesting that admission conditions are satisfied. Evidence must be provided of sufficient health insurance, the seasonal worker must have adequate accommodation, and there must be an employment offer or employment contract which, in particular, stipulates the place and kind of work, the duration of employment, the wage, the working hours per week or month, the duration of paid holidays, other, if any, relevant work conditions, and, if possible, the date that employment will start.

504. If the employer provides the seasonal worker with accommodation, the rent must be adequate and may not be deducted from the wage. In this case, the seasonal worker must receive a rental contract which stipulates the terms of rent. The employer has to report any change in the accommodation of the seasonal worker immediately to the Federal Employment Agency.

505. A work permit has to be applied for by the employer with the Federal Employment Agency.

506. Renewal of a work permit is possible for a single or repeated extension of the employment relationship with the same or a different employer if the maximum period for seasonal work (section 15a(1), sentence 1, No. 1 BeschV) is not exceeded.

B. Denial

507. A work permit has to be revoked or the approval of an application for a work permit has to be denied if one of the following conditions is met. The foreigner is already resident in Germany, unless he or she has entered Germany for the purpose of taking up seasonal employment or the work permit or approval was applied for subsequent, further seasonal employment. The work permit is also denied or revoked if; the seasonal worker has applied for asylum pursuant to Article 16a of the Basic Law or for international protection pursuant to Directive 2011/95/EU; the further effects of filing an asylum application on residence titles, such as cancelling those with an overall validity of up to six months, remain unaffected (section 55(2) AsylG). Denial or revocation also take place if the seasonal worker has not met the obligations resulting from a former decision on admission to seasonal employment. The same applies if insolvency proceedings have been instituted against the employer's enterprise aiming to wind up the enterprise and its business, the employer's enterprise and its business have been wound up in insolvency proceedings, or the institution of insolvency proceedings against the employer assets have been refused for lack of assets and its business has been wound up. The work permit or the approval has also to be denied or revoked if the employer's enterprise does not pursue any economic activity.

508. An application for a work permit is denied if the number of work permits and approvals as determined by the Federal Employment Agency for the relevant period of time has been reached.

II. Temporary Workers

509. Foreigners may not take up employment as temporary workers. The law defines temporary workers as employees whose employer leases them to another employer where these employees are integrated into the working organisation and bound by instructions of that employer (section 1(1) of the Temporary Employment Act).[77] The AufenthG stipulates that approval of an application for a residence title by the Employment Agency must be denied if a foreigner intends to take up employment as a temporary worker (section 40(1), No. 2 AufenthG).

510. Some argue that there must be exceptions to this general rule for cases in which approval by the Employment Agency is not required, such as employment of highly qualified foreigners or in the case a long history of previous employment in Germany (section 19 AufenthG, sections 2 and 9 BeschV).[78]

III. Showman's Assistants

511. Somewhat similar and related to those on seasonal workers are the rules on showman's assistants (section 15b BeschV). The Federal Employment Agency may grant approval for the issuing of a residence title for the purpose of employment in the carny industry for up to a total of nine months per calendar year if the person concerned is employed on the basis of a procedure and selection-agreement between the Federal Employment Agency and the labour administration of the country of origin.

§3. INDEPENDENT ECONOMIC ACTIVITIES

512. As for independent economic activities, the German migration law provides rules on residence for the purpose of self-employment in section 21 AufenthG.

---

77. Temporary Employment Act – Arbeitnehmerüberlassungsgesetz (AÜG); Arbeitnehmerüberlassungs-gesetz of 3 Feb. 1995 (BGBl. I p. 158), last amended by Art. 1 of the Act of 21 Feb. 2017 (BGBl. I p. 258).
78. BeckOK AuslR/Breidenbach, 20. ed. 1 May 2018, AufenthG §40 Nos 2, 3.

A foreigner may be granted a temporary residence permit for the purpose of self-employment if there is an economic interest or a regional need; the economic activity is expected to have a positive effect on the German economy; and the foreigner has personal capital or an approved of loan to realise the business idea. An economic interest exists, in particular, if considerable investments are made or jobs are created. There is a regional need if, e.g., certain services are not provided in the region.

513. The assessment whether these conditions are satisfied has to focus, in particular, on the viability of the business idea for which the application is made, the foreigner's entrepreneurial experience, the level of capital investment, the effects on the employment and training situation and the contribution to innovation and research. The competent authorities for the planned business location, the competent trade and industry authorities, the representative bodies for public-sector professional groups and the competent authorities regulating admission to the profession concerned must be involved in the examination of the application.

514. A temporary residence permit for the purpose of self-employment may also be issued if special privileges apply according to agreements under international law on the basis of reciprocity. Such international agreements exist, e.g., with the Dominican Republic, Indonesia, Iran, Japan, the Philippines, Sri Lanka, Turkey and the United States of America.[79] They limit the scope of discretion of the foreigners authorities.

515. For certain groups of people, residence for the purpose of self-employment is facilitated. A foreigner who has successfully completed his or her studies at a State or State-recognised university or a comparable educational institution in Germany or who holds a temporary residence permit as a researcher or scientist (section 18 or 20 AufenthG) may be issued a temporary residence permit for the purpose of self-employment. No economic interest or a regional need is required, nor do there have to be expected positive effects on the economy or does the foreigner have to have personal capital or an approved loan to realise the business idea. The envisaged self-employment must, however, demonstrate a connection with the knowledge acquired when studying or from the research or scientific activities.

516. In any case, foreigners older than 45 are only issued a temporary residence permit, if there is adequate provision for old age.

517. The period of validity of a temporary residence permit for the purpose of self-employment is limited to a maximum of three years. The general conditions for granting a permanent settlement permit (section 9(2) AufenthG) do not apply. Rather, a permanent settlement permit may be issued after a period of three years, if the foreigner has successfully carried out the planned activity and adequate revenues ensure that there are sufficient means of subsistence for the foreigner and all dependants living in his or her household who need the foreigner's support.

---

79. BeckOK AuslR/Breidenbach, 20. ed. 1 May 2018, AufenthG §21 No. 10.

518. Engaging in a so-called liberal profession, also called independent economic activity, is privileged. An economic activity in a liberal profession includes independent professional exercise of a scientific, artistic, literary, teaching or educational activity, the independent professional occupations of physicians, dentists, veterinary practitioners, lawyers, notaries, patent agents, engineers, architects, trade chemists, accountants, certified auditors, tax consultants, consultant economists, business economists, chartered accountants (attested auditors of books), midwife, massage therapists, physiotherapists, non-medical practitioners, journalists, photo-journalists, interpreters, translators, pilots, scientists, artists, and similar professions (section 18(1), No. 1 Income Tax Act).

519. A foreigner may be issued a temporary residence permit for the purpose of engaging in a liberal profession if there is permission in the form of a permit to practice the profession or confirmation that such a permit will be issued. Issuing a temporary residence permit does not require an economic interest or a regional need. It is also not necessary that there is an expectation that the self-employed activity will have a positive effect on the economy, nor does the foreigner need to have personal capital or an approved loan to realise the business idea as is normally required to be issued a temporary residence permit. However, the competent authorities for the planned business location, the competent trade and industry authorities, the representative bodies for public-sector professional groups and the competent authorities regulating admission to the profession concerned must be included in the examination of the application. The privileges listed in section 21(4) AufenthG do not apply. Therefore, a permanent settlement permit may only be granted if the general conditions are satisfied. Thus, it may not be granted if the applicant has only had a temporary residence permit for three years (section 9 AufenthG).

520. A foreigner who will be or has been issued a temporary residence permit for another purpose may be permitted to pursue a self-employed activity while retaining the aforesaid purpose of residence, if the necessary permits have been issued or if the competent authorities have indicated that such permits will be issued.

521. A large number of foreigners living in Germany are already entitled by law to pursue an independent economic activity. This is the case for holders of a permanent settlement permit (section 9(1) AufenthG), a temporary residence permit for the purpose of protection of the German political interests (section 22, sentence 3 AufenthG). It is also the case for foreigners who have been granted asylum (section 25(1), sentence 4 AufenthG), a refugee or subsidiary protection status (section 25(2), sentence 2 read in conjunction with section 25(1), sentence 4 AufenthG), a residence title for family reasons (section 27(5) AufenthG), a temporary residence permit because of a right to return (section 37(1), sentence 2 AufenthG), a residence title for former Germans or persons treated as such (section 38(4) and section 38(5) AufenthG), or a temporary residence permit in old cases (section 104a

AufenthG). If such a residence title is held by a foreigner, the foreigners authority may also not limit this entitlement by virtue of a discretionary decision.[80]

§4. INVESTMENT ACTIVITIES

522. The Foreign Trade and Payments Act, as well as the Foreign Trade and Payments Ordinance, regulates investments made by nationals of third countries in Germany, especially, if the investment endangers public order or safety.

523. There are no special provisions in migration law on investment activities other than those on self-employment (section 21 AufenthG). These provisions also apply to foreigners who seek entry or residence to conduct investment activities in Germany. Which provisions apply in an individual case depends on whether the intended stay is a short-stay or long-term residence.

524. Just holding shares in a company does not constitute an independent economic activity within the meaning of migration law. This, as a rule, also applies to minority shareholders. If, however, a foreigner has a decisive influence on the decision-making in a company because of his or her shares in the business, migration law assumes a 'comparable independent activity'. If this is the case, a foreign majority shareholder is treated by migration law as being self-employed even if he or she is not acting as a managing director. Migration law also treats foreigners as performing an independent economic activity if several of them who are only minority shareholders together control the company economically and are in a position to issue orders.[81]

525. Section 21 AufenthG does not apply to Turkish nationals who are not subjected to section 21 AufenthG if they intend to enter and reside in Germany for the purpose of founding a company. This follows from section 41(1) of the Additional Protocol and Financial Protocol of 23 November 1970, annexed to the Agreement establishing the Association between the EEC and Turkey that prohibits the Contracting Parties from introducing between themselves any new restrictions on the freedom of establishment and the freedom to provide services, the so-called standstill provision.[82]

---

80. BeckOK AuslR/Breidenbach, 20. ed. 1 May 2018, AufenthG §21 Nos 16–18.

81. https://www.frankfurt-main.ihk.de/existenzgruendung/prozessstruktur/realisierung/vorbereitung/au slaender/.

82. Additional Protocol and Financial Protocol signed on 23 Nov. 1970, annexed to the Agreement establishing the Association between the EEC and Turkey and on measures to be taken for their entry into force – Final Act – Declarations, OJ EEC 1972, L 293/3–56, https://eur-lex.europa.eu/legal-co ntent/EN/TXT/?uri=CELEX%3A21970A1123%2801%29; BeckOK AuslR/Breidenbach, 20. ed. 1 May 2018, AufenthG §21 Rn. 3–7.

Chapter 5. Humanitarian Reasons

§1. HUMANITARIAN GROUNDS

I. Scope of Application

526. There are several reasons which are considered to be humanitarian grounds that justify the issuing of a residence permit to a foreigner. Part 5 the AufenthG provides the rules on residence under international law, for humanitarian or political reasons, or where there is a public interest. The legal terminology used in section 25 of the AufenthG mentions 'humanitarian grounds' as including asylum or refugee status. In other provisions, the reasons for granting a residence permit, such as hardship, personal reasons or lasting integration, may also be regarded as constituting humanitarian grounds.

II. General Provisions

527. A foreigner who is not enforceably required to leave Germany may be issued a temporary residence permit for a temporary stay pursuant to section 25(4) AufenthG if his or her continued presence in Germany is necessary on urgent humanitarian grounds. The duration of stay in Germany can be relevant for assuming urgent humanitarian grounds. This can be the case, in particular, for children who have lived in Germany since they were born and who regard Germany as their home country. To be entitled to a residence title issued on humanitarian grounds, a foreigner must actually be in Germany; it is not possible to make an application from abroad. A temporary residence permit issued for humanitarian reasons may be extended if departure from Germany would constitute exceptional hardship for the foreigner concerned due to the special circumstances of his or her situation. Exceptional hardship can be assumed, if the foreigner, e.g., has to assist and care for a mortally ill relative in Germany. Extension is thus insofar not subject to the regulations as apply to issuance, and the temporary residence permit may be extended even if the competent authority has prohibited an extension in the case of a stay which is of only a temporary nature.

528. A temporary residence permit issued for humanitarian reasons may, in general, be issued and extended in each instance for a maximum of three years, as stipulated in section 26 AufenthG. However, a number of exceptions to this general rule apply in particular in asylum cases. A temporary residence permit for humanitarian reasons may not be extended if any obstacle to departure or other grounds precluding a termination of the right of residence have ceased to apply.

529. Under certain conditions, such as a minimum period of stay in Germany amounting to of five or three years, secure means of subsistence, and sufficient German language skills, a permanent settlement permit may or must be granted to a foreigner who resides in Germany on humanitarian grounds (section 26(3) AufenthG).

530. Humanitarian reasons justifying the issuing of a residence title may also occur in the context of residence for family reasons. According to section 29(3) AufenthG, a temporary residence permit may be granted to the spouse and the minor child of a foreigner who possesses a temporary residence permit in accordance with sections 22, 23(1) or (2) or section 25(3) or (4a), sentence 1, section 25a(1) or section 25b(1) on humanitarian grounds.

531. If there are humanitarian grounds, the supreme *Land* authority may order the deportation of foreigners from specific States or specific categories of foreigners to be suspended in general or with regard to deportation to specific States for a fixed period (section 60a(1) AufenthG).

532. A foreigner may be granted a temporary suspension of deportation if his or her continued presence in Germany is necessary on urgent humanitarian grounds (section 60a(2), sentences 3 and 4 AufenthG).

533. In accordance with Article 33 of Regulation (EC) No. 810/2009, a Schengen visa may be extended up to a total stay of 90 days within an 180-day period if the visa holder has provided proof of force majeure or humanitarian reasons preventing him or her from leaving Germany or if the visa holder provides proof of serious personal reasons justifying the extension of the period of validity of a visa or the duration of stay (section 6(2), sentence 2 AufenthG).

III. Admission from Abroad

534. A foreigner may be issued a temporary residence permit for the purpose of admission from abroad on urgent humanitarian grounds pursuant to section 22 AufenthG.

IV. *Land* Order on Humanitarian Grounds

535. The supreme *Land* authority, which is the competent *Land* ministry, may, pursuant to section 23(1) AufenthG, order a temporary residence permit to be issued on humanitarian grounds to foreigners from specific States or to certain groups of foreigners. Such an order may be issued subject to the proviso that a declaration of commitment to bear the foreigners living expenses is made by a third person (section 68 AufenthG). In order to ensure a nationwide uniform policy, such an order requires the approval of the Federal Ministry of the Interior. The order may provide for the rules on granting of residence for the purpose of temporary protection in section 24 AufenthG to be applied accordingly, either in part or in full (section 23(3) AufenthG).

V. *Land* Order in Cases of Hardship

536. The supreme *Land* authority may order that a temporary residence permit is issued in cases of hardship (section 23a AufenthG) to a foreigner who is enforceably required to leave Germany. This can be done by way of derogation from the rules on the issuing and extending of residence titles in the AufenthG and those in sections 10 and 11 AufenthG on limitations to entry and the granting or extending of a residence title in asylum application cases or an entry and residence ban. The order must be initiated by a petition, a so-called hardship petition, to a Hardship Commission. Depending on the individual circumstances of the case concerned, an order may be issued with due consideration as to whether the foreigner's means of subsistence is assured or a declaration of commitment to bear a foreigner's living expenses (section 68 AufenthG) has been made. Hardship will generally not be considered if a foreigner has committed an offence of considerable severity or if a date has already been set for the foreigner's return. The competence to grant residence represents the public interest only, it does not constitute any rights on the part of the foreigner; there, thus, is no right of a foreigner that the supreme *Land* authority issues such an order.

537. The *Land* governments are authorised to establish a Hardship Commission, which specifies the procedure, grounds for exclusion and requirements that apply to a declaration of commitment, including the conditions to be met by the party submitting such a declaration, and to determine the authority competent to issue orders to other authorities. The details vary according to the individual *Land*. In general, hardship commissions are composed of representatives of the Land parliament, representative authorities of local communities, religious communities, welfare institutions, and integration authorities. The Hardship Commissions can solely act on their own initiative. No third party may request a Hardship Commission to take up a specific individual case or to make a specific decision. A Hardship Commission may decide to file a hardship petition only after establishing that urgent humanitarian or personal grounds justify the foreigner's continued presence in Germany.

538. If a foreigner who is dependent on social welfare benefits and has been issued a temporary residence permit in a case of hardship relocates to the area of responsibility of another institution, the social welfare institution in whose area of responsibility the foreigners authority has issued the temporary residence permit is required to reimburse the costs incurred by the local social welfare institution which has to assume responsibility for the foreigner concerned for a maximum period of three years from the date that the temporary residence permit was issued. The same applies accordingly to other subsistence payments such as unemployment benefits and housing subsidies (section 6(1), sentence 1, No. 2 of Book Two of the Social Code).

VI. Deportation Ban

539. A foreigner should be granted a temporary residence permit, as stated in section 25(3) AufenthG, if a deportation ban applies pursuant to section 60(5) or (7) AufenthG. Such a deportation ban applies if deportation is inadmissible according to the European Convention on Human Rights.[83] This also applies in as far as a foreigner should not be deported to another State if the foreigner faces a substantial and real danger to his or her life and limb or liberty there.

540. A temporary residence permit must not be granted if following his or her departure from Germany, his or her admission to another State is possible and reasonable or if the foreigner has repeatedly or grossly breached the duty to cooperate. It must, further, not be granted where there is a serious reason to believe that the foreigner has committed a crime against peace, a war crime or a crime against humanity within the meaning of international law, has committed an offence of considerable severity, or is guilty of acts contrary to the objectives and principles of the UN, as enshrined in the Preamble and Articles 1 and 2 of the Charter of the UN. A temporary residence permit must also not be issued if a foreigner represents a risk to the general public or a risk to the security of Germany.

VII. Impossibility of Departure

541. A foreigner who is enforceably required to leave Germany may be granted a temporary residence permit pursuant to section 25(5) AufenthG if departure is impossible in fact or in law and the obstacle to deportation is not likely to be removed in the foreseeable future. A temporary residence permit should be issued if deportation has been suspended for eighteen months. A temporary residence permit may only be granted if the foreigner is prevented from leaving Germany through no fault of his or her own. Fault on the part of the foreigner is assumed, in particular, if the foreigner has provided false information, has deceived the authorities with regard to his or her identity or nationality or fails to comply with reasonable demands to remove any obstacle to his or her departure.

§2. Unaccompanied Minor Children

542. Special care is provided for unaccompanied minors.[84] Minors are children and youngsters under the age of 18. Minors are treated as 'unaccompanied minors' if they enter an EU Member State without being accompanied by an adult who is responsible for them, or if they are left there unaccompanied.

---

83. BGBl. 1952 II p. 685.
84. Cf. http://www.bamf.de/EN/Fluechtlingsschutz/UnbegleiteteMinderjaehrige/unbegleitete-minderjae hrige-node.html.

543. If unaccompanied minor foreigners enter and stay in Germany for normal purposes such as visits, tourism or school attendance and do not need specific attendance, the same rules apply as do to adult foreigners.

544. The rules in Book VIII of the Social Code apply to unaccompanied minors. The Child and Youth Welfare Act is codified in this Book. They are thus accommodated, cared for and assisted as is normal under the youth welfare system in the same way that all other minors are. This means that the accommodation, care and assistance that have to be given to unaccompanied minors are not primarily dependent on their status according to the residence law.

545. If special care is needed, unaccompanied minors are first of all taken into care by the youth welfare office that has local responsibility (section 42–42f and section 27 of Book Eight of the Social Code, Article 24 Directive 2013/33/EU). It is ensured that they are accommodated with a suitable person, such as relatives or foster families or placed in youth welfare facilities or in a suitable facility which, as a rule, is a so-called clearing house specialised in the care of unaccompanied minors. The purpose of placement is to ensure that minors grow up in a stable situation.

546. The first step in the immigration procedure is a general examination of the minor's state of health and to establish the minor's age. There are various methods which are used to do this. For instance, by estimating the minor's age after a physical examination or an X-ray of the wrist, jaw or collar bone. Most importantly, the child's best interests in physical or psychological terms needs to be secured. This includes examining whether family reunification with relatives living in Germany is possible. It also includes consideration whether there are close social ties with other unaccompanied minors and it is thus advisable to accommodate them together.

547. The unaccompanied minors are, within fourteen days, allotted to a *Land* which has to ensure that they are accommodated, supplied and cared for and supported in a manner that is suited to serve the child's best interests.

548. The youth welfare office which the minors have been assigned to is responsible for their further care. Minors are accommodated with a suitable person or in a suitable facility, additional medical tests are performed, the need for education is established, and the residence status established. The youth welfare office also takes care of the application to appoint a guardian or curator.

549. The Family Court decides on legal guardianship. In general, legal guardianship lasts until the minor attains the age of majority. The law in the minor's country of origin governs the age when they are treated as grown-up. If this means that majority is attained after the minor becomes 18, guardianship lasts until that age is reached (Articles 7 and 24 of the Introductory Act to the Civil Code).

§3. VICTIMS OF TRAFFICKING IN HUMAN BEINGS

550. Special protection is granted pursuant to section 25(4a) AufenthG to foreigners who are victims of certain crimes. A foreigner who is a victim of a criminal offence pursuant to sections 232–233a of the Criminal Code is granted a temporary residence permit for a temporary stay, even if the foreigner is enforceably required to leave Germany. This includes victims of human trafficking (section 232 Criminal Code), forced prostitution (section 232a Criminal Code), forced labour (section 232b Criminal Code), work exploitation (section 233 Criminal Code), and exploitation through deprivation of liberty while the victim is working as a prostitute, is the subject of exploitative employment conditions, is practising begging or if the victim has committed acts which give rise to criminal proceedings (section 233a Criminal Code).

551. However, a temporary residence permit may only be issued if the public prosecutor's office or the criminal court considers the foreigner's presence in Germany to be appropriate in connection with criminal proceedings relating to that criminal offence, because it would be more difficult to investigate the facts of the case without his or her information, the foreigner has broken all contact with the persons accused of having committed the criminal offence and the foreigner has declared a willingness to testify as a witness in the criminal proceedings relating to the offence. After conclusion of the criminal proceedings, the temporary residence permit should be extended if humanitarian or personal reasons or a public interest requires the foreigner's further presence in Germany.

552. Victims of certain labour law crimes also enjoy protection within the framework of the AufenthG as stipulated in section 25(4b) AufenthG. A foreigner who was a victim of such a criminal offence may be issued a temporary residence permit for a temporary stay, even if he or she is enforceably required to leave Germany. The relevant criminal offences are employment of foreigners without a work permit or residence title under unfavourable working conditions (section 10(1) of the Act to Combat Clandestine Employment), employment of foreigners below the age of 18 who do not possess a residence title which allows them to pursue an economic activity (section 4a(5), sentence 1 AufenthG, section 11(1), No. 3 of the Act to Combat Clandestine Employment), and temporary placement of foreigners without permit (section 15a of the Act on Temporary Employment Businesses). Again, a temporary residence permit may only be issued if the public prosecutor's office or the criminal court considers the temporary presence of the foreigner in Germany to be appropriate in connection with criminal proceedings relating to the relevant criminal offence, because it would be more difficult to investigate the facts of the case without this information and the foreigner has declared a willingness to testify as a witness in the criminal proceedings relating to the offence. The temporary residence permit may be extended until the remuneration owed to the foreigner by the employer has been paid in full, and if it would represent a particular hardship for the foreigner to pursue his or her rights from abroad.

§4. Others

I. Well-Integrated Juveniles and Young Adults

553. Well-integrated juveniles and adolescent foreigners enjoy favourable treatment pursuant to section 25a AufenthG. Juveniles are persons who are 14–18 years old and adolescents are between 18 and 21 years old. A juvenile or adolescent foreigner whose deportation has been suspended should be issued a temporary residence permit if he or she has resided in Germany for four years without interruption either by virtue of having been issued a temporary residence or permanent settlement permit, by virtue of the suspension of a deportation or if they have been given permission to remain pending their asylum decision. Further additional conditions are that the juvenile or adolescent has successfully attended school in Germany for, as a rule, four years or has obtained a recognised vocational or school-leaving qualification. The application for a temporary residence permit must have been filed before the age of 21, and it must appear, on the basis of the foreigner's education and way of life to date, that he or she will be able to become integrated into the way of life in Germany. There must also be no evidence to suggest that the juvenile or adolescent foreigner is not committed to the free democratic basic legal order of Germany.

554. For as long as the juvenile or young adult attends school, vocational training or higher education, claiming public benefits for the purpose of ensuring his or her subsistence does not preclude the issuing of a temporary residence permit. A temporary residence permit will be denied, however, if deportation has been suspended on the basis of false information provided by the juvenile or adolescent or on the grounds of deception by the juvenile or adolescent foreigner concerning his or her identity or nationality.

555. The parents or parent possessing the right of care and custody of a foreign minor who has been issued a temporary residence permit may be granted a temporary residence permit if deportation has not been prevented or delayed because false information has been provided or there has been deceit with regard to identity or nationality or due to a failure to meet reasonable demands to remove any obstacles to departure. In addition, the means of subsistence must be ensured independently by means generated through an economic activity.

556. The other minor children of a foreigner who holds such a temporary residence permit as a parent may be granted temporary residence permits if they live with the foreigner as a family unit. A spouse or registered partner who is living with such a parent in the same household is granted a temporary residence permit if the conditions for granting a temporary residence permit to the parent are met, which means that deportation is not prevented for the aforementioned reasons and the means of subsistence are ensured. The rules for an independent right of residence of spouses in the event of termination of marital cohabitation apply accordingly. Thus, marital cohabitation must have existed for at least three years or the partner has died while marital cohabitation existed in Germany (section 31 AufenthG). A minor, unmarried child who is living with a well-integrated juvenile or young adult as a member of his or her household is also issued a temporary residence permit.

557. A temporary residence permit is not issued to the parent or the parent's partner (section 25a(2) AufenthG) if he or she has been convicted of an offence wilfully committed in Germany. Fines totalling up to fifty daily rates or up to ninety daily rates in the case of offences which, pursuant to the AufenthG or the AsylG, can only be committed by foreigners, such as unlawful entry or residence (section 95 AufenthG), are not taken into consideration as a general principle.

558. A temporary residence permit may be granted before a foreigner leaves Germany even if his or her asylum application has been rejected as being manifestly unfounded (section 10(3), sentence 2, section 25(4) AufenthG, and section 30(3), Nos 1–6 AsylG). This temporary residence permit entitles the holder to pursue an economic activity.

559. Subsequent immigration of dependants to a foreigner who has been issued a residence title as a well-integrated juvenile or adolescent (section 25a(1) AufenthG) is limited in the sense that this is possible only for his or her parents, spouse, and minor children. Subsequent immigration to a foreigner who has been granted a temporary residence for subsequent immigration to a well-integrated juvenile or adolescent foreigner (section 25a(2) AufenthG) is excluded (section 29(3) AufenthG).[85]

II. Lasting Integration

A. *Scope*

560. Privileges somewhat different from those of well-integrated juveniles and adolescent foreigners apply to those foreigners who show lasting integration. Lasting integration might also be called sustainable integration. The privileges associated with lasting integration do not depend on age. Foreigners who show lasting integration are offered residence under facilitated conditions pursuant to section 25b AufenthG. Section 25a AufenthG on the granting of a right to residence in the case of well-integrated juveniles and adolescent foreigners remains unaffected.

561. Some of the requirements that justify the privileges in case of lasting integration must be met only in general or generally. This means that if these requirements are not met in the individual case, other integration achievements can substitute the missing ones, e.g., if the foreigner has shown extraordinary social commitment which ensures a comparable lasting integration into the German society.

---

85. BeckOK AuslR/Hecker, 20. ed. 1 Nov. 2016, AufenthG §25a No. 27.

562. A foreigner whose deportation has been suspended should be granted a temporary residence permit if he or she has become lastingly integrated into the way of life in Germany. This does not presuppose the otherwise general conditions that the foreigner's subsistence is secure (section 5(1), No. 1 AufenthG) and that the foreigner has entered the country with the necessary visa and has already submitted all key information required to issue a residence title along with his or her visa application (section 5(2) AufenthG). To qualify as lastingly integrated, it is, in general, required that a foreigner has resided in Germany for at least eight years or, in the event that a foreigner is living with a minor, unmarried child at least six years without interruption, by virtue of a decision suspending his or her deportation; permission to remain pending the asylum decision; or as a holder of a temporary residence or permanent settlement permit. Furthermore, it is, in general, required, that a foreigner is committed to Germany's free democratic basic order and has acquired a basic level of knowledge of German legal and social system and the way of life in Germany. Moreover, a foreigner must, in general, have an oral command of the German language equivalent to Level A 2 of the Common European Framework of Reference for Languages, unless he or she is unable to fulfil this condition on account of a physical or mental illness or disability or on grounds of old age. The foreigner must be able to provide proof that his or her school-age children are actually attending school.

563. Another general condition is that a foreigner has sufficient means of subsistence by means of pursuing an economic activity or that it is expected that the foreigner will be able to ensure sufficient means of subsistence taking into account his or her education, training, income and family situation.

564. There are several situations in which the ability to ensure one's means of subsistence is not required. Drawing housing benefits, for instance, does not mean that this condition is not satisfied. The 'means of subsistence condition' is waived if a foreigner is unable to fulfil it on account of a physical or mental illness or disability or on grounds of old age. Furthermore, temporary reliance on social benefits is generally not detrimental in the case of students attending a State or State-recognised higher education programme and apprentices who are being trained for a recognised occupation that requires formal training or in a government-sponsored pre-vocational training programme. Temporary reliance on social benefits is generally also not detrimental in the case of families with minor children who are dependent on supplementary social benefits, single parents of minor children who cannot reasonably be expected to take up employment (section 10(1), No. 3 of Book Two of the Social Code), and in the case of foreigners who care for close relatives in need of long-term care.

565. A temporary residence permit is issued and extended for no more than two years. This is a derogation of section 26(1), sentence 1 AufenthG, which provides for different time limits in general.

566. A temporary residence permit may be issued before a foreigner leaves Germany even if his or her asylum application has been rejected as being manifestly unfounded (section 10(3), sentence 2, section 25(4) AufenthG, and section 30(3), Nos 1–6 AsylG).

567. The temporary residence permit entitles the holder to pursue an economic activity.

B. Dependants

568. A spouse, registered partner, and minor, unmarried children living as a family unit with the foreigner from whom they derive their right of residence should be issued a temporary residence permit under similar conditions which apply to that foreigner. These conditions are, in general, that the spouse, registered partner, or child of the foreigner is committed to the German free democratic basic order and has a basic knowledge of the legal and social system and the way of life in Germany. Moreover, his or her oral command of the German language must, in general, be equivalent to Level A 2 of the Common European Framework of Reference for Languages. Those who on account of a physical or mental illness or disability or on grounds of old age are unable to acquire this level are exempted from this requirement. Proof that the school-age children are actually attending school is also required.

569. Another general condition is that the means of subsistence of the spouse, registered partner, or children is ensured, primarily by means of the pursuit of an economic activity or, when considering their education, training, income and family situation, it is to be expected that they will be able to ensure sufficient means of subsistence. Clearly, economic activity is not expected of small children.

570. Here, also, there are several cases in which the ability to ensure one's subsistence is not required. Drawing housing benefits is not detrimental to this condition. The condition is waived if the foreigner is unable to fulfil it on account of a physical or mental illness or disability or on grounds of age. Furthermore, temporarily drawing social benefits is not generally detrimental to securing subsistence in the case of students attending a state or state-recognised higher education institution as well as apprentices undergoing training in a recognised occupation requiring formal training or in a government-sponsored pre-vocational training measure. It is also not detrimental in the case of families with minor children who temporarily rely on supplementary social benefits, single parents of minor children who, pursuant to, cannot reasonably be expected to take up employment (section 10(1), No. 3 of Book Two of the Social Code). Temporarily drawing social benefits is furthermore not generally detrimental to securing subsistence in the case of foreigners caring for close relatives in need of long-term care.

571. The rules for an independent right of residence of spouses that apply in the event of termination of marital cohabitation, such as that the marital cohabitation

has existed for at least three years or the partner has died while marital cohabitation existed in Germany, also apply (section 31 AufenthG).

572. A temporary residence permit is issued and extended for no more than two years. This is a derogation of section 26(1), sentence 1 AufenthG, which provides for different time limits in general.

573. A temporary residence permit may be issued before a foreigner leaves Germany even if his or her asylum application has been rejected as being manifestly unfounded (section 10(3), sentence 2, section 25(4) AufenthG, and section 30(3), Nos 1–6 AsylG).

574. A temporary residence permit entitles the holder to pursue an economic activity.

C. Denial

575. A temporary residence permit for lasting integration must be refused if the foreigner prevents or delays the termination of his or her right of residence by wilfully providing false information, by deceit regarding identity or nationality, or noncompliance with reasonable requirements to cooperate to remove any obstacles to departure. It must also be denied if there is a public interest in expelling a foreigner. This is, e.g., the case if a foreigner has been incontestably sentenced to a term of imprisonment of at least one year for an intentionally committed offence, has been involved in violent activities in the pursuit of political or religious objectives or if a foreigner endorses or promotes crimes against peace, against humanity, war crimes or acts of terrorism of comparable severity (section 54(1) or (2), Nos 1 and 2 AufenthG). The same rules justifying a refusal apply to a foreigner's dependants who have been issued a temporary residence permit for lasting integration.

III. Personal Grounds

576. Special rules make it possible to issue a temporary residence permit for personal reasons to foreigners who are already residing in Germany. A foreigner who is not enforceably required to leave Germany may be issued a temporary residence permit for a temporary stay pursuant to section 25(4) AufenthG if the foreigner's continued presence in Germany is necessary on urgent personal grounds. An example of personal grounds is to finish a training course. To be eligible for this temporary residence permit, a foreigner must already be in Germany. This temporary residence permit may be extended if a foreigner's departure from Germany would constitute an exceptional hardship for him or her due to special circumstances. This is a derogation from the general rules on extension of temporary residence permits in section 8(1) and (2) AufenthG. The extension of this temporary residence permit is not subject to the same conditions which apply to the granting of this permit; a temporary residence permit may be extended even if the competent authority has prohibited an extension in the case of a stay which is only temporary by nature in accordance with the purpose of the right of residence or at the time when the temporary residence permit was last extended.

577. A foreigner may be granted a temporary suspension of deportation if his or her continued presence in Germany is necessary for urgent personal reasons (section 60a(2), sentences 3 and 4 AufenthG). Such urgent personal grounds exist if a foreigner begins or has begun a vocational training at a State-recognised education institution or a similarly regulated occupation which requires formal training in Germany.

IV. Resettlement

578. There are special rules pursuant to section 23(4) AufenthG concerning resettlement refugees.

579. Resettlement is the transfer of refugees from an asylum country to another State that has agreed to admit them and, ultimately, grants them permission to settle there permanently. The United Nations High Commissioner for Refugees (UNHCR) is mandated by its statute and UN General Assembly Resolutions to undertake resettlement.

580. The Federal Ministry of the Interior may order that the Federal Office for Migration and Refugees grant approval for admission to certain persons seeking protection who have been selected for resettlement, so-called resettlement refugees. This has to be done in consultation with the supreme *Land* authorities. No preliminary proceedings take place pursuant to section 68 of the Code of Administrative Court Procedure. The foreigners concerned are issued a temporary residence permit or permanent settlement permit, in accordance with the approval for admission. A permanent settlement permit may be issued subject to a condition restricting their place of residence. A temporary residence permit entitles the holder to pursue an economic activity; a permanent settlement permit entitles the holder to economic activity, anyway (section 23(2), sentences 2–5, and (4) AufenthG, section 9(1), sentence 2 AufenthG).

581. Resettlement refugees are allocated to the *Länder* and the general rules on the allocation of foreigners apply accordingly. These rules provide, e.g., that a foreigner has to take up accommodation and habitual residence in the place to which he or she has been allocated (section 24(3)–(5) AufenthG).

V. Jewish Immigrants

582. In practice, special rules apply to Jewish immigrants especially from the former Soviet Union. For this purpose, section 23(2) AufenthG is applied in order to safeguard Germany's special political interests. The Federal Ministry of the Interior may, in consultation with the supreme *Land* authorities, order the Federal Office for Migration and Refugees to approve of the admission of foreigners from specific States or belonging to a certain group of persons. Making use of this provision expresses acknowledgement of German historic responsibility for Jewish people.[86]

---

86. BeckOK AuslR/Hecker, 20. ed. 1 Nov. 2016, AufenthG §23 Nos 4, 5.

Chapter 6. Asylum

§1. CONDITIONS

I. Refugee Status

A. AsylG: Scope of Application

583. German asylum law distinguishes between political asylum, international protection, subsidiary protection, and temporary protection, and the status of displaced foreigners.

584. The right to asylum within the meaning of the Basic Law and the relevant procedures are specified, in particular, in the AsylG. This Act also applies to asylum in the broader sense of EU and international law. Temporary protection is regulated in the AufenthG. The status of displaced foreigners is regulated in the Act on the Legal Status of Displaced Foreigners in the Federal Territory.[87]

585. The AsylG covers pursuant to its section 1 foreigners applying for protection against political persecution within the meaning of Article 16a(1) of the Basic Law as well as foreigners applying for international protection (Directive 2011/95/EU).[88] International protection within the meaning of Directive 2011/95/EU, the so-called Qualification Directive, comprises the protection against persecution within the meaning of the UN Convention of 28 July 1951 on the Legal Status of Refugees, the 1951 Refugee Convention,[89] and subsidiary protection within the meaning of Article 15 of the Qualification Directive.

586. International protection granted under Council Directive 2004/83/EC[90] is equivalent to international protection as defined in Directive 2011/95/EU that is a recast Directive. The transitional rule in section 104(9) AufenthG that is the legal basis for granting subsidiary protection to foreigners who hold a specific temporary residence permit that was issued before 1 December 2013 has remained unaffected by the entry into force of Directive 2011/95/EU. Section 104(9) AufenthG applies to foreigners who are the subject of a deportation ban under the terms of the European Convention on Human Rights or because the foreigner faces a substantial real

---

87. Act on the legal status of displaced foreigners in the federal territory in the revised version published in the BGBl. Part III, No. 243-1, last amended by Art. 7 of the Act of 30 Jul. 2004 (BGBl. I p. 1950) – Gesetz über die Rechtsstellung heimatloser Ausländer im Bundesgebiet in der im Bundesgesetzblatt Teil III, Gliederungsnummer 243-1, veröffentlichten bereinigten Fassung, das zuletzt durch Artikel 7 des Gesetzes vom 30 Jul. 2004 (BGBl. I p. 1950) geändert worden ist.
88. Directive 2011/95/EU of 13 Dec. 2011 on standards for the qualification of third-country nationals or stateless persons as beneficiaries of international protection, for a uniform status for refugees or for persons eligible for subsidiary protection, and for the content of the protection granted, OJ EU 2011, L 337/9.
89. BGBl. II pp. 559, 560.
90. Council Directive 2004/83/EC of 29 Apr. 2004 on minimum standards for the qualification and status of third-country nationals or stateless persons as refugees or as persons who otherwise need international protection and the content of the protection granted, OJ 2004, L 304/12.

danger to his or her life and limb or liberty in the State where the foreigner would be deported to (sections 25(2), 60(5) or (7) AufenthG).

B. Political Asylum

587. The German federal constitution guarantees political asylum as a fundamental right in its Article 16a. It reads:

Article 16a
[Right of asylum]

1. Persons persecuted on political grounds shall have the right of asylum.
2. Paragraph (1) of this Article may not be invoked by a person who enters the federal territory from a member state of the European Communities or from another third State in which application of the Convention Relating to the Status of Refugees and of the Convention for the Protection of Human Rights and Fundamental Freedoms is assured. The states outside the European Communities to which the criteria of the first sentence of this paragraph apply shall be specified by a law requiring the consent of the *Bundesrat*. In the cases specified in the first sentence of this paragraph, measures to terminate an applicant's stay may be implemented without regard to any legal challenge that may have been instituted against them.
3. By a law requiring the consent of the *Bundesrat*, states may be specified in which, on the basis of their laws, enforcement practices and general political conditions, it can be safely concluded that neither political persecution nor inhuman or degrading punishment or treatment exists. It shall be presumed that a foreigner from such a state is not persecuted, unless he presents evidence justifying the conclusion that, contrary to this presumption, he is persecuted on political grounds.
4. In the cases specified by paragraph (3) of this Article and in other cases that are plainly unfounded or considered to be plainly unfounded, the implementation of measures to terminate an applicant's stay may be suspended by a court only if serious doubts exist as to their legality; the scope of review may be limited, and tardy objections may be disregarded. Details shall be determined by a law.
5. Paragraphs (1) to (4) of this Article shall not preclude the conclusion of international agreements of Member States of the European Communities with each other or with those third states which, with due regard for the obligations arising from the Convention Relating to the Status of Refugees and the Convention for the Protection of Human Rights and Fundamental Freedoms, whose enforcement must be assured in the contracting states, adopt rules conferring jurisdiction to decide on applications for asylum, including the reciprocal recognition of asylum decisions.

588. This right encapsulates the German experience of political and racist persecution under the German terror regime of National-Socialism between 1933 and

1945 when many Germans had to flee Germany and found refuge abroad. In the past decades, this provision has been amended intensively by adding sections two to five in order to structure and reduce immigration into Germany.

589. Political asylum is also guaranteed by most of the constitutions of the German *Länder*. In some of them, the guarantees differ from the federal one. For example, Article 11 of the constitution of Saarland provides that those who have suffered a violation of the fundamental rights as they are laid down in the Saarland constitution enjoy a right to asylum in Saarland. A similar provision is Article 105 of the Bavarian constitution. These provisions share that there is a right to asylum not only in cases of political persecution, but in all cases in which fundamental rights enshrined in the *Land* constitution have been violated in the home country. However, because the federal constitution takes priority over *Land* law, in practical terms, these provisions in the *Land* constitutions do not offer more protection as the federal AsylG also prevails over the *Land* constitutions.

C. Refugee Status

1. Refugee

590. The AsylG describes a person as being a refugee in its section 3(1). A foreigner is a refugee as defined in the Convention of 28 July 1951 on the legal status of refugees if the foreigner, owing to well-founded fear of persecution in the foreigner's country of origin on account of the foreigner's race, religion, nationality, political opinion or membership of a particular social group, resides outside the country (country of origin) whose nationality the foreigner possesses and the protection of which the foreigner cannot, or, owing to such fear does not want to make use of, or where the foreigner used to have the habitual residence as a stateless person and where the foreigner cannot, or, owing to that fear, does not want to return to.

591. A foreigner who is a refugee within the meaning of section 3(1) AsylG is granted refugee status.

2. Acts of Persecution

592. A definition of 'acts of persecution' is found in section 3a AsylG. Such acts must be sufficiently serious by virtue of their nature or repetition as to constitute a severe violation of basic human rights, in particular the rights from which derogation cannot be made under Article 15(2) of the European Convention on Human Rights, such as the prohibition of torture and slavery, or be an accumulation of various measures, including violations of human rights which are sufficiently severe as to affect an individual in a similar manner.

593. Acts of persecution may, among others, be acts of physical or mental violence, including acts of sexual violence. They may also be legal, administrative, police or judicial measures which are, in themselves, discriminatory or which are implemented in a discriminatory manner, or amount to disproportionate or discriminatory prosecution or punishment. The same holds true for a denial of judicial redress resulting in disproportionate or discriminatory punishment. It also applies to prosecution or punishment following a refusal to perform military service in a conflict, where performing military service would include crimes or acts falling under the exclusion clauses as set out in section 3(2) AsylG such as war crimes or crimes against humanity. Acts which are of a gender-specific nature or are directed against children can also qualify as an act of persecution.

3. Lack of Protection

594. There must be a connection between the grounds for persecution and the acts defined as persecution or the lack of protection against such acts (section 3a(1), (2), and (3), section 3(1), No. 1, and section 3b AsylG).

595. The AsylG provides further clarification of the grounds for persecution, such as the concept of race, religion or nationality in its section 3b. These points have to be taken into account when examining the grounds for persecution.

596. The concept of race within the meaning of the AsylG includes, in particular, considerations of skin colour, descent, and membership of a particular ethnic group.

597. The concept of religion includes, in particular, the holding of theistic, non-theistic and atheistic beliefs, the participation in, or abstention from, formal worship in private or in public, either alone or in community with others, other religious acts or expressions of views, or forms of personal or communal conduct based on or mandated by religious belief.

598. The concept of nationality is not confined to citizenship or lack of citizenship, but includes, in particular, membership of a group determined by its cultural, ethnic, or linguistic identity, common geographical or political origins or its relationship with the population of another State.

599. A group is considered to form a particular social group if, in particular, members of that group share an innate characteristic, or a common background that cannot be changed, or share a characteristic or belief that is so fundamental to their identity or conscience that a person should not be forced to renounce it, and that group has a distinct identity in the relevant country, because it is perceived as being different by the surrounding society. A particular social group may include a group based on a common characteristic of sexual orientation. This does not include acts that are punishable under German law, such as sexual abuse of minors. If a person is persecuted solely on account of his or her sex or sexual identity, this may also constitute persecution as a member of a social group.

600. The concept of political opinion includes, in particular, the holding of an opinion, thought or belief on a matter related to the potential agents of persecution (section 3c AsylG) and to their policies or methods, irrespective whether or not the foreigner has acted according to that opinion, thought or belief.

601. When assessing whether an applicant has a well-founded fear of being persecuted it is immaterial whether the applicant actually possesses the racial, religious, national, social or political characteristic leading to persecution, provided that the agent of persecution attributes such a characteristic to the applicant.

4. Agents of Persecution

602. Agents of persecution may include the State authorities, parties or organisations, which control the State or substantial parts of the national territory (section 3c AsylG). If these entities, including international organisations, are demonstrably unable or unwilling to offer protection from persecution, agents of persecution can also be non-State agents, irrespective of whether a power or authorities that exercise state rule exist in the country.

5. Protection Against Persecution

603. Whether there is protection against persecution is assessed by considering whether the State or parties or organisations, including international organisations, controlling the State or a substantial part of the territory of the State, are willing and able to provide such protection, the so-called agents of protection, according to section 3d AsylG.

604. Protection against persecution must be effective and not of a temporary nature. Protection is generally provided when the agents of protection take reasonable steps to prevent persecution, for instance by operating an effective legal system for the investigation, prosecution and punishment of acts constituting persecution or serious harm, and the applicant has access to this legal system for investigation.

605. When assessing whether an international organisation actually controls a State or a substantial part of its territory and actually provides protection against persecution, the relevant legal acts adopted by the EU legislator are used as guidance.

II. Subsidiary Protection Status

606. Another form of protection is the subsidiary protection status. A foreigner is eligible for subsidiary protection according to section 4(1) AsylG, if that foreigner has shown substantial grounds for believing that he or she would face a real risk of suffering serious harm in the country of origin. Serious harm is assumed if the foreigner runs the risk of being subjected to the death penalty or execution, torture or inhuman or degrading treatment or punishment, or if there is a serious and individual threat to a civilian's life or person by reason of indiscriminate violence in situations of international or internal armed conflict.

607. The rules on agents of persecution, agents of protection and on internal protection also apply in relation to subsidiary protection (section 3c–3e AsylG). Persecution, fear of persecution or the well-founded fear of persecution is replaced by the fear of serious harm, the protection against serious harm or the real risk of serious harm. The status accorded to a foreigner who risks serious harm if returned to his or her country of origin is called subsidiary protection.

III. Temporary Protection

608. Temporary protection is granted if the conditions in sections 24 and 2(6) AufenthG are satisfied. Temporary protection within the meaning of section 2(6) of the AufenthG is the granting of a right of residence as provided for in Council Directive 2001/55/EC.[91] This Directive provides an exceptional procedure to provide immediate and temporary protection in cases in which the EU experiences a mass influx or imminent mass influx of displaced persons from third countries who are unable to return to their country of origin. This procedure applies in particular if there is a risk that the asylum system will be unable to process this influx without adverse effects for its efficient operation, and this is in the interests of the persons concerned and other persons requesting protection. In this context, displaced persons are third-country nationals or stateless persons who have had to leave their country or region of origin, or have been evacuated, in particular in response to an appeal by international organisations, and are unable to return to their country or region of origin in safe and durable conditions because of the situation prevailing in that country if those people may fall within the scope of Article 1A of the 1951 UN Refugee Convention or another international or national instrument providing international protection. The idea of providing temporary protection was to protect those who have fled areas of armed conflict or endemic violence as well as those running a serious risk of, or who have been a victim of, systematic or generalised violations of their human rights.

---

91. Council Directive 2001/55/EC of 20 Jul. 2001 on minimum standards for the granting of temporary protection in the case of the mass influx of displaced foreigners and on measures to promote the balanced distribution of the burdens associated with the admission of these persons and the consequences of such admission among the Member States, OJ EC 2001, L 212/12.

609. A foreigner who is granted temporary protection on the basis of a decision of the EU Council and who declares his or her willingness to be admitted to Germany is issued a temporary residence permit that is valid for the entire period that he or she enjoys temporary protection in Germany (section 24(1) AufenthG, Articles 5–6 Directive 2001/55/EC).

610. Those foreigners, to whom temporary protection is granted, will be allocated to one of the *Länder*. The *Länder* may agree on admission quotas for temporary protection and for the allocation of those enjoying temporary protection to the *Länder*.

611. The foreigner who has been granted temporary protection receives a written notification of the rights and obligations which he or she enjoys by virtue of his or her temporary protection status in a language which the foreigner is able to understand.

IV. Other

A. Displaced Foreigners

612. There is a special legal status for so-called displaced foreigners (*heimatloser Ausländer*), which is regulated in the Act on the Legal Status of Displaced Foreigners in the Federal Territory.[92] Displaced foreigners are in particular foreigners, including stateless persons, who have resided in Western Germany or West-Berlin after the Second World War as refugees or persons displaced by the Nazi regime. They are often former forced labourers. Displaced foreigners are to be distinguished from displaced persons, who are sometimes also referred to as displaced foreigners, within the meaning of section 2(6) AufenthG and Directive 2001/55/EC on the mass influx of displaced persons.

613. A displaced foreigner is a foreign national or stateless person who enjoys the care of the Office of the UNHCR. A displaced foreigner is not a German according to section 116 of the Basic Law, whose place of residence on 30 June 1950 fell within the area of application of the Basic Law or in Berlin (West) or who has acquired the legal status of a displaced foreigner by re-immigrating into Germany (sections 1 and 2(3) of the Act on the Legal Status of Displaced Foreigners). The legal status of a displaced foreigner is also enjoyed by anyone who derives his or her nationality from a displaced foreigner and who was lawfully resident in a place where the Act on the Legal Status of Displaced Foreigners applied on 1 January 1991.

---

92. Act on the legal status of displaced foreigners in the federal territory in the revised version published in the BGBl. Part III, No. 243-1, last amended by Art. 7 of the Act of 30 Jul. 2004 (BGBl. I p. 1950) – Gesetz über die Rechtsstellung heimatloser Ausländer im Bundesgebiet in der im Bundesgesetzblatt Teil III, Gliederungsnummer 243-1, veröffentlichten bereinigten Fassung, das zuletzt durch Artikel 7 des Gesetzes vom 30 Jul. 2004 (BGBl. I p. 1950) geändert worden ist.

614. Displaced foreigners lose their status as displaced foreigner if they acquire a new nationality or take up residence outside Germany, unless they return to Germany within a period of two years.

615. The Act on the Legal Status of Displaced Foreigners provides for non-discrimination for those who fall within its personal scope and for far-reaching equal treatment with German nationals, in particular, in the context of schooling, the pursuit of an economic activity and social welfare. They do not need a residence title to reside in Germany (section 12, sentence 2, of the Act on Displaced Persons). However, displaced foreigners do not enjoy the right to vote in general elections. The status as displaced foreigner is inherited by descendants and is lost in the case of a change of citizenship. In 2017, there were approximately 9,065 displaced foreigners in Germany.[93]

B. Diplomatic Asylum

616. Asylum cannot be granted in German diplomatic missions abroad. However, a foreigner may be granted protection for some time in a German mission abroad. If a foreigner applies for asylum in a German mission abroad, the application is forwarded to the Federal Office for Migration and Refugees and processed there.

C. Church Asylum

617. Church Asylum is not a regular topic of German State law. In practice, however, church asylum is sometimes granted by religious communities to foreigners who are to be deported by the State authorities. In quite a lot of cases, church asylum is granted by religious congregations that object to the deportation of foreigners whose application for asylum has been rejected or who are to be deported on other grounds. The congregation provides the concerned foreigners with accommodation on the church's premises. Church asylum can thus, on the one hand, be classed as an act of freedom of religion, freedom of opinion and freedom to demonstrate. On the other hand, it is problematic because it may constitute aiding and abetting irregular stay that is a criminal offence according to migration law.

618. The German authorities have concluded agreements with German churches to the effect that the congregation concerned informs the authorities when church asylum is provided. The foreigners authorities then re-examine the case to establish whether the circumstances of the case amount to hardship. The law enforcement authorities do not enforce deportation during this supplementary procedure.

---

93. https://www.destatis.de/DE/ZahlenFakten/GesellschaftStaat/Bevoelkerung/MigrationIntegration/Au slaendischeBevolkerung/Tabellen/AufenthaltsrechtlicherStatus.html.

Depending on the circumstances of the case, this has resulted in lawful stay or the execution of the deportation measure after finalizing the supplementary procedure.[94]

V. Refusal of Asylum

A. *Internal Protection*

619. If internal protection, as defined by section 3e AsylG, is provided in the country of origin, the assumption is that that person is excluded from refugee status. Thus, a foreigner is not granted refugee status if he or she does not have a well-founded fear of persecution or has access to protection against persecution in a part of the country of origin and if the foreigner can safely and lawfully travel to this part of the country, will be admitted there and can reasonably be expected to settle there. In examining whether a part of the country of origin meets these conditions, the authorities, when deciding on the asylum application, take into account the general circumstances prevailing in that part of the country and the personal circumstances of the applicant (Article 4 of Directive 2011/95/EU). To this end, detailed and accurate information from relevant sources, such as the UNHCR and the European Asylum Support Office as a centre of expertise on asylum,[95] is used.

B. *Self-Created Grounds Subsequent to Fleeing*

620. As a rule, a foreigner is not granted asylum status if the threat of political persecution is based on circumstances resulting from a deliberate decision by the foreigner after leaving his or her country of origin unless this decision is in line with firm convictions on which the foreigner clearly acted while still in his or her country of origin (section 28 AsylG). This exception does not apply if the foreigner, due to age and level of maturity when he or she was in the country of origin, was not yet able to form firm convictions of his or her own.

621. The well-founded fear of persecution or the real risk of suffering serious harm may be based on events that occurred after the foreigner left his or her country of origin and, in particular, on the foreigner's conduct that expresses a continuing conviction or orientation that already existed in the country of origin.

622. If the foreigner files a follow-up application after the withdrawal of or an incontestable rejection of an earlier asylum application by the competent authorities and the new application is based on circumstances created by the foreigner after the

---

94. Erlass: https://fragdenstaat.de/blog/2018/erlass-kirchenasyl-dublin/; https://www.kirchenasyl.de/?po rtfolio=neuigkeiten-in-der-handhabung-von-kirchenasyl.
95. Regulation (EU) No 439/2010 of the European Parliament and of the Council of 19 May 2010 establishing a European Asylum Support Office, OJ EU 2010, L 132/11.

withdrawal or incontestable rejection of the earlier application, that foreigner cannot, as a rule, be granted refugee status in a follow-up procedure.

C. Refugee

623. It has to be noted that a foreigner does not qualify as a refugee if there are serious reasons to believe that he or she has committed a crime against peace, a war crime or a crime against humanity within the meaning of the international instruments defining these crimes (section 3(2) AsylG). The same applies if a foreigner has committed a serious non-political crime outside Germany before being admitted as a refugee. In particular, a brutal act, even if it was supposedly intended to pursue political aims, or a violation of the aims and principles of the UN qualifies as a serious non-political crime. Acts of international terrorism can constitute a violation of the aims and principles of the UN. The same applies to foreigners who have incited others to commit such crimes or acts or have otherwise been involved in such crimes or acts; they also do not qualify as refugee.

624. Likewise, a foreigner also does not qualify as refugee if he or she enjoys the protection or assistance of an organisation or institution of the UN, with the exception of the UNHCR (Article 1, section D of the 1951 UN Refugee Convention). The foreigner does, however, qualify as a refugee, if such protection or assistance is no longer provided and there is no resolution of the General Assembly of the UN as providing a solution for the situation of the affected.

625. Moreover, refugee status is not granted to a foreigner, although he or she qualifies as a refugee, if, for serious reasons, that foreigner is to be regarded as a threat to German security or constitutes a threat to the general public because he or she has been incontestably sentenced to a prison term of at least three years for a crime or a particularly serious offence (section 3(4) ASylG, section 60(8), first sentence AufenthG).

626. Refugee status is also not granted if the Federal Office for Migration and Refugees has decided not to prohibit the deportation of a foreigner because he or she represents a danger to the general public. Such a danger exists if the foreigner has been incontestably sentenced to a term of imprisonment or a term of youth custody of at least one year for one or more intentionally committed offences against life, physical integrity, sexual self-determination or property or for resisting enforcement officers if the criminal offence was committed using violence, using a threat of danger to life or limb, or was committed with guile, or if the offence committed was rape or sexual assault by use of force (section 60(1) and (8) AufenthG, and section 177 of the Criminal Code).

D. Subsidiary Protection

627. A foreigner is not eligible for subsidiary protection, if there are serious grounds to believe that he or she has committed a crime against peace, a war crime or a crime against humanity within the meaning of the international instruments defining such crimes. The same applies if a foreigner has committed a serious crime, is guilty of acts contrary to the objectives and principles of the UN, as defined in the Preamble and Articles 1 and 2 of the UN Charter,[96] or represents a risk to the general public or to Germany's security (section 4(2) AsylG). International terrorism can constitute acts contrary to the objectives and principles of the UN, such as peace and respect for human rights and fundamental freedoms.

628. These grounds for exclusion also apply to foreigners who incite others to commit such crimes or acts or are otherwise involved in such crimes or acts.

E. Temporary Protection

629. No temporary protection is granted if the conditions in section 3(2) AsylG apply. This means that temporary protection is not granted if there are serious reasons to believe that the foreigner has committed a crime against peace, a war crime or a crime against humanity within the meaning of the international instruments defining such crimes. The same applies if a foreigner has committed a serious non-political crime outside Germany before being admitted as a refugee. This is, in particular, the case if the act that was supposedly intended to pursue political aims was brutal, or that foreigner has acted in violation of the aims and principles of the UN. The same also applies to foreigners who have incited others to commit such crimes or acts or have otherwise been involved in such crimes or acts. Temporary protection is also not granted if there are serious reasons to regard a foreigner as a threat to Germany's security or constitutes a threat to the general public because he or she has been incontestably sentenced to a term of imprisonment of at least three years for a crime or a particularly serious offence (section 60(8), sentence 1, and section 24(2) AufenthG). An application for a temporary residence permit will then be denied under these circumstances.

---

96. BGBl. 1973 II pp. 430, 431.

§2. PROCEDURES

I. Asylum Procedure

A. *Form, Scope, Legal Capacity, Contacts and Language*

1. Form

630. An asylum application is deemed to have been made if it is clear from the foreigner's written, oral or otherwise expressed desire that he or she is seeking protection in Germany from political persecution or that the foreigner wishes to be protected from deportation or any other form of removal to a country where he or she would fall victim to persecution or serious harm (section 13, section 3(1) or section 4(1) AsylG).

2. Scope

631. Every asylum application is treated as an application for recognition as an asylum seeker and a person in need of international protection. The latter includes both refugee status and subsidiary protection. A foreigner may state that his or her asylum application is only to be treated as an application for international protection. The foreigner will be informed of the consequences of such limitation. After an application has been filed, the Federal Office for Migration and Refugees has to decide whether or not deportation is permitted (section 60(5) or (7) AufenthG, section 24(2) AsylG).

3. Legal Capacity

632. Legal capacity of foreign minors is regulated in section 12 AsylG. In general, majority is reached at the age of 18.

633. A foreigner who is of full legal age is capable of performing procedural actions within the meaning of the AsylG, provided that he or she should not be treated as legally incapacitated according to the Civil Code or requires supervision and prior approval when conducting legal affairs. When applying the AsylG, the Civil Code determines whether a foreigner is to be regarded as a minor or an adult. If a foreigner is of age according to the law of his or her home country, his or her legal capacity and capacity to enter a contract remains unaffected.

634. Unless there is a decision of a family court that provides otherwise, both parents are authorised to represent a minor child in an asylum procedure. If only one of the parents is in Germany or if the place of residence in Germany of one of the parents is not known, the parent resident in German or whose place of residence in Germany is known represents the minor in an asylum procedure.

4.   Contacts and Counselling

635.   Applicants for asylum and international protection are entitled to contact international organisations. Contact opportunities are secured. The key provision is section 9 AsylG.

636.   A foreigner may contact the UNHCR and the UNHCR may present his or her views regarding an individual application for asylum to the Federal Office for Migration and Refugees. The UNHCR has access to foreigners, including those in detention and in airport transit zones.

637.   At the request of the UNHCR, the Federal Office for Migration and Refugees provides the UNHCR with the information necessary to fulfil his or her tasks (Article 35 of the 1951 UN Refugee Convention).

638.   Decisions on asylum applications and other information given, in particular on the grounds of persecution, may, unless presented in an anonymous form, be transmitted only if the foreigner himself or herself has applied to the UNHCR or if the foreigner's consent is otherwise documented.

639.   The data may be used only for the purpose for which they were transmitted.

640.   These rules apply accordingly to organisations acting in Germany on a mandate of the UNHCR on the basis of an agreement with Germany.

641.   The Federal Office for Migration and Refugees offers counselling to all asylum seekers on the asylum procedure and on return options (section 12a AsylG).

5.   Language

642.   If a foreigner has insufficient command of the German language, an interpreter, translator or other language mediator is provided (section 17 AsylG) to be present at the hearing as standard procedure in order to translate what is said into the foreigner's native language or another language which the foreigner can reasonably be supposed to understand and in which he or she can communicate.

643.   A foreigner has the right to call in a suitable interpreter or translator of his or her choice. This is, however, at the foreigner's own expense.

B. Cooperation Obligations

1. Communications

644. Obligations of a foreigner to cooperate with the authorities are specified in section 10 AsylG.

645. During the asylum procedure, a foreigner has to ensure that the Federal Office for Migration and Refugees, the responsible foreigners authority and any court the foreigner has resorted to can communicate with him or her at all times. This means that a foreigner has to inform these authorities of any change of address without delay.

646. A foreigner has to accept any notification and informal communication at the most recent address indicated in the asylum application or at the address which the foreigner has notified to the authorities at a later date if a foreigner has neither appointed an authorised representative nor designated an authorised receiving agent for the procedure or if notifications or communications cannot be delivered to his or her representative or agent. The same applies if the last known address at which the foreigner resides or is required to reside has been communicated by a public agency. A foreigner has to accept notifications and informal communications of public bodies other than those indicated which are sent to the address at which the foreigner has to accept notifications and informal communications of the Federal Office for Migration and Refugees. If a communication cannot be delivered, it is regarded as having been delivered at the time that is was sent if the communication is returned as undeliverable.

647. Where family members have applied for asylum jointly and where the same address is used for all family members, certain decisions and communications which concern them may be combined in one notice or one communication and delivered to a family member who is of full legal age. The address has to list the names of all family members of full legal age who are affected by the decision or the communication. The decision or communication explicitly states to whom it applies.

648. A reception centre delivers all notifications and informal communications sent to the address of the reception centre to the foreigners concerned. The foreigners concerned have to accept such notifications and informal communications. Post-delivery and distribution hours must be publicly displayed for each working day. A foreigner has to ensure that incoming post can be passed on to him or her by the staff of the reception centre within the time slots identified as mail delivery and distribution hours. When a foreigner receives a notification or informal communication it is classed as 'delivered'. In all other cases, delivery is assumed three days after a notification or informal communication was delivered to the reception centre. The rules on substituted delivery, such as to an adult family member (sections 178–180 of the Code of Civil Procedure), remain unaffected by the aforementioned.

649. Should it be necessary for a communication to be delivered outside Germany, delivery is made by public notice. Section 10(1), sentence 2 and (2) of the Act on Service in Administrative Procedures (*Verwaltungszustellungsgesetz*) on the procedure of public notice apply.

650. At the time of the asylum application, a foreigner is informed of these provisions in writing and has to acknowledge that he or she has received this information.

2.   Facts

651. Additional cooperation requirements exist for the foreigner pursuant to section 15 AsylG.

652. Foreigners are personally required to cooperate in establishing the facts of their case. This also applies to foreigners who are represented by an authorised adviser.

653. A foreigner is required, in particular, to provide the necessary information orally and if also requested in writing to the authorities responsible for implementing the AsylG. A foreigner is also required to inform the Federal Office for Migration and Refugees without delay if he or she has been granted a residence title and to comply with statutory and official orders which require a foreigner to report to specific authorities or institutions or to appear there in person. A foreigner also has to present, hand over and surrender his or her passport or passport substitute, all necessary certificates and any other documents in his or her possession to the authorities responsible for the implementation of the AsylG.

654. An asylum seeker who does not have a valid passport or passport substitute also has to cooperate with the competent authorities to obtain an identity document and to present, hand over or surrender all data carriers in his or her possession, which could be relevant to establish his or her identity or nationality.

655. Furthermore, a foreigner is obliged to undergo any identification measure in accordance with the law.

656. Necessary certificates and other documents include, in particular, all certificates and documents that are not a passport or passport substitute which might help the German authorities to establish a foreigner's identity and nationality, such as visas, residence permits and other border-crossing documents issued by other countries, airline and other transport tickets, documents concerning the travel route from the home country to Germany, the means of transport used and time spent in other countries after leaving the country of origin and before entering Germany, as well as all other certificates and documents which a foreigner uses to substantiate the claim to asylum or international protection or which are relevant for the decisions and measures to be taken according to asylum and foreigners law, including a decision and the enforcement of a removal to another country.

657. The authorities responsible for implementing the AsylG may search a foreigner and the items carried by him or her, if he or she fails to comply with the obligation to present, hand over or surrender the required documents and, on request, data carriers if there are indications that a foreigner has the required documents or data carriers.

658. A foreigner may only be searched by a person of the same sex.

659. The withdrawal of an asylum application does not terminate a foreigner's obligation to cooperate.

C. Competent Authorities

660. The Federal Office for Migration and Refugees decides on asylum applications (section 5(1) AsylG). The Federal Ministry of the Interior appoints the head of the Federal Office for Migration and Refugees (section 5(2) AsylG).

661. In consultation with the respective *Land*, the head of the Federal Office for Migration and Refugees sets up a branch office at each Central Reception Facility for Asylum Applicants (reception centre (*Aufnahmeeinrichtung*)) with a capacity to accommodate 1000 persons or more on a long-term basis (section 5(3) AsylG). He or she may set up additional branch offices in consultation with the *Länder*. Currently, there are a multitude of such branch offices operating in Germany.

662. The head of the Federal Office for Migration and Refugees has arranged with the *Länder* that special reception centres host foreigners whose application is processed in a fast-track procedure pursuant to section 30a AufenthG (special reception centres (*Besondere Aufnahmeeinrichtung*)). Special reception centres are governed by the same rules as reception centres, unless the AsylG or another legal provision stipulates otherwise.

663. Decisions on asylum applications are binding in all matters in which the recognition as being entitled to asylum or to international protection is relevant in law. This does not apply to extradition procedures or to deportation procedures (section 58a AufenthG).

D. Data Protection and Information Procedures

1. Personal Data

664. Special attention is given to personal data and their protection in sections 7 et seq. AsylG. These provisions stipulate in detail which data may be collected, processed and transmitted in which way, to whom, and for which purpose.

665. The authorities responsible for the implementation of the AsylG may, for the purpose of implementing that Act, collect personal data if this is necessary to fulfil their duties. Data which reveal racial or ethnic origin, political opinions, religious or belief convictions, or the membership of a trade union, as well as genetic data, biometrical data that identifies a natural person, health data, and data referring to sexual life or sexual orientation (section 3(9) of the former version of the Federal Data Protection Act; now: section 46, No. 14 of the Federal Data Protection Act and corresponding provisions in the data protection Acts of the *Länder*) may be collected insofar as needed in individual cases.

2. Data Carriers

666. The AsylG provides strict rules on the analysis of data carriers in section 15a.

667. The evaluation of data carriers is only permitted if this is necessary to establish the identity and nationality of a foreigner pursuant to section 15(2), No. 6, and the purpose of the measure cannot be achieved by less intruding means.

3. Identity

668. Identification measures are taken to verify the identity of a foreigner requesting asylum (section 16 AsylG). To do so, a foreigner may only be photographed and the prints of all ten fingers taken. Foreigners younger than 14 may only be photographed. In order to determine a foreigner's country or region of origin, a foreigner's oral statements may be recorded on audio and data media other than at his or her formal hearing. Such recordings may only be made after the foreigner has been informed that this will be done. These recordings are kept at the Federal Office for Migration and Refugees.

669. In order to check the authenticity of a foreigner's documents or identity, the biometric and other data stored electronically in the passport, official passport substitute or other identity documents may be read and the biometric data obtained from the foreigner may be used to compare the biometric data with the data taken from the documents. Biometric data only include fingerprints, a photograph and an iris scan.

E. Place of Application

1. Filing Asylum Application

670. An application for asylum has to be filed at the branch office of the Federal Office for Migration and Refugees assigned to the reception centre responsible for receiving the foreigner. This is stipulated in section 14 AsylG. The Federal Office for Migration and Refugees, in consultation with the authority designated by the supreme *Land* authority, may require a foreigner to file his or her asylum application at another branch office. Before filing an asylum application, the foreigner has to be informed that in the case of withdrawal or incontestable rejection of the application a residence title will be granted prior to the foreigner leaving Germany only if this residence title is for reasons of international law or on humanitarian or political grounds or if a case of entitlement to issuance of a residence title applies (section 10(3) AufenthG). The information has to be made in writing and the foreigner has to acknowledge the receipt of this information.

671. This information on the consequences of a withdrawal or incontestable rejection of the asylum application must be provided without delay if the foreigner is under arrest or has been placed in official custody, in a hospital, a sanatorium or an asylum, or in a youth welfare institution (section 14(2), first sentence, No. 2 AsylG).

672. In certain cases, an asylum application has to be lodged with the Federal Office for Migration and Refugees. This is the case if a foreigner has been granted a residence title with an overall validity of more than six months, is under arrest or has been placed in official custody, in a hospital, a sanatorium or an asylum, or in a youth welfare institution, or if he or she is a minor and his or her legal representative is not required to live in a reception centre.

673. The foreigners authority immediately transmits any written application it has received to the Federal Office for Migration and Refugees. The Federal Office for Migration and Refugees determines which branch office is responsible for the processing of the asylum application.

674. If a foreigner is in detention pending trial, in prison, in custody in preparation of his or her deportation, detention pending deportation because he or she has stayed in Germany for longer than one month without a residence permit after entering the country irregularly, or in detention pending deportation, an application for asylum does not bar the ordering or continuation of custody awaiting deportation. A foreigner must be given an opportunity to contact a legal adviser of his or her choice without delay unless the foreigner already has a legal counsellor. Custody awaiting deportation is terminated as soon as a decision of the Federal Office for Migration and Refugees has been delivered and no later than four weeks after the Federal Office for Migration and Refugees has received an application for asylum. This does not apply if another country has been requested to admit or readmit the foreigner on the basis of EU law or an international agreement on the responsibility for the processing asylum applications, unless the application for asylum has been rejected as inadmissible because a safe third country (section 27 AsylG) is willing to readmit the foreigner or the asylum application is manifestly unfounded.

2. Requesting Asylum

675. Any foreigner requesting asylum with an authority charged with the supervision of cross-border traffic (border authority) is, pursuant to section 18 AsylG, immediately referred to the competent reception centre for the purpose of registration. If the competent reception centre is not known, a foreigner is referred to the nearest one.

3. Border Procedure

676. Any foreigner who does not have the necessary entry documents has to apply for asylum at the border. In the case of unauthorised entry, a foreigner has to immediately report to a reception centre or apply for asylum with the foreigners authority or the police (section 13(3) AsylG).

677. A foreigner is refused entry, if he or she enters Germany from a safe third country. Entry is also refused, if there are indications that another country is responsible for the processing of the asylum application based on EU law or an international agreement and proceedings to admit or readmit have been initiated by the German authorities. A foreigner is also refused entry, if he or she poses a threat to the general public, because the foreigner is the subject of an enforceable custodial sentence of at least three years' imprisonment in Germany on account of a particularly serious criminal offence and if the foreigner left the country less than three years ago.

678. A foreigner is removed, if the border authority finds him or her near the border immediately before or after an illegal entry and if the conditions to refuse entry (section 18(2) AsylG) apply.

679. However, if a foreigner enters Germany from a safe third country, the authorities refrain from refusing entry or from removing the foreigner, if Germany is responsible for the processing of an asylum application based on EU law or an international agreement with a safe third country or if the Federal Ministry of the Interior has so ordered on humanitarian grounds, for reasons of international law or in Germany's political interest.

680. The border authority takes the foreigner's photograph and fingerprints.

4. Entry by Air

681. The procedure for asylum applications in the case of entry by air is regulated in section 18a AsylG.

682. The asylum procedure is conducted prior to a decision on entry, in the case of foreigners arriving from a safe country of origin via an airport who apply for asylum with the border authority, if the foreigner can be accommodated on the airport premises during the procedure or cannot be accommodated on the airport premises because he or she needs hospital treatment. The same applies to foreigners who request asylum with the border authorities at an airport who are unable to prove their identity with a valid passport or other means of identification. The foreigner is immediately given the opportunity to file an asylum application with the branch office of the Federal Office for Migration and Refugees assigned to the border checkpoint. The Federal Office for Migration and Refugees interviews the foreigner in person without delay. The foreigner is then given the opportunity to contact a legal adviser of the foreigner's own choice immediately, unless the foreigner has already secured legal counsel for himself or herself. The reasons to refuse entry remain unaffected, e.g., arrival from a safe third country or another country that is responsible for processing the asylum application (section 18(2) AsylG).

683. If the Federal Office for Migration and Refugees rejects an asylum application because it is manifestly unfounded, the Federal Office for Migration and Refugees warns the foreigner that he or she will be deported in case of entering Germany.

684. If an asylum application is rejected as manifestly unfounded, a foreigner is not allowed to enter Germany. The decision of the Federal Office for Migration and Refugees on the asylum application together with the refusal to grant entry permission is delivered to a foreigner by the border authority.

F. *Procedure Before the Federal Office for Migration and Refugees*

1. Procedure

685. The Federal Office for Migration and Refugees clarifies the facts of the case and compiles the necessary evidence (section 24 AsylG). After the application for asylum has been filed, the Federal Office for Migration and Refugees informs the foreigner in a language that the foreigner can reasonably be supposed to understand about the course of the asylum procedure and about his or her rights and obligations, especially the obligations concerning deadlines and the consequences of missing a deadline.

2. Hearing

686. There is a hearing on the asylum application in which the Federal Office for Migration and Refugees interviews a foreigner in person.

687. A hearing may be dispensed with, if the Federal Office for Migration and Refugees intends to recognise the foreigner's entitlement to asylum or if the foreigner claims to have entered Germany from a safe third country. A hearing may also be dispensed with, if the Federal Office for Migration and Refugees intends to approve an application for asylum which has been limited to international protection (section 13(2), second sentence, AsylG). A hearing will be dispensed with if an asylum application has been filed on behalf of a child younger than 6 who was born in Germany and if the facts of the case have been sufficiently clarified based on the case files of one or both parents.

688. If a large number of foreigners requests asylum at the same time, making it impossible for the Federal Office for Migration and Refugees to conduct hearings in temporal proximity to the filing of applications, another authority discharging tasks defined in the AsylG or in the AufenthG may be authorised by the Federal Office for Migration and Refugees to temporarily conduct hearings. An example of an authority that can be authorised to conduct hearings are the foreigners authorities. Hearings may only be conducted by specially trained public employees who may not wear uniforms during the hearing. Section 5(4) AsylG applies accordingly. Thus, the head of the Federal Office for Migration and Refugees may arrange with the *Länder* that they supply the necessary material and staff resources in order to fulfil their duties in the branch offices. The staff supplied by the *Länder* is bound to the same extent as the staff of the Federal Office for Migration and Refugees by the head's technical instructions. The cooperation is governed by an administrative agreement between the Federation and the *Land*.

3. Hearing Procedures

689. The rules on hearing a foreigner are set out in section 25 AsylG.

690. According to this provision a foreigner has to present the facts justifying his or her fear of political persecution or the risk of serious harm that he or she faces and provide the necessary details. The necessary details include information concerning residence, travel routes, time spent in other countries and whether a procedure aimed at obtaining recognition as a refugee or as a beneficiary of international protection has been lodged with the authorities of another State or Germany or if an asylum application has already been initiated or completed in another country or in Germany. A foreigner also has to relate all other facts or circumstances which preclude deportation or deportation to a specific country.

691. If a foreigner informs the competent authorities of such facts at a later stage, they may be ignored if this would mean a delay in a decision of the Federal

Office for Migration and Refugees. The foreigner has to be informed of this provision. The foreigner has also to be informed that the introduction of facts, evidence, and circumstances which were not considered in the administrative procedure may be left unconsidered by the court if the decision would otherwise be delayed.

692. For a foreigner who is required to reside in a reception centre, a hearing should be arranged in a way that it coincides with the filing of the asylum application. It is not necessary to issue a special summons requiring a foreigner and his or her authorised representative to appear. This provision applies accordingly if a foreigner is informed of the interview date at the time that he or she files the application for asylum or within one week thereafter. If a hearing cannot take place on the same day as the application for asylum is made, a foreigner and his or her authorised representative have to be informed without delay of the date of the interview. If the foreigner fails to appear at the hearing without a valid excuse, the Federal Office for Migration and Refugees decides on the asylum application, on the basis of the record as it stands, taking into account the foreigner's failure to cooperate.

693. In the case of foreigners who are not required to reside in a reception centre, a hearing in person may be dispensed with if a foreigner fails to comply with a summons for a hearing in person without a valid excuse. In this case, a foreigner is given an opportunity to state his or her case in writing within a period of one month. If the foreigner fails to do this, the Federal Office for Migration and Refugees decides on the application for asylum on the basis of the record as it stands, taking into account the foreigner's failure to cooperate. Section 33 AsylG that stipulates that an asylum application is deemed to have been withdrawn if a foreigner fails to pursue it or if a foreigner has returned to his or her country of origin during the asylum procedure, remains unaffected.

694. The interview is not open to the public. It may be attended by any person who can provide proof of his or her identity as a representative of the Federation, of a *Land* or of the UNHCR. The head or the deputy head of the Federal Office for Migration and Refugees may allow another person to attend a hearing.

695. A record of the hearing containing the essential information produced by the foreigner is kept. A copy of this record is given or sent to the foreigner with the Federal Office for Migration and Refugees' decision.

4. Decision

696. After an asylum application has been filed, the Federal Office for Migration and Refugees also has to decide whether a deportation ban exists (section 60(5) or (7) AufenthG).

697. The Federal Office for Migration and Refugees informs the foreigners authority immediately of its decision and the grounds presented by the foreigner or otherwise apparent that justify the suspension of deportation, in particular the need to obtain documents necessary to conduct a removal, or documents which could provide evidence that a temporary residence permit cannot be issued to the foreigner (section 25(3), second sentence, Nos 1–4 AufenthG).

698. If a decision on the asylum application is not taken within six months, the Federal Office for Migration and Refugees informs the foreigner upon request as to when a decision is likely to be taken.

G. Inadmissible and Manifestly Unfounded Applications

1. Inadmissibility

699. Certain applications are inadmissible pursuant to section 29 AsylG. An application for asylum is inadmissible if the asylum application is to be processed by another country according to the Dublin III Regulation,[97] another EU law or another international agreement. The same applies if another EU Member State has already granted the foreigner international protection or if a country that is willing to readmit a foreigner is regarded as a safe third country for that foreigner. Section 29 AsylG also applies if a country that is not an EU Member State that is willing to readmit a foreigner is regarded as a third country where the foreigner is safe from political persecution, or if, in the case of follow-up applications or secondary applications, another asylum application does not have to be processed (sections 70, 71a AsylG).

700. The Federal Office for Migration and Refugees interviews a foreigner in person to establish whether there are reasons to assume its inadmissibility before it decides whether or not an asylum application is admissible. This is not the case if the application is inadmissible because another country is responsible for the procedure due to the Dublin III Regulation. As regards the inadmissibility of follow-up or secondary applications, the Federal Office for Migration and Refugees gives the foreigner an opportunity to submit both a statement in writing of the facts and evidence which are in the foreigner's possession (section 71(3) AsylG).

701. If a foreigner fails to attend the interview regarding the admissibility of his or her asylum application, the Federal Office for Migration and Refugees decides on the basis of the record as it stands. This does not apply if a foreigner proves without delay that the failure was due to circumstances beyond his or her control. In this case, the procedure is to be continued.

---

97. Regulation (EU) No 604/2013 of the European Parliament and of the Council of 26 Jun. 2013 establishing the criteria and mechanisms for determining the Member State responsible for examining an application for international protection lodged in one of the Member States by a third-country national or a stateless person, OJ EU 2013, L 180/31.

702. According to section 24(1a) AsylG, specially trained public employees from other authorities may be requested to carry out hearings with foreigners regarding the admissibility of their applications.

2. Manifest Unfoundedness

703. According to section 30 AsylG, an asylum application is considered manifestly unfounded if the conditions to grant asylum and the conditions to grant international protection are obviously not met.

704. In particular, an asylum application is manifestly unfounded if it is obvious from the circumstances of the individual case that the only purpose for a foreigner's stay in Germany are economic or in order to evade a general emergency situation in his or her country of origin.

705. An unfounded asylum application is rejected as manifestly unfounded if key aspects of the foreigner's statements are unsubstantiated or contradictory, obviously do not correspond to the facts or are based on forged or falsified evidence. This is also the case if the foreigner misrepresents or refuses to state his or her identity or nationality in the asylum procedure or the foreigner has filed another asylum application or asylum request using different personal data. Manifestly unfounded is also an unfounded asylum application filed in order to avert an imminent termination of the right of residence although the foreigner has had sufficient opportunity to file an asylum application earlier. An asylum application is also rejected as manifestly unfounded if the applicant has grossly violated the obligation to cooperate, unless the foreigner is not responsible for this violation or there are important reasons why he or she has not been able to cooperate. Moreover, it applies if a foreigner has enforceably been expelled. An unfounded application is furthermore classed as manifestly unfounded if it has been filed on behalf of a foreigner without legal capacity under the AsylG, or is considered to have been filed after the asylum applications made by the parents or by the parent with the sole right of custody have been incontestably rejected (section 14a AsylG).

706. Furthermore, an unfounded asylum application is rejected as manifestly unfounded if, for serious reasons, the foreigner is to be regarded as a threat to the security of the Federal Republic of Germany or constitutes a threat to the general public because that foreigner has been incontestably sentenced to a term of imprisonment of at least three years for a crime or a particularly serious offence. The same applies if there are serious reasons to believe that a foreigner has committed a crime within the meaning of section 3(2) AsylG such as war crime or a serious non-political crime. An unfounded asylum application is also rejected as being manifestly unfounded in cases where the Federal Office for Migration and Refugees has decided not to issue a decision prohibiting deportation (section 60(1) and (8), third sentence AufenthG).

707. An application filed with the Federal Office for Migration and Refugees is also rejected as manifestly unfounded if, due to its content, it does not constitute an asylum application (section 13(1) AsylG).

H. Fast-Track Procedure

708. The special fast-track procedures which aim at speeding up the asylum application proceedings are provided for in section 30a AsylG.

709. The Federal Office for Migration and Refugees may use fast-track procedures for asylum applications which are processed in a branch office assigned to a special reception centre (section 5(5) AsylG) in a number of cases. Fast-track procedures may be used if a foreigner is a national of a safe country of origin. This also applies if a foreigner has clearly misled the authorities as to his or her identity or nationality by presenting false information or documents or by withholding relevant documents or has in bad faith destroyed or disposed of an identity or travel document that would have helped establish the foreigner's identity or nationality, or if the circumstances clearly give reason to believe that this is so. It also applies if a foreigner has filed a follow-up application, has made an application merely in order to delay or frustrate the enforcement of an earlier or imminent decision which would result in the foreigner's deportation, or refuses to be fingerprinted.[98] It also applies if a foreigner has been expelled because this was justified by serious reasons of public security and order or if there were serious reasons to believe that a foreigner constituted a serious threat to public security and order.

710. If the Federal Office for Migration and Refugees applies this fast-track option it decides on the asylum application within one week of it being filed. If it is not able to decide on the merits of the case within this period, the asylum application is transferred to a non-fast-track procedure.

711. Foreigners whose applications are being processed under fast-track procedures are required to live in a special reception centre that is responsible for their reception pending the Federal Office for Migration and Refugees' decision on their asylum application. This obligation continues to exist until a foreigner leaves Germany or until the deportation warning or deportation order is enforced, should the procedure be discontinued or the asylum application be rejected on obvious grounds. The latter can be the case if the asylum application is rejected i.e., as being

---

98. Regulation (EU) No 603/2013 of the European Parliament and of the Council dated 26 Jun. 2013 on the establishment of Eurodac for the comparison of fingerprints for the effective application of Regulation (EU) No 604/2013 establishing the criteria and mechanisms for determining the Member State responsible for examining an application for international protection lodged in one of the Member States by a third-country national or a stateless person and on requests for the comparison with Eurodac data by Member States' law enforcement authorities and Europol for law enforcement purposes, and amending Regulation (EU) No 1077/2011 establishing a European Agency for the operational management of large-scale IT systems in the area of freedom, security and justice, OJ EU 2013, L 180/1.

manifestly unfounded, inadmissible because a third country that is not an EU Member State is willing to readmit the foreigner, or in deportation cases (section 29(1), No. 4, and section 71(4) AsylG). The general rules on the termination of an obligation to reside in a reception centre, on release from it, and on the distribution of asylum applicants within a *Land* remain unaffected (sections 48–50 AsylG).

I. Termination of Proceedings

1. Content of Decision

712. Decisions adopted by the Federal Office for Migration and Refugees are issued in writing in accordance with section 31 AsylG. They contain a justification in writing of the decision. Contestable decisions are delivered to the persons concerned without delay. If no authorised representative has been appointed, a translation of the decision and the information on the available legal remedy in a language the foreigner can reasonably be assumed to understand must be enclosed. The rights and duties are communicated to those who are granted asylum status or international protection or in whose case the Federal Office for Migration and Refugees has issued a deportation ban.

713. If an asylum application is rejected for the sole reason that a foreigner has entered Germany from a safe third country or another country is responsible for the asylum procedure, the decision together with the deportation order is delivered to the foreigner in person. It may also be delivered to the foreigner by the authority responsible for the deportation or for carrying out the deportation. If the foreigner has an authorised representative or has named an authorised receiving agent, a copy of the decision is forwarded to the representative or agent.

714. In decisions on admissible asylum applications and in decisions rejecting an asylum application as manifestly unfounded because, due to its content, it does not constitute an asylum application, must include an express statement whether the foreigner has been granted refugee status or subsidiary protection or whether the foreigner is granted asylum. In cases of an application limited to international protection, the limited application is decided upon (section 13(2), second sentence AsylG).

715. In decisions on admissible asylum applications and in decisions rejecting an application as manifestly unfounded because, due to its content, it does not constitute an asylum application and in decisions on inadmissible asylum applications it is specified whether the conditions for a deportation ban are met (section 60(5) or (7) AufenthG). This may be dispensed with if a foreigner is granted asylum or international protection.

716. If an asylum application is rejected as inadmissible only because a foreigner has entered Germany from a safe third country, granting accessory refugee status or subsidiary protection to family members is not excluded (section 31(4), and section 26(5), section 26(1)–(4) AsylG).

717. If a foreigner is granted asylum status or international protection for families (section 26(1)–(3) AsylG), the determination of the conditions for a deportation ban should be dispensed with. This is to reduce the Federal Office for Migration and Refugees' workload.

718. If an asylum application is rejected as inadmissible because another country is responsible for the processing of that application according to the Dublin III Regulation, a foreigner is informed in a decision which country is responsible for the processing of his or her asylum application.

2.   Decision in Case of Withdrawal or Abandonment

719. The decision in case of withdrawal or abandonment of an asylum application is regulated in section 32 AsylG.

720. If the proceedings have been abandoned (section 33 AsylG), the Federal Office for Migration and Refugees decides on the basis of the record as it stands. If the asylum application is abandoned for a child (section 14a(3) AsylG) or is withdrawn, the Federal Office for Migration and Refugees states in its decision that the asylum procedure has been discontinued and whether a deportation ban exists.

3.   Suspension of Proceedings

721. Suspension of the proceedings is provided for in section 32a AsylG.

722. An asylum procedure is suspended as long as a foreigner enjoys temporary protection. As long as the procedure is suspended, the foreigner's legal status is not determined by the AsylG, but by the AufenthG.

723. An asylum application is deemed to be withdrawn if a foreigner does not notify the Federal Office for Migration and Refugees within one month of the expiry of the foreigner's temporary residence permit that he or she intends to continue the asylum procedure.

4.   Abandonment

724. An asylum application is pursuant to section 33 AsylG deemed to have been withdrawn if the foreigner fails to pursue it.

725. It is presumed that the foreigner has failed to pursue the procedure, if the foreigner fails to comply with a request to present information which is important for the application or with a request to attend a hearing, has gone underground or has violated the geographic restriction of the permission to remain pending the asylum decision to which the foreigner is subject on account of the obligation to live in a reception centre. The foreigner is deemed to have gone underground when the foreigners authority cannot find the foreigner despite the foreigner's obligation to enable constant contact.[99]

726. This presumption does not apply if a foreigner proves without delay that the failure or action was due to circumstances beyond his or her control. In this case, the asylum procedure is continued. If the procedure was conducted as a fast-track procedure, the period of one week within which a decision on the asylum application is to be made reassumes.

727. An asylum application is also deemed to have been withdrawn if a foreigner has travelled to his or her country of origin during the asylum procedure.

728. A foreigner is informed in writing of the legal consequences of a withdrawal and has to acknowledge the receipt of this information.

729. The Federal Office for Migration and Refugees discontinues the asylum procedure when an asylum application is considered to have been withdrawn. Foreigners whose asylum procedure has thus been discontinued may apply for its resumption. The foreigner has to make this application in person at the branch office of the Federal Office for Migration and Refugees assigned to the reception centre where the foreigner was required to reside before the asylum procedure was discontinued. If the foreigner files a new asylum application, this application is treated as an application to resume the asylum procedure. The Federal Office for Migration and Refugees resumes the examination of the asylum application where it left off. The asylum procedure is not to be resumed and an application for resumption is treated as a follow-up application (section 71 AsylG) if the asylum procedure was discontinued at least ten months before the application for resumption was filed. If this is the situation, *restitutio in integrum* remains possible. An asylum procedure is also not resumed if it has already been resumed on a former occasion, resumption can only be applied for once.

730. If a procedure is resumed and the asylum application was being processed in a fast-track procedure before its discontinuation, the period of one week within which a decision on the asylum application is to be made begins to run again.

731. The rules on appeals against a deportation warning, such as filing within one week and written procedure (section 36(3) AsylG), apply accordingly to appeals against decisions not to resume the asylum procedure (section 33(5), sentence 6 AsylG).

---

99. Deutscher Bundestag Druksache 18/7538, p. 17.

J. Follow-Up and Secondary Application

1. Follow-Up Application

732. Follow-up applications are dealt with by section 71 AsylG.

733. If, after the withdrawal or incontestable rejection of a previous asylum application, a foreigner files a new asylum application, this new application is called a follow-up application. However, a new asylum procedure is only conducted if the conditions that apply to the resumption of an asylum procedure in section 51(1)–(3) of the Administrative Procedure Act are met. This can be the case in particular if the relevant facts have changed in the meantime, e.g., because the political situation in the country of origin has deteriorated and the foreigner would not be safe there anymore. The relevant new circumstances are examined by the Federal Office for Migration and Refugees. The same applies to a child's application for asylum if the child's representative waived the processing of the asylum application (section 14a(3) AsylG).

734. A foreigner has to make a follow-up application in person at the branch office of the Federal Office for Migration and Refugees assigned to the reception centre where the foreigner was required to reside during the previous asylum procedure. If, in the meantime, a foreigner has temporarily left Germany, the rules on residence in the AsylG apply accordingly. This includes the rules on allocation, residence in reception centres and employment restrictions (sections 47–67). If a foreigner is under arrest or has been placed in official custody in a hospital, a sanatorium or an asylum, or in a youth welfare institution, or if a foreigner can prove that he or she is unable to appear in person, a follow-up application is filed in writing. A follow-up application is filed in writing with the central office of the Federal Office for Migration and Refugees if the branch office where the foreigner was required to reside during the previous asylum procedure no longer exists or if a foreigner was not required to reside in a reception centre during the previous asylum procedure.

735. There is no referral to a reception centre for registration procedures, as required in an initial asylum application procedure (section 19(1) AsylG).

736. In a follow-up application a foreigner has to give his or her address as well as the facts and evidence to fulfil the conditions of resumption. A foreigner has to provide this information in writing upon request. A hearing may be dispensed with and the rules on delivery apply accordingly (section 10 AsylG).

737. Special facilitating rules on deportation apply in cases of unsuccessful follow-up applications.

738. If a foreigner's right of residence during the previous asylum procedure was geographically restricted, the most recent geographical restrictions continue to apply, unless decided otherwise. The rules on the ordering and expiry of geographical restrictions apply accordingly (section 59a and 59b AsylG).

2.   Secondary Application

739.   Secondary applications are dealt with in section 71a AsylG. Secondary applications are asylum applications filed by foreigners in Germany after having unsuccessfully applied for asylum in a safe third country where EU law on the responsibility for the processing of asylum applications applies, such as the Dublin III Regulation, or which has concluded an international agreement with Germany.

740.   If a foreigner files a secondary application, a further asylum procedure is only carried out if Germany is responsible for carrying out the asylum procedure and the conditions of resumption (section 51(1)–(3) of the Administrative Procedure Act) are met. Whether this is the case is determined by the Federal Office for Migration and Refugees.

741.   The general procedural provisions governing an initial asylum application, such as the rules on the filing of an asylum application, family unity, or accommodation and distribution (sections 12–25, 33 and 44–54 AsylG) apply accordingly to the procedure for determining whether the new asylum application has to be processed. A hearing may be dispensed with if not needed to determine that a new asylum application does not have to be processed.

742.   There are special rules that apply to deportation in the case of a secondary application.

743.   Geographical and employment restrictions and residence rules apply accordingly (sections 56–67 AsylG).

744.   If a foreigner files another asylum application after the withdrawal or the incontestable rejection of his secondary application, the rules on a follow-up application apply (section 71 AsylG).

II.   Review of a Decision Rejecting an Application for Asylum

A.   Administrative Appeals

745.   Special rules which are set out in sections 11 et seq. AsylG govern the administrative procedure in asylum cases.

746.   As a general rule, administrative acts are reviewed upon application in a second administrative procedure, called an administrative appeal, before an appeal to a court is possible. However, there is no right to file an administrative appeal against measures and decisions issued in accordance with the AsylG. This is to speed up the asylum procedure.

747. The Federal Ministry of the Interior, however, may temporarily suspend decisions of the Federal Office for Migration and Refugees under the AsylG for certain countries of origin for a period of up to six months if the assessment of the asylum and deportation situation requires special clarification. This suspension decision may be extended (section 11a AsylG).

B. Appeals of Airport Decisions

748. Special rules apply when an asylum applicant appeals a decision rejecting his or her asylum application filed at an airport pursuant to section 18a(3)–(5) AsylG.

749. The border authority immediately sends a copy of its decision and the administrative file of the Federal Office for Migration and Refugees to the competent administrative court in order to speed up the procedure.

750. Any application for temporary relief within the meaning of the Code of Administrative Court Procedure must be filed within three days from the date the decisions of the Federal Office for Migration and Refugees and of the border authority are delivered. This application may be filed with the border authority. The foreigner must be informed of this possibility as well as the possibility to appeal a decision (section 58 of the Code of Administrative Court Procedure). The decision should be issued in writing.

751. An order to suspend deportation may only be issued if there are serious doubts as to the legality of the administrative act against which an appeal has been filed (section 36(4) AsylG). If an application is filed in time, a refusal to grant entry permission must not be enforced prior to a court decision (section 36(3), ninth sentence AsylG).

752. If an application is aimed at obtaining entry and, in the case of entry, against the deportation warning, the court order allowing a foreigner to enter Germany also serves the purpose of a decision that suspends deportation.

753. A foreigner is allowed to enter Germany if the Federal Office for Migration and Refugees informs the border authority that it is not able to decide the case within a short time or the Federal Office for Migration and Refugees has not adopted a decision on the asylum application within two days of it being filed. The same applies if a court has not ruled on the merits of an application for temporary relief pursuant to the Code of Administrative Court Procedure (section 18(4) AsylG)

within two weeks. It also applies if the border authority has not requested a judicial order for detention (section 15(6) AufenthG) or the judge has refused to order or extend a detention measure.

C. Court Proceedings

1. Time Limits

754. Court proceedings in asylum cases are regulated by sections 74 et seq. AsylG. These provisions aim at speeding up proceedings in particular by introducing shorter time limits, distributing the workload among courts, and limiting the admissibility of legal remedies. On the other hand, the law tries to uphold rule of law standards to safeguard the rights of foreigners.

755. Action against decisions pursuant to the AsylG must be lodged (section 74 AsylG) no later than two weeks after the decision was delivered. An application for temporary relief (section 80(5) of the Code of Administrative Court Procedure) must be filed within one week; if such an application is lodged, the action against the asylum decision must also be brought within one week (section 34a(2), first and third sentences, and section 36(3), first and tenth sentences AsylG).

756. The plaintiff has to submit the facts and evidence on which an action is based within a period of one month after the decision was delivered to the plaintiff. A court may reject statements and evidence submitted after this time limit has expired and may decide without any further investigations whether admitting them would, according to the free conviction of the court, delay the termination of the legal proceeding, if the party has not provided a sufficient justification for the delay and the parties have been informed about the consequences of a failure to observe a time limit, unless the court can establish the facts easily without the cooperation of the parties (section 87b(3) of the Code of Administrative Court Procedure). The plaintiff has to be informed of this obligation and the consequences of a failure to observe the time limit. The submission of new facts and evidence arising after the administrative decision on the asylum application was adopted remains unaffected.

2. Limited Suspensory Effect

757. As a rule, action in an administrative court procedure has suspensory effect. However, contrary to this general rule, an action brought against a decision adopted under the AsylG only has suspensive effect in few cases. These are actions against a rejection of the asylum application not based on special rules, in particular, if the asylum application was rejected because it is unfounded rather than manifestly unfounded (section 38(1) AsylG). This also applies to actions against a revocation or withdrawal of asylum status, refugee status, subsidiary protection, or a deportation ban (section 73, 73b and 73c AsylG).

758. However, actions brought against decisions of the Federal Office for Migration and Refugees to revoke or withdraw asylum or refugee status do not have suspensive effect if the status was revoked or withdrawn because, for serious reasons, the foreigner is to be regarded as a threat to Germany's security or constitutes a threat to the general public because he or she has been incontestably sentenced to a term of imprisonment of at least three years for a crime or a particularly serious offence (section 60(8), first sentence, AufenthG), or the foreigner has committed a serious act such as a war crime or a crime against humanity (section 3(2) AsylG). An action also has no suspensive effect if a status has been revoked or withdrawn, because the Federal Office for Migration and Refugees has decided not to grant a request for a prohibition of deportation because the foreigner represents a danger to the general public because that foreigner has been incontestably sentenced to a term of imprisonment or a term of youth custody of at least one year for one or more intentionally committed offences against life, physical integrity, sexual self-determination or property or for resisting enforcement officers if the criminal offence was committed using violence, using a threat of danger to life or limb, or was conducted out of guile, or if the crime committed was rape or sexual assault by use of force (section 60(1) and (8) AufenthG, and section 177 of the Criminal Code). The same applies accordingly when an action is brought against the decision to revoke or withdraw subsidiary protection because there are serious grounds to believe that the foreigner has committed a serious act, such as a war crime or a crime against humanity (section 4(2) AsylG). Elimination of suspensive effect must be especially ordered by the authority which has issued the administrative act (section 80(2), first sentence, No. 4 of the Code of Administrative Court Procedure).

3. Single Judge and Chamber

759. In disputes resulting from the AsylG, a Chamber should, pursuant to section 76 AsylG, as a rule, refer a legal dispute to one of its members for a decision as an individual judge, unless the case presents particular difficulties of a factual or legal nature or the legal question has fundamental significance. A Chamber consists of three professional judges. In oral proceedings, there are also two honorary judges.

760. In cases where a Chamber has already conducted oral proceedings, a dispute may not be referred to an individual judge unless a provisional, partial or interlocutory judgment has been passed in the meantime.

761. After having heard the parties involved, an individual judge may refer the dispute back to the Chamber if it is clear, due to a substantial change in the proceedings, that the legal question has fundamental significance. It is not possible to refer the matter to an individual judge a second time.

762. In temporary relief proceedings, a member of a Chamber decides as an individual judge. The individual judge refers the dispute to the Chamber if the legal question has fundamental significance or if the judge intends to deviate from previous rulings by a Chamber.

763. There is an initial probationary period, meaning that a judge may not act as an individual judge within the first six months of his or her appointment.

4. Decision of the Court

764. In disputes resulting from a decision adopted under the AsylG, a court has, according to section 77 AsylG, to base its decision on the factual and legal situation at the time of the last oral proceedings. If the case is decided without an oral proceeding, the decision is based on the situation at the time the decision is taken. Again, the court may reject belated submissions of facts or evidence, unless it can establish the facts easily without the cooperation of the parties (section 87b(3) of the Code of Administrative Court Procedure, section 74(2), second sentence, AsylG).

765. The court decides without a presentation of the facts and the reasons for its decision, if it follows the statements and justification of the administrative act against which the appeal was filed. This is stated as such in the decision. A decision without a presentation of the facts is also permitted if the parties concerned unanimously renounce such a presentation.

5. Legal Remedy

766. If an administrative court rejects an action brought in connection with a legal dispute resulting from a decision adopted under the AsylG as manifestly inadmissible or manifestly unfounded, its judgment is incontestable according to section 78 AsylG. The same applies if only the plaintiff's action against a decision on the asylum application has been rejected as being manifestly inadmissible or manifestly unfounded, while the remainder of the plaintiff's action has been rejected as inadmissible or unfounded.

767. In all other cases, the parties concerned are entitled to file an appeal against the administrative court's judgment if a right to appeal is granted by the higher administrative court. A right to appeal is only granted if the legal question is of fundamental significance or the decision deviates from a decision of the Higher Administrative Court, the BVerwG, the Joint Panel of the Highest Federal Courts or the Federal Constitutional Court. It is also granted if one of the parties claims that there has been a particular serious flaw in the proceedings, such as an incorrect composition of the court or a violation of the rules on the public nature of the proceedings and if such a defect exists (section 138 of the Code of Administrative Court Procedure).

768. A request for an appeal has to be made within one month after the judgment was delivered. This request has to be filed with the administrative court. It has to indicate the decision that needs to be appealed. The request must state the reasons why a right to appeal should be granted. Filing the request for an appeal stays the legal force of a decision.

769. The Higher Administrative Court decides whether to grant an appeal request. This court is not required to give any reasons for its decision. The original decision becomes final upon rejection of the request for a right to appeal. If the Higher Administrative Court grants the appeal request, the application procedure is continued in the form of appellate proceedings; there is no need to file an appeal.

770. A request for revision directed against the judgment of the Administrative Court is inadmissible if the judgment of the Administrative Court has become incontestable (section 134 of the Code of Administrative Court Procedure).

771. Most appeals have to be filed within two weeks from the moment that a court decision was delivered (section 84(2) of the Code of Administrative Court Procedure).

6. Special Provisions Governing Appeals

772. In the proceedings before the Higher Administrative Court, statements and evidence which the plaintiff has failed to submit within a period of one month after the decision of the Administrative Court was delivered to him or her may only be admitted if, according to the free decision of that court, this will not delay the proceedings or if any delay has been duly justified by the plaintiff (section 128a of the Code of Administrative Court Procedure, section 74(2), first sentence, and section 79 AsylG).

773. A referral that would mean that the Court of First Instance has to review the case again is not allowed (section 130(2) and (3) of the Code of Administrative Court Procedure, section 79 AsylG).

7. Inadmissibility of Complaints

774. A complaint against decisions on cases brought under the AsylG is inadmissible according to section 80 AsylG. This does not apply to complaints against non-admission of revision (section 133(1) of the Code of Administrative Court Procedure). Complaints are special legal remedies against court decisions within court procedures, not against the final judgment. An example is a decision whether or not to summon and question a specific witness.

8.   Suspension and Withdrawal

775. A court action is suspended if a foreigner is granted temporary protection. Suspension has no influence on time limits for filing or justifying appeals. The action is regarded as withdrawn if the plaintiff does not notify the court within one month of the expiry of the temporary residence permit for temporary protection that he or she intends to pursue legal proceedings (section 32a(1) and section 80a AsylG, section 24 AufenthG).

776. The Federal Office for Migration and Refugees informs the court without delay of the issuing and expiry of a temporary residence permit for temporary protection.

777. In legal proceedings instigated pursuant to the AsylG, an action is deemed to have been withdrawn if the plaintiff, despite a request by the court, has failed for a period exceeding one month to pursue the proceedings (section 81 AsylG). The plaintiff has to bear the costs of the proceedings. As court proceedings as such are free of charge, these costs entail only the out-of-court costs such as a lawyer's fees and travel expenses. The court has to inform the plaintiff of these consequences.

9.   Inspection of Files

778. In proceedings for temporary relief, a request to access to files at the court's registry is granted. These files may be handed over to the authorised lawyer to take to the lawyer's home or office if this does not delay the proceedings (section 82 AsylG). This also applies to the dispatching of files.

10.   Special Panels

779. Disputes under the AsylG should be aggregated by special panels composed of judges in accordance with section 83 AsylG.

780. The *Land* governments may instal, in accordance with statutory instruments, special judicial bodies at the administrative courts, to deal with disputes under the AsylG. They are also competent to determine the seat of such bodies. The *Land* governments may confer this power on other authorities, such as the *Land* Ministry of Justice. The judicial bodies should have their seat close to the relevant reception centres.

781. The *Land* governments are authorised to issue statutory instruments allocating legal disputes under the AsylG to a single administrative court if they concern the districts of several administrative courts and deal with specific countries of origin, if this is relevant to the proceedings related to these disputes. The *Land* governments may confer this power on other authorities, which, again, can be the *Land* Ministry of Justice.

11. Notification

782. The court may, in accordance with section 83a AsylG, informally notify the foreigners authority of the outcome of proceedings. The court must inform the foreigners authority of the outcome if the proceedings deal with the lawfulness of a deportation warning or a deportation order adopted pursuant to the AsylG.

12. Costs

783. Court costs (fees and expenses) are not charged in disputes pursuant to the AsylG, as stipulated in section 83b AsylG. However, costs caused by the fault of the plaintiff may be charged to the plaintiff. This applies to additional court expenses caused, e.g., by lies of the plaintiff.

13. Entry and Residence Bans

784. The provisions on court proceedings in the AsylG and the rules on the geographic competence of the Administrative Court (section 52, No. 2, sentence 3 of the Code of Administrative Court Procedure) also apply to appeals against certain decisions adopted by the Federal Office for Migration and Refugees imposing a time limit on a ban on entry and residence, in the case of a deportation warning or a deportation order (section 83c AsylG, section 75, No. 12 AufenthG).

III. Unaccompanied Minor Asylum Claimants

785. In addition to the general rules on unaccompanied minor foreigners there are special rules that govern the status of unaccompanied minor asylum seekers.

786. Establishing the residence status of a minor includes a decision whether an asylum application has been lodged. If asylum is to be applied for, the youth welfare office or the guardian has to lodge the application in writing on behalf of the unaccompanied minor. The Federal Office for Migration and Refugees is responsible for the implementation of the procedure. Under asylum law, upon reaching the age of 18, a foreigner is responsible for the continuation of his or her procedure regardless of what the age of majority is according to the law of his or her country of origin. A guardian will, however, offer assistance if needed (sections 12 and 14 AsylG). If it is clear that an asylum application is weak, the competent foreigners authority may also grant temporary suspension of deportation (section 60a AufenthG). If this is not possible, the foreigners authority will consider other possibilities under migration law.

787. In the asylum procedure, specially commissioned case-officers who are trained to take a sensitive approach take care of an asylum application, as unaccompanied minors are regarded as being a particularly vulnerable group of asylum seekers. Child-specific grounds for flight are given particular attention (Directive 2013/32/EU; Article 2(I) Directive 2011/95/EU). Such child-specific grounds for flight can be i.e., genital mutilation, forced marriage, domestic violence, trafficking in human beings, or forced recruitment as a child soldier.

788. In the case of deportation, before deporting (section 58(1a) AufenthG) an unaccompanied foreign minor, the competent authority must ensure that the minor will be handed over to a member of the minor's family, to a person who has a right of care and custody or to an appropriate reception centre when returned.

IV. Safe Country of Origin and Safe Third Country

A. Safe Country of Origin

789. Special rules apply to foreigners coming from safe countries of origin pursuant to section 29a AsylG. Safe countries of origin are defined in Article 16a(3) of the Basic Law.

790. By a law requiring the consent of the *Bundesrat*, a list of States may be drawn up in which, on the basis of their laws, enforcement practices and general political conditions, it can be safely concluded that neither political persecution nor inhuman or degrading punishment or treatment exists. A State that is listed as 'safe' justifies the presumption that a foreigner from that State is not persecuted, unless the foreigner presents evidence justifying the conclusion that, contrary to this presumption, he or she is persecuted on political grounds in his or her country of origin.

791. Thus, as a rule, an asylum application lodged by a foreigner from a safe country of origin is rejected as manifestly unfounded. However, an asylum application is not rejected for this reason if a foreigner produces facts or evidence, which gives reason to believe that this foreigner faces serious harm in the country of origin in spite of the general situation there. This serious harm consists of political persecution on account of the foreigner's race, religion, nationality, political opinion or membership of a particular social group. The same applies if a foreigner faces the death penalty or an execution, torture or inhuman or degrading treatment or punishment, or a serious and individual threat to his or her life or person by reason of indiscriminate violence in situations of international or internal armed conflict (section 3(1) and section 4(1) AsylG).

792. A parliamentary law provides a list of safe countries of origin. A law adding countries to this list also has to be passed by parliament. In addition to the EU

Member States, safe countries of origin are those listed in Annex II of the AsylG.[100] These are, at present, Albania, Bosnia and Herzegovina, Ghana, Kosovo, North Macedonia, Montenegro, Senegal, and Serbia.

793.   Every two years, and by 23 October 2017 for the first time, the Federal Government submits to the German *Bundestag* a report explaining whether or not the requirements for the classification of the States listed as safe countries of origin continue to be met.[101]

794.   The Federal Government determines by statutory instrument that does not require the consent of the *Bundesrat* that a country listed is no longer to be classed as a safe country of origin if changes in its legal or political situation give reason to believe that the requirements to be regarded as a safe country of origin (Article 16a(3), first sentence of the Basic Law) have ceased to exist. The instrument expires no later than six months after it entered into force, so that the *Bundestag* and *Bundesrat* can exercise their normal right of control again. If a decision would apply to an EU Member State, this will require an amendment of Article 16a of the Basic Law.

B. Safe Third Countries

795.   Protection is limited by the concept of safe third countries (Article 16a(2) of the Basic Law, section 26a AsylG).

796.   According to Article 16a(1) of the Basic Law there is no right to asylum for a person who enters Germany from a safe third country. Safe third countries are, according to Article 16a(2) of the Basic Law, the EU Member States and third States in which the application of the Convention Relating to the Status of Refugees and the Convention for the Protection of Human Rights and Fundamental Freedoms is assured.

797.   Any foreigner who has entered Germany from a safe third country will not be granted asylum (Article 16a(2), first sentence of the Basic Law).

798.   This does not apply if a foreigner was lawfully resident in Germany at the time that he or she entered Germany from a safe third country, there are indications that Germany is responsible for the processing of an asylum application according to EU law, i.e., the Dublin III rules, or an international agreement. This exclusion from the asylum procedure also does not apply if a foreigner has not been refused entry or has been removed on account of an order by the Federal Ministry of the

---

100. BGBl. I 2015 p. 1725.
101. Cf. Deutscher Bundestag Drucksache 19/299 of 15 Dec. 2017: Erster Bericht zu der Überprüfung der Voraussetzungen zur Einstufung der in Anlage II zum Asylgesetz bezeichneten sicheren Herkunftsstaaten.

Interior on humanitarian grounds, in compliance with international law or to protect the political interests of Germany (section 18(4), No. 2 AsylG).

799.   In addition to the EU Member States, safe third countries are those listed in Annex I of the AsylG.[102] These are, at present, Norway and Switzerland.

800.   The Federal Government determines by statutory instrument that does not require the consent of the *Bundesrat* that a country listed as a safe third country is no longer deemed to be safe if changes in its legal or political situation give reason to believe that the requirements mentioned in Article 16a(2), first sentence of the Basic Law have ceased to exist. This instrument expires no later than six months after it entered into force, so that *Bundestag* and *Bundesrat* can exercise their normal right of control again. If the decision concerns an EU Member State, an amendment of Article 16a of the Basic Law is required.

801.   A foreigner who is already safe from political persecution in another third country will not be granted asylum status in Germany (Article 27 AsylG).

802.   If a foreigner holds a travel document issued by a safe third country or by another third country as provided for in the Convention Related to the Status of Refugees, it is presumed that a foreigner was safe from political persecution in the country that issued one of those documents.

803.   If, before entering Germany, a foreigner has lived for more than three months in another third country where he or she is not threatened by political persecution, it is presumed that the foreigner was safe there. This does not apply if a foreigner provides plausible evidence that deportation to another country where the foreigner is threatened by political persecution could not be ruled out with reasonable certainty.

804.   If a foreigner entering Germany from a safe third country applies for asylum, measures to terminate an applicant's stay may be implemented without regard to any legal challenge that may have been instituted against those measures.

---

102. BGBl. I 2008 p. 1822.

§3. LEGAL POSITION

I. Asylum Seekers

A. Residence

1. Permission to Remain Pending the Asylum Decision

805. The right of residence pending an asylum procedure is regulated in sections 55 et seq. AsylG.

806. Foreigners seeking asylum are permitted, pursuant to section 55 AsylG, to remain in Germany while their asylum procedure is pending, once they have been issued an arrival certificate. They are issued a 'permission to remain pending the asylum decision' certificate (*Aufenthaltsgestattung*). In cases where an arrival certificate has not been issued, filing an application equates to permission to remain pending the asylum decision.

807. Filing an asylum application automatically cancels any exemption from the obligation to hold a residence title and cancels any existing residence title with an overall validity of up to six months. Filing an asylum application also cancels the effects of an application for a residence title, Thus, in this case, an application for a residence title does not have the effect that the foreigner's residence is deemed to be permitted up to the moment that the foreigners authority adopts its decision. A deportation is also not considered to have been suspended if the application for a residence permit is filed too late. The equivalent effect takes place for an extension of a residence title, and, thus, if a foreigner applies for an extension of his or her residence title or for a different residence title before the current residence title expires, the current residence title is not deemed to remain in force from the time its expires until the time of the decision by the foreigners authority (section 81(3) and (4) AufenthG). However, if a foreigner has applied for an extension of a residence title with an overall validity of more than six months, that residence title remains in force from the moment it expires until the time of the decision by the foreigners authority, even if the foreigner applies for asylum (section 55(2) AsylG, section 81(4) AufenthG).

808. To the extent that acquiring or exercising a right or a privilege depends on the length of stay in Germany, such as granting a permanent settlement permit, the duration of lawful residence pending the asylum decision is only counted if the asylum applicant is granted asylum or international protection.

2. Registration Certificate

809. Within three working days of filing an asylum application, a foreigner is issued a certificate confirming the right to remain pending the asylum decision unless the foreigner already has a residence title. A photograph of the asylum applicant and his or her personal information are recorded on the certificate. This is provided for in section 63 AsylG. If the asylum applicant is not required to reside in a reception centre (section 63(3), second sentence, AsylG), then the asylum seeker is informed that he or she needs to apply to the responsible foreigners authority within three working days from filing the asylum application to obtain the required certificate (section 63(1) first sentence, AsylG). The responsible foreigners authority is the one in the district where the asylum applicant has to stay pending the asylum decision or in the district where the foreigner has to take up residence.

810. The certificate is valid for a limited period. As long as the asylum applicant is required to reside in a reception centre, it is valid for no more than three months. In all other cases it is valid for no more than six months.

811. The Federal Office for Migration and Refugees is responsible for issuing certificates to asylum applicants who are not accommodated in a reception centre. Otherwise, this responsibility lies with the foreigners authority of the district where an asylum applicant may lawfully reside pending the asylum decision or where the asylum applicant has to take up residence. Conditions and changes to geographic restrictions and the relevant orders (section 59b AsylG) may be endorsed on the certificate by the authorities which have imposed these conditions or changes.

812. A certificate should be withdrawn when the permission to remain pending the asylum decision expires.

813. The certificate contains the date of issuing an arrival certificate; the date on which the asylum application was filed; and the date and place of the foreigner's birth and his or her nationality. A photograph and two fingerprints are stored in the certificate (section 78a(5) AufenthG).

3.   Arrival Certificate

814. A foreigner who has requested asylum and who has been photographed and fingerprinted in line with the provisions of the AsylG or of the AufenthG but who has not filed an application for asylum will be issued with a registration certificate for asylum seekers without delay. This document is called arrival certificate (*Ankunftsnachweis*) pursuant to section 63a AsylG. It contains a number of visibly displayed items of information: surname and first names, maiden name, photograph, date of birth, place of birth, abbreviation of the nationality, sex, height and eye colour, responsible reception centre, serial number of the certificate (arrival certificate number), issuing authority, date of issue, holder's signature, duration of validity, extension note, file number issued by the registration authority (Central Register of Foreigners), note stating the surnames and first names of accompanying minor

children and young persons, note that the items of information are based on information furnished by the foreigner, note stating that the certificate does not suffice to
meet the holder's obligation to have and present identification papers, machine-
readable zone, and barcode.

815. Besides some formal information, the machine-readable zone contains the
following information: surname and first names; date of birth; nationality; sex; the
serial number of the certificate (arrival certificate number); and the duration of its
validity. The barcode is generated automatically and contains the information that is
visible on the certificate, a digital signature and the number issued by the Central
Register of Foreigners. A child aged 10 or over at the time the arrival certificate is
issued has to sign his or her own certificate.

816. The certificate is issued for no longer than six months. In exceptional cases,
it is extended for a maximum of three months at any time, if the certificate holder
does not have an appointment with the branch office of the Federal Office for Migration and Refugees to file an asylum application before the expiry of the period of
six months or the extended period of three months. The same applies if the asylum
seeker has an appointment with the branch office of the Federal Office for Migration and Refugees albeit not within the period of six months or the extended period
of three months. It also applies if the foreigner fails to attend the appointment for
reasons beyond the asylum seeker's control.

817. The reception centre responsible for an asylum seeker is also responsible
for the issuing, changing of address or extension of an arrival certificate, unless the
branch office of the Federal Office for Migration and Refugees assigned to this
reception centre assumes responsibility for the taking of a photograph and the fingerprints of the foreigner or the processing of the foreigner's personal data. If the
asylum seeker is no longer required to live in the reception centre, the responsibility
for the issuing of a certificate rests with the foreigners authority in whose district
the asylum applicant is required to stay or to take up residence. If there is no obligation to remain in a reception centre, responsibility rests with the foreigners
authority in whose district the foreigner is actually staying.

818. The validity of the arrival certificate expires as soon as the six month period
expires, when the certificate confirming permission to remain pending the asylum
decision in accordance with section 63 AsylG is issued, or upon expiry of permission to remain pending the asylum decision in accordance with section 67 AsylG.
This is the case, for instance, when a deportation order becomes enforceable or
when a deportation order is communicated to the asylum seeker. When the certificate confirming permission to remain pending the asylum decision is issued, the
arrival certificate is withdrawn by the authority that has issued the certificate confirming permission to remain pending the asylum decision.

819. The holder is required to present the arrival certificate to the reception centre, the Federal Office for Migration and Refugees or the foreigners authority if it
contains incorrect information. The holder is also required, upon request, to return

the arrival certificate to authorities of the reception centre, the Federal Office for Migration and Refugees or the foreigners authority upon receiving a new arrival certificate or permission to remain pending the asylum decision. The same authorities must be informed in the event that an arrival certificate is lost and, if it is found, the foreigner must return it to them. If the arrival certificate holder's identity cannot be established without doubt or unauthorised changes have been made to an arrival certificate, the holder has to return it without delay to the aforementioned authorities.

4. Identification Documents

820. For the duration of the asylum procedure an asylum applicant has to comply with the requirement to have and present identification papers by having and presenting the certificate confirming permission to remain pending the asylum decision (section 64 AsylG).

821. The certificate confirming permission to remain does not authorise an asylum applicant to cross a border.

822. After an asylum seeker has filed an asylum application, the passport or passport substitute is returned to him or her pursuant to section 65 AsylG. This is the case if it is not needed in the further course of the asylum procedure and if the asylum applicant already has a residence title or if the foreigners authority grants the asylum seeker a residence title for subsequent immigration of dependants pursuant to the AufenthG, because, for instance, the asylum applicant is married.

823. The passport or passport substitute may be returned to the asylum applicant temporarily if this is necessary for him or her to travel. Travel can be necessary if there is an urgent public interest, if a refusal would constitute undue hardship, or if this is necessary because the asylum seeker has been granted permission to work, attend school or an occupational training (section 58(1) AsylG) or if this is necessary in order to renew a passport or to prepare the asylum applicant's departure. This also applies to travel after the expiry of a geographic restriction (section 59a AsylG).

5. Alert

824. In order to establish a foreigner's whereabouts, an alert may be entered pursuant to section 66 AsylG in both the Central Register of Foreigners and the police search systems if the foreigner's whereabouts are unknown and if the asylum seeker fails to arrive within one week at the reception centre to which he or she has been referred or if the foreigner has left the reception centre and has failed to return within one week. The same applies if the asylum applicant has failed to comply within one week with an allocation order or an order to live in, to move to or to take up habitual residence in a specific municipality or accommodation (section 60(2), first sentence AsylG). It also applies if the asylum applicant cannot be reached at the address he or she has given or at the address of the accommodation where he or she is required to reside. These conditions are met if a message that is delivered to that address does not reach the asylum seeker within two weeks of sending it to him or her.

825. The reception centre, the foreigners authority in whose district the asylum applicant is required to stay or take up residence, and the Federal Office for Migration and Refugees are all responsible for the issuing of an alert. The actual alert may only be issued by a person employed by one of these authorities who has special authority to do so.

6. Expiry

826. Permission to remain pending the asylum decision expires pursuant to section 67 AsylG if the foreigner is refused entry because the asylum application is made by a foreigner who has entered Germany after travelling through a safe third country, if there are indications that another country is responsible for the processing of the asylum application according to EU law or a treaty and proceedings to admit or readmit have been initiated, if the asylum applicant poses a threat to the general public, as he or she is the subject of an enforceable custodial sentence of at least three years of imprisonment in Germany on account of a particularly serious criminal offence and if the asylum applicant left Germany less than three years ago. If such conditions apply, permission to remain pending the asylum decision also expires if the asylum seeker is removed after the border authority has found him or her in the border area immediately before or after illegal entry (section 18(2) and (3) AsylG). It also expires in one of the following circumstances: (i) the foreigner fails to file an asylum application within two weeks of being issued an arrival certificate; (ii) upon delivery of the Federal Office for Migration and Refugees' decision to the asylum applicant following the withdrawal of the asylum application; (iii) if a deportation notification that has been issued pursuant to the provisions of the AsylG because the asylum applicant is to be regarded as a threat to the security of Germany or constitutes a threat to the general public in Germany (section 60(9) AufenthG) has become enforceable; (iv) if a deportation order has been issued authorising deportation to a safe third country, another country that is responsible for the processing of the asylum application procedure or following the withdrawal of the asylum application (section 34a AsylG) has become enforceable; (v) if an announcement of a deportation order has been made by the supreme *Land* authority in order to avert a special danger to the security of Germany or a terrorist threat or if the Federal Ministry of the Interior assumes responsibility due to a special interest of the Federation (section 58a AufenthG); and (vi) if a decision of the Federal Office for Migration and Refugees on the asylum application has become incontestable.

827. If the appointment at the branch office of the Federal Office for Migration and Refugees for the purpose of filing the asylum application (section 23(1) AsylG) falls outside the time limit of two weeks of issuing an arrival certificate (section

67(1), first sentence, No. 2, AsylG) permission to remain pending the asylum decision only expires according to section 67 AsylG if the foreigner has not filed an asylum application by the date of the appointment.

828. Permission to remain pending the asylum decision becomes effective again, if the procedure which had been discontinued because the asylum application had been deemed to have been withdrawn (section 33(5), first sentence, AsylG) is resumed. It also becomes effective again if the foreigner files the asylum application after the time limit of two weeks following the issuing of an arrival certificate (section 67(1), first sentence, No. 2 or second sentence AsylG).

7.   Residence Title

829. The chance that an asylum seeker is issued a residence title is small. Neither the arrival certificate nor the permission to remain pending the asylum decision are residence titles. Asylum seekers have, in general, to complete the asylum procedure before a residence title can be issued.

830. Pursuant to section 10 AufenthG, an asylum applicant may only be granted a residence title before the asylum procedure has legally been completed with the approval of the supreme *Land* authority, and if a vital German interest thus requires. There is only one exception to this rule which is when the foreigner has a right to be granted a residence title, which may be the case, e.g., for subsequently immigrating dependants.

831. A residence title issued or extended by the foreigners authority after an asylum seeker has entered Germany may be extended in accordance with the provisions of the AufenthG, irrespective of whether the asylum seeker has applied for asylum.

832. A foreigner whose asylum application has been incontestably rejected or who has withdrawn the asylum application may be granted a residence title prior to leaving Germany only in accordance with the provisions on residence under international law or on humanitarian or political grounds (Part 5 AufenthG). If the asylum application has been rejected as manifestly unfounded for reasons such as that the key aspects of the foreigner's statements are unsubstantiated or contradictory, obviously do not correspond to the facts or are based on forged or falsified evidence or because the foreigner has filed another asylum application or asylum request using different personal data (section 30(3), Nos 1–6 AsylG), no residence title may be issued before the foreigner leaves Germany. These rules do not apply, however, in cases of entitlement to issuance of a residence title. Also, if the foreigner meets the requirements for issuance of a temporary residence permit because a deportation ban applies under the terms of the European Convention on Human Rights or because the foreigner would face a substantial danger to his or her life and limb or liberty in the state where the foreigner would be deported (section 60(5) and (7), section 25(3) AufenthG) a residence title may be issued before the foreigner leaves

Germany even if the asylum application has been rejected as being manifestly unfounded in accordance with section 30(3), Nos 1–6 AsylG.

B. Allocation

1. Reception Centre

833. Asylum seekers are not entitled to reside in a specific *Land* or a specific place of their free choice (section 55(1), sentence 2 AsylG).

834. Any person who lodges his or her asylum application with a foreigners authority or the police of a *Land* has to be referred to the competent reception centre immediately, or, if that is not known, to the nearest one, for the purpose of registration (section 19 AsylG).

835. The foreigners authority and the police take the asylum applicant's photograph and fingerprints (section 16(1) AsylG).

836. An asylum applicant who has entered Germany without authorisation, arriving from a safe third country may be removed to that country without being referred to a reception centre (section 57(1) and (2) AufenthG). In this case the competent foreigners authority orders the removal of the asylum applicant as soon as it has been ascertained that removal can be carried out.

837. The rules on arrest and detention remain unaffected.

2. Residence Obligation

838. Asylum applicants are required, pursuant to section 20 AsylG, to comply with a referral to a reception centre immediately or as specified by the competent authority (section 18(1) or section 19(1) AsylG). A failure to comply with this requirement means that the asylum application is deemed to have been withdrawn and the asylum procedure is discontinued; appeals against this decision have to be filed within one week of notification (section 33(1), (5), and (6) AsylG). This does not apply if the foreigner proves, without delay, that the failure to report was due to circumstances beyond his or her control. The authority with which the asylum seeker has requested asylum informs him or her in writing of the obligation to comply with the referral and the legal consequences of a failure to do so. The asylum applicant has to acknowledge the receipt of this information. If it is impossible to inform the asylum applicant, he or she is escorted to the reception centre.

839. The authority referring an asylum applicant to a reception centre immediately informs the reception centre in writing of the referral, the asylum request and the information provided to the foreigner. The reception centre informs the assigned branch office of the Federal Office for Migration and Refugees immediately, or no later than one week after receiving the information whether the foreigner has been admitted to the reception centre.

3. Documents

840. Any authority referring an asylum applicant to a reception centre takes that persons' passport or passport substitute and all necessary certificates and other documents which are in the foreigner's possession for safekeeping and forwards them to the reception centre without delay (section 15(2), Nos 4 and 5, and section 21 AsylG).

841. If an asylum applicant reports directly to the reception centre responsible for accommodating him or her, these documents are taken into safekeeping by the reception centre. The reception centre responsible for accommodating an asylum applicant forwards the documents without delay to the assigned branch office of the Federal Office for Migration and Refugees. Copies of the documents taken for safekeeping are provided to the asylum applicant at his or her request.

842. These documents are returned to the asylum applicant when they are no longer needed for the asylum procedure or for measures terminating the right of residence.

4. Registration

843. Registration requirements are found in section 22 AsylG.

844. Every asylum applicant is required to file an asylum application with a branch office of the Federal Office for Migration and Refugees and has to register in person at a reception centre. This reception centre accommodates the asylum applicant or refers him or her to the reception centre responsible for his or her accommodation. In the case of a referral, the asylum applicant's fingerprints and photograph are taken, if possible.

845. The *Land* government or its designated agency may determine that registration is to be effected at a specific reception centre and that any asylum applicant referred from another *Land* has to initially report to a specific reception centre.

846. The asylum applicant's fingerprints and photograph are taken during his or her stay in the specific reception centre. If an asylum application is lodged with the border authority, a foreigners authority or the police of a *Land* (sections 18(1) and 19(1) AsylG), the asylum applicant is referred to this specific reception centre.

847. Asylum applicants are required to comply with a decision referring them to the reception centre mentioned in that decision immediately or before the expiry of the deadline specified by the reception centre. If the asylum applicant fails to comply with this requirement, section 33(1), (5), and (6) AsylG applies accordingly. According to this provision failure to report at a reception centre as requested means that the asylum application is deemed to have been withdrawn and the asylum procedure is discontinued. Appeals against this ex legem withdrawal have to be filed within one week of notification of the decision informing the asylum applicant hereof. This does not apply if the asylum applicant proves without delay that the failure to report can be ascribed to circumstances beyond his or her control. The authority where the asylum application has been lodged has to inform the foreigner in writing of these obligations and the legal consequences of non-compliance. The asylum applicant has to acknowledge the receipt of this information. The authority referring the asylum applicant to a reception centre also has to inform the reception centre immediately and in writing of the referral, the asylum request and the information provided to the foreigner. The reception centre immediately, in any case within a week after receiving this information, informs the assigned branch office of the Federal Office whether the asylum applicant has been admitted to the reception centre (section 20(1), fourth sentence, and (2) AsylG).

5. Admitted Persons

848. Any asylum applicant who has been admitted under EU law or an international agreement on the processing of an asylum application has the same status as a foreigner who has applied for asylum. The former is required to proceed, upon or immediately after entry, to the agency named by the Federal Ministry of the Interior or by its designated agency (section 22a AsylG).

6. Filing an Application at the Reception Centre

849. Any foreigner who has been received by the reception centre is, pursuant to section 23 AsylG, required to report in person and without delay or on the date determined by the reception centre to the branch office of the Federal Office for Migration and Refugees for the purpose of filing an asylum application.

850. If a foreigner fails to report as specified, an asylum application is deemed to have been withdrawn and the asylum procedure is discontinued. The reception centre informs the foreigner in writing of this legal consequence of a failure to report. Appeals against this notification have to be filed within one week of notification (section 33(1), (5), and (6) AsylG). This does not apply if the foreigner proves, without delay, that the failure to report was due to circumstances beyond his or her control. The reception centre informs its assigned branch office of the Federal Office for Migration and Refugees without delay that the foreigner has been admitted to the reception centre.

7.   Setting Up and Maintaining a Reception Centre

851. Accommodation and distribution rules are found in sections 44 et seq. AsylG.

852. The *Länder* are required to set up and maintain reception centres necessary to accommodate persons requesting asylum and to provide the necessary number of places in the reception centres for new asylum applicants who are allocated to them on the basis of their respective admission quotas on a monthly basis.

853. The Federal Ministry of the Interior or the authority designated by it, which is the Federal Office or Migration and Refugees, informs the *Länder* each month of the number of new asylum applicants, the prospective trend and the prospective need for accommodation.

854. Section 45 of Book Eight of the Social Code[103] that specifies that special permission is required to operate an institution where children and adolescents are cared for all or part of the day or are accommodated does not apply to reception centres. Operators of reception centres should require persons working in these centres to supervise, look after, educate or train minors or carry out other activities where they are likely to come in contact with minors, to submit, prior to their hiring or before taking up long-term voluntary work, and at regular intervals, police certificates of good conduct (section 30(5) and 30a(1) of the Central Criminal Register Act). Operators of reception centres must not employ persons or volunteers who have incontestably been convicted of a criminal offence such as child abuse, sexual crimes or human trafficking (sections 171, 174–174c, 176–180a, 181a, 182–184g, 225, 232–233a, 234, 235 or 236 of the Criminal Code) to supervise, look after, educate or train minors or carry out other activities where they are likely to come in contact with minors. The operator of a reception centre viewing the police certificate of good conduct (section 30(5) and 30a(1) of the Central Criminal Register Act) may only record the fact that the certificate has been viewed, its date and whether or not the person concerned was incontestably convicted of one of the aforementioned criminal offences. If a person whose police certificate has been viewed does not carry out activities with minors, the data are to be deleted without delay. In all cases the data is deleted no later than six months after the person concerned has worked with minors for the last time.

8.   Admission Quota

855. The *Länder* may agree to define a key to distribute persons requesting asylum among the individual *Länder*. This is the admission quota (section 45 AsylG). Until such an agreement has been reached or if such an agreement should cease to

---

103. Article 1 of the Act dated 26 Jun. 1990, BGBl. I p. 1163.

exist, the admission quota for the current calendar year is based on the key calculated for the previous calendar year in line with tax revenues and population and published in the Federal Gazette by the office of the Joint Education and Research Conference. This is the so-called Koenigstein key (*Königsteiner Schlüssel*) which refers to the fiscal capacity and the number of inhabitants of the respective *Land*.

856. Two or more *Länder* may agree that persons requesting asylum who are to be admitted by a specific *Land* in line with its admission quota, are admitted by another *Land*. Such an agreement has at least to contain information regarding the size of the group of persons covered by the agreement between the *Länder* and an appropriate compensation for costs. Such an agreement does not affect the admission quota.

857. Persons requesting asylum who are under arrest or have been placed in official custody, admitted into hospital, a sanatorium or an asylum, or in a youth welfare institution are not required to live in a reception centre. This is also the case for minors and their legal representative. All these people are not counted in the admission quotas for the individual *Länder* (section 14(2), first sentence, Nos 2 and 3, section 45, section 52 AsylG). The same applies to unmarried minor children and family members and persons admitted for humanitarian reasons (section 14a and 51 AsylG).

9.   Responsible Reception Centre

858. The special reception centre which has space available under the terms of the admission quota and where the branch office of the Federal Office for Migration and Refugees assigned to it processes asylum applications from the foreigner's country of origin is, pursuant to section 46 AsylG, responsible for the reception of foreigners who have filed a manifestly unfounded asylum application (section 30a(1) AsylG). As for the rest, the reception centre where the foreigner has registered is responsible for receiving the foreigner, if it has space available under the terms of the admission quota and if the branch office of the Federal Office for Migration and Refugees assigned to it processes asylum applications from the foreigner's country of origin. Where these prerequisites are not met, the reception centre designated by the Federal Ministry of the Interior is responsible for receiving the foreigner. If several special reception centres could be responsible for receiving such a foreigner, the Federal Ministry of the Interior will determine the responsible special reception centre.

859. Upon request by a reception centre, the Federal Office for Migration and Refugees as the central distributing agency designated by the Federal Ministry of the Interior indicates which reception centre is responsible for receiving the foreigner. This is based on the admission quotas, the available vacancies according to these quotas and finally the processing capacities of the competent branch office of

the Federal Office for Migration and Refugees with regard to the foreigners' countries of origin. If more than one reception centre meets the aforementioned criteria, the nearest one is designated to be responsible for receiving the foreigner.

860. Where responsibility derogates from such measures, following an agreement between *Länder*, the reception centre required to receive the foreigner in question pursuant to the agreement becomes responsible upon actually receiving the foreigner. As far as circumstances permit, the agreement is taken into account when distributing foreigners.

861. The reception centre that has requested the redistribution of asylum applicants only has to inform the central distributing agency of the number of asylum applicants and their respective countries of origin. Asylum applicants and their family members are reported as a group.

862. The *Länder* ensure that the central distributing agency, at all times, has the information needed to determine which reception centre is responsible, in particular information on how many foreigners have arrived and departed, how full each reception centre is and how many vacant places each reception centre has.

863. If there are no vacant places in the reception centres of a *Land* which is nevertheless required under the quota system to accept foreigners, the government of the *Land* concerned or an authority designated by it informs the central distributing agency which reception centre is responsible for admitting foreigners.

10.   Residence

864. Foreigners who have to file their asylum application with a branch office of the Federal Office for Migration and Refugees (section 14(1) AsylG), are required to live for a period of up to eighteen months, in the reception centre responsible for accommodating them. This is stipulated in section 47 AsylG. The period is only up to six months for minors and their parents or other persons with the right of custody as well as the minor's major, unmarried siblings. The same applies if the asylum applicant is under arrest or subjected to another form of official custody, has been admitted into a hospital, a sanatorium or an asylum or in a youth welfare institution (section 14(2), first sentence, No. 2 AsylG) if they are released or dismissed from the latter accommodation before the Federal Office for Migration and Refugees has taken a decision on their asylum application. In certain cases, such as in the event of deceiving about their identity or violating their cooperation obligations, foreigners are required to live in a reception centre for more than eighteen months.

865. Foreigners from a safe country of origin are required to live in the reception centre responsible for accommodating them until the Federal Office for Migration and Refugees has decided on their asylum application. If their asylum application has been rejected as manifestly unfounded or as inadmissible, they remain in the reception centre until they leave Germany or until the deportation warning or deportation order is enforced. The provisions on the termination of the obligation to reside in a reception centre, on the release from a reception centre and on the distribution within a *Land* (sections 48–50 AsylG) apply as normal.

11.   Prolonged Residence

866.   The *Länder* may regulate that asylum applicants are required to live in the reception centre responsible for receiving them until the Federal Office for Migration and Refugees has decided on their asylum application or, should the application be rejected as manifestly unfounded or as inadmissible, until they leave Germany or until the deportation warning or deportation order is enforced (section 47(1b) AsylG). This requirement may last for no longer than twenty-four months. The provisions on the termination of the obligation to reside in a reception centre, on the release from a reception centre and on the distribution of asylum applicants within a *Land* (sections 48–50 AsylG) apply as normal. In particular, section 50(1), sentence 1, No. 1, AsylG applies, pursuant to which the asylum applicant can leave the reception centre if it is impossible for the Federal Office for Migration and Refugees to decide or to decide at short notice that the application is inadmissible or manifestly unfounded.

12.   Children's Residence

867.   If the parents of a minor unmarried child are required to live in a reception centre, the child may also live in that reception centre, even if the child has not filed an asylum application.

13.   Contacts

868.   During the period of obligatory residence in a reception centre, the asylum applicant is required to ensure that the competent authorities and courts can contact him or her.

14.   Information

869.   Within fifteen days of the filing of an asylum application, the reception centre informs the asylum applicant, if possible in writing and in a language, which the asylum applicant can reasonably be assumed to understand, of his or her rights and obligations under the Act on Benefits for Asylum Applicants. Together with this information, the reception centre also informs the asylum applicant who is able to provide legal aid and which organisations can advise on accommodation and medical care.

15. Termination of Residence Obligation

870. The obligation to live in a reception centre ends, pursuant to section 48 AsylG, if the asylum applicant is required to take up residence in another place or in other accommodation, has been granted asylum status or international protection (section 1(1), No. 2 AsylG), or if he or she qualifies for a residence title under the AufenthG. The latter is the case if the asylum applicant has married or entered into a civil partnership in Germany.

871. The obligation to reside at a reception centre is terminated pursuant to section 49 AsylG if a deportation warning is enforceable and it is impossible to enforce deportation at short notice. This is also the case if the foreigner is issued a temporary residence permit for temporary protection (section 24 AufenthG).

872. The obligation may also be terminated for reasons of public health, for other reasons of public security and order, or other compelling reasons.

873. Asylum applicants are released from the reception centre immediately and relocated within the *Land* concerned if the Federal Office for Migration and Refugees informs the responsible *Land* authority that it is impossible to decide or to decide at short notice whether the asylum application is inadmissible or manifestly unfounded or whether deportation of the asylum applicant or one of his or her family members is prohibited under the terms of the European Convention on Human Rights or if deportation to another State would mean that the asylum applicant faces a substantial and real danger to life, limb or liberty (section 60(5) or (7) AufenthG, section 26(1)–(3), and section 50 AsylG). The same applies if an administrative court rules that the action brought against the decision of the Federal Office for Migration and Refugees has suspensive effect.

874. Relocation may also be required if the obligation to live in the reception centre ends for other reasons, such as illness or for family reasons.

875. The *Land* government or the authority designated by it is authorised to regulate distribution by means of a statutory instrument if this is not regulated by *Land* law.

16. Allocation Decision

876. The responsible *Land* authority informs the Federal Office for Migration and Refugees within three working days in which district of the foreigners authority the asylum applicant is to take up residence after the distribution procedure.

877. The responsible *Land* authority takes the allocation decision. The allocation decision is a written decision that includes information on the legal remedy available. A justification of the allocation decision is not required. This is also the case for a hearing of the foreigner. When adopting the allocation decision the situation of family members (section 26(1)–(3) AsylG) and other equally important humanitarian reasons are taken into consideration.

878. The allocation decision is delivered to the asylum applicant in person. As appropriate, the authorised representative receives a copy of the allocation decision.

879. The asylum applicant has to proceed, without delay, to the designated reception centre in the allocation decision.

880. If an asylum applicant is not or no longer required to live in a reception centre, the situation of family members or other equally important humanitarian reasons is taken into account when allocating asylum applicants to the *Länder* (section 51 AsylG). Allocation of such persons is realised at the asylum applicant's request. The responsible authority of the *Land* where the asylum applicant has requested residence decides on the request.

17. Collective Accommodation

881. Foreigners who have filed an asylum application and are not or no longer required to live in a reception centre, should, as a rule, be housed in collective accommodation. This is stipulated in section 53 AsylG. In this context, both the public interest and the asylum applicant's interests are taken into account.

882. The obligation to live in collective accommodation ends when the Federal Office for Migration and Refugees has recognised the asylum applicant as a person who has been granted asylum status or when a court has required the Federal Office for Migration and Refugees to recognise the foreigner, even if an appeal has been made, as long as the foreigner is able to prove that he or she has found accommodation elsewhere and that this will not result in additional costs for a public authority. The same applies in cases where the Federal Office for Migration and Refugees or a court has granted an asylum applicant international protection. In these cases, this obligation also ends for family members.

883. The special provisions relating to care and protection in reception centres apply as normal (section 44(3) AsylG).

18. Notification

884. The foreigners authority in whose district the asylum applicant is required to stay or to take up residence immediately informs, pursuant to section 54 AsylG, the Federal Office for Migration and Refugees of the address where a summon may be served on the foreigner and of any alert to determine the foreigner's place of residence.

19.   Geographic Restrictions

885.   Geographic restrictions apply pursuant to section 56 AsylG.

886.   Permission to remain pending the asylum decision is limited to the district of the foreigners authority where the reception centre responsible for receiving the asylum applicant is located.

887.   If the asylum applicant is required to take up residence in the district of another foreigners authority, permission to remain pending the asylum decision is limited to that district.

888.   An asylum applicant who is required to live in a reception centre may be permitted pursuant to section 57 AsylG by the Federal Office for Migration and Refugees to leave the area specified in the permit issued pending the asylum decision temporarily if compelling reasons so require. Permission should be granted without delay in order to enable the asylum applicant to keep appointments with authorised representatives, the UNHCR and organisations providing welfare services to refugees.

889.   The asylum applicant does not need permission to attend appointments with the authorities or court hearings where his or her personal appearance is required. The asylum applicant does have to inform the reception centre and the Federal Office for Migration and Refugees of such appointments.

890.   An asylum applicant who is not or no longer required to live in a reception centre may be allowed, pursuant to section 58 AsylG, by the foreigners authority to temporarily leave the area where he or she is required to remain pending the asylum decision or to remain in the district of another foreigners authority. Permission is granted if an urgent public interest applies, if it is necessary for compelling reasons or if refusing permission would constitute undue hardship for the asylum applicant. As a general rule, permission is granted if the foreigner intends to take up employment as permitted (section 61(2) AsylG) or if this is necessary for the purposes of school attendance, basic and advanced occupational training or to study at a State or State-recognised university or comparable educational establishment. This permission requires the consent of the foreigners authority where the asylum applicant habitually resides.

891.   An asylum applicant may leave the area for which permission to remain pending the asylum decision has been granted without permission temporarily, if a court has ordered the Federal Office for Migration and Refugees to grant the asylum applicant the status of asylum or international protection, or if this is necessary to determine whether deportation is prohibited under the terms of the European Convention on Human Rights or whether deportation to another State would mean that the asylum applicant would face a substantial and real danger to life, limb or liberty (section 60(5) or (7) AufenthG), even if this decision is still contestable. This also applies to family members.

892. The foreigners authority of a district or a municipality belonging to a district may grant an asylum applicant permission to stay temporarily anywhere within the district.

893. In order to take local circumstances into account, *Land* governments may provide by statutory instrument that asylum applicants do not need permission to stay temporarily in an area encompassing the jurisdiction of multiple foreigners authorities or the area encompassing a whole *Land*, or to stay in another *Land*, provided there is agreement between the governments of the *Länder* concerned.

20.   Enforcement of Geographic Restrictions

894. If necessary, the obligation to leave the area of Germany where the asylum applicant is staying without permission of the foreigners authority and in breach of a geographic restriction may, even without prior notification, be enforced by means of direct force (section 59 AsylG, section 12(3) AufenthG). The travel route and means of transport are determined by the authorities.

895. An asylum applicant is arrested and taken into custody following a court order confirming the obligation to leave if it cannot be guaranteed that an asylum applicant would voluntarily comply with the obligation to leave. This also applies if geographic restrictions are in force after the permission to remain pending the asylum decision has expired (section 59a(2) AsylG) and if it would otherwise be considerably more difficult or even impossible to enforce this obligation.

896. These measures fall under the responsibility of the police forces of the *Länder*, the border authority where the asylum applicant requests asylum, the foreigners authority in whose district the foreigner is staying, the reception centre where the asylum applicant is registered, and the reception centre which has received the asylum applicant.

21.   Expiry of Geographic Restrictions

897. An asylum applicant who has been given permission to remain pending the asylum decision in the district where the reception centre responsible for the asylum applicant is located no longer applies when that asylum applicant has resided in Germany for three months without interruption by virtue of his deportation having been suspended. The same applies if the foreigner has been issued a temporary residence or permanent settlement permit or has been permitted to remain in Germany pending the asylum decision (sections 56, 59a AsylG).

898. The geographic restriction remains in place as long as an asylum applicant has to live in the reception centre which is responsible for receiving him or her. Geographic restrictions remain in place when the permission to remain pending the asylum decision expires, but no longer than the point in time just mentioned. However,

geographic restrictions no longer apply when residence is regarded as legal because asylum, refugee, or subsidiary protection status has been granted, but the temporary residence title has not yet been issued section 25(1) third sentence or section 25(2), second sentence AufenthG or when a residence title is issued.

22. Special Reasons for Geographic Restrictions

899. In any case, the responsible foreigners authority may order that permission to remain pending the asylum decision is subject to geographic restrictions, if the asylum applicant has been sentenced incontestably for a criminal offence which can only be committed by foreigners, such as unlawful entry or residence in Germany, there are facts indicating that the foreigner has violated the Narcotics Act, or withdrawal of a foreigner's right of residence is imminent. The same applies if a foreigner constitutes a significant risk to Germany's internal security or to the life and limb of others. In these cases, the rules on imposing and enforcing the geographic restrictions apply accordingly (sections 59b, 56, 58, 59 and 59a(2) AsylG).

23. Residence Restrictions

900. Further residence restrictions apply pursuant to section 60 AsylG.

901. Asylum applicants who are not or no longer required to live in a reception centre and whose subsistence is not secured are required to take up residence as specified in the allocation decision (section 50(4) AsylG). This is a so-called residence restriction. Responsibility for the execution of these measures rests with the *Land* authority, which is responsible according to the distribution. The decision on the residence restriction is adopted at the same time as the allocation decision.

902. Where asylum applicants are distributed among the *Länder* for family or equivalent humanitarian reasons (section 51 AsylG), the residence restriction is the place of residence according to the distribution decision. Responsibility for the correct enforcement of these decisions rests with the *Land* authority which is responsible for deciding on the family or humanitarian issue (section 51(2), sentence 2 AsylG). The decision establishing the residence restriction should be taken at the same time as the allocation decision. Asylum applicants may temporarily leave the place mentioned in the residence restriction without permission.

903. Asylum applicants who are not or no longer required to live in a reception centre and whose subsistence is not secured, may be required to live in or to move to a specific municipality or private or public accommodation, or to take up habitual residence in private or public accommodation in the district of another foreigners authority of the same *Land*.

904. An interview with the asylum applicant is required if the asylum applicant has to live in a specific municipality or private or public accommodation and has stayed there for more than six months. The hearing is deemed to have taken place if the asylum applicant or his or her legal representative has been given the opportunity to comment on the accommodation arrangements within a period of two weeks. A hearing is not necessary if it conflicts with compelling reasons of public interest. Responsibility for these residence restrictions and interviews rests with the foreigners authority which is responsible for the district in which the municipality or private or public accommodation is located.

C. Economic Activity

905. Asylum applicants are not allowed to take up paid employment pursuant to section 61 AsylG as long as they are required to stay in a reception centre. Taking up paid employment has to be permitted if the asylum procedure has not been terminated within nine months and further conditions are met such as the approval of the Federal Employment Agency. Foreigners whose deportation has been suspended since at least six months may be granted permission to take up paid employment.

906. An asylum applicant who has stayed in Germany for three months on the basis of permission to remain pending the asylum decision may be permitted to take up employment if the Federal Employment Agency has granted its approval or a statutory instrument stipulates that taking up employment is permissible without the approval of the Federal Employment Agency. Previous periods of tolerated or lawful residence are counted as part of the waiting period. The rules in the AufenthG on approval of employment for a foreigner (sections 39, 40(1), No. 1 and (2) and sections 41 and 42 AufenthG) apply accordingly.

907. However, an asylum applicant from a safe country of origin who has applied for asylum after 31 August 2015 is not permitted to work pending the asylum decision.

D. Social and Health Benefits

1. Medical Examination

908. Asylum applicants who are required to stay in a reception centre or in shared accommodation are required to undergo a medical examination for communicable diseases including an x-ray of the respiratory organs pursuant to section 62 AsylG. The supreme health authority of the *Land* or an authority designated by it determines the extent of and the physician who will conduct the medical examination.

909. The authority responsible for the asylum applicant's accommodation is informed of the medical examination results. If the medical examination shows that

the asylum applicant has or may have a notifiable disease such as cholera, diphtheria or tuberculosis (section 6 of the Infection Protection Act (*Infektionsschutzgesetz,* IfSG)) or is infected with a notifiable pathogen such as the various hepatitis viruses or the measles virus (section 7 of the Infection Protection Act), the Federal Office for Migration and Refugees is also informed of the examination result.

2.   Benefits

910.   The AsylbLG[104] establishes the rules determining which benefits asylum seekers receive during the asylum procedure.

911.   Most asylum seekers and their direct dependants are entitled to social benefits while they live in Germany if they have been granted permission to remain there pending their asylum decision (section 1 AsylbLG). Asylum applicants who intend to enter Germany via an airport and who have not or not yet been granted entry, but are already actually in the country, are also entitled to social benefits. The same applies to such foreigners who hold a temporary residence permit for the following specific reasons. This reason can be an order of the supreme *Land* authority or temporary protection status because of a war in their country of origin (sections 23(1), 24 AufenthG). The reason can also be a temporary stay (section 25(4), sentence 1 AufenthG), or the fact that their deportation has been suspended (section 25(5) AufenthG) if the decision on the temporary suspension of deportation was adopted no longer ago than eighteen months. Entitled to receive benefits are also foreigners who are in fact staying in Germany and who hold a temporary suspension of deportation (section 60a AufenthG). The same applies to those who are enforceably required to leave Germany, even when the deportation warning is not or not yet enforceable. The same entitlement applies to foreign and in fact in Germany staying spouses, registered partners or minor children of any of these persons (section 1(1), Nos 1–5 AsylbLG) without themselves meeting the conditions for entitlement which these persons fulfil. Entitled are also foreigners who are in fact staying in Germany and who file a follow-up application or a secondary application.

912.   Asylum applicants are not entitled to receive benefits pursuant to the AsylbLG for the period when they have been granted a different residence title which is valid for more than six months. This exception does not apply to holders of a residence permit that has been issued following an order of the supreme *Land* authority due to a war in their country of origin (section 23(1) AufenthG) or who have been granted a temporary protection status (section 24 AufenthG) for pressing humanitarian or personal reasons or substantial public interests (section 25(4), sentence 1

---

104. Asylbewerberleistungsgesetz in der Fassung der Bekanntmachung vom 5 Aug. 1997 (BGBl. I p. 2022), das zuletzt durch Artikel 4 des Gesetzes vom 17 Jul. 2017 (BGBl. I p. 2541) geändert worden ist (AsylbLG) – Asylum Seekers Benefits Act in the version of the publication of 5 Aug. 1997 (BGBl. I p. 2022), last amended by Art. 4 of the Law of 17 Jul. 2017 (BGBl. I p. 2541) (AsylbLG).

AufenthG), or whose deportation has been suspended (section 25(5) AufenthG) if the decision on suspending deportation temporarily was adopted within the past eighteen months. These asylum applicants remain entitled to receive benefits pursuant to the AsylbLG.

913. Foreigners who are enforceably required to leave Germany, even when the deportation warning is not or not yet enforceable, and who have been granted international protection by another EU Member State or a third country taking part in the distribution mechanism under the Dublin III Regulation are not entitled to benefits pursuant to the AsylbLG when the international protection continues to exist (section 1(4) AsylbLG). They only receive limited aid to bridge the time until exit. This aid is furthermore limited to two weeks and must be granted only once within two years. Further aid is possible in special circumstances of special hardship. Aid should be granted in kind. The costs for the return journey may be covered. All this aid is to be granted as a loan.

914. The entitlement to benefits ends with the departure of the asylum applicant or at the end of the month in which the entitlement for the benefit ends. It also ends when the Federal Office for Migration and Refugees for Migration and Refugees has recognised the asylum applicant as being entitled to asylum or a court has ruled that the Federal Office for Migration and Refugees must recognise the asylum applicant as such, even if that decision is not yet incontestable.

915. The entitlement to benefits of minor children who have been issued a temporary residence permit because deportation has been suspended because departure is impossible in fact or in law and who live with their parents in a household community also ends if the entitlement to benefits ends for a parent who holds a temporary residence permit because deportation has been suspended, because departure is impossible in fact or in law (section 25(5) AufenthG).

3.   Limitations to Benefits

916. Limitations to social benefits entitlements are found in section 1a AsylbLG. Certain beneficiaries receive benefits pursuant to the AsylbLG only in as far as that is irrefutably necessary according to the circumstances in the individual case. This applies to beneficiaries who hold a temporary suspension of deportation (section 60a AufenthG) or who are enforceably required to leave Germany, even when the deportation warning is not or not yet enforceable (section 1(1), Nos 4 and 5 AsylbLG). These limitations also apply to such person's dependants entitled to benefits because they are their spouse, registered partner or minor children and do not personally fulfil the specific conditions for entitlement to these benefits (section 1(1), No. 6 AsylbLG). The limitations also apply to foreigners who have entered Germany in order to receive benefits pursuant to the AsylbLG.

917. Even more strict limitations apply to beneficiaries who are enforceably required to leave Germany, even when the deportation warning is not or not yet enforceable (section 1(1), No. 5 AsylbLG), for whom a date of exit and a possibility of exit are determined. These persons are not even entitled to the benefits in special cases, to cover basic needs, basic personal needs, nor to other benefits (sections 2, 3, and 6 AsylbLG) from the day following that determined date onwards unless exit could not take place on grounds which they are not responsible for. They are granted only benefits covering their needs for food and accommodation, including heating, and bodily and health care until the date of their exit or the performance of their deportation. They can also be granted benefits of garment and household products (section 3(1), sentence 1 AsylbLG) only in as far as there are special circumstances in the individual case. Such benefits should be furnished in kind.

918. The same applies to beneficiaries who hold a temporary suspension of deportation (section 60a AufenthG) or who are enforceably required to leave Germany, even when the deportation warning is not or not yet enforceable, for whom measures to terminate residence cannot be performed for reasons which they themselves are responsible for. Their entitlement to benefits in special cases, for basic needs, basic personal needs, and any other benefit ceases to exist the day after the deportation warning or a deportation order becomes enforceable. Such person's spouse, registered partner or minor children who do not meet these conditions themselves receive benefits pursuant to the AsylbLG only in as far as that is irrefutably necessary according to the circumstances in the individual case.

919. Beneficiaries holding a permission to remain pending the asylum decision or who are enforceably required to leave Germany, even when the deportation warning is not or not yet enforceable, for whom by way of derogation from the regular responsibility pursuant to the Dublin III Regulation[105] another EU Member State or a third country taking part in the distribution mechanism is responsible also receive benefits only in as far as that is irrefutably necessary according to the circumstances in the individual case. This also applies to persons holding a permission to remain pending the asylum decision or who are enforceably required to leave Germany, even when the deportation warning is not or not yet enforceable, who have been granted international protection or a residence title on other grounds by another Member State or a third country taking part in the distribution mechanism under the Dublin III Regulation when the international protection or the residence title granted on other grounds continues to exist.

920. Beneficiaries who have been issued a permission to remain pending the asylum decision or who file a follow-up application or a secondary application receive only benefits covering their needs for food and accommodation, including heating, and bodily and health care until the date of their exit or the performance of their deportation if they do not comply with certain obligations. This is the case if they do not comply with their obligations to cooperate by not submitting, delivering

---

105. Dublin III, Regulation (EU) No 604/2013 of the European Parliament and of the Council of 26 Jun. 2013 establishing the criteria and mechanisms for determining the Member State responsible for examining an application for international protection lodged in one of the Member States by a third-country national or a stateless person, OJ L 180 of 29 Jun. 2013, p. 31.

or ceding documents for establishing their identity which are in their possession (section 15(2), Nos 4 and 5 AsylG), have not attended an appointment granted for the formal application at the competent branch of the Federal Office for Migration and Refugees or at the Federal Office for Migration and Refugees, or have refused to state their identity or nationality in the asylum procedure (section 30(3), No. 2, second alternative AsylG). These limitations do not apply, however, if they are not responsible for the violation of their obligations to cooperate or for not attending the appointment or they were not able to comply with the obligations to cooperate or to attend the appointment for important reasons. The limitation of benefits ends as soon as they have performed the missing act of cooperation or attended the appointment for the formal application.

921. Asylum seekers may receive a number of benefits in special cases (section 2 AsylbLG). Beneficiaries who have resided in Germany with no substantial interruption for more than fifteen months and have not, themselves, influenced the period of stay by abusing legal rights receive benefits under Book Twelve of the Social Code. This book covers general social welfare benefits. The competent authority decides on the form of benefits when beneficiaries are provided collective accommodation on the basis of the local circumstances. Minors who live with their parents in the same household also receive benefits under Book Twelve of the Social Code if at least one parent in that household is entitled to benefits.

4. Kinds of Benefits

922. Benefits are defined in section 3 AsylbLG. Beneficiaries receive benefits to cover the needs for food, accommodation, heating, garment, health care and household products. This category is called basic needs. In addition, the beneficiaries are granted benefits to cover personal needs of daily life. This category is called basic personal needs.

923. When accommodation is provided in reception centres, the basic needs are covered in kind. If garments cannot be provided, vouchers or another comparable cashless account system is used. Household products can be provided by way of lending.

924. As far as this is reasonably possible basic personal needs should be provided in kind. As far as basic personal needs cannot be satisfied with reasonable administrative effort, they may also be granted in the form of vouchers, any other comparable cashless account systems or as cash payments.

925. When accommodation is provided outside of reception centres, the basic needs and the basic personal needs are in general covered by cash payments. The cash amount per month to cover all basic personal needs is (as of 1 January 2020) for single beneficiaries usually EUR 153. For two adult beneficiaries who live together as partners in a shared household this amount is EUR 139 each. For each additional adult beneficiary without his or her own household the amount is EUR

122. For juvenile beneficiaries older than 14 the amount is EUR 80 until they are 18. Children are entitled to benefits from the age of 6 until they are 14. They are entitled to EUR 99. Children who are younger than 6 are entitled to EUR 86.

926. The competent authority decides on the individual amount of money that is necessary to cover the basic personal needs beneficiaries who are held in custody to secure departure or who are in pre-trial detention if these needs are covered otherwise in total or in part.

927. As a rule, cash payments are primarily made to cover also the basic needs if, as a rule, cash payments are primarily granted for also covering the basic needs if accommodation is provided outside of reception centres. The basic need amounts (as of 1 January 2020) per month for single beneficiaries to EUR 198, for two adult beneficiaries who live together as partners in a collective household to EUR 177 each, for additional adult beneficiaries without own household to EUR 158, for other juvenile beneficiaries who have reached the age of 14 until they have reached the age of 18 it amounts to EUR 200, for children entitled to benefits from the beginning of the age of 6 until they have reached the age of 14 to EUR 174, for children entitled to benefits until they have reached the age of 6 the amount is EUR 132.

928. Basic needs benefits may be provided in the form of a cashless account system, vouchers or paid in kind in as far as this is necessary according to the circumstances. The costs for accommodation, heating and household products are provided separately, either in the form of a cash payment or a payment in kind. The basic personal needs are covered by cash payments. Household products can be provided by way of lending. If all basic personal needs are covered by cash payments, the amount of cash paid per month is the same as for those who have been accommodated in a reception centre. The competent authority decides on the individual amount of cash to cover the basic personal needs of those who are held in custody to secure their departure or in pre-trial detention if the needs are covered otherwise in total or in part. The basic personal needs may also be provided for, as far as possible, in kind if accommodation is shared with others.

929. Needs for education and participation in the social and cultural life in the community are provided for in addition to the benefits for basic needs and basic personal needs. They amount to the same as is provided for in the general social welfare rules (section 34, 34a, and 34b of Book Twelve of the Social Code).

930. The sum to be paid for all basic personal needs and basic needs are updated on 1 January of each year by way of a regulation (sections 28a, 40 of Book Twelve of the Social Code). The Federal Ministry of Labour and Social Affairs publishes the new figures which are authoritative for the following calendar year in the Federal Gazette on 1 November of each calendar year at the latest. The sum to be paid for all basic personal needs and the amount of the basic needs are also updated when the results of a new national income and consumption survey are available.

931. Benefits in cash are paid to the beneficiary or to an authorised member of full age of the household in person. Cash equivalents are delivered to that person. A benefit is granted proportionally if the benefits are not granted for a full month. In this case the month is calculated as having thirty days. Benefits in cash are provided in advance for one month at the most. *Land* law may not deviate from this.

5.   Medical Benefits

932. Benefits in the case of illness, pregnancy, and birth are provided for in section 4 AsylbLG.

933. The necessary medical and dental treatment, including the supply of medicines and dressings, as well as other benefits needed for convalescence, recovery from or relief of an illness or the consequences of an illness are provided if the illness or pain is acute. Preventive vaccinations (sections 47, 52(1), sentence 1, of Book Twelve of the Social Code) and any medically necessary medical check-ups are provided to ensure early prevention and detection of diseases. Dental treatment is only provided in individual cases if this cannot be delayed for medical reasons.

934. Expectant mothers and women in childbed enjoy medical treatment and nursing care, midwife assistance, medicines, dressings and remedies as required.

935. The competent authority ensures the supply of these health benefits. It also ensures that the beneficiaries are offered the required vaccinations at an early stage. For the services that are provided by doctors or dentists in private practice, the prices charged are those in the agreements concluded with the doctor's or dentist's private practice (section 72(2) and section 132e(1) of Book Five of the Social Code). The competent authority decides which agreement is used.

6.   Working Opportunities

936. Working opportunities are regulated in section 5 AsylbLG.

937. Working opportunities, such as household activities, interpreting, or gardening, in particular for maintenance and operation of the centre or institution, should be provided in reception centres (section 44 AsylG) and in comparable institutions. Assuming these responsibilities does not affect the obligation of the beneficiaries to perform activities that ensure their self-sufficiency. In addition, working opportunities should be provided, as far as possible, by state, local, and charitable institutions inasmuch as the work to be done would otherwise not, not to the same extent or not at that time be performed.

938. With the exception of self-sufficiency activities an expense compensation of EUR 80 per hour is paid for the work that is performed. If the beneficiary provides evidence that the costs to make use of these working opportunities are higher, the expense compensation is also higher.

939. The working opportunity is organised in such a way – in terms of time slots and locations – that it can reasonably be made use of. At the very least, it has to be organised by the hour. Beneficiaries may not be obliged to perform unreasonable work, e.g., work which they cannot perform due to an illness or disability or if the work would endanger the ordinary care for a child or if there is another reason why it cannot be expected of the beneficiary to perform such work (section 11(4) of Book Twelve of the Social Code). An example of such a reason is that the beneficiary is or is to be employed on the general labour market, or is attending a vocational training or a study.

940. Beneficiaries who are fit for work, albeit not gainfully employed, and who are no longer of school age are obliged to engage in a working opportunity if such an opportunity is offered. There is no right to benefits in special cases, to basic benefits and to other benefits (sections 2, 3, and 6 AsylbLG), if an offer has been rejected without reason. In such a case, benefits are only paid to the extent that they cover the needs for food and accommodation, including heating, and body and health care. Other basic benefits are covered only in as far as this is required by the special circumstances of an individual case. Such benefits should be provided in kind (section 1a(2), sentences 2–4 AsylbLG). The beneficiary is informed accordingly beforehand.

941. Neither employment within the meaning of labour law nor an employment relationship within the meaning of the statutory health and pension insurance are established. The prohibition of employment while staying in a reception centre (section 61(1) AsylG) in the German asylum and foreigners law do not preclude the pursuit of a working opportunity. The rules on occupational safety and the principles that govern the limitation of employees' liability, however, apply accordingly.

7.   Labour Market Programme Refugees Integration Measures

942. Working opportunities are also offered on the basis of the Labour Market Programme Refugees Integration Measures. This is regulated in section 5a AsylbLG.

943. Beneficiaries who are fit for work, but not gainfully employed and who have reached the age of 18 and are not subject to full-time compulsory education may be assigned to working opportunities which are provided for within the scope of the Refugee Integration Programme with Additional Cost Compensation implemented by the Federal Employment Agency. This does not apply to beneficiaries holding a permit to remain pending the asylum decision who come from a safe country of origin. This is also the case for beneficiaries whose deportation has been suspended temporarily or who are enforceably required to leave Germany.

944. Beneficiaries are obliged to participate in a refugee integration measure if this is reasonable. Section 11(4) of Book Twelve of the Social Code applies accordingly. Therefore, when assessing whether a request is reasonable, the following circumstances are taken into account as reasons why a beneficiary should be exempted from the obligation to engage in a refugee integration measure. These circumstances are illness, need of care or needs of those who are raising and caring for a child. An important reason for not engaging in such a measure may, in particular, be that the beneficiary is (to be) employed on the general labour market or is attending a vocational training or a study (section 11(4), sentence 1, No. 3 of Book Twelve of the Social Code).

945. Non-compliance with a refugee integration measure that is classed as 'reasonable' means that beneficiaries are not entitled to benefits in special cases, to basic benefits and to other benefits (sections 2, 3, and 6 AsylbLG) once they have been informed in writing of the legal consequences of a refusal. In these cases, beneficiaries are only entitled to benefits that cover the needs for food and accommodation, including heating, and body and health care. Other basic benefits are only covered if and in as far as this is required due to special circumstances in the individual case. Benefits are then provided in kind (section 1a(2), sentences 2–4 AsylbLG). This legal consequence does not occur if the beneficiary presents and provides evidence that there is an important reason that justifies his or her refusal.

946. The selection of suitable participants is coordinated with the institutions responsible for the refugee integration measures before the assignment of a foreigner to a specific programme.

947. The authorities which are competent according to the AsylbLG may collect the personal data of beneficiaries that are necessary for the performance of their tasks, including data on past education, vocational qualifications and present employment, on language skills, and on an integration course or a measure of a job-related German language training programme that a beneficiary is or has attended.

948. These authorities may also transmit data to the institutions responsible for refugee integration measures in as far as this is necessary for the fulfilment of their tasks.

949. Institutions responsible for refugee integration measures may transmit data to the authorities which are competent according to the AsylbLG in as far as this is necessary for the selection of participants, the assignment of a beneficiary to a specific integration measure, registration of correct participation or for the certification when the programme has been completed successfully. Institutions responsible for refugee integration measures have to inform the authorities, which are competent according to the AsylbLG, about facts which are relevant for the enjoyment of benefits according to the AsylbLG, for instance a refusal to engage in a refugee integration measure.

8. Further Integration Measures

950. Other integration measures are specified in section 5b AsylbLG.

951. The authority, competent according to the AsylbLG, may also oblige certain categories of beneficiaries who are fit for work but not in paid employment, who have reached the age of 18 and are no longer subject to full-time compulsory schooling, to attend an integration course. Notification of this obligation has to be in writing. This applies to asylum applicants who have permission to remain pending the asylum decision and who are expected to be given permission to remain lawfully and permanently in Germany. The same applies to asylum applicants who have been granted a temporary suspension of their deportation because their continued presence in Germany is necessary on urgent humanitarian or personal grounds or due to an important public interest. The same holds true for asylum applicants who are enforceably required to leave Germany, but have been issued a temporary residence permit because their departure is impossible in fact or in law and the obstacle to deportation is not likely to be removed in the foreseeable future (section 44(4), sentence 2, Nos 1–3, section 60a(2), sentence 3, and section 25(5) AufenthG).

952. Beneficiaries are not entitled to benefits in special cases, to basic benefits or to other benefits (sections 2, 3, and 6 AsylbLG) if they refuse, despite an instruction in writing about the legal consequences, to engage in an integration course which is classed as reasonable for them. This is also the case if they fail to duly attend an integration course which is classed as reasonable for them. If either of these situations occurs, a beneficiary only receives benefits covering the need for food and accommodation, including heating, and bodily and health care. Other basic benefits are granted only in as far as there are special circumstances in an individual case. These benefits are provided in kind (section 1a(2), sentences 2–4 AsylbLG). This legal consequence does not occur if the asylum beneficiary presents and provides evidence that there is an important reason for his or her behaviour. Examples are illness, need of care or the upbringing and care for a child. An important reason for not engaging in an integration measure may, in particular, exist if the beneficiary takes or has taken up employment on the general labour market, or has started a vocational training or a study (section 11(4), sentence 1, No. 3 of Book Twelve of the Social Code).

953. The authority, competent according to the AsylbLG, may collect the data of beneficiaries that is necessary for the fulfilment of these tasks, including data on language skills and participation in an integration course or a job-related German language skills training programme.

9. Other Benefits

954. Other benefits are specified in section 6 AsylbLG.

955. Other benefits may, in particular, be granted if they are indispensable in an individual case to cover living or health expenses and, if necessary, to cover the needs of children or to comply with an administrative law obligation to cooperate. These benefits are granted in kind. In exceptional circumstances they are cash payments.

956. Holders of a temporary residence permit for temporary protection on the basis of a decision by the EU Council who have special needs, e.g., unaccompanied minors or those who have suffered torture, rape or other severe forms of psychological, physical or sexual violence, are granted the necessary medical and any other assistance that they might need (Directive 2001/55/EC, section 24(1) AufenthG).

10. Income and Assets

957. Income and assets are dealt with in section 7 AsylbLG.

958. Income and assets which are at the disposal of an asylum applicant have to be used by the beneficiary and his or her dependants who share the same household before an asylum applicant is eligible for a benefit according to the AsylbLG. Relations that involve a shared household similar to marriage or a registered partnership may not be treated more favourably than married couples (section 20 of Book Twelve of the Social Code). Beneficiaries who are accommodated in a facility where benefits are paid in kind have to reimburse any benefit received by them and their dependants to the institution that has paid the benefit for the costs made by that institution. The sum due corresponds with a benefit for basic needs (section 3(2), sentence 2 AsylbLG) and the costs of accommodation, heating, and household energy. The *Länder* may determine a lump sum for the cost of accommodation and heating or authorise the competent authority to do so.

959. Not to be taken into account as income according to the AsylbLG are the following means. A basic pension within the meaning of the Federal Law on War Pensions and any law that provides that the Federal Law on War Pensions applies by analogy, a basic pension or aid within the meaning of the Federal Indemnification Law for damages to life, body or health up to the amount of a comparable basic pension within the meaning of the Federal Law on War Pensions, an indemnification for damages other than pecuniary loss (section 253(2) of the Civil Code), an expense compensation for engaging in a work opportunity (section 5(2) AsylbLG), an additional expense compensation which is paid to a beneficiary who participates in a refugee integration measure (section 5a AsylbLG), and a travel allowance which is granted by the Federal Office for Migration and Refugees to ensure that the beneficiary can participate in an integration course or in a job-related German language training programme.

960. When applying these rules, a certain part of the income of the beneficiary is not taken into account, which means that this part remains at the disposal of the beneficiary. This is 25% of the income from employment, at the most, however, in the amount of 50% of the relevant category of needs of the amount for covering all basic personal needs and the basic needs. From the income are also deduced taxes paid on the income, compulsory social security contributions including payments towards the promotion of employment, contributions to public or private insurances or similar institutions, as far as these contributions are required by law, and the expenses necessary for the attainment of the income.

961. If a beneficiary has a financial claim against a third party, the competent authority may transfer that claim to itself (section 93 of Book Twelve of the Social Code).

962. An allowance of EUR 200 for the asylum applicant and each family member who live in the same household is deduced from a beneficiary's assets. Property is not taken into consideration if it is indispensable to engage in or continue a vocational training or employment.

11. Liability of Third Persons

963. Benefits in view of liability of third persons are dealt with in section 8 AsylbLG.

964. Benefits pursuant to the AsylbLG are not granted as far as the necessary living expenses are covered from elsewhere. This is, in particular, the case if there is a commitment to cover these expenses (section 68(1), sentence 1 AufenthG). If there is such a commitment, the competent authority covers any costs related to illness and disabilities and in any other situation if this is provided for in the *Land* law.

965. A monthly allowance of up to double the amount of all basic personal needs benefits (section 3(1), sentence 8 AsylbLG), may be paid to a person who has made a commitment (section 68(1), sentence 1 AufenthG) to cover an asylum applicants living expenses (section 1(1) AsylbLG) for a period of six months. This period can be longer if the situation of the liable person is to be classed as exceptional justifying reliance on public funds.

12. Notification

966. Beneficiaries who take up employment or a self-employed gainful activity have to report this to the competent authority at the latest on the third day after taking up the gainful activity (section 8a AsylbLG).

13.   Relationship with Other Benefit Provisions

967. The relationship to other provisions is regulated by section 9 AsylbLG.

968. Beneficiaries do not receive benefits under general social welfare law (Book Twelve of the Social Code) or comparable *Land* laws.

969. The AsylbLG applies without prejudice to benefits received from other sources, in particular from breadwinners, providers of social benefits and the *Länder* to the extent that they are obliged to set up and maintain reception centres (section 44(1) AsylG).

970. The rules on the obligation to cooperate in general welfare law, such as providing all necessary data or undergoing medical treatment (sections 60–67 of the First Book of the Social Code), also apply beneficiaries.

971. Several other rules of general social welfare law also apply within the context of asylum seeker's benefits. This is the case for the rules on withdrawal, revocation, and repeal of an administrative act and on the refunding of benefits unjustly paid (sections 44–50 Book Ten of the Social Code). It also applies for the obligation of dependants, breadwinners and other persons to provide information (section 99 Book Ten of the Social Code) and on the refunding of claims between providers of benefits (sections 102–114 Book Ten of the Social Code).

972. Sections 117 and 118 of Book Twelve of the Social Code on information obligations and administrative assistance, as well as the regulations adopted on the basis of section 120(1) of Book Twelve of the Social Code or section 117 of the Federal Social Assistance Act are applied accordingly.

14.   Supplementary Provisions

973. Supplementary provisions are found in section 11 AsylbLG.

974. Information must be provided by a beneficiary on any return or move-on scheme benefit received under the AsylbLG. Where appropriate, engagement in such programmes is promoted.

975. Beneficiaries who are resident in a part of Germany where they should not be staying due to a geographic limitation under asylum or foreigners law may normally only be granted a travel allowance by the authority that is competent for the actual location to cover the costs of travel to the place of lawful residence. This benefit may be provided in kind.

976. Until an arrival certificate has been issued (section 63a AsylG), beneficiaries only receive benefits to cover their need for food and accommodation, including heating, bodily and health care (sections 3 and 6 AsylbLG). If, however, there are special circumstances, they are eligible for benefits to cover basic needs. These benefits are provided in kind.

977. Basic and other benefits (sections 3–6 AsylbLG) replace these reduced benefits, even if the beneficiary has not been issued an arrival certificate, if the procedure to establish the identity of an asylum applicant has been completed and the beneficiary has been registered with the authorities of the reception centre which the foreigner has been assigned to, and it is not his or her fault that an arrival certificate has not been issued.

978. A beneficiary is not considered to be responsible that an arrival certificate has not been issued if the reception centre responsible for the issuance of that arrival certificate lacks the technical infrastructure to issue these certificates. A beneficiary is, however, considered to be responsible for if an arrival certificate has not been issued because the beneficiary has violated the obligation to cooperate (section 15(2), Nos 1, 3, 4, 5, or 7 AsylG). This also applies to beneficiaries who are enforceably required to leave Germany after they have entered Germany irregularly from a safe third country on completion of the identification procedure, as provided for by the AsylG or the AufenthG. This also applies to beneficiaries who have filed a follow-up or a secondary application and are subject to an accommodation obligation (section 71(2), sentence 2, or section 71a(2), sentence 1 AsylG read in conjunction with sections 47–50 AsylG).

979. The competent authority examines the personal data of asylum applicants who receive benefits according to the AsylbLG to ensure that the data in its possession correspond with the personal data that is in the possession of the foreigners authority. For this examination, it may transmit name, first or given name, date and place of birth, nationality, sex, marital status, address, status of residence, and times of residence of these persons as well as the commitments for these persons engaged into the competent foreigners authority. The foreigners authority is responsible for the synchronisation of the data transmitted and transmits the result of the synchronisation to the competent authority. In addition, the foreigners authority transmits changes of the data to the competent authority. Regular conformity checks may also be performed using automated data synchronisation.

980. An objection or legal action lodged against an administrative act withdrawing in full or in part a benefit within the meaning of the AsylbLG or revoking or limiting a right to a benefit (section 1a or section 11(2a) AsylbLG) do not have suspensory effect.

981. The AsylbLG also contains rules on statistics (section 12), provisions on *Land* law, the competence of local authorities, and the remuneration of costs between providers of benefits (section 10–10b AsylbLG).

E. Sanctions

1. Fines

982. The rules on fines are set out in section 13 AsylbLG.

983. It is an administrative offence to wilfully or negligently not submit a report on having engaged in paid employment or self-employed economic activity as provided for in section 8a of the AsylblG. This is also the case if a report is not submitted correctly or in full. The fine for these administrative offences is a maximum of EUR 5,000.

2. Limitation of Benefits

984. Benefits are or can be limited in several cases if the beneficiary does not comply with his or her obligations, such as participating in an integration measure or engaging in a working opportunity.

985. The duration of limitations to benefits is stipulated by section 14 AsylbLG. As a general rule, the enjoyment of a benefit within the meaning of the AsylbLG can be limited for a period of six months. This period can be extended if a beneficiary continues to fail to comply with a duty imposed on him or her (section 14 AsylbLG).

II. Persons Granted Asylum Status

A. Status in General

986. The general legal status of persons granted asylum status is defined in section 2 AsylG.

987. In Germany those who have been granted asylum status enjoy the rights set out in the 1951 Geneva Convention relating to the status of refugees. Examples of these rights are the right to non-discrimination and access to courts. As the 1951 Geneva Convention relating to the status of refugees only provides minimum standards, provisions granting a more favourable legal status to persons granted asylum status remain unaffected.

988. Foreigners who were granted asylum status in the former German Democratic Republic, including East Berlin, before its accession to the Federal Republic of Germany in 1990 are treated as persons who have been granted asylum status.

989. The AsylG still distinguishes between the status of a person who has been granted political asylum according to the German Basic Law and that of refugees who have been granted international protection. Due to a gradual alignment of the two statuses in the past, nowadays there is hardly any difference between them in practice. However, as political asylum is a fundamental right according to Article 16a(1) of the Basic Law, violations of the right to political asylum as such can be brought before the Federal Constitutional Court by way of a constitutional complaint, whereas a constitutional complaint concerning a violation of the status of refugee according to ordinary law also requires a violation of constitutional rights, such as the free development of one's personality protected by Article 2(1) of the Basic Law to be admissible. The practical consequences are, however, minimal.

B. Residence Title

990. A foreigner is issued a temporary residence permit according to section 25(1) AufenthG if he or she is entitled to asylum, unless the foreigner has been deported on the ground of a particularly serious interest of deportation pursuant to section 54(1) AufenthG. A temporary residence permit according to section 25(2) AufenthG is issued if the Federal Office for Migration and Refugees has granted the foreigner the status of refugee within the meaning of section 3(1) AsylG or subsidiary protection within the meaning of section 4(1) AsylG. This does not apply if the foreigner has been expelled on serious grounds relating to public safety and order. Residence is deemed to be permitted up to the time that the temporary residence permit is issued.

991. A foreigner who enjoys temporary protection on the basis of a decision of the EU Council and who declares willingness to be admitted into Germany is granted a temporary residence permit for the duration of his or her temporary protection (section 24(1) AufenthG, Articles 5, 4, and 6 Directive 2001/55/EC). A temporary residence permit is not issued if, for serious reasons, the foreigner is to be regarded as a threat to Germany's security or constitutes a threat to the general public because he or she has incontestably been sentenced to a term of imprisonment of at least three years for a crime or a particularly serious offence (section 60(8), sentence 1, and section 24(2) AufenthG).

C. Allocation

1. Residence

992. There are rather strict residence rules for certain categories of persons, for instance those who have been granted political asylum or refugee status set out in section 12a AufenthG. These residence rules apply to foreigners who were recognised or initially granted a temporary residence permit after 1 January 2016.

993. In order to promote their lasting integration in Germany, certain foreigners are obliged to take up habitual residence for a period of three years, from the moment of recognition or the issuing of a temporary residence permit, in the *Land* to which they were allocated for the purpose of processing their asylum application or in the context of their admission procedure. Habitual residence as it is used here is called place of residence. The allocation to a *Land* applies to foreigners who have been recognised as being entitled to asylum or who have been granted refugee status. It also applies to foreigners who have been granted subsidiary protection and those who have been issued an initial temporary residence permit for the purpose of admission from abroad in accordance with international law, on urgent humanitarian grounds or in order to protect Germany's political interests. Furthermore, it applies to those to whom a deportation ban applies under the terms of the European Convention on Human Rights or because a foreigner faces a substantial and real danger to life and limb or liberty in the State to which the foreigner would be deported.

994. This does not apply where the foreigner, the foreigner's spouse, registered partner, or minor child takes up or has taken up employment of at least fifteen hours per week with full social security coverage, on account of which that person has an income amounting to at least the average monthly needs for an individual person which is provided as general social welfare benefit (sections 20 and 22 of Book Two of the Social Code). The same also applies if that person takes up or has taken up vocational training or is pursuing a study or is in a training relationship.

995. A foreigner who is the subject of a residence obligation and who is living in a reception centre or other temporary accommodation may, within six months of recognition or admission, but no later than three years, is obliged, for the purpose of being provided with suitable accommodation, to take up residence in a specific place if this does not interfere with the foreigner's lasting integration in Germany. Insofar as, in an individual case, it is not possible to allocate suitable accommodation within six months, this period may be extended with a further six months.

996. In order to promote their lasting integration in Germany, foreigners subject to a residence obligation are obliged, within six months of recognition or the issuing of the first temporary residence permit, but no later than three years, to take up residence in a specific place if this can help them acquire suitable accommodation, acquire sufficient oral command of the German language equivalent to Level A 2 of the Common European Framework of Reference for Languages and take up paid employment, taking into account the local conditions on the vocational training and labour market.

997. Foreigners who are the subject of a residence obligation may, in order to prevent social exclusion, also be obliged, until the expiry of a three-year period, not to take up residence in a specific place, in particular if it is to be expected that they will not use German as their main language of communication there. A decision to this effect must take the situation on the local vocational training and labour market into consideration.

998. Any residence obligation imposed on a foreigner or allocation decision must be revoked upon application by the foreigner concerned, if he or she provides

proof, in the event of a residence obligation or allocation decision to take up residence in a specific place or to take up residence at another place, or in the event of an obligation not to reside at a place, that the foreigner or his or her spouse, registered partner, or minor child is employed for at least fifteen hours a week with full social security coverage and generates an income which secures the foreigner's subsistence. The same holds true if a foreigner provides evidence that any one of the aforementioned family members has obtained a vocational training place or has been accepted by a higher education institution. This also is the case if the foreigner's spouse, registered partner, or minor, unmarried children reside elsewhere. Furthermore, the same rules apply to prevent hardship, in particular, if hardship has been established by the competent youth welfare office that estimates that the local child and youth welfare benefits and measures of child and youth welfare, such as assistance in case of psychological needs (Book Eight of the Social Code), would be adversely affected, acceptance by another *Land* has been confirmed on other urgent, personal grounds or comparable unreasonable restrictions would arise for the person concerned on other grounds.

999.   In the event of revocation to prevent hardship (section 12a(5), sentence 1, No. 2 AufenthG), a foreigner must be subjected to an obligation to take up residence in a specific place or not to take up residence in a specific place (section 12a(3) or (4) AufenthG) for at the most three years (section 12a(1) AufenthG). Due account has to been given to the foreigner's interests.

1000.   Objections and actions filed against an obligation to take up residence at a specific place or not to take up residence in a specific place (section 12a(2)–(4) AufenthG) do not have suspensory effect.

2.   Temporary Protection

1001.   Foreigners who have been granted temporary protection are allocated to the various *Länder* (section 24(1), (3)–(5) AufenthG). The *Länder* may agree on admission and allocation quotas for those who have been granted temporary protection. The allocation to the *Länder* is carried out by the Federal Office for Migration and Refugees. Unless another formula for allocation has been agreed on among the *Länder*, the formula for the allocation of asylum applicants applies.

1002.   The supreme *Land* authority or the body appointed by it decides on an allocation ruling. The *Land* governments are authorised to regulate the allocation within a *Land* in statutory instruments, and can assign this authorisation to other bodies using a statutory instrument. Section 50(4) AsylG applies accordingly. This means that the responsible *Land* authority adopts an allocation decision. An allocation decision is issued in writing and includes information on the available legal remedy. A justification and a hearing are not required. The allocation decision has to take into account the domestic situation of family members and any other, equally important, humanitarian reason. The allocation ruling is not contestable. Any legal action does not have suspensory effect.

1003. A foreigner who has been granted temporary protection is not entitled to stay in a specific *Land* or a specific place and has to take up accommodation and habitual residence in the place to which he or she has been allocated.

D. *Economic Activity*

1004. A temporary residence permit granted to a foreigner who is entitled to asylum, who has been granted refugee status or who enjoys subsidiary protection entitles the holder to pursue an economic activity (section 25(1), sentence 4 AufenthG).

1005. Foreigners who have been granted temporary protection are subject to specific rules on employment. Self-employment may not be excluded. Employment conditions are found in section 4(2) and section 24(6) AufenthG. Thus, a residence title entitles the holder to pursue an economic activity insofar as this is provided for in the AufenthG or if the residence title expressly permits the pursuit of an economic activity. The residence document must indicate whether the pursuit of an economic activity is permitted. A foreigner who does not possess a temporary residence permit for the purpose of employment is only permitted to take up employment if the Federal Employment Agency has granted its approval or a statutory instrument stipulates that taking up the employment concerned is permissible without the approval of the Federal Employment Agency. Any restrictions imposed by the Federal Employment Agency in granting approval must be specified on the residence document.

§4. POSITION OF FAMILY MEMBERS

I. Scope of Asylum Application

1006. The rules on family members are set out in, in particular, section 14a AsylG. When an application for asylum is filed at a branch office of the Federal Office for Migration and Refugees or at the Federal Office itself, the application also includes every unmarried minor child of the asylum applicant who resides in Germany at the time without the right to freedom of movement under the Freedom of Movement Act/EU or without a residence title, if the child has not already filed an application for asylum.

1007. If a foreigner's unmarried minor child enters Germany or is born thereafter the asylum application is made, the Federal Office for Migration and Refugees is notified immediately, if one parent has permission to remain pending the asylum decision. The same applies if one parent is residing in Germany after the asylum procedure has been completed without a residence title or with a temporary residence permit for a foreigner who is enforceably required to leave Germany because the foreigner's departure is impossible in fact or in law and the obstacle to deportation is not likely to be removed in the foreseeable future (section 25(5) AufenthG).

Such notification is the responsibility of both the child's representatives (section 12(3) AsylG) and the foreigners authorities. As soon as the Federal Office for Migration and Refugees has received the notification, the application for asylum is considered to have been filed on behalf of that child.

1008. The child's representative may waive the processing of an asylum application for the child until the decision of the Federal Office for Migration and Refugees is delivered by stating that the child faces no threat of persecution or serious harm. The representative may also limit the application for asylum to the application for international protection.

1009. These rules also apply if the application for asylum was filed before 1 January 2005 and the child was resident in Germany at that time, arrived later or was born there.

II. Asylum Status for Family Members

1010. The rules on the asylum status for families and international protection for family members are set out in section 26 AsylG.

1011. The spouse or registered partner of a person who has been granted asylum status is granted asylum upon application if the recognition of the foreigner's asylum status is incontestable; the marriage or civil partnership with the person who has been granted asylum status already existed in the country where the person who has been granted asylum status is politically persecuted; the spouse or registered partner entered the country before the foreigner was granted asylum status; or if the foreigner filed the asylum application immediately after entry and there is no reason to repeal or withdraw the recognition of asylum status.

1012. It is irrelevant for the purpose of granting asylum status to a spouse that a marriage is invalid according to German law. It is also irrelevant if the marriage has been annulled because of minority at the time it was concluded. The latter does not apply in favour of the partner who was of age at the time of marriage.

1013. A child of a foreigner who was a minor and unmarried at the time the asylum application was filed, is granted asylum status if the foreigner's asylum status is incontestable and there is no reason to repeal or withdraw this status.

1014. The parents of a minor unmarried person who has been granted asylum or another adult who enjoys a right of care (Article 2(j) of Directive 2011/95/EU) are granted asylum upon application if: the recognition of the foreigner's asylum status is incontestable; the family (Article 2(j) of Directive 2011/95/EU) already existed in the country where the person who has been granted asylum status was politically persecuted; the family member entered Germany before the person was granted asylum status; or if the application for asylum was filed immediately after entry, there is no reason to repeal or withdraw the recognition of the asylum status, and there is a right of care and custody for the person who has been granted asylum status.

1015. This also applies accordingly to minor and unmarried siblings of a minor who has been granted asylum status with the exception of the requirement of the right of care and custody for the person who has been granted asylum status.

1016. These rules do not apply to family members who, for serious reasons, are to be regarded as a threat to Germany's security or who constitute a threat to the general public because they have been incontestably sentenced to a term of imprisonment of at least three years for a crime or a particularly serious offence (section 60(8), first sentence AufenthG). They also do not apply where there are serious reasons to believe that a foreigner has committed a crime against peace, a war crime or a crime against humanity within the meaning of the international instruments drawn up for the purpose of establishing provisions regarding such crimes; a serious non-political crime that was committed outside Germany before being admitted as a refugee, in particular a brutal act, even if it was supposedly intended to pursue political aims, or acted in violation of the aims and principles of the UN (section 3(2) AsylG). Moreover, these rules do not apply if the Federal Office for Migration and Refugees has decided not to prohibit deportation, because the foreigner represents a danger to the general public following an incontestable sentence to a term of imprisonment or a term of youth custody of at least one year for one or more intentionally committed offences against life, physical integrity, sexual self-determination or property or for resisting enforcement officers if the criminal offence was committed using violence, using a threat of danger to life or limb, or with guile, or if the offence is rape or sexual assault by use of force or threats (section 177 of the Criminal Code, section 60(8), third sentence AufenthG, section 60(1) AufenthG). Family asylum within the meaning of section 26(2) and (3) AsylG is not granted in the case of children of foreigners who themselves have been granted family asylum.

1017. Family asylum is also granted to family members of a person who has been granted international protection. Refugee status or subsidiary protection replaces asylum status. However, family members are not granted subsidiary protection if there are grounds for exclusion because of serious crimes, such as war crimes, or other serious reasons such as posing a threat to Germany's security (section 4(2) AsylG).

1018. Family asylum is not granted to family members if a foreigner has suffered persecution or faces serious harm within the meaning of the AsylG by these family members, or if the foreigner has already suffered persecution or serious harm.

III. Subsequent Immigration to Persons Granted Subsidiary Protection Status

1019. Where dependants subsequently immigrate to join a foreigner who is the subject of a residence or allocation obligation for foreigners granted asylum or an equivalent status (section 12a(1)–(4) AufenthG), the obligation or allocation decision also applies to the dependants who join the person with an asylum status (section 12a(6) AufenthG). This is possible for, at most, until the three years period that applies to the foreigner expires, unless the competent authority orders otherwise. The rules concerning the revocation upon application by the foreigner apply accordingly to these subsequently immigrating dependants.

Chapter 7. Other Grounds

§1. RIGHT OF RETURN

A. General Approach

1020. In certain cases there is a special right of return to Germany and exceptions apply to the general conditions on the issuing of a temporary residence permit. This can be the case for young foreigners, forced marriage and for foreigners who receive a pension from a German institution.

B. Young Foreigners

1021. A foreigner whose habitual residence as a minor was in Germany can be issued a temporary residence permit for the reason of return to Germany (section 37 AufenthG). This right of return requires that a foreigner has resided lawfully in Germany for eight years prior to his or her departure and has attended school in Germany for six years. Furthermore, an application for this temporary residence permit must be filed after a foreigner has reached the age of 15 and before reaching the age of 21, and within five years of departure. Derogations from these requirements are possible in order to prevent particular hardship.

1022. The requirements of having lawfully resided in Germany for eight years prior to departure and of attending a school in Germany for six years may be waived if a foreigner has acquired a recognised school-leaving qualification in Germany. However, a foreigner's means subsistence must be ensured through the foreigner's own economic activity or by a five-year maintenance commitment into which a third party has entered.

1023. This temporary residence permit entitles the holder to pursue an economic activity.

C. Victims of Forced Marriage

1024. The law further facilitates the right of return in cases of forced marriage (section 37(2a) AufenthG). Derogations from the requirements for the right of return are possible in these cases. This applies to the requirement of lawful residence in Germany for eight years, school attendance, filing the application within the said time limits, and secure means of subsistence if the foreigner has been unlawfully forced into marriage by means of violence or threat of serious harm and has been prevented from returning to Germany. The foreigner must file an application for a temporary residence permit no more than three months after the coercive situation has ended and within five years of departure. It must furthermore appear, on the basis of the foreigner's education and way of life to date, that the foreigner will be able to become integrated into German society.

1025. If a foreigner fulfils the requirements of lawful residence in Germany for eight years prior to departure and school attendance in Germany for six years, the conditions for return because of forced marriage are even less difficult to meet. A foreigner will be granted a temporary residence permit if he or she has been unlawfully forced into marriage by means of violence or threat of serious harm and has been prevented from returning to Germany, if the foreigner files the application for a temporary residence permit no more than three months after the coercive situation has ended and within ten years of departure. Here, too, derogations from these requirements are possible in order to prevent particular hardship. The requirements of lawful residence in Germany for eight years prior to departure and attending school in Germany for six years may be waived if the foreigner has acquired a recognised school-leaving qualification in Germany (section 37(2a) and (2) AufenthG).

1026. In all return cases, a temporary residence permit may be denied, if a foreigner has been expelled or could have been expelled when leaving Germany, if there is a public interest in expelling the foreigner. A temporary residence permit may also be denied as long as the foreigner is a minor and personal care in Germany is not assured.

1027. The fact that a foreigner's means of subsistence are no longer ensured on the basis of the foreigner's own economic activity or that the maintenance commitment no longer applies due to the expiry of the five-year period does not preclude the extension of a temporary residence permit.

D. Pensioners

1028. A foreigner who receives a pension from a German institution will generally be granted a temporary residence permit if the pensioner resided lawfully in Germany for at least eight years prior to departure.

§2. FORMER GERMANS

1029. Residence titles for former Germans can be obtained in a facilitated manner as stipulated in section 38 AufenthG. A former German is a person who once was a German citizen, but has lost this citizenship on grounds of law. This can happen, e.g., by renunciation of citizenship, by acquiring a foreign citizenship, or by joining the armed forces of a foreign State (sections 17 et seq. of the Citizenship Act (*Staatsangehörigkeitsgesetz*)).

1030. A former German will be issued a permanent settlement permit if he or she has been habitually resident as a German in Germany for five years before having lost the German citizenship. A former German will be issued a temporary residence permit if he or she has been habitual resident in Germany for at least one year when having lost the German citizenship.

1031. The application for such a residence title must be filed within six months of obtaining knowledge of the loss of German citizenship. If a foreigner who is lawfully resident in Germany, but does not possess a residence title, applies for a residence title, residence is deemed to be permitted up to the time of the decision of the foreigners authority. If the application is filed too late, deportation is deemed to have been suspended from the time the application is made up to the time of the decision of the foreigners authority (section 81(3), and section 38(1), sentence 3 AufenthG).

1032. A former German who is habitually resident abroad may be issued a temporary residence permit if he or she has sufficient command of the German language.

1033. In special cases, a residence title may be granted by way of derogation from the general conditions on granting residence titles such as secure means of subsistence or a visa obligation (sections 5, 38(3) AufenthG). A special case can exist, e.g., if a former German is unable to procure secure means of subsistence through no fault of his or her own.

1034. This temporary residence permit entitles the holder to pursue an economic activity. The pursuit of an economic activity is permitted within a period of six months of obtaining knowledge of the loss of German citizenship and, if an application is filed, until the foreigners authority's makes a decision on the application.

1035. The same conditions apply to a foreigner who, for reasons beyond his or her control, has been treated as a German by the German authorities to date.

§3. LONG-TERM RESIDENTS IN OTHER EU MEMBER STATES

1036. Granting and extending temporary residence permits to long-term residents of other EU Member States is facilitated extensively. A foreigner who has the status of a long-term resident in another EU Member State is granted a temporary residence permit if he or she wishes to stay in Germany for a period in excess of ninety days (section 38a(1) AufenthG). The general rule that a temporary residence permit may not be extended if the competent authority has prohibited an extension (section 8(2) AufenthG) does not apply, and, therefore, the extension of a temporary residence permit issued to foreigners who have the status of a long-term resident in another EU Member State must not be prohibited and remains possible.

1037. Such a temporary residence permit will not be issued to foreigners who are dispatched by a service provider in connection with the cross-border provision of services, who intend to provide any other form of cross-border services or wish to work in Germany as a seasonal worker or to take up employment as a cross-border worker.

1038. This temporary residence permit entitles its holder to take up employment if the Federal Employment Agency has granted its approval (section 39(2) AufenthG), or if either the Ordinance on Employment, or an intergovernmental agreement provide that employment may be taken up without prior approval of the Federal Employment Agency. This temporary residence permit entitles its holder to take up self-employment, provided the general requirements for self-employment of foreigners (section 21 AufenthG) are met. These requirements are, *inter alia*, that there is an economic interest or a regional need, the activity is expected to have positive effects on the economy and the foreigner has personal capital or an approved loan to realise his or her business plan.

1039. Where a residence title is issued for study or another educational purpose, the general requirements for granting a residence title for further education (section 16 AufenthG) and another educational purpose, such as basic and advanced vocational training (section 17 AufenthG) apply accordingly. Thus, *inter alia*, a residence title also extends to measures in preparation of a study and compulsory training, and the restrictive rules on the pursuit of an economic activity apply. In the case of another educational purpose (section 17 AufenthG), a residence title is issued without prior approval of the Federal Employment Agency.

1040. A temporary residence permit for long-term residents in another EU Member States may be provided with a subsidiary provision stipulating the duration and form of occupational activity and restricting employment to specific plants or regions for no longer than twelve months (section 38a(4) AufenthG). This period begins when the holder is permitted to take up employment for the first time. After this period has expired, a temporary residence permit entitles the holder to pursue an economic activity.

§4. PUBLIC INTERESTS

1041. There is a special possibility to issue a temporary residence permit for the pursuit of a public interest to foreigners already in Germany.

1042. A foreigner who is not enforceably required to leave Germany may be granted a temporary residence permit for a temporary stay according to section 25(4) AufenthG if the foreigner's continued presence in Germany is necessary due to a substantial public interest. The foreigner must already be in Germany. This temporary residence permit may be extended if departure from Germany would constitute exceptional hardship for the foreigner due to special circumstances inherent to the case concerned. This is a derogation of the general rules on the extension of temporary residence permits in section 8(1) and (2) AufenthG. Thus, extending the temporary residence permit is, in this case, not subject to the same conditions that apply to issuing of a temporary residence permit and the temporary residence permit may be extended even if the competent authority has prohibited an extension in the case of a stay which is only temporary by nature in accordance with the purpose of residence or at the time the temporary residence permit was last extended.

1043. A foreigner may be granted a temporary suspension of deportation if his or her continued presence in Germany is necessary due to substantial public interests (section 60(2), sentence 3 AufenthG).

1044. A Schengen visa may be extended by a further 90 days within the 180-day period concerned as a national visa to safeguard Germany's interests (section 6(2), sentence 2 AufenthG, Regulation (EC) No. 810/2009).

§5. POLITICAL GROUNDS

1045. Political reasons can be relevant in in migration law decisions.

1046. A foreigner who is not enforceably required to leave Germany may be granted a temporary residence permit for a temporary stay according to section 25(4) AufenthG if his or her continued presence in Germany is necessary due to substantial public interests. Such a public interest could exist, e.g., if the stay of a foreigner is justified by political reasons, for instance public security.

1047. A temporary residence permit on political grounds may in general be issued and extended in each instance for a maximum of three years, as stipulated in section 26 AufenthG. The temporary residence permit on political grounds may not be extended, however, if an obstacle to departure or other grounds precluding termination of the right of residence have ceased to apply.

1048. Under certain conditions, such as residence during a period of five or three years, secure means of subsistence, and sufficient command of the German language, a permanent settlement permit may or must be granted (section 26(3) AufenthG).

1049. A foreigner will be granted a temporary residence permit for the purpose of admission from abroad if the Federal Ministry of the Interior or the body designated by it has declared, so as to protect Germany's political interests, that a foreigner is to be admitted (section 22 AufenthG). In this case, the temporary residence permit entitles its holder to pursue an economic activity. An example of a case in which a political interest was discussed was to allow whistle-blower Edward Snowden to be interrogated in Germany by a parliamentary committee of inquiry.

1050. The supreme *Land* authority may order a temporary residence permit to be issued to foreigners from specific States or to certain groups of foreigners in order to protect Germany's political interests (section 23(1) AufenthG). This order may be issued subject to the proviso that a declaration of commitment to bear the foreigner's living expenses is submitted. In order to ensure a nationwide uniform approach, the order requires prior approval of the Federal Ministry of the Interior. The order of the supreme *Land* authority may provide that the rules on the granting of residence permission for temporary protection in section 24 AufenthG are to be applied accordingly, either in part or in full.

1051. Furthermore, in order to safeguard Germany's special political interests, the Federal Ministry of the Interior may, in consultation with the supreme *Land* authorities, order foreigners from specific States or certain categories of foreigners to be granted approval for admission by the Federal Office for Migration and Refugees (section 23(2) AufenthG). There is no administrative appeal against this decision (section 68 of the Code of Administrative Court Procedure). The foreigners concerned are issued a temporary residence permit or a permanent settlement permit, in accordance with the approval for admission. The permanent settlement permit may be issued subject to a condition restricting the permissible place of residence. The temporary residence permit entitles the holder to pursue an economic activity; the permanent settlement permit entitles the holder to economic activity, anyway (section 9(1), sentence 2 AufenthG). Here, too, the order may provide that the provisions on granting temporary protection in section 24 AufenthG are to be applied accordingly, either in part or in full.

1052. A temporary residence permit may be granted to the spouse and the minor child of a foreigner who possesses a temporary residence permit in accordance with sections 22, 23(1) or (2) or section 25(3) or (4a), sentence 1, section 25a(1) or section 25b(1) AufenthG in order to safeguard political interests of the Federal Republic of Germany (section 29(3) AufenthG). These temporary residence permits are those for admission from abroad, granted on the ground of a *Land* or federal order for specific groups of foreigners, when a deportation ban applies to avoid particular danger to a foreigner, for victims of human trafficking, for well-integrated juveniles and young adults, or to those who are lastingly integrated into Germany.

1053. In order to safeguard the political interests of the Federal Republic of Germany, the supreme *Land* authority may order the deportation of foreigners from specific States or of categories of foreigners to be suspended in general or with regard to deportation to specific States for a fixed period of time (section 60a(1) AufenthG).

1054. In accordance with Regulation (EC) No. 810/2009, Schengen visas may be extended by a further 90 days within the 180-day period concerned as a national visa to safeguard Germany's interests (section 6(2), sentence 2 AufenthG).

§6. INTERNATIONAL LAW

1055. International law is of high relevance in decision adopted in accordance with migration law. Residence titles can be granted or extended in several cases, if this is required according to international law, e.g., the European Convention on Human Rights or bilateral agreements.

1056. A temporary residence permit for international law reasons may, in general, be issued and extended in each instance for a maximum of three years, as provided for in section 26 AufenthG.

1057. Under certain conditions, such as a stay of five or three years, secure means of subsistence, and sufficient command of the German language, a permanent settlement permit may or must be granted (section 26(3) AufenthG).

1058. A foreigner may be issued a temporary residence permit for the purpose of admission from abroad in accordance with international law according to section 22 AufenthG.

1059. The supreme *Land* authority may also order that a temporary residence permit is issued to foreigners from specific States or to certain groups of foreigners in accordance with international law (section 23(1) AufenthG). This order may be issued subject to the proviso that a declaration of commitment to bear the foreigner's living expenses (section 68 AufenthG) is submitted. In order to ensure a nationwide uniform approach, the order requires the approval of the Federal Ministry of the Interior. Again, the order may provide that the rules on granting residence permission for the purpose of temporary protection in section 24 AufenthG are to be applied accordingly, either in part or in full.

1060. A temporary residence permit may be issued to the spouse and the minor child of a foreigner who has been issued a temporary residence permit in accordance with sections 22, 23(1) or (2) or section 25(3) or (4a), sentence 1, section 25a(1) or section 25b(1) AufenthG for reasons of international law (section 29(3) AufenthG). Again, these temporary residence permits are: temporary residence permits for admission from abroad; temporary residence permits issued to specific groups of foreigners on the ground of a *Land* or federal order; temporary residence permits issued when there is a deportation ban to avoid particular danger to the foreigner; temporary residence permits issued to victims of human trafficking, well-integrated juveniles and young adults, and to foreigners who are lastingly integrated.

1061. If justified by reasons of international law, the supreme *Land* authority may order that the deportation of foreigners from specific States or of categories of foreigners is suspended in general or with regard to the deportation to specific States for a fixed period of time (section 60a(1) AufenthG).

1062. In accordance with Regulation (EC) No. 810/2009, Schengen visas may be extended by a further 90 days within the 180-day period concerned as a national visa for reasons of international law (section 6(2), sentence 2 AufenthG).

Part IV. Loss of Right of Residence

Chapter 1. Conditions under Which the Right of Residence Might Be Lost

§1. REQUIREMENT TO LEAVE GERMANY

1063. A foreigner loses the right of residence in Germany if the conditions enumerated in sections 50 et seq. AufenthG occur.

1064. Section 50 AufenthG stipulates the basic requirements to leave Germany. Foreigners are obliged to leave Germany if they do not possess or no longer possess the necessary residence title and a right of residence does not exist or no longer exists under the EEC/Turkey Association Agreement.

1065. A foreigner has to leave Germany without delay or, if a period has been allowed for departure, by the end of this period.

1066. A foreigner can only comply with the obligation to leave Germany by entering another EU Member State or another Schengen State if the foreigner's entry into and residence in that State is permitted. If this is the case, a foreigner who is obliged to leave Germany must proceed to the territory of that State without delay.

1067. A foreigner who is obliged to leave Germany and who intends to change his or her address or to leave the district that falls under the foreigners authority's competence for more than three days he or she has to notify the foreigners authority accordingly beforehand.

1068. The passport or passport substitute of a foreigner who is required to leave Germany is taken into custody until departure.

1069. For the purpose of terminating the right of residence of a foreigner, the police may use their search tools for wanted persons in order to determine the foreigner's whereabouts and to apprehend him or her, if the foreigner's whereabouts are not known. A foreigner, subject to an entry and residence ban that has been issued because he or she has been expelled, removed or deported or has not fulfilled the obligation to leave the country within the period allowed for departure (section 11 AufenthG), may be reported for the purpose of refusal of entry and, in the event of being found in Germany, for the purpose of the foreigner's apprehension. An alert may be entered into the Central Register of Foreigners and in the police search systems (section 66 AsylG) on a foreigner who has been allocated to certain residence after having entered Germany unlawfully (section 15a and section 50(6) AufenthG).

§2. TERMINATION OF LAWFUL STAY

I. Expiry of Residence Title

1070. Foreigners no longer possess the necessary residence title if their residence title expires (section 51 AufenthG). There can be many reasons for this.

1071. A residence title expires upon expiry of its period of validity, upon the occurrence of an invalidating condition, for instance, the condition to be employed in a specific employment relationship. A residence title also expires upon its withdrawal, and revocation. It also expires when a foreigner is expelled and upon announcement of a deportation order, which can be issued to avert a special danger to Germany's security or a terrorist threat (section 58a AufenthG).

1072. Moreover, a residence title expires if a foreigner files an application for asylum after being granted a residence title for the purpose of admission from abroad or by order of the supreme *Land* authority or the Federal Ministry of the Interior, e.g., for urgent humanitarian reasons or to protect Germany's political interests (sections 22, 23 AufenthG). A residence title also expires if the foreigner files an application for asylum after having been granted a residence title following the adoption of a deportation ban where deportation is not permitted under the terms of the European Convention on Human Rights[106] or deportation would take place to a State in which the foreigner faces a substantial and real danger to life and limb or liberty (section 60(5) and (7) AufenthG). Furthermore, a residence title expires if a foreigner files an application for asylum after having been granted a residence title because the foreigner's continued presence in Germany is necessary on urgent humanitarian or personal grounds or due to substantial public interests, because the foreigner has been the victim of the criminal offence of human trafficking (sections 232–233a of the Criminal Code) or labour exploitation (section 10(1) or 11(1), No. 3 of the Act to Combat Clandestine Employment, section 15a of the Act on Temporary Employment Businesses), or because the foreigner's departure is impossible in fact or in law (section 25(3)–(5) and section 51(1), No. 8 AufenthG). If an asylum application has been lodged with the competent authorities, a foreigner will, as a matter of principle, be granted permission to remain pending the asylum decision. This right of stay is governed by asylum law.

1073. Furthermore, a residence title expires when a foreigner leaves Germany for a reason which is not of a temporary nature or if a foreigner leaves Germany and fails to re-enter it within six months or within a longer period set by the foreigners authority.

---

106. BGBl. 1952 II p. 685.

II. Exceptions from Expiry

1074. A visa issued for several entries or with a period of validity in excess of ninety days does not expire in the aforementioned cases (section 51(1), Nos 6 and 7 AufenthG). The validity of an ICT Card for ICT (section 19 AufenthG) does not expire if an ICT leaves Germany for a reason which is not temporary by nature or fails to re-enter Germany within six months or within a longer period set by the foreigners authority, if the reason for departure is to carry out part of the ICT in another EU Member State (Directive 2014/66/EU). In these cases, section 51(1), Nos 6 and 7 AufenthG does not apply. The validity of a temporary residence permit for the purpose of full-time studies at a State or State-recognised university or a comparable educational institution (section 16 AufenthG) or for the purpose of research (section 18d AufenthG) does not expire if a student or researcher leaves Germany for a reason which is not temporary by nature or fails to re-enter Germany within six months or within a longer period set by the foreigners authority, if the student or researcher has left Germany to carry out part of his or her study or research project in another EU Member State (Directive (EU) 2016/801). Again, section 51(1), Nos 6 and 7 AufenthG does not apply.

1075. The provision of section 51(1), Nos 6 and 7 AufenthG does also not apply in certain cases for holders of a long-term residence permit. Thus, even longer absences from Germany do not lead to the loss of a long-term residence permit. The permanent settlement permit of a foreigner who has lawfully resided in Germany for at least fifteen years and the permanent settlement permit for a foreigner's cohabiting spouse do not expire, even if the holder of that permit has left Germany for a reason which is not temporary by nature or fails to re-enter Germany within six months or within a longer period set by the foreigners authority (section 51(1), Nos 6 and 7 AufenthG) if that person's means of subsistence are secure and there is no public interest in expelling that foreigner (section 54(1), Nos 2–5 or (2), Nos 5–7 AufenthG). There is a public interest to expel a foreigner if he or she poses a threat to Germany's free democratic basic order or its security. A public interest is also assumed if the holder of the residence permit was one of the leaders of an organisation which has been incontestably banned in Germany because its purpose or activities contravenes criminal law or endanger Germany's constitutional order or the concept of international understanding. There also is a public interest to expel a foreigner if that person is involved in violent activities to pursuit his or her political or religious objectives or calls publicly for the use of violence or threatens to use violence, incites others to hatred against segments of the population, incites others to undertake arbitrary measures against segments of the population, maliciously disparages segments of the population and thus attacks the human dignity of others. The same applies if the foreigner endorses or promotes crimes against peace, against humanity, war crimes or acts of terrorism of comparable severity. There furthermore is a public interest to expel a foreigner who prevents another person from participating in life in Germany on an economic, cultural or social level by reprehensible means, in particular through the use or threat of violence. It also applies if the foreigner forces or attempts to force another person into entering into marriage, or repeatedly performs religious or traditional acts which aim at concluding a relationship equivalent to marriage between two persons one of whom has not yet reached the age of 18 (section 11(2), sentences 1 and 2 of the Civil Status Act) and which constitute a severe contravention of this provision; such acts constitute a severe contravention if they involve a person under the age of 16. A public interest in expelling a foreigner also exists if that foreigner, in the course of an interview to clarify reservations concerning entry or continued residence, fails to inform the German diplomatic mission abroad or the foreigners authority of previous stays in Germany or another State, or intentionally provides no, incorrect or incomplete information on key points regarding links to persons or organisations suspected of supporting terrorism or threatening Germany's free, democratic order or security.

1076. A permanent settlement permit issued to the spouse of a German does not expire if the spouse of a German leaves Germany for a reason which is not temporary by nature or fails to re-enter Germany within six months or within a longer period set by the foreigners authority. Section 51(1), Nos 6 and 7 AufenthG therefore does not apply, unless there is a public interest in expelling the foreigner as outlined (section 54(1), Nos 2–5 or (2), Nos 5–7, and section 51(2), sentence 2 AufenthG). Upon request, the foreigners authority competent for the place of a foreigner's last habitual residence issues a certificate confirming the continued validity of a permanent settlement permit.

1077. A residence title does not expire, even if a foreigner leaves Germany and fails to re-enter it within six months or within a longer period set by the foreigners authority (section 51(1), No. 7 AufenthG), if the specified period is exceeded solely because a foreigner is in compulsory military service in his or her country of nationality and re-enters Germany within three months of discharge from military service.

1078. A longer period for leaving Germany is generally granted by the foreigners authority pursuant to section 51(1), No. 7 AufenthG if a foreigner who has been issued a permanent settlement permit, intends to leave Germany for reasons that are temporary by nature, or residence outside Germany serves Germany's interests.

1079. A residence title does not expire, even if a foreigner leaves Germany for a reason which is not temporary by nature or fails to re-enter Germany within six months or within a longer period set by the foreigners authorities (section 51(1), Nos 6 and 7 AufenthG) in certain cases. It does not expire if the foreigner's habitual residence as a minor was in Germany and the foreigner lawfully resided in Germany for eight years prior to departure and attended a school in Germany for six years. The residence title does also not expire if the foreigner has been forced into marriage by means of violence or threat of serious harm, has been prevented from returning to Germany and re-enters Germany within three months after the coercive situation has ended and at the latest within ten years of departure (section 37(1), sentence 1, No. 1, and section 51(4), sentence 2 AufenthG).

1080. An exemption from the requirement to hold a residence title expires the moment that a foreigner is expelled; removed; or deported (section 51(5) AufenthG). The rules on time limits for a re-entry and residence ban (section 11(2)–(5) AufenthG) apply accordingly.

1081. Geographic and other restrictions and conditions which can be imposed on a foreigner according to the Residence and other Acts remain in force after a residence title expires or deportation is suspended until they are lifted or the foreigner complies with the obligation to leave Germany.

1082. If a person who is entitled to asylum or a foreigner whom the Federal Office for Migration and Refugees has incontestably granted refugee status leaves Germany, a residence title does not expire as long as that foreigner possesses a valid travel document for refugees that has been issued by a German authority. There is no right to have a residence title extended on the basis of the recognition as a person entitled to asylum or by virtue of having been incontestably granted refugee status by the Federal Office for Migration and Refugees if a foreigner has left Germany and the competence to issue a travel document has been transferred to another State.

III. Long-Term Residents/EU

1083. Special information and consultation procedures apply to the termination of the status of a long-term resident in another EU Member State who have been issued a temporary residence permit allowing them to stay in Germany for a period in excess of ninety days (section 38a(1) AufenthG).

1084. Before the competent authority can revoke this temporary residence permit, expel or adopt a decision ordering deportation of a foreigner who has been issued such a temporary residence permit is to avert a specific danger to the security of Germany or a terrorist threat (section 58a AufenthG), the authorities of the EU Member State that has issued the long-term resident permit has to be given an opportunity to submit an opinion in these proceedings, if deportation to an area where this status cannot be acquired is under consideration (section 91c(2) and section 51(8) AufenthG). The EU Member State's opinion is taken into consideration by the competent German authority if it was received in time.

1085. Insofar as the authorities of other Schengen States must be notified about decisions on the annulment or revocation of visas (Article 34 of the Visa Code (Regulation (EC) No. 810/2009)) taken by the foreigners authorities, this is done via the Federal Office for Migration and Refugees. The authorities charged with policing cross-border traffic notify the authorities of the other Schengen States immediately of their decisions in these cases.

1086. The EU long-term residence permit only expires in a limited number of cases which are enumerated in section 51(9), Nos 1–5 AufenthG. It expires if revoked on account of fraudulent misrepresentation, threats or bribery (section

51(9), No. 1 AufenthG) or if the foreigner is expelled or is served with a deportation order that has been issued to avert a specific danger to Germany's security or a terrorist threat (section 58a AufenthG and section 51(9), No. 2 AufenthG). It also expires if the foreigner acquires the legal status of a long-term resident in another EU Member State (section 51(9), No. 5 AufenthG).

1087. The EU long-term residence permit further expires, according to section 51(9), No. 3 AufenthG, if the foreigner is resident for a period of twelve consecutive months outside the EU; the period is twenty-four consecutive months for a foreigner who previously held an EU Blue Card and for the foreigner's dependants who previously held a temporary residence permit for subsequent immigration of spouses (section 30 AufenthG) or children (section 32 AufenthG), for a child born in Germany (section 33 AufenthG) or for subsequent immigration of parents and other dependants (section 36 AufenthG). It also expires if the foreigner remains outside Germany for a period of six years (section 51(9), No. 4 AufenthG).

1088. In these two latter cases, the privileges set out in section 51(2)–(4) AufenthG apply accordingly to certain foreigners and, thus, their EU long-term residence permit does not expire. This is the case if the foreigner has lawfully resided in Germany for at least fifteen years or has exceeded the specified period solely because serving compulsory military service in his or her country of nationality and has re-entered Germany within three months after the termination of the military service. The same applies if the foreigner has been unlawfully forced into marriage by means of violence or threat of serious harm. The privileges also apply to a foreigner who has intended to leave Germany for reasons of a temporary nature only or whose stay outside Germany serves Germany's interests; in these cases, the foreigners authority will set a longer period of time in which the foreigner may stay outside Germany.

IV. EU Blue Card

1089. EU Blue Card holders also enjoy some privileges. While section 51(1), No. 7 AufenthG stipulates in general that a residence title expires if a foreigner leaves Germany and fails to re-enter within six months or within a longer period set by the foreigners authority, this fixed period is extended for them and their dependants. By way of derogation from section 51(1), No. 7 AufenthG, the period is twelve months for holders of an EU Blue Card and holders of a temporary residence permit issued to dependants of EU Blue Card holders for subsequent immigration of spouses (sections 30 AufenthG) or children (section 32 AufenthG), for children born in Germany (section 33 AufenthG) and for subsequent immigration of parents and other dependants (section 36 AufenthG).

V. Permanent Settlement Permit

1090. The period during which a holder of a permanent settlement permit who has resided lawfully in Germany for at least fifteen years and his or her spouse can reside outside Germany is twelve months if he or she is 60 years or older (section 51(10), sentence 2 AufenthG).

§3. REVOCATION OF RESIDENCE TITLES

1091. A residence title expires if it is revoked. The conditions justifying revocation are enumerated in section 52 AufenthG. Residence titles can be revoked only for a limited number of reasons. They can be withdrawn if they were issued unlawfully. Article 34 of the EU Visa Code uses the terms revocation and annulment. A Schengen visa is annulled if it becomes evident that the conditions for issuing it were not met at the time when it was issued, in particular if there are serious grounds for believing that the visa was fraudulently obtained. A visa will be revoked if it becomes evident that the conditions for issuing it are no longer satisfied. A visa is, in principle, annulled or revoked by the competent authorities of the Member State which issued it. A visa may also be annulled or revoked by the competent authorities of another Member State, in which case the authorities of the Member State that issued the visa must be informed thereof.

1092. When the competent authorities revoke the following residence titles, section 52 AufenthG applies. This is the case for: national visas (section 6(3) AufenthG), temporary residence permits (section 7 AufenthG), EU Blue Cards (section 18b AufenthG), ICT Cards (section 19 AufenthG), Mobile ICT Cards (section 19b AufenthG), permanent settlement permits (section 9 AufenthG), and EU long-term residence permits (section 9a AufenthG). While all these residence titles can be withdrawn if they have been issued unlawfully, they can only be revoked if at least one of the following conditions is satisfied.

1093. Such a residence title can be revoked if the foreigner no longer possesses a valid passport or passport substitute, if the foreigner changes or loses his or her nationality or if the foreigner has not yet entered Germany.

1094. The residence titles can also be revoked if the foreigner's recognition as a person entitled to asylum, as a refugee or as a person entitled to subsidiary protection has ended or has become null and void (section 52(1), sentence 1, No. 4 AufenthG).

1095. Revocation is also possible if the foreigners authority establishes, after having issued a temporary residence permit because a deportation ban applies under the terms of the European Convention on Human Rights[107] or the foreigner faces a substantial real danger to life and limb or liberty in the state in which the foreigner

---

107. BGBl. 1952 II p. 685.

would be deported, that these conditions are no longer met (section 52(1), No. 5, section 25(3), sentence 1, section 60(5) or (7) AufenthG). The same applies if, after being issued such a temporary residence title, the foreigner fulfils one of the grounds for exclusion pursuant to section 25(3), sentence 2, Nos 1–4 AufenthG; these grounds exist where there is serious reason to believe that the foreigner has committed a crime against peace, a war crime or a crime against humanity within the meaning of the international instruments which have been drawn up for the purpose of establishing provisions regarding such crimes, or has committed an offence of considerable severity, is guilty of acts contrary to the objectives and principles of the UN, as enshrined in the Preamble and Articles 1 and 2 of the Charter of the UN, or represents a risk to the general public or a risk to Germany's security. Revocation is also possible if, after having issued such a temporary residence title, the Federal Office for Migration and Refugees decides that the conditions for granting it are no longer met (section 42, sentence 1 AsylG).

1096. In the cases covered by section 52(1), sentence 1, Nos 4 and 5 AufenthG, a residence title of the dependants living with the foreigner as a family may also be revoked, if they have no independent right to a residence title.

1097. Further reasons for revocation are enumerated in section 52(2)–(6) AufenthG.

1098. A national visa, a temporary residence permit or an EU Blue Card which have been issued for the purpose of employment are revoked if the Federal Employment Agency revokes the approval of employment because the foreigner is employed on less favourable terms than comparable German workers (section 41 AufenthG). The same applies if one of the situations stipulated in section 40 AufenthG, for instance unlawful placement or recruitment, has occurred. If one of the situations in that provision occurs, a national visa or a temporary residence permit which has not been granted for the purpose of employment must be revoked to the extent that they permit employment.

1099. An ICT Card (section 19 AufenthG), a Mobile ICT Card (section 19b AufenthG) or a residence title allowing subsequent immigration of dependants to join a holder of an ICT Card or a Mobile ICT Card may be revoked if a foreigner no longer satisfies the conditions for its issuance, or has violated the rules of another EU Member State on the mobility of ICT (Directive 2014/66/EU). If an ICT Card or Mobile ICT card is revoked, the residence title granted to the dependant must be revoked at the same time, unless a dependent has an independent right to a residence title.

1100. A temporary residence permit issued for study purpose (section 16b(1), (5) or (7) AufenthG), for instance for full-time or part-time study at a State or State-recognised university or a comparable educational institution or to attend a preparatory language course or a preparatory company traineeship, may be revoked according to section 52(3) AufenthG. This is the case if a foreigner pursues an economic activity without the necessary permit, fails to make adequate progress with his or her study, bearing in mind the average length of time required to complete that particular study programme and the foreigner's personal situation, or if the foreigner no longer satisfies the conditions under which the temporary residence permit for this kind of study can be issued. The educational institution concerned may be consulted to verify whether a foreigner makes adequate progress with his study.

1101. A temporary residence permit issued for the purpose of research (section 18d AufenthG) or for mobile researchers (section 18f AufenthG) may be revoked if the research establishment with which the foreigner has concluded an admission agreement loses its recognised status and the foreigner acted in such a way that this has led to the loss of that status. It may also be revoked if a foreigner no longer conducts or is no longer permitted to conduct research at the research establishment or the foreigner no longer satisfies the conditions according to which a temporary residence permit for research purposes can be issued or it would have been permitted to conclude an admission agreement with the foreigner in the first place.

1102. A temporary residence permit for training purposes in a study-related training programme EU (section 16e AufenthG) or to participate in an EU voluntary service scheme (section 19e AufenthG) may be revoked if a foreigner no longer meets the conditions under which a temporary residence permit can be issued.

1103. A temporary residence permit issued to a foreigner who is a victim of human trafficking (sections 232–233a of the Criminal Code, section 25(4a), sentence 1 AufenthG) or labour exploitation (section 25(4b), sentence 1 AufenthG) should be revoked if that foreigner was not or is no longer prepared to testify in the criminal proceedings, the information provided by the foreigner in the proceedings (section 25(4a), sentence 2, No. 1 AufenthG, section 25(4b), sentence 2, No. 1 AufenthG) is considered by the public prosecutor's office or the criminal court to be in all reasonable probability incorrect or the foreigner no longer satisfies the conditions to be issued a residence title according to section 25(4a) or (4b) AufenthG on account of other circumstances.

1104. A temporary residence permit issued because a foreigner is a victim of human trafficking (sections 232–233a of the Criminal Code, section 25(4a), sentence 1 AufenthG) should also be revoked if the victim has voluntarily re-established contact with the persons accused of having committed the criminal offence (section 25(4a), sentence 2, No. 2 AufenthG).

1105. A temporary residence permit for long-term residents in another EU Member State (section 38a AufenthG) should be revoked if the status as a long-term resident in another EU Member State is lost.

§4. Loss of Asylum

I. Asylum Status and Refugee Status

1106. The recognition as a person enjoying asylum or refugee status ceases to have effect according to section 72 AsylG if a foreigner voluntarily or by accepting or renewing a national passport or by any other action places him- or herself anew under the protection of the State of which the foreigner is a national. They also cease to have effect if a foreigner voluntarily returns to and settles in the country the foreigner left or stayed away from for fear of persecution. The same applies if a foreigner after losing his or her nationality has voluntarily regained it or if a foreigner has obtained a new nationality upon application and enjoys the protection of the State the nationality of which he or she has acquired. It also ceases to have effect if a foreigner renounces the recognition as a person enjoying asylum or refugee status or withdraws an application for either of these statuses before the decision of the Federal Office for Migration and Refugees becomes incontestable. A foreigner has to return the notification of recognition and the travel document to the foreigners authority without delay.

1107. The rules on revocation and withdrawal of asylum and refugee status are set out in section 73 AsylG.

1108. Recognition of asylum and refugee status is revoked without delay if the conditions on which such recognition is based have ceased to exist. This is the case if, after the conditions on which the recognition is based have ceased to exist, the foreigner can no longer refuse to claim the protection of the country of which he or she is a citizen. The same applies under these circumstances if a stateless person is able to return to the country of his or her habitual residence. Recognition is not revoked, however, if a foreigner has compelling reasons, based on earlier persecution, to refuse to return to the country of which he or she is a citizen, or, in the case of a stateless person, his or her former country of habitual residence.

1109. Recognition of asylum or refugee status is withdrawn if it was granted on the basis of incorrect information or withholding essential facts, if recognition is not possible on any other ground.

1110. The conditions justifying the granting of asylum or refugee status are reviewed regularly. No more than three years after the decision on grating asylum or refugee status becomes incontestable, it is examined whether the conditions for revocation or withdrawal exist. If the requirements for revocation or withdrawal are met, the Federal Office for Migration and Refugees informs the foreigners authority of this fact no later than one month after the favourable decision has become incontestable for three years. If they are not met, the foreigners authority does not have to be informed. The foreigners authority is also informed which family members derive their asylum or refugee status from a foreigner and whether the conditions for revocation exist in their case. If no revocation or withdrawal follows the examination, a later decision is possible unless the asylum or refugee status is revoked or withdrawn because a foreigner is to be regarded as a threat to German security or constitutes a threat to the general public because he or she has been incontestably sentenced to a term of imprisonment of at least three years for a crime or a particularly serious offence (section 60(8), first sentence AufenthG) or there are serious reasons to believe that a foreigner has committed a serious act such as a war crime or a crime against humanity (section 3(2) AsylG), or because the Federal Office for Migration and Refugees has decided not to prohibit deportation as the foreigner represents a danger to the general public because he or she has been incontestably sentenced to a term of imprisonment or youth custody of at least one year for one or more intentionally committed offences against life, physical integrity, sexual self-determination or property or for resisting enforcement officers if the criminal offence was committed using violence, using a threat of danger to life or limb, or with guile, or if the offence committed is that of rape or sexual assault by use of force or threat (section 60(1) and section 60(8), third sentence AufenthG, section 177 of the Criminal Code).

1111. For the same security reasons, the recognition of asylum or refugee status enjoyed by family members (section 26(1)–(3) and (5) AsylG), is revoked, if the family member is to be regarded a threat to the security of Germany or the general public (section 26(4), first sentence, and (5) AsylG). The status of a person enjoying asylum is furthermore revoked, if the asylum status of the person from whom the status recognition was derived has expired, has been revoked or withdrawn and if that foreigner could not be granted asylum for another reason. It is irrelevant if the marriage is invalid according to German law or has been annulled because one of partners was a minor at the time of marriage (section 26(1), sentence 2 AsylG).

1112. If the asylum or the refugee status is revoked or withdrawn, a decision is taken as to whether the conditions to be granted subsidiary protection or to impose a deportation ban (section 60(5) or (7) AufenthG) are fulfilled.

1113. A foreigner is informed in writing of a planned decision to revoke or withdraw asylum or refugee status and is given the opportunity to respond to that decision. The foreigner may be requested to respond in writing within one month. If the foreigner fails to respond within this period, the decision is adopted on the basis of the record as it stands and the foreigner is informed of the legal consequences. Communications or decisions of the Federal Office for Migration and Refugees which require action by a certain deadline are delivered to the foreigner in person. If the recognition of a right to asylum or refugee status is incontestably revoked or withdrawn or no longer in effect for other reasons, a foreigner has to return the notification of recognition and the travel document to the foreigners authority without delay (section 72(2) AsylG).

1114. Special rules that apply in the case of a foreign recognition as a refugee are set out in section 73a AsylG. If the responsibility for issuing a passport to a foreigner who has been granted refugee status by a foreign country has been transferred from a foreign country to Germany, the foreigner's legal status as a refugee in Germany ceases to have effect if one of the circumstances listed in section 72(1)

AsylG applies. An example of such a condition is voluntary return to the country of persecution. A foreigner has to surrender the passport to the foreigners authority without delay. The foreigner's legal status as a refugee in Germany is withdrawn, if the requirements to be granted refugee status are not or no longer met. The rules in section 73 AsylG on revocation and withdrawal of asylum and refugee status to be granted by Germany apply accordingly. Thus, in these cases, the reasons for ending the recognition by the German authorities also apply to the foreign recognition. However, a special act by the German authorities is not required and cessation of the status is a matter of operation of the law.

II. Subsidiary Protection Status

1115. Subsidiary protection status is revoked according to section 73b AsylG when the circumstances which led to the granting of that status have ceased to exist or have changed to such a degree that protection is no longer required. This does not apply, however, if a foreigner has compelling reasons, based on earlier persecution, to refuse to return to the country of which he or she is a citizen, or, if the foreigner is a stateless person, his or her country of habitual residence (section 73(1), sentence 3, and section 73b(1), sentence 2, AsylG).

1116. In deciding on revocation, it is taken into account whether the change of circumstances is so significant and lasting that the person eligible for subsidiary protection no longer faces a real risk of serious harm (section 4(1) AsylG).

1117. Subsidiary protection status is withdrawn if a foreigner was or is not eligible for subsidiary protection because he or she has committed a serious criminal act such as a war crime or a crime against humanity (section 4(2) AsylG) or if the foreigner's misrepresentation of or omission to communicate facts or the use of false documents were decisive to grant subsidiary protection status.

1118. Most of the rules governing the procedures to revoke and withdraw asylum and refugee status also apply to the revocation and withdrawal of subsidiary protection status (section 73(2b), sentence 3, and (2c)–(6) AsylG).

§5. CESSATION OF DEPORTATION BANS

1119. Withdrawal and revocation of a deportation ban in the asylum context are regulated by section 73c AsylG.

1120. The decision that deportation is not permitted under the terms of the European Convention on Human Rights or if deportation to another State where a foreigner faces a substantial real danger to his or her life and limb or liberty (section 60(5) or (7) AufenthG) is withdrawn if and when it is inaccurate. It is revoked if and when the conditions that bar deportation no longer exist.

1121. Most of the procedural rules on revocation and withdrawal of asylum and refugee status also apply to the ending of a deportation ban (section 73(2c)–(6) AsylG).

§6. EXPULSION

I. Weighing of Interests

1122. A foreigner loses his or her right of residence following expulsion (*Ausweisung*). Expulsion in German legal terms is the order to leave Germany. The actual transfer to another country, which might entail bodily force, is called deportation (*Abschiebung*).

1123. A foreigner whose stay endangers public safety and order, the free democratic basic order or another significant interest of Germany will be expelled according to section 53 AufenthG if, after weighing the interests of the foreigner's departure against the foreigner's individual interests to remain in Germany, which is to be conducted taking into account all of the circumstances of the particular case, there is an overriding public interest in the foreigner leaving Germany.

1124. When weighing these interests in accordance with the circumstances of a particular case, consideration must be given to, in particular, the length of the foreigner's stay, the foreigner's personal, economic and other ties in Germany and in the country of origin or in another State that is prepared to receive him or her, the consequences of expulsion for the foreigner's dependants as well as whether the foreigner has abided by the law.

1125. A foreigner who has been recognised as being entitled to asylum, who enjoys the status of a foreign refugee, who possesses a travel document issued by an authority in Germany in accordance with the 1951 UN Convention on the Legal Status of Refugees,[108] may be expelled only if the foreigner on serious grounds represents a serious threat to the safety of Germany or a terrorist threat or if the person represents a danger to the public because he or she has been unappealably sentenced because of a serious crime (section 53(3a) AufenthG).

1126. A foreigner who has been granted subsidiary protection status pursuant to section 4(1) AsylG may only be expelled if he or she has committed a serious crime or represents a danger to the public or the safety of Germany (section 53(3b) AufenthG).

1127. A foreigner who has filed an application for asylum may be expelled only under the condition that the asylum procedure has been concluded with an incontestable decision that the foreigner is not a person entitled to asylum recognition or international protection. The condition that there is an incontestable decision is

---

108. BGBl. 1953 II p. 559.

waived, however, if there are facts justifying expulsion because the personal conduct of the person concerned at that time represents a serious threat to public safety and order which affects a fundamental interest of society and expulsion is essential to protect that interest (section 53(3) and (4) AufenthG) or if a deportation warning that has been issued in accordance with the rules in the AsylG has become enforceable.

II. Particularly Serious Interest in Expulsion

1128. Not the least in the interest of the foreigner, the AufenthG scrupulously describes relevant interests in expulsion. The law distinguishes between a particularly serious public interest (section 54(1) AufenthG) and a serious interest (section 54(2) AufenthG).

1129. Several circumstances listed in section 54(1) AufenthG make up a particularly serious public interest. There is a particularly serious public interest in expelling a foreigner within the meaning of section 53(1) AufenthG if the foreigner has been incontestably sentenced to a term of imprisonment or youth custody of at least two years for one or more intentionally committed offences or if preventive detention has been ordered in connection with the most recent incontestable conviction. The same applies if a foreigner has been incontestably sentenced to a term of imprisonment or youth custody of at least one year for one or more intentionally committed offences against life, physical integrity, sexual self-determination or property, for resisting or using force against enforcement officers, for certain offences at the expense of a social security agency or for an offence against the Narcotic Act.

1130. There is also a particularly serious public interest in expelling the foreigner if he or she poses a threat to the free democratic basic order or German security. This is assumed to be the case if there is reason to believe that a foreigner is or has been a member of an organisation which supports terrorism or he or she supports or has supported such an organisation or is preparing or has prepared a serious violent offence endangering the State (section 89a(1) and (2) of the Criminal Code), unless the foreigner recognisably and credibly distances him- or herself from the activity which endangered the State. The same particularly serious public interest exists if a foreigner was one of the leaders of an organisation which was incontestably banned because its purpose or activity are classed as criminal by the law or acts are directed against the constitutional order or the concept of international understanding (Article 9(2) of the Basic Law). The same applies if a foreigner is involved in violent activities in the pursuit of political or religious objectives or calls publicly for the use of violence or threatens to use violence. It also applies if a foreigner incites others to hatred against members of the German population. This is assumed to be the case where a foreigner exerts a targeted and permanent influence on other people in order to incite or increase hatred against members of certain ethnic groups or religions, or publicly, in a meeting or by disseminating written text in a manner which is suited to disturb public safety and law and order, incites others to undertake arbitrary measures against segments of the population, maliciously disparages segments of the population and thus attacks the human dignity of others or endorses or promotes crimes against peace, against humanity, war crimes or acts of terrorism of a comparable severity. In all of these cases, too, the particularly serious public interest in expelling a foreigner ceases to exist if that foreigner recognisably and credibly distances him- or herself from these actions.

III. Serious Interest in Expulsion

1131.   There are a lot of reasons why there is a serious interest in expelling a foreigner which are enumerated in section 54(2) AufenthG. Although the impact is less than that of a particularly serious interest it is still of considerable importance.

1132.   There is a serious interest in expelling the foreigner where the foreigner has been incontestably sentenced to a prison term of at least six months for one or more intentionally committed offences.

1133.   Furthermore, the serious interest in expelling the foreigner exists if the foreigner has been incontestably sentenced to youth custody for at least one year for one or more intentionally committed offences and enforcement of the penalty has not been suspended on probation.

1134.   The same applies if the foreigner has committed or attempted to commit, as a perpetrator or participant, a serious offence under section 29(1), sentence 1, No. 1 of the Narcotics Act such as dealing extensively with prohibited narcotics, uses heroin, cocaine or a comparably dangerous narcotic drug and is not prepared to undergo the necessary treatment which serves his or her rehabilitation or he or she evades such treatment.

1135.   Furthermore, there is a serious interest in expelling the foreigner who prevents another person from participating in life in Germany on an economic, cultural or social level by reprehensible means, in particular through the use of or threat with violence.

1136.   The same applies if the foreigner forces or attempts to force another person into marriage, or repeatedly performs religious or traditional acts which aim at concluding a relationship equivalent to marriage between two persons one of whom has not yet reached the age of 18 (section 11(2), sentences 1 and 2 of the Civil Status Act) and constitute a severe contravention of this provision. Such acts constitute a severe contravention if they are involving a person under the age of 16.

1137.   The same serious interest applies if the foreigner, in the course of an interview to clarify reservations concerning entry or continued residence, fails to inform the German diplomatic mission abroad or the foreigners authority of previous stays in Germany or other states, or intentionally provides no, false or incomplete information on key points regarding links to persons or organisations suspected of supporting terrorism or threatening Germany's free, democratic order or security. Expulsion on this basis is, however, permissible only if the foreigner is expressly informed prior to the interview of the security-related purpose of the interview and the legal consequences of refusing to provide information or of providing false or incomplete information.

1138. There is also a serious interest in expelling the foreigner, if the foreigner, in the course of an administrative procedure conducted by the authorities of a Schengen State in Germany or abroad, has provided false or incomplete information in order to obtain a German residence title, a Schengen visa, an airport transit visa, a passport substitute, eligibility for exemption from the passport requirement or the suspension of deportation or, notwithstanding a legal obligation, has failed to cooperate in measures taken by the authorities responsible for implementing the AufenthG or the Convention Implementing the Schengen Agreement. Again, expulsion on this basis is permissible only if the foreigner was informed beforehand of the legal consequences of such action.

1139. Moreover, a serious interest in expelling a foreigner exists where he or she has committed a breach of legal provisions, court rulings or orders which are not only isolated or minor, or has committed an offence outside of Germany which is to be regarded as an intentionally committed serious offence in Germany.

IV. Particularly Serious Interest in Remaining

1140. The AufenthG also lists a foreigner's interest in remaining, so that a fair balancing of the interests is possible. This list is found in section 55 AufenthG. Here, similar to the distinction regarding public interests in section 54 AufenthG, the law distinguishes between a particularly serious individual interest and a serious individual interest, both in remaining in Germany.

1141. According to section 55(1) AufenthG, there is a particularly serious individual interest in remaining in Germany if the foreigner possesses a permanent settlement permit and has lawfully resided in Germany for at least five years.

1142. The same applies if the foreigner possesses a temporary residence permit and was born in Germany or entered Germany as a minor and has lawfully resided in Germany for at least five years.

1143. Spouses and registered partners are somewhat privileged: For them a particularly serious interest in remaining already exists if they possess only a temporary residence permit, have lawfully resided in Germany for at least five years and cohabit with a foreigner as a spouse or in a registered partnership if that foreigner possesses a permanent settlement permit and has lawfully resided in Germany for at least five years or possesses a temporary residence permit and was born in Germany or entered Germany as a minor and has lawfully resided in Germany for at least five years (section 55(1), Nos 3, 1 and 2 AufenthG).

1144. The same particularly serious individual interest in remaining in Germany exists where the foreigner cohabits with a German dependant in a family unit or a registered partnership, exercises his or her rights of care and custody for a minor, unmarried German or exercises his or her right of access to that minor.

1145. A particularly serious individual interest also exists where the foreigner enjoys the status of being entitled to subsidiary protection, or has been issued a temporary residence permit as a resettlement refugee or for temporary protection.

1146. The same applies if the foreigner has been granted a temporary residence permit as a victim of a criminal offence of human trafficking where humanitarian or personal reasons or public interests require the foreigner's further presence in Germany (sections 232–233a of the Criminal Code and section 25(4a), sentence 3 AufenthG).

1147. A particularly serious individual interest also exists if the foreigner has been granted a temporary residence permit pursuant to section 29(2) or (4) AufenthG, these being subsequently immigrated spouses and children of foreigners who have been granted a status as resettlement refugees, enjoying subsidiary protection, asylum, refugee status or temporary protection.

V. Serious Interest in Remaining

1148. A serious individual interest in remaining exists, according to section 55(2) AufenthG, in particular if one of the following circumstances occur. This list is not exhaustive, and other circumstances may also constitute a serious interest in remaining depending on the specific case.

1149. The individual interest in remaining is serious if the foreigner is a minor and has been issued a temporary residence permit.

1150. The same applies if a foreigner has been issued a temporary residence permit and has resided in Germany for at least five years, exercises his or her rights of care and custody for an unmarried minor residing lawfully in Germany or his or her right of access to that minor.

1151. There is also a serious individual interest in remaining if a foreigner is a minor and his or her parents or parent with rights of care and custody reside or resides lawfully in Germany.

1152. A serious interest in remaining also exists where consideration has to be given to the best interests or the well-being of a child.

1153. If a foreigner has been issued a temporary residence permit as a victim of human trafficking (sections 232–233a of the Criminal Code and section 25(4a), sentence 1 AufenthG), there is also a serious individual interest in remaining in Germany.

VI. Pending Application Procedures

1154. Special rules apply in view of pending application procedures. Residence on the basis of section 81(3), sentence 1, and (4), sentence 1 AufenthG is only considered lawful residence in the context of determining whether there is a particularly serious interest or a serious interest in remaining if there is a positive decision on an application to be issued a residence title or have a residence title extended. This is the case if residence is considered to be permitted until the foreigners authority adopts its decision if the foreigner does not possess a residence title, is legally resident in Germany, and has applied for a residence title. Likewise, if a foreigner applies for an extension of his or her residence title or for a different residence title before the current residence title expires, the current residence title is deemed to remain in force from the moment it expires until a decision is adopted by the foreigners authority.

Chapter 2. Legal and Administrative Procedures

§1. PROCEDURES

1155. Basic structures of the general procedures on foreigners leaving Germany are provided for by section 46 AufenthG.

1156. The foreigners authority may adopt measures to facilitate the departure of a foreigner who is enforceably required to leave Germany. It may, in particular, oblige a foreigner to take up residence at a designated place. Other measures entail, e.g., the obligation to appear regularly before control authorities.

1157. On the other hand, a foreigner may be prohibited from leaving Germany in appropriate application of section 10(1) and (2) of the Passport Act. This relates to foreigners who endanger the security or other serious interests of Germany, intend to evade criminal punishment, act contrary to laws against misuse of narcotics, to laws on taxes, tariffs, imports or exports, or who wants to evade a statutory maintenance duty.

1158. A foreigner may otherwise be prohibited from leaving Germany only if he or she intends to enter another State without possessing the necessary documents and permits. The departure ban is lifted as soon as the reason for its imposition ceases to apply.

§2. COSTS

1159. The costs relating to deportation, removal, a refusal to grant entry permission and the enforcement of a geographic restriction are specified in section 67 AufenthG. They include transport costs and other travel costs for the foreigner within Germany and to a destination outside Germany, the administrative costs arising in connection with preparing and enforcing such a measure, including the costs of custody awaiting deportation, translation and interpreting costs and the costs for accommodation, food and other services for the foreigner, and all costs which are made if it is necessary that a foreigner is escorted by officials, including staff costs.

1160. The costs for which a transport carrier is liable (section 66(3), sentence 1 AufenthG) include transport costs and other travel costs made by the foreigner within Germany and to a destination outside Germany (section 67(1), No. 1, and (2) AufenthG). They also include administrative costs and expenditure for accommodation, food and other services and translation and interpreting costs which are incurred until the admission decision is enforced, and all costs which are made because it is necessary for officials to escort the foreigner, including staff costs (section 67(1), No. 3, and (2) AufenthG), unless the transport carrier provides the necessary escort for the foreigner.

1161. These costs (section 67(1) and (2) AufenthG) are charged by the competent authority by means of a payment order for the amount of the costs actually incurred.

Part V. Sanctions

Chapter 1. Sanctions

§1. Administrative Sanctions

I. The Basic Structure

1162. The German legal system of offences and their sanctions distinguishes between criminal offences, which are punishable with penal sanctions, and administrative offences, which are sanctioned with administrative sanctions. Basically, and bearing in mind that there are further means of enforcement, one might say that administrative offences can be sanctioned with fines, while penal sanctions can be either fines or imprisonment. Administrative offences are, in general, regarded as being less severe than criminal ones.

II. Administrative Offences in the AufenthG

A. *General Rules*

1163. The AufenthG provides an enumeration of administrative offences and the sanctions, i.e., fines, for those offences in section 98. Administrative sanctions which are not fines may be, *inter alia*, a prohibition to enter Germany, expulsion, a territorial restriction, an order to leave Germany or revocation of a residence title. These sanctions are described in their respective contexts.

1164. Administrative offences listed in the AufenthG are, in most cases, punishable by a fine of up to EUR 1,000, in some cases the fine may be up to EUR 500,000. Usually, the fines imposed are much less than the theoretically possible top amount, as any sanction has to be proportional and has to take the individual circumstances of the given case into account.

1165. According to section 98(5) AufenthG, an administrative offence may be punishable in the cases covered by section 98(2a), No. 1 AufenthG with a fine of up to EUR 500,000, in the cases covered by section 98(2a), Nos 2–4 AufenthG with a fine of up to EUR 30,000, in the cases covered by section 98(2), No. 2, (3), No. 1, and 5b AufenthG with a fine of up to EUR 5,000, in the cases covered by section

98(1) and (2), Nos 1, 2a and 3 and (3), No. 3 AufenthG with a fine of up to EUR 3,000 and in the other cases with a fine of up to EUR 1,000.

1166. Administrative fines are mostly imposed for failure to comply with the requirements to submit documents, to provide information and to notify the competent authorities, but also violations of residence obligations or an obligation to attend an integration course. Administrative offences subject to higher fines are violations of employment rules.

1167. An attempt to commit an administrative offence may be punishable in certain cases (section 98(4), (2), No. 2, and (3), No. 3 AufenthG).

B. Specific Administrative Offences

1168. Punishable is the attempt not to submit the necessary documents to the authorities policing cross-border traffic (section 98(4), (2), No. 2, and section 13(1), sentence 2 AufenthG). Punishable is also the attempt to unlawfully enter or leave Germany not using an approved border-crossing point or outside the stipulated hours. Furthermore, failing to carry a passport or passport substitute (section 13(1), 98(4), and (3), No. 3 AufenthG) is an administrative offence. The fine in all those cases is up to EUR 3,000.

Anyone who negligently commits an act specified in section 95(1), No. 1 or 2 or (2), No. 1 (b) AufenthG is deemed to have committed an administrative offence (section 98(1) AufenthG). The fine is up to EUR 3,000.

This applies to negligently residing in Germany without the necessary identification documents (section 95(1), No. 1, and sections 3(1), 48(2) AufenthG).

Equally punishable is negligently residing in Germany without the necessary residence title if the foreigner is enforceably required to leave Germany, has not been granted a period for departure or this has expired and deportation has not been suspended (section 95(1), No. 2, and section 4(1), sentence 1 AufenthG).

The same applies to negligently residing in Germany in contravention of a ban on entry because of having been expelled, removed or deported (section 95(2), No. 1(b), and section 11(1) AufenthG).

It equally applies to negligently residing in Germany in contravention of a ban on entry and residence which has been imposed against the foreigner for not having fulfilled the obligation to leave the country within the period allowed for departure (section 95(2), No. 1(b), and section 11(6), sentence 1 AufenthG).

Punishable is also to negligently residing in Germany in contravention of an enforceable order to leave the country under certain conditions. These conditions are that a ban on entry and residence has been imposed on a foreigner who does not possess a residence title and whose asylum application was rejected as manifestly unfounded, subsidiary protection was not granted, or no prohibition of deportation due to the European Convention of Human Rights or substantial concrete danger to life and limb or liberty in the country to which deportation would take place applies or whose asylum application repeatedly did not lead to a follow-up asylum procedure (section 95(2), No. 1(b), and section 11(7), sentence 1 AufenthG).

Anyone is deemed to have committed an administrative offence who, possessing a right of residence in accordance with the EEC/Turkey Association Agreement, fails to furnish evidence of this by providing the necessary documents (section 98(2), No. 1 AufenthG). The fine is up to EUR 3,000.

Anyone is deemed to have committed an administrative offence who fails to submit to those policing cross-border traffic the necessary documents (section 98(2), No. 2, and section 13(1), sentence 2 AufenthG). The fine is up to EUR 5,000.

An administrative fine of up to EUR 3,000 is to be imposed on a person who fails to submit, on time or at all, a necessary, specified document. The same applies if a person fails to allow, on time or at all, his or her face to be checked against the photograph on the document (section 98(2), No. 2a, and section 47a, sentences 1, 2, and 3 AufenthG).

Anyone is deemed to have committed an administrative offence who, in contravention of section 48(1) or (3), sentence 1 AufenthG, fails to submit, on time or at all, a document or paper or a data carrier. The same applies if a person fails to surrender the item, or fails to do so in good time, or fails to leave, or leave in good time, the item with the competent authorities (section 98(2), No. 3, and section 48(1) or (3), sentence 1 AufenthG). Section 48(1) and (3), sentence 1 AufenthG obliges foreigners to produce these items and to cooperate, e.g., if this is necessary to implement a measure according to the AufenthG. It also obliges Germans who have also a foreign citizenship to produce these items which refer to their foreign citizenship in certain defined cases. The fine is up to EUR 3,000.

An administrative offence is committed by those who act in contravention of an enforceable order to take an integration course (section 98(2), No. 4, section 44a(1), sentence 1, No. 3, sentence 2 or 3 AufenthG). The fine is up to EUR 1,000.

Anyone who wilfully or recklessly commissions a foreigner on a sustained basis to perform paid work or services for gain, who may not pursue an economic activity or perform other paid work or services (section 98(2a), No. 1) is liable to a fine of up to EUR 500,000.

Anybody who wilfully or recklessly fails to provide notification, provides incorrect notification or fails to provide the required employer notification on a short-term mobility ICT in good time (section 98(2a), No. 2, and section 19c(1), sentence 2 or 3 AufenthG) is liable to a fine of up to EUR 30,000.

Equally considerable is the fine for not providing adequate employer information in cases of a Mobile ICT Card. Anyone who wilfully or recklessly fails to provide the required notification or provides an incorrect or incomplete notification or fails to provide in good time notification of the required employer information Mobile ICT Card is deemed to have committed an administrative offence (section 98(2a), No. 3, and section 19d(7) AufenthG). The fine is up to EUR 30,000.

The same applies to a person who wilfully or recklessly does not provide the required notification, or does not do so correctly, completely, in the prescribed manner or in good time, if the foreigner does not undertake or discontinues the vocational training for which suspension of a deportation order has been granted (section 98(2a), No. 4, and section 60a(2), sentence 7 AufenthG). The fine is also up to EUR 30,000.

A fine of up to EUR 5,000 is to be imposed on a foreigner who wilfully or negligently pursues a self-employed activity without the necessary permit (section

98(3), No. 1 AufenthG). This is specified in section 4a(3), sentence 4 and (4), section 6(2a), section 7(1), sentence 4, first half sentence, section 16a(3), sentence 1, section 16b(3), also in conjunction with (7), sentence 3, section 16b(5), sentence 3, second half sentence, section 16c(2), sentence 3, section 16d(1), sentence 4(3), sentence 2 and (4), sentence 3, section 16f(3), sentence 4, section 17(3), sentence 1, section 20(1), sentence 4, also in conjunction with (2), sentence 2, section 23(1), sentence 4, first half sentence and section 25(4), sentence 3, first half sentence, (4a), sentence 4 first half sentence and (4b), sentence 4, first half sentence AufenthG.

The law provides for an administrative fine of up to EUR 1,000 for anybody who wilfully or negligently contravenes an enforceable condition subject to which the visa or temporary residence permit was issued or which has been imposed on the, stay of a foreigner who does not require a residence title (section 98(3), No. 2, and section 12(2), sentence 2 or (4) AufenthG).

Equally, a fine of up to EUR 1,000 is to be imposed on a person who wilfully or negligently does not take up residence in the *Land* in which he or she is obliged to take up residence or does not do so for the prescribed length of time (section 98(3), No. 2a, and section 12a(1), sentence 1 AufenthG).

Anyone is deemed to have committed an administrative offence who wilfully or negligently contravenes an enforceable order on residence obligations (section 98(3), No. 2a, and section 12a(2), (3) or (4), sentence 1, or section 61(1c) AufenthG). The fine is up to EUR 1,000.

Also, any person is deemed to have committed an administrative offence who wilfully or negligently enters or leaves Germany outside an approved border-crossing point or outside the stipulated traffic hours. The same applies if the person fails to carry a passport or if a passport as required (section 98(3), No. 3, and section 13(1) AufenthG). The fine in these cases is up to EUR 3,000.

It is also an administrative offence to wilfully or negligently contravene an enforceable order on facilitating departure, on monitoring or on restrictions on the stay of a foreigner who is enforceably required to leave Germany (section 98(3), No. 4, section 46(1), section 56(1), sentence 2 or (3) or section 61(1e) AufenthG). The law prescribes a fine up to EUR 1,000.

Furthermore, anyone is deemed to have committed an administrative offence who wilfully or negligently fails to provide a notification, provides an incorrect notification or fails to provide a notification in good time on monitoring (section 98(3), No. 5, and section 56(1), sentence 1 AufenthG). The fine is up to EUR 1,000.

Liable to a fine of up to EUR 1,000 is anyone who, in violation of section 82(6), sentence 1 AufenthG, also in conjunction with section 60d(3), sentence 4 AufenthG, fails to provide a notification on time or at all (section 98(2), No. 5 AufenthG). This relates to notification of early termination of vocational training or economic activity.

Anyone is deemed to have committed an administrative offence who wilfully or negligently contravenes a geographic restriction (section 98(3), No. 5a, and section 56(2) or section 61(1), sentence 1 AufenthG). The fine is up to EUR 1,000.

It also is an administrative offence to wilfully or negligently fail to file one of the required applications on behalf of a foreigner lacking legal capacity (section 98(3), No. 6, and section 80(4) AufenthG). The fine is also up to EUR 1,000.

No one may wilfully or negligently contravene a statutory instrument pursuant to section 99(1), No. 3a, letter d, Nos 7, 10 or 13a, sentence 1, (j), insofar as such statutory instrument refers to section 98(3), No. 7 AufenthG as to fines for a specific offence; this provision relates to notification and documentary obligations (section 98(3), No. 7, and section 99(1), No. 3a, letter d, Nos 7, 10 or 13a, sentence 1, (j) AufenthG). The fine for this administrative offence is up to EUR 1,000.

1169. These provisions do not affect Article 31(1) of the Convention relating to the Status of Refugees, pursuant to which the Contracting States do not impose penalties, on account of their irregular entry or presence, on refugees who, coming directly from a territory where their life or freedom was threatened, enter or are present in their territory without authorisation, provided they present themselves, without delay, to the authorities and show good cause for their irregular entry or presence (section 98(6) AufenthG).

III. Administrative Offences in the AsylG

1170. Provisions on administrative offences are contained in section 86 AsylG.

1171. Any foreigner who violates a residence restriction in the asylum procedure (sections 56, 59b(1), and section 71a(3) AsylG), is deemed to have committed an administrative offence. Such an administrative offence may be punished with a fine of up to EUR 2,500.

§2. Penal Sanctions

1172. Penal sanctions on offences relating to migration law are provided for in the German Criminal Code, the AufenthG, and the AsylG.

1173. Penal sanctions can be either a fine or imprisonment. If certain conditions are met, a number of further sanctions can be imposed, such as confiscation or disqualification from exercising a profession. Usually, if the perpetrator has committed the offence for the first time, the punishment will by far not reach the top possible amount. There is also the possibility to suspend the enforcement of a sentence for a probationary period for sentences of imprisonment up to two years. In the case of a sentence of imprisonment up to six months, suspending enforcement is obligatory.

I. Penal Sanctions in the AufenthG

1174. A variety of offences relating to the AufenthG are punishable as a criminal offence according to section 95 AufenthG.

1175. Punishable with up to one year's imprisonment or a fine is anyone who wilfully resides in Germany without the necessary identification documents (section 95(1), No. 1, and sections 3(1), 48(2) AufenthG).

1176. Equally punishable is a person who wilfully resides in Germany without the necessary residence title if he or she is enforceably required to leave Germany, has not been granted a period for departure or this has expired, and the deportation has not been suspended (section 95(1), No. 2, and section 4(1), sentence 1 AufenthG). An act carried out without the necessary residence title is deemed equivalent to an act carried out on the basis of a residence title obtained by threat, bribery or collusion or by furnishing incorrect or incomplete information (section 95(6) AufenthG).

1177. Equally punishable is a person who wilfully enters Germany not possessing the required passport or passport substitute or not possessing the residence title as required (section 95(1), No. 3, section 14(1), No. 1 or 2, section 3(1), and section 4(1) AufenthG). An attempt is also punishable (section 95(3) AufenthG). An act carried out without the necessary residence title is deemed equivalent to an act carried out on the basis of a residence title obtained by threat, bribery or collusion or by furnishing incorrect or incomplete information (section 95(6) AufenthG).

1178. Equally punishable with up to one year's imprisonment or a fine is a person who wilfully contravenes an enforceable order of a prohibition to leave the country or of a prohibition or restriction of political activity (section 95(1), No. 4, section 46(2), sentence 1 or 2, section 47(1), sentence 2 or (2) AufenthG).

Equally punishable is a person who wilfully fails to furnish an item of information or furnishes incorrect or incomplete information on identity data where the offence is not punishable pursuant to a more severe provision (section 95(1), No. 5, section 49(2), section 95(2), No. 2 AufenthG).

The same punishment of up to one year's imprisonment or a fine applies to a person who wilfully fails to tolerate a required identification measures (section 95(1), No. 6, section 49(10) AufenthG).

Equally punishable is a person who wilfully and repeatedly fails to meet an obligation to report to the authorities during monitoring or repeatedly contravenes geographic restrictions or other conditions imposed on their stay The same applies to a person who wilfully fails to meet the obligation to take up residence in a designated facility despite having been notified repeatedly as to the legal consequences or uses certain means of communication or does not abide by specific contact bans in contravention of section 56(4) AufenthG (section 95(6a), section 56 AufenthG).

1179. Equally punishable with up to one year's imprisonment or a fine is a person who wilfully and repeatedly breaches a geographic restriction imposed on a stay in Germany while enforceably required to leave the country (section 95(1), No. 7, section 61(1) or (1c) AufenthG).

1180. Equally punishable is a person who wilfully belongs to an organisation or group in Germany which consists primarily of foreigners and whose existence, aims or activities are concealed from the authorities in order to avert the prohibition of that organisation or group (section 95(1), No. 8 AufenthG).

1181. The same punishment also applies to anyone who wilfully commits an act of specified economic activity and requires a residence title in order to reside in Germany, but only possesses a residence title in the form of a Schengen visa (section 95(1a) AufenthG, section 404(2), No. 4 of Book Three of the Social Code, section 98(3), No. 1, section 4(1), sentence 1, and section 6(1), No. 1 AufenthG). The attempt is also punishable (section 95(3) AufenthG).

1182. Anyone is punishable with up to three years' imprisonment or a fine who wilfully enters or resides in Germany in contravention of a ban on entry because of having been expelled, removed or deported (section 95(2), No. 1(a) and (b), and section 11(1) AufenthG). It equally applies to wilfully entering or residing in Germany in contravention of a ban on entry and residence which has been imposed against the foreigner for not having fulfilled the obligation to leave the country within the period allowed for departure (section 95(2), No. 1(a) and (b), and section 11(6), sentence 1 AufenthG). It furthermore applies to wilfully entering or residing in Germany in contravention of an enforceable order to leave the country in the following cases: if a ban on entry and residence has been imposed on a foreigner who does not possess a residence title and whose asylum application was rejected as manifestly unfounded, subsidiary protection was not granted, or no prohibition of deportation due to the European Convention of Human Rights or substantial concrete danger to life and limb or liberty in the country to which deportation would take place applies or whose asylum application repeatedly did not lead to a follow-up asylum procedure (section 95(2), No. 1(a) and (b), and section 11(7), sentence 1 AufenthG). The attempt to enter Germany in all of these cases is also punishable (section 95(3) AufenthG).

1183. Equally punishable is a person who wilfully contravenes an enforceable court order to carry the technical device necessary to permanently monitor his or her location and not to impair its functionality, thereby preventing the competent authority from constantly locating him or her (section 95(2), No. 1a, section 56a(1) and (3) AufenthG). The offence is only prosecuted upon an application made by that competent authority (section 95(7) AufenthG).

1184. Equally punishable is a person who wilfully furnishes or uses false or incomplete information in order to procure a residence title or a suspension of deportation for themselves or for another. The same applies if this is done in order to prevent the expiry or subsequent restriction of a residence title or the suspension of deportation. It furthermore applies to a person who knowingly uses a document procured in this manner for the purpose of deceit in legal matters. Objects related to such an offence may be confiscated (section 95(2), No. 2, and (4) AufenthG).

1185. These provisions of criminal punishment do not affect Article 31(1) of the Convention relating to the Status of Refugees, pursuant to which the Contracting

States do not impose penalties, on account of their illegal entry or presence, on refugees who, coming directly from a territory where their life or freedom was threatened, enter or are present in their territory without authorisation, provided they present themselves without delay to the authorities and show good cause for their illegal entry or presence (section 95(5) AufenthG).

1186. Where these acts are offences that can only be committed as a principal by a foreigner, Germans can be punishable for abetting or aiding the principal (sections 25–31 of the Criminal Code).

II. Penal Sanctions in the AsylG

1187. The AsylG also contains provisions on criminal offences.

1188. Incitement to submit fraudulent applications for asylum is a punishable crime according to section 84 AsylG.

1189. Anyone who incites or helps a foreigner to provide incorrect or incomplete information during the asylum procedure before the Federal Office for Migration and Refugees or during the judicial proceedings in order for the applicant to be granted asylum status or international protection status is punishable with a term of imprisonment of up to three years or a fine. In particularly serious cases a prison sentence of up to five years or a fine can be imposed on the perpetrator. As a rule, a case is considered particularly serious if the perpetrator receives or expects to receive financial advantage for such an act or repeatedly acts or acts on behalf of more than five foreigners.

1190. Anyone who is motivated to commit such acts by a commercial interest or acts as a member of a gang formed for the purpose of committing such offences on a recurring basis is punishable by a prison sentence of between six months and ten years. An attempt is punishable. Whoever commits such an act for the benefit of a family member, however, is exempted from punishment.

1191. Anyone who, motivated by commercial interests and as a member of a gang formed for the purpose of committing such offences on a recurring basis, commits such offences is punishable by a term of imprisonment of between one and ten years; in less serious cases the penalty is imprisonment for six months to five years (section 84(1) and section 84a AsylG).

1192. Other offences are punishable according to section 85 AsylG.

1193. Anyone who fails, despite an obligation to proceed without delay to the place designated in an allocation decision, to report immediately to the authority indicated in that decision is punishable by a term of imprisonment of up to one year or a fine (sections 85, 50(6), 71a(2), sentence 1 AsylG).

The same applies to anyone who repeatedly violates residence restrictions (sections 85, 56(1) or 59b(1), 71a(3) AsylG).

1194. It also applies to anyone who fails to comply, within the time given, with an enforceable order to live in or move to a specific municipality or accommodation or to take up habitual residence and accommodation in a particular district (sections 85, 60(2), sentence 1, section 71a(3) AufenthG) or to pursue paid employment whilst required to stay in a reception centre (sections 85, 61(1), 71a(3) AufenthG).

§3. DETENTION, CUSTODY, ALLOCATION AND RESTRICTIONS

I. Detention and Custody

A. *Detention Pending Exit from the Federal Territory*

1195. Detention of a foreigner is permissible according to section 15(5) and (6) AufenthG in the context of refusal of entry. In order to ensure that a refusal to enter Germany is effective after a judicial order to refuse entry has been issued and cannot be enforced immediately, the foreigner concerned should be taken into custody. This is called detention pending exit from the federal territory (*Zurückweisungshaft*). A judicial order is required. Custody may be ordered for up to six months, in certain cases, such as cases in which the foreigner hinders his or her deportation, it may be extended with a maximum of twelve months (section 62(4), section 15(5) AufenthG). If a judge declines to issue a judicial order or to extend the period of detention, a foreigner who wishes to enter the federal territory may not be refused entry at the border.

1196. A foreigner who has reached Germany by air and has not entered Germany, but has been refused entry at an international airport, is taken to the transit area of that airport or to a place of accommodation from which departure from Germany is possible if detention pending exit from the federal territory is not applied for. A foreigner's stay in the transit area of an airport or the aforementioned accommodation requires a judicial order that is handed down no later than thirty days after arrival at the airport or, should it be impossible to ascertain the time of arrival, after the competent authorities become aware of the foreigner's arrival. The judicial order is issued to ensure that the foreigner leaves Germany. It is only permitted if exit is to be expected within the term set out in the order. Again, if a judge declines to issue a judicial order or to extend the period of detention, the foreigner who wishes to enter the federal territory may not be refused entry at the border.

B. *Custody Awaiting Deportation*

1. Principle of Proportionality

1197. Custody awaiting deportation is a special form of detention regulated in section 62 AufenthG.

1198. Custody awaiting deportation is not permitted if the purpose of custody can be achieved by other, less severe means which are also sufficient. The detention has to be limited to the shortest possible duration. Minors and families with minors may be taken into custody awaiting deportation only in exceptional cases and only for as long as this is reasonable taking into account the well-being of the child.

2. Custody to Prepare Deportation

1199. A foreigner is placed in custody by judicial order to enable the preparation of expulsion, if a decision on expulsion cannot be reached immediately and subsequent deportation would be much more difficult or impossible without prior detention. This is called 'custody to prepare deportation' (section 62(2) AufenthG). The duration of custody to prepare deportation should not exceed six weeks. If expulsion is ordered, no new judicial order is required for the continuation of custody until the ordered term of custody has expired.

3. Custody to Secure Deportation

1200. A foreigner can be placed in custody by judicial order for the purpose of safeguarding his or her deportation. This is called custody to secure deportation.

1201. Custody to secure deportation is permitted if a foreigner is enforceably required to leave Germany on account of having entered Germany unlawfully or if there is the risk of absconding. It is also permitted if custody has been ordered on the basis of a deportation order which has been issued according to section 58a AufenthG, but is not immediately enforceable. these are the cases in which a deportation order has been issued without a prior expulsion order for a foreigner on the basis of a prognosis based on facts in order to protect against a particular danger to Germany's security or against a terrorist threat (sections 58a, 62(3), sentence 1, No. 1a, and (4) AufenthG).

1202. Custody to secure deportation can also be ordered if the period allowed for departure has expired and a foreigner has changed his or her place of residence without notifying the foreigners authority of his or her new address. The same applies if a foreigner has failed to appear at the location stipulated by the foreigners authority on the date fixed for deportation, if this is attributable to the foreigner concerned.

1203. Custody to secure deportation can also be ordered if a foreigner has evaded the execution of a deportation measure by any other means or if there are, in an individual case, reasons based on evidence, such as that the foreigner has deceived the authorities regarding his or her identity, and there is thus a well-founded suspicion that the foreigner intends to evade deportation by absconding. This is called risk of absconding.

1204. Concrete evidence for the risk of absconding may be constituted if a foreigner, notwithstanding being informed of the notification obligation, has, in the past, already misled the authorities by changing his or her place of residence, not only on a temporary basis, without notifying the competent authority of his or her new address. It may also be assumed if a foreigner deceives the authorities regarding his or her identity, in particular by withholding or destroying identity or travel documents or claiming a false identity. The same applies if a foreigner has refused or failed to cooperate to establish his or her identity if it can be concluded from the particular circumstances of the case that the foreigner intends to actively prevent his or her deportation from Germany. In addition, the conclusion that a foreigner will prevent his or her deportation is also justified if a foreigner has paid considerable sums of money to a third person who, in return, engages in criminal activities (section 96 AufenthG) to secure the foreigner's unlawful entry if the sum are so relevant given the foreigner's circumstances that the foreigner will prevent deportation to ensure that the expenses were not made in vain. If a foreigner has explicitly declared that he or she intends to evade deportation, there is evidence that a foreigner poses a significant threat to the life and limb of others or to significant legally protected internal security interests.

1205. By way of exception, order for custody to secure deportation because a foreigner is enforceably required to leave Germany on account of having entered Germany unlawfully may be waived if a foreigner declares credibly that he or she does not intend to evade a deportation order (section 62(3), sentence 2 AufenthG). Custody to secure deportation is not permitted if it is established that it will not be possible to carry out deportation within the next three months for reasons beyond the foreigner's control. By way of derogation from this rule, however, a foreigner who possesses a significant threat to the life and limb of others or to a significant legally protected internal security interest may be taken into custody to secure his or her deportation even if the foreigner cannot be deported within the next three months.

1206. Custody to secure deportation may be ordered for up to six months. If a foreigner hinders his or her deportation, it may be extended by a maximum of twelve months. It may also be extended by a maximum of twelve months if custody was ordered on the basis of a deportation order which was issued pursuant to section 58a AufenthG even if it is not immediately enforceable. This is the case if a deportation order has been issued without a prior expulsion order because, a prognosis based on facts indicates that this is necessary in order to protect Germany against a particular danger to its security or a terrorist threat (sections 58a, 62(3), sentence 1, No. 1a, and (4) AufenthG), and if the transmission of the documents, required by the third country obliged or willing to admit the foreigner, is delayed. A period of custody to prepare deportation counts towards the overall duration of custody to secure deportation.

1207. Where deportation has failed, the deportation order remains unaffected until the period allowed for deportation has expired, insofar as the conditions justifying the detention order in the first place remain unchanged.

1208. The authority responsible for the detention application may detain a foreigner without a prior judicial order and place such foreigner in temporary custody where there is a strong suspicion that the conditions allowing to place the foreigner in custody by judicial order for the purpose of safeguarding deportation apply, it is not possible to obtain the judicial decision on the order for custody to secure deportation beforehand and there is a well-founded suspicion that the foreigner intends to evade the order for custody to secure deportation. The authorities responsible for the detention application are the foreigners authority, the police authority, and the customs authority. The foreigner has to be brought before the court without delay for a decision on the order for custody to secure deportation.

Foreigners may be taken into custody by judicial order for a maximum of fourteen days for the purpose of deportation on further specific grounds (section 62(6) and (4), sentence 1 AufenthG). This can be done in order to enforce an order to appear in person at the diplomatic representation or before authorised officials of the State whose nationality they putatively possess or to enable a medical examination to determine their fitness to travel. However, before such a custody measure can be imposed, it is also required that the foreigner has, without being excused, failed to appear in person before the responsible authority in violation of an order to do so for the first time or an order to appear in person before the responsible authority (section 82(4), sentence 1 AufenthG) and was informed in advance of the possibility of being taken into custody (custody to enforce cooperation). It is not possible to extend the length of custody to enforce cooperation. A period of custody to enforce cooperation counts towards the overall duration of custody to secure deportation. The rules in section 62a(1) AufenthG on separate accommodation apply accordingly in these cases.

4. Enforcement

1209. Special rules apply as to how custody awaiting deportation is to be enforced. These rules are found in section 62a AufenthG.

1210. A person in detention awaiting deportation is to be accommodated separately from prisoners serving a criminal sentence. If more than one member of a family is detained, they have to be accommodated separately from other detainees awaiting deportation. They are guaranteed adequate privacy.

1211. Detainees awaiting deportation are permitted to contact their legal representative, family members, the competent consular authorities and the relevant aid and support organisations.

1212. In the case of minors in detention awaiting deportation, the needs of persons of their age are to be taken into account (Article 17 of Directive 2008/115/EC).[109] Thus, minors in detention must have the possibility to engage in leisure activities, including play and recreational activities appropriate to their age, and must have, depending on the length of their stay, access to education. Unaccompanied minors must, in as far as possible, be accommodated in institutions with staff and facilities which take into account the needs of a person of their age. The best interest of the child is the primary consideration in the context of detention of minors awaiting deportation.

1213. Particular attention must be paid to the situation of vulnerable persons. Upon application, staff of relevant aid and assistance organisations is permitted to visit detainees awaiting deportation. Detainees awaiting deportation are informed of their rights and obligations and the house rules of the facility.

C. Custody to Secure Departure

1214. Section 62b AufenthG provides the rules that apply to custody to secure departure (*Ausreisegewahrsam*).

1215. The rules on custody to secure departure apply notwithstanding the conditions applicable to custody to secure deportation in section 62(3) AufenthG that regulates custody if, e.g., a foreigner is enforceably required to leave Germany on account of having entered Germany unlawfully or if a foreigner has evaded deportation.

1216. According to the provisions on custody to secure departure a foreigner may be placed in custody for no more than ten days by judicial order for the purpose of ensuring that the deportation can be carried out if the period allowed for departure has expired, unless the foreigner was prevented through no fault of his or her own from leaving or the period allowed for departure has been exceeded by an insignificant amount of time, deportation can be performed within this period of time, and the foreigner has displayed behaviour which leads one to expect that the foreigner will make the deportation more difficult or impossible by violating a statutory obligation to cooperate or the foreigner has deceived the authorities regarding his or her identity or nationality. The same applies if the foreigner has been sentenced because of a wilful crime; fines of up to fifty daily rates are disregarded. It also applies if the deadline for leaving the country has expired by more than thirty days. Temporary custody without prior judicial order is possible if strong suspicion

---

109. Article 17 of Directive 2008/115/EC of 16 Dec. 2008 on common standards and procedures in Member States for returning illegally staying third-country nationals, OJ EC 2008, L 348/98.

exists that these prerequisites apply, a judicial order cannot be obtained beforehand and reasonable suspicion exists that the foreigner will escape the order of custody to secure departure. The foreigner has to be brought before a judge promptly to secure a decision about the order of custody to secure departure.

1217. The ordering of custody to secure departure is waived if the foreigner credibly asserts or it is obvious that the foreigner does not intend to evade deportation.

1218. Custody to secure departure is enforced in the transit area of an airport or in accommodation from which the foreigner's subsequent departure is possible without overcoming a longer distance to the border-crossing point.

1219. Section 62(1) and (4a) AufenthG and section 62a AufenthG apply accordingly in cases of custody to secure departure. If a deportation cannot be executed, it remains unaffected until the period allowed for deportation has expired, insofar as the conditions for the issuing the detention order remain unchanged (section 62(4a) and section 62b(3) AufenthG).

1220. The rules on the enforcement of custody awaiting deportation laid in section 62a AufenthG also apply to custody to secure departure. An example is the rule that custody, as a general rule, has to take place in a specialised detention facility. If that is not possible then a foreigner awaiting a deportation order can be put in custody in another appropriate custodial institution. Adequate privacy must be guaranteed for families and contact with legal representatives must be permitted.

D. Supplementary Custody

1221. There is also the possibility of the so-called supplementary custody pursuant to section 62c AufenthG. This is custody to prepare a deportation warning pursuant to section 34 AsylG. As a matter of principle, it requires a court order. A foreigner who is staying in Germany in contravention of a ban on entry and residence pursuant to section 11(1), sentence 2 AufenthG and does not hold a permit to enter Germany for a brief period (section 11(8) AufenthG) has to be taken into custody to prepare a deportation warning if the following conditions are met. The foreigner is a serious threat to life or limb of third persons or important legally protected rights of domestic security or if the foreigner has been expelled because of an especially serious interest in expelling pursuant to section 54(1) AufenthG such as threatening the free democratic basic order or the security of Germany. This custody must not be imposed if it is not necessary for preparing a deportation warning. Special rules determine the end of such custody (section 62c(2) AufenthG).

II. Allocation

1222. There are special rules on the territorial allocation of foreigners who have entered Germany unlawfully.

1223. Foreigners who enter the country unlawfully without applying for asylum and who, when their unlawful entry has been detected, cannot be placed in custody pending deportation and foreigners who are deported or expelled directly from custody must, according to section 15a AufenthG, be allocated to the *Länder* before the competent authorities decide on the suspension of deportation or the issuing of a residence title. They are not entitled to be allocated to a specific *Land* or a specific town or location. Allocation to the *Länder* is carried out by the Federal Office for Migration and Refugees, a central allocation agency that is appointed by the Federal Ministry of the Interior. Unless the *Länder* have agreed on another formula for allocation, the formula for the allocation of asylum applicants applies. Each *Land* appoints up to seven authorities who are competent to request allocation by the central allocation agency and to admit the allocated foreigners. If a foreigner provides evidence prior to the adoption of an allocation decision that there the spouses or parents and their minor children live in a shared household, or that there are other compelling reasons which conflict with an allocation to a certain place, due consideration should be paid to this fact in the allocation procedure.

1224. The foreigners authorities may require foreigners to present themselves to the authority requesting allocation. This does not apply when due consideration has to be accorded to compelling reasons that a foreigner has to be allocated to a certain place. An allocation obligation is not contestable; any legal actions contesting the allocation obligation do not have suspensory effect.

III. Territorial Restrictions

1225. Under specific circumstances, far-reaching territorial restrictions can or may be imposed on a foreigner according to section 61 AufenthG.

1226. The stay of a foreigner who is enforceably required to leave Germany is restricted in geographic terms to the territory of the *Land* concerned. This geographic restriction may be waived if the foreigner is entitled to take up employment as a skilled worker and is not employed under less favourable terms than German nationals employed in an equivalent position (section 39(2), sentence 1, No. 1, and section 61(1) AufenthG). A geographic restriction may also be waived if this is necessary to attend school, to participate in basic and advanced vocational training or to study at a State or State-recognised university or a comparable educational institution. The same applies if this preserves the family unit.

1227. If the deportation of a foreigner is suspended for one week, because removal or deportation has failed, custody pending deportation is not ordered and Germany is obliged to readmit a foreigner by virtue of section 60a(2a), and section

61(1a) AufenthG, residence is restricted to the administrative district of the most recently responsible foreigners authority. A foreigner must proceed to such location without delay after re-entering Germany. If it is impossible to determine which foreigners authority is responsible, section 15a AufenthG on the allocation of foreigners who have entered Germany unlawfully applies accordingly. This means that the Federal Office for Migration and Refugees decides on the allocation.

1228. A geographic restriction expires if a foreigner has resided in Germany for three months without interruption either by virtue of holding a temporary residence or permanent settlement permit or by virtue of the deportation having been suspended or the foreigner has been issued a permission to remain pending the asylum decision.

1229. However, and notwithstanding these rules, a geographic restriction limiting where a foreigner who is enforceably required to leave Germany may stay, may be ordered if that foreigner has been incontestably convicted of a criminal offence, with the exception of those offences which can only be committed by foreigners, there is evidence that justify the conclusion that the foreigner has committed an offence in the Narcotics Act or if measures have be taken which will mean that termination of a foreigner's stay is imminent.

1230. An order restricting a foreigner's geographic location to the district of a foreigners authority should be imposed if the foreigner through his or her own action has created an obstacle to his or her deportation by intentionally providing incorrect information, or through deceit concerning his or her identity or nationality or if the foreigner has failed to comply with reasonable requirements to cooperate in such a way that the obstacles to deportation are removed.

1231. A foreigner who is enforceably required to leave Germany and whose means of subsistence are not ensured is obliged to take up his or her habitual residence at a specific place. If the foreigners authority does not order any other measure, this is the place where the foreigner was residing when the decision to temporarily suspend a deportation was taken. The foreigners authority may amend the residence restriction ex officio or at the foreigner's request. Consideration must be given to the fact that a foreigner lives with his or her family members and of any other humanitarian ground of comparable importance. A foreigner may leave the place determined in the residence restriction without obtaining permission temporarily.

1232. The *Länder* may also establish departure facilities for foreigners who are enforceably required to leave Germany. The authorities of these departure facilities must promote a willingness to leave Germany voluntarily by providing support and counselling, access to the competent authorities and courts. They should also ensure the implementation of the departure procedure.

§4. Expulsion, Deportation and Removal

I. Legal System and Terminology

1233. There are different ways to enforce the obligation to leave Germany. In German legal terminology, these are called removal (*Zurückschiebung*) and deportation (*Abschiebung*). This terminology differs slightly from the terminology used in EU law; translation leads to further variations. Removal and deportation are factual activities and can include bodily force. Expulsion (*Ausweisung*) is not part of that concept, but is used to refer to the administrative order to leave the country which is enforceable by removal or deportation or by voluntary departure of the foreigner.

II. Removal

1234. One way of enforcing an obligation to leave Germany is removal (*Zurückschiebung*) that is regulated by section 57 AufenthG.

1235. A foreigner who is apprehended following unlawful entry into Germany after crossing an external border will be removed from Germany. External borders are borders with States other than an EU Member State (Article 2, No. 2 of Regulation (EU) No 2016/399).

1236. A foreigner who is enforceably required to leave Germany and who will be readmitted by another EU Member State, Norway or Switzerland under the terms of an intergovernmental admission agreement with those States that was in force on 13 January 2009 should be removed to that State. This is also the case if a foreigner is apprehended by the border authority in the vicinity of the border in close chronological proximity to unlawful entry into Germany, there are indications that another EU Member State is responsible for conducting an asylum procedure by virtue of EU law or an international treaty and an admission or readmission process is initiated.

1237. Foreigners holding an EU long-term residence permit or a corresponding legal status in another EU Member State who are eligible for international protection in another EU Member State may only be deported to that Member State. Deportation is not permitted if there are serious reasons to assume that the foreigner poses a threat to Germany's security or to the general public because he or she has been incontestably sentenced to a term of imprisonment of at least three years for a crime or a particularly serious offence (section 60(8), section 58(1b), sentence 1, and section 57) according to section 60(2), (3), (5) and (7) AufenthG on custody awaiting deportation remain unaffected.

1238. Prior to removal, foreigners who were employed but were not permitted to pursue an economic activity (section 4a(5), section 59(8), and section 57 AufenthG) have to be notified of their rights. Two examples are: back payments to be made by the employer and the right to lodge a complaint against the employer (Article 6(2) and Article 13 of Directive 2009/52/EC).[110]

1239. The prohibitions to execute a deportation measure in section 60(1)–(5) and (7)–(9) AufenthG also apply to removal orders. The most important prohibition is that a foreigner may not be deported to a State where his or her life or liberty is under threat on account of the foreigner's race, religion, nationality, membership of a certain social group or political convictions. A foreigner may also not be deported to a State where he or she faces a substantial real danger to life and limb or liberty. A foreigner may not be deported to a State where he or she awaits a criminal procedure for a criminal offence and a danger of imposition or enforcement of the death penalty exists. Under these circumstances removal is only possible according to the rules on extradition.

1240. The rules on custody awaiting deportation in section 62 AufenthG apply in removal cases as well as the rules on enforcement of custody awaiting deportation in section 62a AufenthG (section 57(3) AufenthG).

III. Deportation

A. *Conditions for Deportation*

1241. The rules governing deportation (*Abschiebung*) are set out in section 58 AufenthG.

1242. A foreigner will be deported if the requirement to leave Germany is enforceable, no period for departure has been ordered or if this period has expired and it is not certain that the foreigner will leave Germany voluntarily or supervision of departure appears necessary on grounds of public security and order. If one of the conditions in section 59(1), sentence 2 AufenthG becomes applicable within the period allowed for departure, the foreigner will be deported before this period has expired. This is the case where a shorter period may be set or if this period may be waived altogether because this is, in an individual case, vital to safeguard an overriding public interest, in particular if there is a well-founded suspicion that a foreigner intends to evade deportation, or poses a serious danger to public safety or order.

1243. Before deporting an unaccompanied foreign minor, the competent authorities must ensure that in the State to which he or she is to be returned, the minor will be handed over to a member of his or her family, to a person possessing the right of care and custody or to an appropriate reception centre (section 58(1a) AufenthG).

---

110. Article 6(2) and Art. 13 of Directive 2009/52/EC of the European Parliament and of the Council of 18 Jun. 2009 providing for minimum standards on sanctions and measures against employers of illegally staying third-country nationals, OJ EC 2009, L 168/24.

1244. Foreigners holding an EU long-term residence permit or a corresponding legal status in another EU Member State and who are eligible for international protection in another EU Member State may only be deported to the Member State granting protection. This restriction does not apply if there are serious reasons to regard a foreigner as a threat to Germany's security or a threat to the general public, because that foreigner has been incontestably sentenced to a term of imprisonment of at least three years for a crime or a particularly serious offence (section 60(8), sentence 1, and section 58(1b), sentence 1 AufenthG). However, even in the case of a dangerous foreigner, section 60(2), (3), (5) and (7) AufenthG, and section 58(1b), sentence 2 AufenthG may prohibit deportation of that foreigner. Thus, e.g., a foreigner may not be deported to a State where he or she faces serious harm (section 4(1) AsylG) or runs the risk that a death penalty is executed. A foreigner may also not be deported to a State where he or she faces a substantial real danger to life and limb or liberty.

1245. The requirement to leave Germany is enforceable if a foreigner has entered Germany unlawfully. It is also enforceable if a foreigner has not yet applied for the necessary initial residence title or has not yet applied for its extension or, despite an application having been submitted, residence is not permitted prior to decision of the foreigners authority (section 81(3), and section 58(2), sentence 1, No. 2 AufenthG) or, where a foreigner applies for an extension of the residence title or for a different residence title before the current residence title expires and the existing residence title is not considered to retain its validity from the time it expires until the time of the decision of the foreigners authority (section 81(4), and section 58(2), sentence 1, No. 2 AufenthG). The same applies if the foreigner is obliged to leave Germany by virtue of a ruling on his or her return adopted by the competent authorities of another EU Member State (Article 3 of Council Directive 2001/40/EC),[111] provided that the ruling concerned is recognised by the competent German authority.

1246. Otherwise, the obligation to leave Germany is only enforceable if the decision refusing to grant a residence title or another administrative act requiring the foreigner to leave Germany because he or she does not possess or no longer possesses the necessary residence title and there is no right of residence or that residence title no longer exists under the EEC/Turkey Association Agreement (section 50(1) AufenthG) takes effect.

1247. Supervision of deportation is necessary, in particular if the foreigner is, by virtue of a judicial order, in detention or another form of public custody; has failed to leave Germany within the period allowed for departure; has been expelled on the ground of a particularly serious interest in expulsion within the meaning of section 54(1), section 53, and section 58(3), No. 3 AufenthG, or if a foreigner is destitute,

---

111. Article 3 of Council Directive 2001/40/EC of 28 May 2001 on the mutual recognition of decisions on the expulsion of third country nationals, OJ EC 2001, L 149/34.

does not possess a passport or passport substitute, has intentionally submitted incorrect information in order to deceive the foreigners authority or has refused to provide information, or has indicated that he or she will not comply with an obligation to leave Germany.

1248. The authority executing the deportation has the power to briefly detain the person to be deported in order to bring him or her to the border or airport and to search the foreigner's home (section 58(4)–(10) AufenthG).

B. *Deportation Order*

1249. While, in general, a deportation order (*Abschiebungsanordnung*) may only be issued on the basis of an expulsion order, there are cases in which an expulsion order is not needed and a deportation order can be issued without a prior expulsion order and deportation can be executed. These cases are enumerated in section 58a AufenthG.

1250. The supreme *Land* authority may issue a deportation order without a prior expulsion order based on the assessment of facts, in order to avert a special danger to the security of Germany or a terrorist threat. The deportation order is immediately enforceable; no notice of intention to deport is necessary.

1251. The Federal Ministry of the Interior may assume responsibility if there is a special interest on the part of the Federation. The supreme *Land* authority must be notified accordingly. Deportation orders issued by the Federation are enforced by the Federal Police.

1252. A deportation order may not be enforced if the conditions in section 60(1)–(8) AufenthG on a deportation ban are satisfied. An example of such conditions is that the foreigner faces a substantial real danger to life and limb or liberty in the State where he or she would be deported to. The notice of intention to deport a foreigner should specify the State to which the foreigner will be deported and should inform the foreigner that he or she may also be deported to another State, which the foreigner is permitted to enter or which is obliged to admit the foreigner. The existence of deportation bans and grounds for the temporary suspension of deportation does not preclude the actual issuing of the deportation order in the first place. The State to which the foreigner may not be deported has to be specified in the deportation order. If an administrative court establishes the existence of a deportation ban, the validity of the deportation order remains unaffected (section 58a(3), sentence 2, and section 59(2) and (3) AufenthG). An assessment in this context is carried out by the authority deciding on the deportation order. This authority is not bound by the findings reached in this connection in other proceedings.

1253. When a deportation order has been served, a foreigner must be given an opportunity to contact a legal adviser of his or her own choice without delay, unless the foreigner has secured the services of a lawyer beforehand. The foreigner must be informed of this right, the legal consequences of a deportation order and the available legal remedies. An application for temporary relief as provided for by the Code of Administrative Courts Procedure has to be filed within seven days after a deportation order has been served. Deportation may not be enforced until this period has expired and, if an application for temporary relief is filed in time, until the court has decided on that application.

C. Deportation Warning

1254. Before executing deportation, section 59 AufenthG requires that a deportation warning (*Abschiebungsandrohung*) is issued. This gives a foreigner some time to adjust to the situation and prepare for the necessary steps.

1255. Thus, a notice of intention to deport a foreigner must be served specifying a reasonable period of between seven and thirty days for voluntary departure. By way of exception, a shorter period may be set or such a period may be waived altogether if, in individual cases, this is vital to safeguard an overriding public interest. Example of an overriding public interest are a well-founded suspicion that the foreigner intends to evade deportation and if a foreigner poses a serious danger to public safety or order.

1256. Under these conditions, serving a notice of intention to deport may also be waived if the foreigner's residence title has expired, because it has been withdrawn or revoked or because the foreigner has been expelled (section 51(1), Nos 3–5, and section 59(1), sentence 3, No. 1 AufenthG), or if the foreigner has already been informed, in accordance with the requirements in section 77 and section 59(1), sentence 3, No. 2 AufenthG, of the obligation to leave Germany. Such requirements include, as a matter of principle, that the information has been given in writing, is motivated and a translation of its operative part is provided upon application.

1257. Taking into account the particular circumstances of each case, the period allowed for departure may be extended as appropriate or a longer period may be set. This does not affect the possibility and conditions that deportation is suspended (section 60a(2) AufenthG). If an obligation to leave or a notice of intention to deport ceases to be enforceable, the period allowed for departure is interrupted and begins to run again when the obligation or notice becomes enforceable once more. No new setting of a period is required. When the period allowed for voluntary departure expires, the foreigner must not be informed of the date of the deportation.

1258. A notice of intention to deport should specify the State to which a foreigner is to be deported and should inform the foreigner that he or she may also be deported to a State which he or she is permitted to enter or which is obliged to admit him or her.

1259. The existence of a deportation ban and grounds justifying the temporary suspension of deportation does not preclude issuing a notice of intention to deport.

The State to which the foreigner may not be deported has to be specified in a notice of intention to deport. If an administrative court establishes the existence of a deportation ban, the validity of a notice of intention to deport remains otherwise unaffected.

1260. Once a notice of intention to deport can no longer be appealed, the foreigners authority has, for the purpose of further decisions on deportation or the suspension of deportation, to ignore any circumstances which represent an obstacle to deportation to a State specified in the notice of intention to deport which occurred before the notice of intention to deport could not be appealed. Any other circumstances cited by the foreigner which represent an obstacle to deportation, or to deportation to a specified State, may be ignored. The provisions enabling a foreigner to contest the validity of these circumstances through a court of law by means of a legal action or the temporary relief procedure in the Code of Administrative Procedure remain unaffected.

1261. It is not necessary to set a deadline if a foreigner has, by virtue of a judicial order, been placed in detention or another form of public custody (section 58(3), No. 1, and section 59(5) AufenthG). Under these circumstances, a foreigner is deported directly from the place of detention or public custody. An impending deportation should be announced at least one week beforehand.

1262. A foreigner is issued a certificate confirming that a period for departure has been set (section 59(1) AufenthG).

1263. If the foreigners authority has concrete reasons to suspect that a foreigner is a victim of human trafficking or labour exploitation, it has to, by derogation from rules on the notice of intention in section 59(1), sentence 1 AufenthG, set a period to leave Germany which gives a foreigner sufficient time to decide whether he or she is prepared to testify as a witness in the criminal proceedings related to these offences (section 25(4a), sentence 2, No. 3 or section 25(4b), sentence 2, No. 2, and section 59(7), sentence 1 AufenthG). A period of at least three months is allowed for departure. The foreigners authority may refrain from setting a period to leave Germany or may annul or reduce the period allowed for departure, if a victim's presence in Germany is a danger to public safety and order or any other substantial interest of Germany, or if a victim has voluntarily re-established contact with the persons accused of having committed the criminal offence of human trafficking after being duly informed of the prevailing arrangements, programmes and measures that are available to victims of human trafficking.

1264. This obligation to inform the victim in the context of a deportation warning is stipulated in section 59(7) AufenthG. It requires the foreigners authority or a body authorised by it, for instance a non-governmental relief organisation, to duly inform the victim of the prevailing arrangements, programmes and measures that are available to victims of human trafficking (section 25(4a), sentence 1, and section 59(7), sentence 4 AufenthG).

1265. Prior to deportation, victims of human trafficking or labour exploitation who were employed although not entitled to pursue an economic activity, have to be notified of their rights. Examples of such rights are back payments to be made by the employer and the right to lodge a complaint against the employer (Article 6(2) and Article 13 of Directive 2009/52/EC).[112]

IV. Prohibition of Deportation

1266. Of major importance in German migration law are the rules prohibiting and temporarily suspending deportation. This applies to their practical impact as well as to their relevance for a correct understanding of the spirit of the law, in particular its humanitarian approach. These rules, however, are not easy to locate in the AufenthG, or to fit into the systematic structure of the law. Section 60 AufenthG provides for the prohibition of deportation.

1267. The 1951 UN Convention relating to the Status of Refugees[113] prohibits the deportation of a refugee to a State where that foreigner's life or liberty is under threat on account of the foreigner's race, religion, nationality, membership of a certain social group or political conviction. This also applies to persons who are entitled to asylum and to foreigners who have been incontestably granted refugee status or who have been accorded the status of foreign refugee in Germany on other grounds or who have been granted foreign refugee status outside Germany in accordance with the 1951 UN Convention relating to the Status of Refugees.

1268. When a foreigner invokes the ban on deportation in the 1951 UN Convention relating to the Status of Refugees, the Federal Office for Migration and Refugees has to establish in an asylum procedure whether the conditions stated in section 60(1), sentence 1 AufenthG apply and whether he foreigner must be granted refugee status. Cases that fall under this deportation ban are the cases in which a foreigner may not be deported to a State where his or her life or liberty is under threat on account of his or her race, religion, nationality, membership of a certain social group or political conviction. It does not apply, however, to cases covered by section 60(1), sentence 2 AufenthG, and, thus, it does not apply to persons who are entitled to asylum and to foreigners who have been incontestably granted refugee status or who enjoy the status of foreign refugees on other grounds in Germany or who have been granted foreign refugee status outside Germany in accordance with the 1951 UN Convention relating to the Status of Refugees. A decision adopted by the Federal Office for Migration and Refugees is only contestable as provided for in the AsylG.

---

112. Article 6(2) and Art. 13 of Directive 2009/52/EC of the European Parliament and of the Council of 18 Jun. 2009 providing for minimum standards on sanctions and measures against employers of illegally staying third-country nationals, OJ EC 2009, L 168/24.
113. BGBl. 1953 II p. 559.

1269. Foreigners may not be deported to a State where they face serious harm (section 4(1) AsylG). Section 60(1), sentences 3 and 4 AufenthG on the procedure before the Federal Office for Migration and Refugees applies accordingly.

1270. If a foreigner may not be deported to a State where the foreigner is wanted for a criminal offence and there is a danger that the death penalty is imposed or enforced, the rules on extradition apply accordingly, in particular the Act on International Mutual Assistance in Criminal Matters.

1271. If a formal request for extradition or a request for arrest combined with a notification of intent to file a request for extradition has been received from the authorities of another State, deportation of a foreigner to this State prior to a decision on extradition is only permitted with the approval of the authority which is responsible for approving extradition requests according to section 74 of the Act on International Mutual Assistance in Criminal Matters. This authority is primarily the Federal Ministry of Justice.

1272. A foreigner may not be deported if deportation is not permitted by the European Convention on Human Rights (section 60(5) AufenthG).[114] This means that the foreigner has to be protected against inhumane, degrading and cruel treatment, in particular against torture and the death penalty.

1273. A general danger that a foreigner may face prosecution and punishment in another State and, in the absence of any rules to the contrary in section 60(2)–(5) AufenthG, a real danger of lawful punishment under the legal system of another State does not, however, preclude deportation (section 60(6) AufenthG). These rules do apply if there is a danger that the death penalty is imposed or enforced, or that the foreigner might be exposed to cruel, inhumane or degrading punishment.

1274. A foreigner should not be deported to another State where he or she faces a substantial real danger to life and limb or liberty. A substantial real danger for health reasons only exists if there is life-threatening or serious illness which would significantly worsen if the foreigner were deported. It is not necessary that medical care in the destination State is comparable to medical care in Germany. Sufficient medical care generally exists if this is only available in parts of the State of destination. Substantial real danger to life and limb or liberty to which the population or segment of the population to which the foreigner belongs are generally exposed have to receive due consideration in decisions on temporary suspension of deportation for reasons of international law, on humanitarian grounds or to safeguard the political interests of Germany (section 60a(1), sentence 1, and section 60(7), sentence 5 AufenthG).

1275. In certain cases concerning public safety, the prohibition of deportation in section 60(1) AufenthG does not apply. When this is the case, is set out in section 60(8) AufenthG. There is no prohibition of deportation according to section 60(8)

---

114. BGBl. 1952 II p. 685.

and (1) AufenthG if a foreigner may not be deported to a State where a foreigner's life or liberty is under threat on account of his or her race, religion, nationality, membership of a certain social group or political convictions or if a foreigner is entitled to asylum, has been incontestably granted refugee status or who enjoys the status of foreign refugees on other grounds in Germany or has been granted foreign refugee status outside Germany in accordance with the 1951 UN Convention relating to the Status of Refugees if there are serious reasons why a foreigner is to be regarded as a threat to Germany's security or poses a threat to the general public because he or she has been incontestably sentenced to a term of imprisonment of at least three years for a crime or a particularly serious offence. The same applies if the foreigner satisfies the conditions in section 3(2) AsylG. This is the case if he or she has committed a serious offence such as a war crime or a crime against humanity. Application of this deportation prohibition may be waived if a foreigner represents a danger to the general public because he or she has been incontestably sentenced to a term of imprisonment or a youth custody of at least one year for one or more intentionally committed offences against life, physical integrity, sexual self-determination or property or for resisting enforcement officers if the criminal offence was committed using violence, using a threat of danger to life or limb, or with guile, or if the offence committed is rape or sexual assault by use of force or threat (section 177 of the Criminal Code).

1276. If there is a threat to public safety (section 60(8) AufenthG), a foreigner who has filed an application for asylum may, by way of derogation of the AsylG, be served an intention to deport and be duly deported. Section 60(2)–(7) AufenthG prohibiting deportation to States where a foreigner would risk a real severe danger remains unaffected.

1277. If a foreigner who cannot be deported to specific States as stipulated in section 60(1) AufenthG is to be deported, a notice of intention to deport must be served and a reasonable period must be allowed for departure. The States to which a foreigner may not be deported must be specified in the notice of intention to deport.

V. Suspension of Deportation

1278. Suspension of Deportation is of considerable importance as it affects rather a lot of foreigners (about 166,000 in 2017).[115] It is provided for in section 60a–60d AufenthG. The technical expression in German law is *Duldung*.

1279. For reasons of international law or on humanitarian grounds or to safeguard the political interests of Germany, the supreme *Land* authority may order the deportation of foreigners from specific States or of certain categories of foreigners defined by any other means to be suspended in general or with regard to deportation

---

115. Destatis, https://www.destatis.de/DE/ZahlenFakten/GesellschaftStaat/Bevoelkerung/MigrationInte gration/AuslaendischeBevolkerung/Tabellen/AufenthaltsrechtlicherStatus.html.

to specific States in particular for a maximum of three months. Section 23(1) AufenthG applies to a period in excess of six months. This means that a decision to prolong the suspension requires the approval of the Federal Office for Migration and Refugees.

1280. The deportation of a foreigner is suspended for as long as deportation is impossible in fact or in law and no temporary residence permit is granted.

1281. The deportation of a foreigner is also suspended if the public prosecutor's office or the criminal court considers the foreigner's temporary presence in Germany to be appropriate in connection with criminal proceedings relating to a criminal offence, because it would be more difficult to investigate the facts of the case without the foreigner's information.

1282. A foreigner may be granted a temporary suspension of deportation if his or her continued presence in Germany is necessary on urgent humanitarian or personal grounds or due to substantial public interests.

1283. Suspension of deportation for reasons of vocational training must be granted pursuant to section 60c AufenthG if a foreigner begins or has begun vocational training in a State-recognised education programme or a similarly regulated occupation which requires formal training in Germany, the conditions of section 60a(6) AufenthG prohibiting the pursuit of economic activities are not satisfied and no measures that will terminate a foreigner's right of residence are imminent. In these cases, suspension of deportation is granted for the duration of the vocational training specified in the training contract. In these cases, however, suspension of deportation is not granted and suspension of deportation granted for these reasons expires if a foreigner has been convicted for an offence intentionally committed in Germany. No account is as a rule to be taken of fines of a total of up to fifty daily rates or of up to ninety daily rates in the case of criminal offences which can, under the AufenthG or the AsylG, only be committed by foreigners. If a foreigner does not undertake or discontinues his or her training, the training institute is obliged to notify the competent foreigners authority in writing immediately, generally within one week, of this fact. This notification must include the facts to be notified, when they arose, as well as the surname, given names and the nationality of a foreigner. The suspension of deportation granted because of urgent personal reasons, i.e., vocational training, expires if a foreigner no longer undertakes or discontinues his or her training. If the training relationship is terminated before completion or is discontinued, a foreigner is granted a one-time suspension of deportation for six months for the purpose of seeking another training place in order to begin vocational training as provided for in section 60a(2), sentence 4 AufenthG. Suspension of deportation granted for vocational training is extended by six months for the purpose of seeking employment which matches the acquired professional qualification if, after successfully completing a vocational training for which suspension of deportation was granted, the foreigner is not employed by the organisation where he or she has been trained. Suspension of deportation granted to enable a foreigner to seek employment may not be extended for this purpose. Other reasons to suspend deportation provided for in section 60a AufenthG can still apply. Similar and special rules apply for suspension of deportation for reasons of employment pursuant to section 60d AufenthG; these will cease to apply on 1 December 2023.

1284. Similar and special rules apply to the suspension of deportation for reasons of employment pursuant to section 60d AufenthG. These rules will cease to apply on 1 December 2023.

1285. Where the official recording of the acknowledgement of paternity or the mother's consent to carry out a procedure in case of specific indications of wrongful acknowledgement of paternity (section 85a and section 60a(2), sentence 12 AufenthG) is suspended, the deportation of the foreigner acknowledging paternity, of the foreign mother or the foreign child is suspended until that procedure has been concluded by means of an enforceable decision.

1286. The deportation of a foreigner is suspended for one week if the foreigner's removal or deportation has failed, custody awaiting deportation was not ordered and Germany is legally obliged to readmit a foreigner, in particular by Article 6(1) of Council Directive 2003/110/EC on, among other, readmittance of foreigners whose removal to the country of destination was unsuccessful.[116] Suspension for this reason is not extendible. The foreigner must be granted permission to enter Germany.

1287. For as long as a foreigner who has been issued a temporary residence permit is a well-integrated juvenile or a young adult (section 25a(1) AufenthG) is a minor, the deportation of that minor's parents or the parent possessing the sole right of care and custody as well as of the minor children who live as a family with the parents or the parent with the sole right of care and custody should be suspended.

1288. It is assumed that deportation is not precluded on health grounds. A foreigner must substantiate that he or she suffers an illness which might impede deportation by submitting a medical certificate signed by a qualified medical professional. This medical certificate should, in particular, document the factual circumstances on the basis of which the professional assessment was made, the method of establishing the facts, the specialist's medical assessment of the disease pattern (diagnosis), the severity of the illness and how the medical condition will presumably develop, in the light of the medical assessment, in due course.

1289. A foreigner is obliged to submit that medical certificate immediately to the competent authority. If the foreigner fails to submit that medical certificate immediately, the competent authority may not take a foreigner's submissions regarding the illness into account, unless he or she was prevented, through no fault of his or her own, from obtaining the required medical certificate or if there is other factual

---

116. Article 6(1) of Council Directive 2003/110/EC of 25 Nov. 2003 on assistance in cases of transit for the purposes of removal by air, OJ EC 2003, L 321/26.

evidence of a life-threatening or serious illness which would be significantly worsened by deportation. If a foreigner submits a medical certificate and the competent authority then orders a medical examination, the competent authority may decide not to take the illness into consideration if the foreigner does not comply with the order without adequate reasons. The foreigner must be informed of the obligations and of the legal consequences of any breach of these obligations (section 60a(2d) AufenthG).

1290. Suspension of deportation does not affect a foreigner's obligation to leave Germany.

1291. A foreigner must be issued a certificate confirming the suspension of deportation.

1292. The suspension of deportation ends when a foreigner leaves Germany. Suspension is revoked when the circumstances preventing deportation cease to apply. A foreigner will be deported without delay when suspension ends, without a new notice of intention to deport specifying a deadline, unless suspension is extended. If deportation has been suspended for more than one year, prior notice of at least one month has to be served if the authorities intend to deport a foreigner by way of revocation. The foreigner has to be notified again if the suspension is extended for more than one year. This obligation to notify the foreigner at least one month before deportation can be executed does not apply if it is the foreigner who has created an obstacle to deportation by intentionally providing incorrect information or deceit concerning his or her identity or nationality or if a foreigner fails to comply with a reasonable request to cooperate with a view to removing any obstacle to his or her deportation.

1293. A foreigner whose deportation has been suspended may not pursue an economic activity if that foreigner has entered Germany to obtain benefits under the AsylbLG. The same applies if measures to terminate a foreigner's stay cannot be carried out for reasons for which the foreigner is responsible. A foreigner whose deportation has been suspended is also not permitted to pursue an economic activity if he or she is a national of a safe country of origin and an asylum application which was filed after 31 August 2015 has been rejected.

1294. Foreigners are, in particular, responsible if their residence cannot be terminated due to their deceit concerning their identity or nationality or by providing incorrect information.

1295. There is a special status for foreigners whose identity is undetermined. This is provided for in section 60b AufenthG. A foreigner who is enforceably required to leave Germany will be granted suspension of deportation in the form of a person with undetermined identity. This is the case if deportation cannot be enforced on grounds which the foreigner him- or herself is responsible for because the foreigner has created the obstacle to deportation by deception or wrong information about his or her identity or citizenship. The same applies if the foreigner does not perform reasonable efforts to obtain the necessary passport. The reasonable efforts are described in detail in section 60b(3) AufenthG. Persons with undetermined identity enjoy a less favourable status, e.g., they may not be allowed to perform gainful economic activity and are subject to residence restrictions (sections 60b(5), 61(1d) AufenthG).

VI. Deportation in Cases of Refusal of Asylum

A. *Asylum Application*

1. Deportation Order

1296. There are special provisions in the AsylG on deportation of foreigners whose asylum application has been refused.

1297. The Federal Office of Migration and refugees will issue a written deportation warning if a foreigner is not granted asylum status, refugee status, or subsidiary protection, the conditions justifying a prohibition of deportation are not met (section 60(5) and (7) AufenthG), and a foreigner does not hold a residence title. A hearing prior to issuing a deportation warning is not required. The moment that a deportation warning has been delivered to a foreigner is the moment from which that foreigner is required to leave Germany.

1298. A deportation order within the meaning of section 34a AsylG is adopted if the foreigner is to be deported to a safe third country or to a country responsible for the processing of the asylum application. The Federal Office for Migration and Refugees orders the foreigner's deportation to this country as soon as it has been ascertained that deportation can be carried out. This is also the case if a foreigner has filed an application for asylum in another country which is responsible for the processing of their asylum application according to EU law, an international agreement, or if a foreigner withdraws an asylum application before the Federal Office for Migration and Refugees has made a decision. No prior notification of deportation or the deadline for deportation is required. If it is not possible to order a foreigner's deportation, the Federal Office for Migration and Refugees notifies the foreigner that he or she will be deported to the country in question.

2. Application of Temporary Relief

1299. Appeals against a deportation order by way of temporary relief are to be filed within one week of notification. Deportation is not permitted until there is a court decision if the appeal has been filed in time. Applications for temporary relief against decisions of the Federal Office for Migration and Refugees setting time limits for entry or residence bans are to be filed within one week of the notification. This does not affect the enforceability of a deportation order.

3. Safe Third Countries

1300. If another EU Member State has already granted a foreigner international protection or if another safe third country is willing to readmit a foreigner (section 29(1), Nos 2 and 4 AsylG), the Federal Office for Migration and Refugees notifies that foreigner that he or she will be deported to that country.

1301. There are special procedural rules in section 36 AsylG that apply to cases where an application for asylum is inadmissible (section 29(1), Nos 2 and 4 AsylG) or manifestly unfounded. In these cases, the foreigner is given one week to leave Germany.

1302. The Federal Office for Migration and Refugees sends the persons involved a copy of their asylum file along with the decision. The administrative file is transmitted without delay to the competent administrative court along with proof of delivery.

1303. Appeals against the deportation warning in temporary relief procedures are to be filed within one week of notification. The deportation warning has to be enclosed with the appeal. A foreigner is informed of this. The rules in section 58 of the Code of Administrative Court Procedure on the information of legal remedies apply accordingly. The most important rule is that the time limit is at least one year if the information has not been provided or has been provided incorrectly. The decision is taken in a written procedure. An oral court hearing in which the action is heard at the same time is not permitted. The decision is to be taken within one week after the expiry of the one week period for leaving the country. The chamber of an administrative court may extend the time limit one week at a time. A second and additional extension of the time limit is only permitted for serious reasons, in particular if the court is not able to take a decision earlier due to an unusual heavy workload. No deportation is permitted prior to a court decision if the appeal has been filed in time. A decision is taken when the operative provisions of that decision have been signed by the judge or the judges and are available at the registry of the chamber. Applications for temporary relief against decisions by the Federal Office for Migration and Refugees to order or set time limits for an entry or residence ban (section 11(2) and (7) AufenthG) also have to be filed within one week of their notification. This does not affect the enforceability of a deportation warning.

1304. The procedural rules for appeal cases granted by court decision are set out in section 37 AsylG.

1305. In these cases a decision of the Federal Office for Migration and Refugees regarding the inadmissibility of an application (section 29(1), Nos 2 and 4 AsylG) and the deportation warning become ineffective if an administrative court grants the appeal in a temporary relief procedure. The Federal Office for Migration and Refugees then continues the asylum procedure.

1306. If, in the case of an asylum application which was turned down as manifestly unfounded, the administrative court grants an appeal in temporary relief procedures, the deadline for leaving the country expires thirty days after the incontestable conclusion of the asylum procedure.

1307. These rules do not apply, if, due to a decision of the administrative court, deportation to one of the countries mentioned in the deportation warning becomes enforceable. This is relevant if several countries are listed in the deportation warning.

4. Rejection of Asylum

1308. In those cases where a foreigner is not granted asylum status by the Federal Office for Migration and Refugees, a foreigner is given thirty days to leave the country (section 38 AsylG). If this decision is contested, the deadline for leaving the country is thirty days after the incontestable conclusion of the asylum procedure.

1309. If an asylum application is withdrawn prior to the decision of the Federal Office for Migration and Refugees, a foreigner is given one week to leave the country.

1310. If an asylum application is withdrawn, if action is brought or if the processing of the asylum application is waived, a foreigner may be given up to three months to leave the country if he or she agrees to do so voluntarily.

5. Notification

1311. Further requirements on the exchange of information between are set out in section 40 AsylG.

1312. The Federal Office for Migration and Refugees has to inform the foreigners authority of the district where the foreigner is required to stay or take up residence immediately of any enforceable deportation warning and immediately provide it with any documents required for deportation. It does the same if an administrative court has ruled that the suspensive effect of court action applies only with regard to deportation to the country where the court action is based (section 60(5) or (7) AufenthG). This also applies if the Federal Office for Migration and Refugees discontinues the asylum procedure.

1313. The Federal Office for Migration and Refugees informs the foreigners authority immediately if an administrative court rules that an action against the deportation notice is to have a suspensive effect in cases in which the deportation warning has been issued after a foreigner has withdrawn his or her asylum application (section 38(2) AsylG).

1314. If the Federal Office for Migration and Refugees serves a deportation order (section 34a AsylG) to a foreigner, the Federal Office informs the authority responsible for the deportation immediately of this delivery.

6. Reasons Precluding Deportation

1315. The foreigners authority is bound by a decision of the Federal Office for Migration and Refugees or an administrative court concerning the existence of reasons precluding deportation in the European Convention on Human Rights or if a foreigner is deported to another State where he or she will face a substantial real danger to his or her life and limb or liberty (section 60(5) or (7) AufenthG and section 42 AsylG). The foreigners authority decides whether one of the reasons precluding deportation has arisen or has ceased to exist at a later stage. This decision does not mean that a decision taken by the Federal Office for Migration and Refugees has to be suspended.

7. Deportation Warning

1316. If a foreigner possessed a residence title, a deportation warning which is enforceable under the terms of the AsylG may, as is stipulated in section 43 AsylG, not be enforced until that foreigner is enforceably required to leave the country under the terms of the AufenthG (section 58(2), second sentence AufenthG).

1317. If a foreigner has applied for an extension of a residence title with an overall validity of more than six months, a deportation warning is not enforceable until the application has been rejected. In other cases, applying for a residence title does not preclude deportation (section 81 AufenthG).

1318. Where family members (section 26(1)–(3) AsylG) have filed an asylum application simultaneously or in each case immediately upon their entry, the foreigners authority may temporarily suspend deportation in order to enable the family to leave the country together. The foreigners authority issues a certificate confirming the suspension of deportation to the foreigner.

B. *Follow-Up and Secondary Application*

1. Follow-Up Application

1319. In cases of unsuccessful follow-up asylum applications, special facilitating rules on deportation apply. If the conditions for resuming the processing of an asylum application (section 51(1)–(3) of the Administrative Procedure Act) are not met, the rules on deportation warnings, manifestly unfounded asylum applications and inadmissible applications because another country has already granted protection apply accordingly (sections 34, 35, and 36 AsylG). If an asylum applicant can be deported to a safe third country, a deportation order is issued (section 34a AsylG). These provisions facilitate the deportation of foreigners.

1320. If, after a deportation warning or a deportation order that has been issued according to the AsylG has become enforceable following the filing of a previous asylum application, the foreigner files a follow-up application which does not lead to a new asylum procedure, a new time limit and a new deportation warning or deportation order is not required in order to enforce deportation. Deportation may only be enforced after a notification by the Federal Office for Migration and Refugees that the conditions for resumption (section 51(1)–(3) of the Administrative Procedure Act) are not satisfied, unless the foreigner is to be deported to the safe third country.

1321. This also applies, if, in the meantime, the foreigner has temporarily left Germany. A foreigner who has entered Germany unlawfully from a safe third country may be removed to that country without prior notification by the Federal Office for Migration and Refugees (section 57(1) and (2) AufenthG).

1322. For purposes of deportation (section 71(5) and (6) AsylG) the responsibility for the execution of measures adopted in accordance with the laws on foreigners also lies with the foreigners authority in whose district the foreigner is resident.

1323. A follow-up application does not preclude an order to take the foreigner into custody awaiting deportation unless a further asylum procedure is carried out.

2.   Secondary Applications

1324. In cases of secondary asylum applications section 71(8) AsylG applies accordingly, Thus, a secondary application does not preclude an order to take a foreigner into custody awaiting deportation unless a further asylum procedure is carried out.

1325. The deportation of a foreigner is deemed to be temporarily suspended in the case of a secondary application.

1326. If a new asylum application is not processed, the deportation rules in sections 34–36 and 42–43 AsylG apply accordingly.

§5. MONITORING

I. Measures

1327. Monitoring foreigners who are required to leave Germany is possible for internal security reasons. The relevant rules are provided for by section 56 AufenthG.

1328. A foreigner subject to an expulsion order or a deportation order because he or she poses a particular threat is, under certain conditions, obliged to report to the police station which is responsible for the foreigner's place of residence at least once a week, unless the foreigners authority stipulates otherwise. This obligation to report to the police authorities may be imposed if a foreigner is enforceably required to leave Germany and there is a public interest in expelling the foreigner. This is the case if an expulsion order was issued because a foreigner is a threat to the free democratic basic order or the security of Germany or is involved in violent activities in the pursuit of political or religious objectives (section 54(1), Nos 2–5 AufenthG). A deportation order must have been issued because a foreigner poses a particular danger to Germany's security or poses a terrorist threat (section 58a AufenthG). The same obligation to report to the police authorities may be imposed if a foreigner is enforceably required to leave Germany if there is a public interest in expelling the foreigner as mentioned (section 56(1), sentence 2, No. 1 AufenthG). This also applies if a public interest in expelling the foreigner exists for reasons other than an interest in expulsion, and if the order to report to the police authorities is necessary to avert a danger to public safety and order (section 56(1), sentence 2, No. 2 AufenthG).

1329. The foreigner's right of residence is restricted in these cases to the district of the foreigners authority concerned, unless the foreigners authority stipulates otherwise.

1330. The foreigner concerned may be obliged to live in a different place of residence or in specified accommodation located outside the district of the foreigners authority concerned, if this appears expedient in order to hinder or prevent activities which have led to the expulsion order and to facilitate monitoring compliance with the rules on organisations and associations or other statutory conditions and obligations.

1331. In order to hinder or prevent activities which have led to the adoption of an expulsion order (section 54(1), Nos 2–5 AufenthG), an order within the meaning of section 56(1), sentence 2, No. 1 AufenthG or a deportation order (section 58a AufenthG), a foreigner may also be obliged not to get in contact with certain people or members of a specific group, not to keep company with them, not to employ them, train or house them and to refrain from using certain means of communication or communication services, insofar as means of communication remain at the foreigner's disposal and these restrictions are necessary in order to avert a significant risk to Germany's internal security or to the life and limb of others.

1332. Any obligations imposed on a foreigner who is required to leave German adopted in the context of monitoring that foreigner for internal security reasons (section 56(1)–(4) AufenthG) are suspended if a foreigner is placed in custody. An order to reside in a different place or in certain accommodation is immediately enforceable (section 56(3) and (5) AufenthG). The same applies to an order not to contact specific people or members of a specific group, not to keep company with them, not to employ them, train or house them and to refrain from using certain means of communication or communication services (section 56(4) and (5) AufenthG).

II. Electronic Location Monitoring

1333. In order to protect public safety in certain circumstances, electronic location monitoring is possible according to section 56a AufenthG.

1334. To prevent serious threats to internal security or to the life and limb of others, foreigners who are the subject of a geographic restriction (section 56(2) and (3) AufenthG) or a contact ban (section 56(4) AufenthG) may be required, by court order, to carry the technical devices necessary to permanently monitor their location at all times, keep the devices ready for service, and not impair their functionality.

1335. This order may be issued for no longer than three months. It may be extended by three-month periods at the most, provided that the requirements continue to be met. If the conditions that justified the order in the first place cease to exist, the measure has to be stopped immediately.

1336. The foreigners authority collects and stores, with the help of the technical devices that a foreigner carries and in an automated manner, data on a foreigner's location and on any impairments of the data collection.

1337. To the extent that this is technically possible, it must be ensured that no location data are collected in the foreigner's home other than that the foreigner is or is not present. The *Land* governments may determine by statutory instrument that an authority other than the foreigners authority collects and stores this data. Such authorisation may be transferred, by statutory instrument, from the *Land* governments to the supreme *Land* authorities responsible for the enforcement of the AufenthG.

1338. Without the consent of the person concerned, the data may only be used to the extent necessary to establish violations of a geographic restriction (section 56(2) and (3) AufenthG) or a contact ban (section 56(4) AufenthG). They may be used to prosecute a violation of a geographic restriction which is an administrative offence (section 56(2) or section 61(1), sentence 1, and section 98(3), No. 5a AufenthG). The same applies if a foreigner repeatedly fails to meet an obligation to report to the authorities, repeatedly violates a geographic restriction or another condition restricting a foreigner's stay, a failure to comply with the obligation to take up residence in a designated facility despite having been notified repeatedly as to the legal consequences of such a failure, to use a certain means of communication or a specific contact ban (section 56 and section 95(1), No. 6a AufenthG). These are criminal offences. The data that is collected may also be used to establish violations of an enforceable court order to prevent a serious threat to Germany's internal security or to the life and limb of others (section 56a(1) AufenthG) and to prosecute the criminal offence of entering Germany in violation of an entry and residence ban (section 11(1), (6), sentence 1, or (7), sentence 1, and section 95(2), No. 1a AufenthG). Furthermore, this data may also be used to avert a current threat to the life, limb or liberty of a third person, to prosecute serious crimes against the life and limb of a third person, the preparation of a serious violent offence endangering the State (section 89a of the Criminal Code) or to set up a terrorist organisation (section 129a of the Criminal Code). Finally, the data may be used to maintain the functionality of the technical devices used to collect the data.

1339. To comply with the purpose limitation requirement (section 56a(4) AufenthG), data must be processed automatically and are to be protected, especially against unauthorised disclosure. The data stored on a foreigner's location and on impairments of the data collection (section 56a(3), sentence 1 AufenthG) must be deleted no later than two months after their collection, insofar as they are not used for the purposes stated in section 56a(4) AufenthG, this includes establishing violations of a geographic restriction and the aversion of a current threat to the life, limb or liberty of a third person. Any retrieval of data must be logged. The log data must be deleted after twelve months. If location data is collected in the home of the person concerned other than that the person is present or not, this data may not be used and must be deleted immediately after observing that this data has been logged. A written record has to be made hereof and that this data has been deleted. This record may be used exclusively for the purpose of data protection monitoring. It must be deleted when data protection monitoring is completed.

Chapter 2. Sanctions Against Persons Helping Illegal Entry and Residence

§1. HUMAN SMUGGLING

I. Inciting or Assisting Unlawful Entry

1340. The AufenthG provides penal sanctions in cases of human smuggling. According to section 96 AufenthG a person is punishable who incites another person to commit or assists that person in the commission of an act pursuant to section 95(1), No. 3 or (2), No. 1(a) AufenthG and receives a pecuniary advantage or the promise of a pecuniary advantage in return. The same applies if the person acts in such a manner repeatedly or for the benefit of several foreigners. The punishment is imprisonment of three months to five years, in less serious cases imprisonment of up to five years or a fine. This crime refers to wilfully entering Germany not possessing a required passport or passport substitute or not possessing the residence title required (section 95(1), No. 3, section 14(1), No. 1 or 2, section 3(1), and section 4(1) AufenthG). It also applies to wilfully entering Germany in contravention to a ban on entry because of having been expelled, removed or deported (section 95(2), No. 1(a), and section 11(1) AufenthG). It equally applies to wilfully entering Germany in contravention to a ban on entry and residence which has been imposed against the foreigner for not having fulfilled the obligation to leave the country within the period allowed for departure (section 95(2), No. 1(a), and section 11(6), sentence 1 AufenthG). It furthermore applies to wilfully entering Germany in contravention to an enforceable order to leave the country if a ban on entry and residence has been imposed on a foreigner in one of the following circumstances: the foreigner does not possess a residence title and his or her asylum application was rejected as manifestly unfounded; the foreigner was not granted subsidiary protection; there does not apply any prohibition of deportation on the ground of the European Convention of Human Rights or because of a substantial concrete danger to life and limb or liberty in the country to which deportation would take place; or the foreigner's asylum application repeatedly did not lead to a follow-up asylum procedure (section 95(2), No. 1(a), and section 11(7), sentence 1 AufenthG).

II. Inciting or Assisting Unlawful Residence

1341. Punishable is anyone who incites another person to commit or assists that person in committing an act pursuant to section 95(1), Nos 1, 2, (1a) or (2), No. 1(b) or No. 2 AufenthG (section 96(1), No. 2 AufenthG) and receives a pecuniary advantage or the promise of a pecuniary advantage in return. The punishment is imprisonment of three months to five years, in less serious cases it is imprisonment of up to five years or a fine. Inciting or assisting refers to the following acts.

Punishable is inciting or assisting wilfully residing in Germany without the necessary identification documents (section 95(1), No. 1, and sections 3(1), 48(2) AufenthG).

Punishable is inciting or assisting wilfully residing in Germany without the necessary residence title if the foreigner is enforceably required to leave Germany, has not been granted a period for departure or this has expired, and the deportation has not been suspended (section 95(1), No. 2, and section 4(1), sentence 1 AufenthG). An act carried out without the necessary residence title is deemed equivalent to an act carried out on the basis of a residence title obtained by threat, bribery or collusion or by furnishing incorrect or incomplete information (section 95(6) AufenthG).

Punishable is inciting or assisting wilfully committing an act of specified economic activity while requiring a residence title in order to reside in Germany, but only possessing a residence title in the form of a Schengen visa (section 95(1a) AufenthG, section 404(2), No. 4 of Book Three of the Social Code, section 98(3), No. 1, section 4(1), sentence 1, and section 6(1), No. 1 AufenthG).

Punishable is inciting or assisting wilfully residing in Germany in contravention to a ban on entry because of having been expelled, removed or deported (section 95(2), No. 1(b), and section 11(1) AufenthG). This equally applies to wilfully entering or residing in Germany in contravention to a ban on entry and residence which has been imposed against the foreigner for not having fulfilled the obligation to leave the country within the period allowed for departure (section 95(2), No. 1(b), and section 11(6), sentence 1 AufenthG). It furthermore applies to wilfully entering Germany in contravention to an enforceable order to leave the country if a ban on entry and residence has been imposed on a foreigner in one of the following circumstances: the foreigner does not possess a residence title and his or her asylum application was rejected as manifestly unfounded; the foreigner was not granted subsidiary protection; there does not apply any prohibition of deportation on the ground of the European Convention of Human Rights or because of a substantial concrete danger to life and limb or liberty in the country to which deportation would take place; or the foreigner's asylum application repeatedly did not lead to a follow-up asylum procedure (section 95(2), No. 1(a), and section 11(7), sentence 1 AufenthG).

Punishable is inciting or assisting furnishing or using false or incomplete information in order to procure a residence title or a suspension of deportation for oneself or for another. The same applies in case of inciting or assisting furnishing or using false or incomplete information in order to prevent the expiry or subsequent restriction of a residence title or the suspension of deportation. It also applies to inciting or assisting knowingly using a document procured in this manner for the purpose of deceit in legal matters (section 95(2), No. 2 AufenthG).

III. Aggravating Circumstances

1342. In all of the aforementioned cases of incitement and assistance, the person responsible can be punished with a prison sentence of between six months and ten years if that person has acted for gain, as a member of a gang which has been formed for the purpose of habitually committing such offences, or if that person has subjected the smuggled person to potentially fatal, inhumane or humiliating treatment or a risk of sustaining severe damage to that person's health (section 96(2), Nos 1, 2, and 5 AufenthG).

The same applies to anyone who carries a firearm when committing the crimes, if the offence concerns an act listed in section 95(1), No. 3 or (2), No. 1(a) AufenthG (section 96(2) AufenthG). This section covers wilfully entering Germany whilst not possessing the required passport or passport substitute or not possessing a residence title as required (section 95(1), No. 3, section 14(1), No. 1 or 2, section 3(1), and section 4(1) AufenthG). It also applies to wilfully entering Germany in contravention of an entry ban issued following expulsion, removal or deportation (section 95(2), No. 1(a), and section 11(1) AufenthG). It equally applies to wilfully entering Germany in contravention of an entry and residence ban which was imposed because the foreigner has failed to fulfil the obligation to leave the country within the period allowed for departure (section 95(2), No. 1(a), and section 11(6), sentence 1 AufenthG). It furthermore applies to wilfully entering Germany in contravention to an enforceable order to leave the country if a ban on entry and residence has been imposed on a foreigner in one of the following circumstances: the foreigner does not possess a residence title and his or her asylum application was rejected as manifestly unfounded; the foreigner was not granted subsidiary protection; there does not apply any prohibition of deportation on the ground of the European Convention of Human Rights or because of a substantial concrete danger to life and limb or liberty in the country to which deportation would take place; or the foreigner's asylum application repeatedly did not lead to a follow-up asylum procedure (section 95(2), No. 1(a), and section 11(7), sentence 1 AufenthG).

Aggravating circumstances also exist, if the perpetrator of these offences carries another type of weapon and uses that weapon in connection with one of these offences (section 96(2), No. 4 AufenthG). Equally, a person awaits the same punishment of imprisonment between six months and ten years if he or she acts in favour of a minor and unmarried foreigner who enters Germany without being accompanied by a person possessing the right of personal care and custody or a third person who has taken over care of or custody for the minor if the person receives a pecuniary advantage or the promise of a pecuniary advantage in return (section 96(1), No. 1(a), and (2), sentence 2 AufenthG).

An attempt is punishable in all of the aforementioned cases (section 96(3) AufenthG).

In several cases, these provisions apply accordingly to breaches of another EU Member State's or Schengen State's immigration rules. Section 96(1), No. 1(a), No. 2, (2), sentence 1, Nos 1, 2 and 5 and (3) AufenthG, concerning aggravated forms of human smuggling, are applicable to contraventions of statutory rules on the entry of foreigners into the territory of the EU Member States or of a Schengen State and the rules on residence as a foreigner in those territories. This presupposes that these violations correspond to the acts specified in section 95(1), No. 2 or 3 or section 2, No. 1 AufenthG and the offender supports a foreigner who is not a national of an EU Member State or of another State party to the EEA Agreement (section 96(4) AufenthG).

Section 74a of the Criminal Code applies to all of these offences (section 96(5) AufenthG). Thus, objects may be the subject of a deprivation order, if, at the time of the decision, the person who owns them or has a right to them contributed at least recklessly to the objects being used as the means of the crime or if they were the object of the crime of human smuggling or its preparation. This also holds true if a person has acquired the objects in a reprehensible manner in the full knowledge of the circumstances, which would have allowed for their confiscation.

Anyone responsible for the death of a person who is smuggled into Germany (section 96(1) AufenthG), is, pursuant to section 97(1) AufenthG, punishable with a prison sentence of no less than three years. This also applies to smuggling foreigners into one of the other EU Member States or a Schengen State (section 96(4) AufenthG). Less serious such cases are punishable with a prison sentence of between one year and ten years. Here, too, section 74a of the Criminal Code applies to all of these offences (section 97(4) AufenthG). Thus, objects may be the subject of a deprivation order, if, at the time of the decision, the person who owns them or has a right to them contributed at least recklessly to the objects being used as the means of the crime or if they were the object of the crime of human smuggling or its preparation. This also holds true if a person has acquired the objects in a reprehensible manner in the full knowledge of the circumstances, which would have allowed for their confiscation.

Anyone acting for gain as a member of a gang which has been formed for the purpose of habitually smuggling foreigners into Germany (section 96(1) AufenthG), is, pursuant to section 97(2) AufenthG, punishable with a prison sentence of between one and ten years. This is also the penalty for smuggling foreigners into one of the other EU Member States or the Schengen States (section 96(4) AufenthG). Less serious cases are punishable with a prison sentence of between six months and ten years. Section 74a of the Criminal Code applies to all of these offences (section 97(4) AufenthG). Thus, again, objects may be the subject of a deprivation order, if, at the time of the decision, the person who owns them or has a right to them contributed at least recklessly to the objects being used as the means of the crime or if they were the object of the crime of human smuggling or its preparation. This also holds true if a person has acquired the objects in a reprehensible manner in the full knowledge of the circumstances, which would have allowed for their confiscation.

§2. Human Trafficking

I. Measures

1343. Human trafficking is a crime that can be punished pursuant to sections 232 et seq. of the Criminal Code. The Criminal Code distinguishes between various forms of human trafficking in several specified provisions. It uses a variety of terms to indicate specifics of criminal behaviour, such as forced prostitution, forced labour, exploitation of labour. Also, the term human trafficking itself has a specific meaning in German criminal law, The provisions pay special attention to persons who are in a foreign country.

In some cases (section 232, 232a(1)–(5), sections 232b, 233(1)–(4), and section 233a of the Criminal Code) a court may adopt a supervision order (section 68(1) and section 233b of the Criminal Code).

II. Forms of Human Trafficking

1344. Human trafficking in its specific meaning is a punishable crime under section 232 of the Criminal Code. An attempt to commit the offence is punishable.

Whoever recruits, transports, transfers, harbours or receives another person by taking advantage of that person's personal or financial predicament or helplessness on account of being in a foreign country, or that person is under 21 years of age, incurs a penalty of imprisonment for a term of between six months and five years if one of the following purposes is pursued with the act. The person is to be exploited by way of engaging in prostitution or performing sexual acts on or in the presence of the offender or a third person, or having sexual acts performed on them by the offender or a third person. The person is to be exploited by way of employment, begging or committing criminal offences. Exploitation through employment occurs if the employment, in serving the ruthless pursuit of profit, takes place under working conditions, which are strikingly different to those of others performing the same or a similar activity. This is called exploitative employment. It is also human trafficking if the purpose of the act is to hold the person in slavery, bonded labour, debt bondage or under corresponding or similar conditions. The same applies if the purpose is to illegally remove an organ from that person.

Whoever, with respect to another person who is to be exploited in the manner just referred to recruits, transports, transfers, harbours or receives that person by force, by threat of serious harm or by deception incurs a penalty of imprisonment for a term of between six months and ten years. The same applies if the offender abducts that person or gains physical control over him or her or encourages a third person to gain physical control over him or her.

The penalty is six months to ten years imprisonment, if the victim is under 18 at the time of the offence. The same punishment applies if the offender seriously physically ill-treats the victim or, by committing the offence or an act committed during the offence, at least recklessly places the victim in danger of death or at risk of serious damage to health. The offender is also liable to the punishment of six months up to ten years imprisonment if he or she acts on a commercial basis or as a member of a gang whose purpose is the continued commission of such offences.

III. Forced Prostitution

1345. Forcing someone into prostitution is a punishable crime under section 232a of the Criminal Code. In all forms of forced prostitution, an attempt is also punishable.

A person commits the crime of forced prostitution who, by taking advantage of another person's personal or financial predicament or helplessness on account of being in a foreign country, causes that person or causes another person under 21 years of age to engage in or continue to engage in prostitution. The same applies if the offender causes those persons under such circumstances to perform sexual acts, by way of which they are exploited, on or in the presence of the offender or a third person or to allow sexual acts to be performed on them by the offender or a third person. The penalty is imprisonment for a term of between six months and ten years. The penalty is imprisonment for a term of between one year and ten years if the victim is under 18 at the time of the offence. The same increased punishment applies if the offender seriously physically ill-treats the victim or, by committing the offence or an act committed during the offence, at least recklessly places the victim in danger of death or at risk of serious damage to health. The offender is also liable to the punishment of one year up to ten years imprisonment if he or she acts on a commercial basis or as a member of a gang whose purpose is the continued commission of such offences. In less serious cases, the penalty is imprisonment for a term of between three months and five years.

Causing another person by force, by threat of serious harm or by deception to engage or continue to engage in prostitution or to perform specific sexual acts is even more severely punishable. The specified acts are sexual acts on or in the presence of the offender or a third person. The increased punishment is imprisonment for a term of between one year and ten years. It is imprisonment for a term of at least one year if the victim is under 18 at the time of the offence. This determination of a specific minimum term means that the punishment may not be reduced even if mitigating circumstances exist on the side of the offender. The same increased punishment applies if the offender seriously physically ill-treats the victim or, by committing the offence or an act committed during the offence, at least recklessly places the victim in danger of death or at risk of serious damage to health. The offender is also liable to the punishment of at least one year of imprisonment if he or she acts on a commercial basis or as a member of a gang whose purpose is the continued commission of such offences. However, in less serious cases of the act performed by force, threat of serious harm or by deception, the punishment is imprisonment for a term of between six months and ten years.

It is also punishable to make use of such prostitution. Whoever performs sexual acts on or allows sexual acts to be performed on them for a consideration by a person engaging in prostitution commits a crime if the following circumstances apply. The person engaging in prostitution must have been the victim of human trafficking in the form of exploitation by way of engaging in prostitution or performing sexual acts on or in the presence of the offender or a third person, or having sexual acts performed on them by the offender or a third person, Alternatively, the person must be a victim of forced prostitution. The crime also presupposes that the offender, in performing the action, takes advantage of that person's personal or financial predicament or helplessness on account of being in a foreign country. The penalty is imprisonment for a term of between three months and five years. Whoever voluntarily reports such an offence committed against a person engaging in prostitution as described to the competent authority or voluntarily occasions such a report to be made incurs no such penalty, unless the act had already been discovered, in whole or in part, at the time and the offender knew this or based on a reasonable assessment of the circumstances, should have expected this.

IV. Forced Labour

1346. Forced labour is a punishable crime under section 232b of the Criminal Code. In all forms of forced labour, an attempt is also punishable.

The crime of forced labour commits anyone who, by taking advantage of another person's personal or financial predicament or helplessness on account of being in a foreign country, causes that person or causes another person under 21 years of age to engage in or continue to engage in exploitative employment. As stated in section 232(1), sentence 2 of the Criminal Code, exploitation through employment occurs if the employment, in serving the ruthless pursuit of profit, takes place under working conditions, which are strikingly different to those of others performing the same or a similar activity. The crime of forced labour also commits who, again by taking advantage of another person's personal or financial predicament or helplessness on account of being in a foreign country, causes that person or causes another person under 21 years of age to enter into slavery, bonded labour, debt bondage or corresponding or similar conditions. The same applies if, under the said conditions, the offender causes the victim to engage in or continue to engage in begging as a result of which that person is exploited.

The penalty in all of these cases is imprisonment for a term of between six months and ten years. However, the penalty is imprisonment for a term of between one year and ten years if the victim is under 18 at the time of the offence. The same increased punishment applies if the offender seriously physically ill-treats the victim or, by committing the offence or an act committed during the offence, at least recklessly places the victim in danger of death or at risk of serious damage to health. The offender is also liable to the punishment of one year up to ten years imprisonment if he or she acts on a commercial basis or as a member of a gang whose purpose is the continued commission of such offences. In less serious cases, the penalty is imprisonment for a term of between three months and five years.

The penalty is imprisonment for a term of between one year and ten years in even more serious circumstances. This is the case for anybody who, by force, by threat of serious harm or by deception, causes another person to engage in or continue to engage in exploitative employment. Again, exploitative employment occurs if the employment, in serving the ruthless pursuit of profit, takes place under working conditions which are strikingly different to those of others performing the same or a similar activity (section 232(1), sentence 2 of the Criminal Code), This more serious form of the crime of forced labour also commits who, by force, by threat of serious harm or by deception, causes another person to enter into slavery, bonded labour, debt bondage or corresponding or similar conditions or to engage in or continue to engage in begging as a result of which that person is exploited.

The penalty is stricter in certain aggravated cases. It is imprisonment for a term of at least one year if the victim is under 18 at the time of the offence. Again, this determination of a specific minimum term means that the punishment may not be reduced even if mitigating circumstances exist on the side of the offender. The same increased punishment applies if the offender seriously physically ill-treats the victim or, by committing the offence or an act committed during the offence, at least recklessly places the victim in danger of death or at risk of serious damage to health. The offender is also liable to the punishment of at least one year of imprisonment if he or she acts on a commercial basis or as a member of a gang whose purpose is the continued commission of such offences. However, in less serious cases of the act performed by force, threat of serious harm or by deception, the punishment is imprisonment for a term of between six months and ten years.

V. Work Exploitation

1347. Work exploitation is a punishable crime under section 233 of the Criminal Code. The crime is also called 'exploitation of labour'. An attempt is punishable in all cases of work exploitation.

Anyone who, by taking advantage of another person's personal or financial predicament or helplessness on account of being in a foreign country, exploits that person or exploits a person under 21 years of age, by way of that person engaging in employment within the meaning of section 232(1), sentence 2 of the Criminal Code commits the crime of work exploitation. This, again, means exploitative employment, which occurs if the employment, in serving the ruthless pursuit of profit, takes place under working conditions, which are strikingly different to those that are enjoyed by others performing the same or a similar activity. It is also work exploitation if, under the said circumstances of predicament, helplessness or young age, the offender exploits the person by way of that person begging or committing criminal offences, The penalty is imprisonment for a term not exceeding three years or a fine. In less serious cases, the penalty is imprisonment of up to two years or a fine.

The penalty is imprisonment of six months to ten years, if the victim is under 18 years of age at the time of the offence. The same penalty applies if the offender seriously physically abuses the victim or places the victim at least with gross negligence in danger of death or a serious injury through the offence or an act performed when committing the offence. It also applies if the offender subjects the victim to economic need or considerably increases an already existing economic need by withholding the reward normal for the activity performed by the victim. Furthermore, the penalty applies if the offender acts as a member of a gang whose purpose is the continued commission of such offences. In less serious cases, the penalty is imprisonment from three months to five years.

Anyone is liable to imprisonment of up to two years or a fine who aids and abets an act of exploitative employment (section 232(1), sentence 2 of the Criminal Code) by acting as an intermediary to arrange exploitative employment, renting out business premises, or renting out living space to the person to be exploited. This does not apply if the offence is already punishable with a more severe punishment under another provision.

VI. Exploitation Involving Deprivation of Liberty

1348. Exploitation by taking advantage of deprivation of liberty is a punishable crime under section 233a of the Criminal Code. This crime does not make particular reference to situations of migration. In practice, however, victims of such crimes are often migrants. The attempt to commit the offence is punishable.

Anyone commits the crime of exploitation involving deprivation of liberty who imprisons another person or otherwise subjects another person to deprivation of liberty and exploits that person in that situation in specific ways. These are having that person engage in prostitution, begging, commit criminal offences, or engage in exploitative employment. Such exploitative employment, as has already been stated above, occurs if the employment, in serving the ruthless pursuit of profit, takes place under working conditions which are strikingly different to those of others performing the same or a similar activity (section 232(1), sentence 2 of the Criminal Code). The penalty is imprisonment from six months to ten years. In less serious cases, the penalty is imprisonment from three months to five years.

The penalty is imprisonment from one to ten years if the victim is under 18 years of age at the time of the offence, the offender seriously physically ill-treats the victim or, by committing the offence or an activity committed during the offence, at least recklessly places the victim in danger of death or at risk of serious damage to health. The same increased penalty applies if the offender, by withholding from the victim, in full or in part, the usual consideration paid for the activity he or she is engaged in, places the victim in financial hardship or substantially exacerbates any existing financial hardship. The increased penalty also applies if the offender acts as a member of a gang whose purpose is the continued commission of such offences (section 233(2), Nos 1–4 of the Criminal Code). In less serious cases, the penalty is imprisonment from six months to ten years.

Part VI. Legal Remedies and Procedural Safeguards

Chapter 1. Legal Remedies in Refusal of Right to Enter, Stay or Reside Cases

1349. In general, all administrative acts of the German authorities are open to legal recourse. Usually, the administrative courts are the competent courts to deal with these cases. There are some limits to the right to appeal certain administrative acts, which can be found in section 83 AufenthG.

A denial to issue a national visa and a passport substitute at the border cannot be appealed. When an application for a national visa or a passport substitute is rejected at the border, a foreigner is informed of the possibility of filing an application with the competent diplomatic mission abroad.

Should a visa application be rejected, the applicant is to be informed of the main reasons for this rejection. Every applicant is entitled to take legal recourse against the diplomatic mission's decision.[117]

The refusal to suspend deportation is not contestable.

An order and the imposition of a time limit on a ban on entry and residence by the Federal Office for Migration and Refugees is not contestable.

While, as a general rule, objections against legal actions have suspensory effect and may therefore not be implemented until a decision on the objection has been adopted, suspensory effect can be withheld in a number of migration law cases pursuant to section 84 AufenthG.

There is no suspensory effect when an objection or legal action is lodged against a refusal to issue or extend a residence title, measures verifying, establishing and documenting a person's identity (section 49 AufenthG). There also is no suspensory effect of an objection or of a legal action lodged against a condition that obliges a foreigner to reside in a departure facility or a conditions imposed to secure and enforce the enforceable obligation to leave the country (section 61(1e) AufenthG). This is also the case for an objection against the amendment or rescission of a subsidiary provision concerning the pursuit of an economic activity, the revocation of the foreigner's residence title (section 52(1), sentence 1, No. 4 AufenthG), the cases covered by section 75(2), sentence 1 AsylG which includes grave crimes committed by a foreigner. There is also no suspensory effect of legal action against the revocation or withdrawal of the recognition of a research establishment for the purpose

---

117. https://www.auswaertiges-amt.de/en/einreiseundaufenthalt/visabestimmungen-node#content_6.

of concluding admission agreements for researchers (section 18d AufenthG). The same is also the case for objections against departure bans (section 46(2), sentence 1 AufenthG), the decision imposing a ban on entry and residence with a time limit (section 11 AufenthG), a ban on entry and residence (section 11(6) AufenthG), and a decision that wrongfully determines the acknowledgement of paternity (section 85a(1), sentence 2 AufenthG).

Likewise, an action filed against an order containing a ban on entry and residence (section 11(7) AufenthG) does not have a suspensory effect.

Notwithstanding suspensory effect, an objection or legal action does not affect the operative effect of an expulsion or any other administrative act terminating lawful residence.

For purpose of pertaining admission or the pursuit of an economic activity, the residence title is deemed to remain in force until expiry of the deadline for raising an objection or instituting legal action, during judicial proceedings concerning a permissible application for the institution or restoration of suspensory effect or for as long as the submitted legal remedy has a suspensory effect.

The lawfulness of residence is not interrupted if an administrative act is revoked by an official decision or by an incontestable court ruling.

Chapter 2. Legal Remedies in Detention Cases

1350. The local court (*Amtsgericht*) decides on detention matters. The foreigner as well as the foreigners authority can file a complaint against a decision of a local court with the district court (*Landgericht*) pursuant to section 58 of the Act on Court Procedure in Family Matters and Non-litigious Matters (*Gesetz über das Verfahren in Familiensachen und in den Angelegenheiten der freiwilligen Gerichtsbarkeit*). There is a further remedy before the Federal Supreme Court (*Bundesgerichtshof*) to contest the decision in a legal complaint procedure against a decision of the district court to in section 70(3), No. 3 of the Act on Court Procedure in Family Matters and Non-litigious Matters.

Chapter 3. Other Legal Remedies

1351. There are ample legal procedures before a court of law to contest an administrative decision. As a matter of principle, there is a great variety of actions and complaint procedures, which can be used to contest all administrative actions that violate individual rights before a court. In the law on foreigners, some of these measures have been limited in order to speed up procedures. They are dealt with in the individual contexts.

A constitutional complaint to the Federal Constitutional Court is an extraordinary remedy that can be used by a foreigner where his or her fundamental rights have been violated.

Part VII. Access to the Labour Market

Chapter 1. Overview of Applicable Legislation

1352. Foreigners holding a residence title may pursue an economic activity unless there is a law prohibiting such activity. This principle is set out in section 4a(1) AufenthG. While there are many provisions prohibiting economic activity of foreigners, especially in the AufenthG itself, the principle is meant to facilitate labour migration. The economic activity may be restricted by law. The pursuit of an economic activity going beyond a ban or restriction requires permission.

Every residence title must indicate whether the pursuit of an economic activity is permitted and whether it is subject to any restrictions (section 4a(3) AufenthG). Further details are detail with in more detail above in Chapter 4.

An important institution in procedure to obtain permission to access the German labour market is the Federal Employment Agency. This agency has to give its approval before the foreigners authorities in general can issue a residence permit that includes the right to participate in the labour market.

Access of foreigners to the labour market is primarily regulated by the AufenthG and the AsylG. The rules in these Acts are supplemented by those in the Ordinance on Employment.

The Act to Combat Clandestine Employment, in section 1(3), explicitly declares it to be illegal employment if an employer illicitly employs a foreigner or as a hirer lets him or her become active. It also constitutes illegal employment if a foreigner illicitly carries out gainful activities.

EU law governs the access of EU citizens and persons with an equivalent status to the German labour market.

Rules on the labour conditions that apply to foreign workers are found in the AEntG. These rules aim at guaranteeing fair labour conditions for all workers and fair conditions of economic competition.

Within the field of its competence, the Federal Ministry of Labour and Social Affairs may regulate certain issues by means of statutory instruments. This competence is spelled out in section 42 AufenthG. For some statutory instruments, the Federal Ministry of Labour and Social Affairs needs the consent of the *Bundesrat*, through which the *Länder*, pursuant to Article 50 of the Basic Law, participate, *inter alia*, in the adoption of legislation and the administration of Germany. This is, e.g., the case when determining the types of employment for which no approval is necessary from the Federal Employment Agency or the exceptions for nationals of certain States. For certain other ordinances, the Ministry of Labour and Social Affairs does not need the consent of the *Bundesrat*. Examples are ordinances regulating the conditions and the procedure for the Federal Employment Agency to grant its approval.

Furthermore, the Federal Ministry of Labour and Social Affairs may issue instructions to the Federal Employment Agency on the implementation of the provisions of the AufenthG and the statutory instruments issued in connection with it, of the provisions enacted by the EU on access to the labour market and of the intergovernmental agreements on the employment of workers.

Chapter 2. Conditions to Work as an Employed Person

§1. CONDITIONS

1353. Various conditions apply to a foreigner who wishes to work in Germany as an employee. These conditions are found in a large number of provisions in the AufenthG and the AsylG. They are dealt with primarily above.[118]

The basic requirements for access to the labour market are set out in section 39 AufenthG.

A residence title which permits a foreigner to take up employment may only be granted with the approval of the Federal Employment Agency, unless pursuant to a law, on the basis of the Employment Ordinance or an international instrument it is provided that such approval is not necessary. Approval to work may be granted if provided for by a law, in the Employment Ordinance, or in an intergovernmental agreement.

The Federal Employment Agency may approve to taking up employment by a skilled worker if a number of requirements are met such as equal terms of employment, The approval for employment of a skilled worker is granted without an examination of priority – the labour market test – unless the Employment Ordinance stipulates otherwise. This means that it is not examined whether there are no German workers available for the type of employment concerned, and also no foreigners who already have the same legal status as German workers with regard to the right to take up employment or other foreigners who are entitled to preferential access to the labour market under EU law.

The skilled worker must not be employed on terms less favourable than those that apply to comparable German workers. It must be qualified employment to which the skilled worker is qualified by his or her qualification or, in the case of professions in science and engineering, medical doctors, and information and communications technology professionals, pursues an employment commensurate to his or her qualification. Furthermore, it must be a national employment and the specific requirements, if any, in view of the pursuit of the employment stipulated in the Employment Ordinance must be met.

The approval is granted without an examination of priority – the labour market test – unless the Employment Ordinance stipulates otherwise. This means that it is not examined whether there are no German workers available for the type of employment concerned, and also no foreigners who already have the same legal status as German workers with regard to the right to take up employment or other foreigners who are entitled to preferential access to the labour market under EU law.

The Federal Employment Agency may approve the pursuit of an employment by a foreigner regardless of his or her qualification as a skilled worker if the foreigner is not employed on terms less favourable than apply to comparable German workers. Furthermore, no German workers, foreigners having the same legal status as German workers with regard to the right to take up employment or other foreigners

---

118. *See* Part III, Ch. 4 and Ch. 6, §3, I, C and II, D.

who are entitled to preferential access to the labour market under EU law are available (examination of priority, also called labour-market test), as far as such examination is prescribed by the Employment Ordinance.

The employer must furnish the Federal Employment Agency with information on pay, working hours and other terms and conditions of employment. Upon request of the Federal Employment Agency the employer who employs or has employed the foreigner has to furnish this information within one month.

The general rules on granting approval for employment by a foreigner (section 39(1) AufenthG), the rules on granting approval for employment by a foreigner regardless of his or her qualifications as a skilled worker (section 39(3) AufenthG) and the obligation to provide information to the Federal Employment Agency (section 39(4) AufenthG) also apply if approval is required for foreigners whose residence purpose is not employment but study, international obligations, humanitarian or political rights or the right of return set out in Chapter 2 Parts 3, 5 or 7 of the AufenthG.

The rules that apply to the pursuit of an employment by a foreigner regardless of his or her qualification as a skilled worker (section 39(3) AufenthG) apply accordingly to the granting of a seasonal work permit. That means that the Federal Employment Agency may approve the pursuit of employment as a seasonal worker if the foreigner is not employed on terms less favourable than apply to comparable German workers. Furthermore, no German workers, foreigners having the same legal status as German workers with regard to the right to take up employment or other foreigners who are entitled to preferential access to the labour market under EU law are available (examination of priority), as far as such examination is prescribed by the Employment Ordinance. As for the rest, the legal provisions governing the approval by the Federal Employment Agency shall be applied to the work permit in the absence of any law or statutory instrument to the contrary. The Federal Employment Agency may determine demand-oriented admission figures with regard to approving the granting of a residence title for seasonal work and a seasonal work permit.

§2. DENIAL

1354. Under certain circumstances, the approval of issuing a temporary residence permit to take up employment must or may be denied as is stipulated by section 40 AufenthG.

The approval by the Federal Employment Agency is denied if the employment has been realised through an unlawful placement or recruitment or if the foreigner intends to take up employment as a temporary worker (section 1(1) of the Act on Temporary Employment Businesses).

The approval may be denied if a foreigner has culpably violated section 404(1) or (2), Nos 2–13 of Book Three of the Social Code, sections 10, 10a or 11 of the Act to Combat Clandestine Employment or section 15, 15a or section 16(1), No. 2 of the Act on Temporary Employment Businesses.

Approval may also be denied if there are so-called important personal grounds that relate to the foreigner. Examples of 'important personal grounds' are the pursuit of activities that violate the rights of employees or calling for illegal strikes.

Furthermore, approval may be denied if the future employer or the future employer's representative, as authorised by statutes or law, has been the subject of an incontestable fine within the past five years for a breach of section 404(1) or (2), No. 3 of Book Three of the Social Code, or if either of them has been the subject of an incontestable fine or convicted to a term of imprisonment for a breach of sections 10, 10a or 11 of the Act to Combat Clandestine Employment or of section 15, 15a or section 16(1), No. 2 of the Act on Temporary Employment Businesses. This applies accordingly to the host entity in the case of an ICT.

Approval to issue an ICT Card or a Mobile ICT Card may be denied if the employer or the host entity has failed to meet its legal obligations regarding social security, taxation, labour rights or working conditions. It may also be denied if insolvency proceedings have been instituted against the assets of the undertaking by which the foreigner is employed or against the host entity's assets aiming to wind up the undertaking or the entity and its business. Furthermore, the approval may be denied if the undertaking by which the foreigner is employed or the host entity and its business have been wound up in insolvency proceedings or the institution of insolvency proceedings against the assets of the undertaking by which the foreigner is employed or against the host entity's assets has been refused for lack of assets, and its business has been wound up. Also, the approval may be refused in the case that the undertaking by which the foreigner is employed or the host entity does not pursue any economic activity or the presence of the ICT is aimed at or results in affecting labour management disputes or negotiations.

In all of these cases, as is stipulated in section 41 AufenthG, the approval may be revoked and the seasonal work permit may be withdrawn. This is also the case if the foreigner is employed on less favourable terms than comparable German workers.

Chapter 3. Sanctions Against Illegal Participation in the Labour Market

§1. SANCTIONS AGAINST EMPLOYERS

I. Payment Obligations

1355. While under general rules contracts concluded contrary to legal obligations usually are void, the AufenthG provides for a privileged position of the foreign employee who has been illegally employed. Normally, the employee would not have any right of pay by the employer, because the labour contract would be void since it is illegal. This, however, would privilege the employer who has acted contrary to the law. Also, the foreign worker would in practice need social welfare support by the social authorities. Therefore, section 98a AufenthG provides for a substitute right of pay.

An employer is obliged to pay the agreed remuneration to a foreigner he or she has employed without the required employment authorisation under transitional rules that apply to Member States during the initial period of their membership of the EU (section 284(1) of Book Three of the Social Code) or for which the employer has no authorisation for that foreigner to pursue an economic activity (section 4a(5) AufenthG). For the purpose of remuneration, it is assumed that a foreigner has been employed by the employer for three months; this assumption can be rebutted by the employer.

The agreed remuneration is considered to be the usual remuneration unless the employer agreed a lower or higher remuneration with the foreigner on a permissible basis.

A contractor who has commissioned another contractor to perform work or render services is liable for fulfilling the obligation of the latter contractor in the same way as a surety, which has waived the defence of unexhausted remedies. This means that the first contractor is directly liable and may not refuse to fulfil the obligation until the foreigner has unsuccessfully tried to recover the claims by means of forced execution against the commissioned contractor. The same applies to a contractor who has commissioned another contractor to perform work or render services. The liability does not apply if the contractor provides evidence that he or she was able to assume, on the basis of due diligence, that the employer has not employed any foreigner who lacks the authorisation for employment required under transitional rules for new EU Member States (section 284(1) of Book Three of the Social Code) or the authorisation to pursue an economic activity required (section 4a(5) AufenthG).

A foreigner who has been employed within the scope of application of the AufenthG without the authorisation for employment required under the transitional rules for workers that apply to EU Member States during their initial period of membership of the EU (section 284(1) of Book Three of the Social Code) may institute legal proceedings against his or her former employer before a German court competent in labour matters to uphold his or her right to remuneration. The same applies if a foreigner has been employed without the authorisation required to pursue an economic activity that applies to foreigners in general (section 4a(5) AufenthG).

In all of these cases, the provisions of the Posted Workers Act remain unaffected. These regulate e.g., equal pay, working hours, non-discrimination, and the applicability of collective labour agreements.

II. Administrative Offences

A. *Residence Act*

1356. Several provisions make violations of labour market rules an administrative offence. Some of these administrative offences are found in section 98(2a), Nos 1–4 AufenthG.

Anyone is deemed to have committed an administrative offence who wilfully or recklessly commissions a foreigner on a sustained basis to perform paid work or services for gain if that foreigner may not pursue an economic activity or perform other paid work or services (section 98(2a), No. 1, and section 4a(5), sentence 1 AufenthG). The fine is up to EUR 500,000.

Likewise, a person is deemed to have committed an administrative offence who wilfully or recklessly fails to provide a notification, provides an incorrect notification or fails to provide the required employer notification on short-term mobility ICT in good time (section 98(2a), No. 2, and section 4a(5), sentence 3, No. 3, or section 19a(1), sentence 2 or 3 AufenthG). The fine, here, is up to EUR 30,000.

It is also an administrative offence to wilfully or recklessly fail to provide the required notification or to provide incorrect or incomplete notification or to fail to provide notification in good time of the required employer information on Mobile ICT Card (section 98(2a), No. 3, and section 19d(7) AufenthG). The fine is up to EUR 30,000.

Furthermore, anyone is punishable who wilfully or recklessly does not give the required notification, or does not do so correctly, completely, in the prescribed manner or in good time, if the foreigner does not undertake or discontinues the vocational training for which suspension of deportation has been granted (section 98(2a), No. 4, and section 60a(2), sentence 7 AufenthG). The fine for this administrative offence is up to EUR 30,000.

B. *Social Code*

1357. Further administrative offences in the field of labour law relating to foreigners are punishable according to the terms in section 404 Book Three of the Social Code.

Anyone commits an administrative offence who, as a contractor, commissions another contractor to render services or perform works of whom he or she knows or negligently does not know that this contractor in fulfilling the order employs a foreigner in contravention of section 284(1) Book Three of the Social Code or section

4a(5), sentence 1 AufenthG. The same applies if the contractor commissions a sub-contractor or tolerates that a sub-contractor becomes active who employs a foreigner in contravention of section 284(1) Book Three of the Social Code or section 4a(5), sentence 1 AufenthG. Section 284(1) Book Three of the Social Code refers to citizens of the EU who require a work permit in Germany because the transitional period of their Member State joining the EU has not yet elapsed section 4a(5), sentence 1 AufenthG refers to the required temporary residence title permitting economic activity (section 404(1), No. 1 Book Three of the Social Code).

Furthermore, anyone commits an administrative offence who wilfully or negligently employs a foreigner in contravention of section 284(1) Book Three of the Social Code or section 4a(5), sentence 1 AufenthG. The same applies to anyone who wilfully or negligently does not furnish information correctly in contravention of section 39(4), sentence 2 AufenthG. This latter provision obliges the future or present employer of a foreigner who requires or has obtained approval for such employment to furnish the Federal Employment Agency with information on pay, working hours and other terms and conditions of employment (section 404(1), No. 2 Book Three of the Social Code).

In all of these cases, the offender is liable to a fine up to EUR 500,000.

C. Act on Temporary Employment Businesses

1358. Further administrative offences relating to employment of foreigners are contained in the Act on Temporary Employment Businesses (*Arbeitnehmerüberlassungsgesetz*). Section 16 of the Act on Temporary Employment Businesses provides that anyone commits an administrative offence who wilfully or negligently lets a foreign posted worker become active who is posted to him or her but does not possess the required residence title. The same applies if such foreign posted worker does not hold a permission to remain pending the asylum decision or a suspension of deportation which entitle to economic activity or does not possess a permit pursuant to section 284(1) Book Three of the Social Code. As stated above, section 284(1) Book Three of the Social Code refers to citizens of the EU who require a work permit in Germany because the transitional period of their Member State joining the EU has not yet elapsed. This administrative offence may also be punished with a fine of up to EUR 500,000.

III. Criminal Offences

A. Act to Combat Clandestine Employment

1359. Several laws make violations of rules on the employment of foreigners a criminal offence. This is the case for sections 10, 11 of the Act to Combat Clandestine Employment.

Section 10 of the Act to Combat Clandestine Employment relates to employment of foreigners without permit or without residence title and on unfavourable working conditions. Whosoever commits an act indicated in section 404(2), No. 3 Book

Three of the Social Code, which refers to the work permissions required, and employs the foreigner under working conditions which are in clear discrepancy to those of German workers performing the same or a similar activity is liable to imprisonment up to three years or to a fine. In especially serious cases the penalty is imprisonment from six months to five years. An especially serious case typically occurs if the offender acts on a commercial basis or out of gross self-seeking.

Section 10a of the Act to Combat Clandestine Employment refers to employment of foreigners without residence title who are victims of human trafficking. Anyone is liable to imprisonment of up to three years or to a fine for employing a foreigner who does not possess the required residence title allowing for an economic activity and thereby takes advantage of a situation in which the foreigner is because of a third person's act constituting human trafficking (section 232a(1)–(5) or section 232b of the Criminal Code).

Section 11 of the Act to Combat Clandestine Employment refers to economic activity of foreigners without permit or without residence title on a larger scale or of minor foreigners. Anyone is liable to imprisonment up to one year or a fine who simultaneously employs more than five foreigners who do not possess the required permission to work (section 284(1) Book Three of the Social Code) or commissions them with rendering services or performing works. The same applies to anyone who persistently repeats a wilful act of such employment. It also applies to anyone who persistently repeats a wilful act of not providing the required notification of employment to the authorities (section 98(2a) AufenthG). Equally punishable is anyone who employs a person under 18 years of age who does not possess the required residence title allowing for economic activity. The penalty is up to three years imprisonment or a fine if the offender acts out of gross self-seeking (section 11(2) of the Act to Combat Clandestine Employment).

B. Act on Temporary Employment Businesses

1360. Further criminal offences relating to employment of foreigners are found in sections 15–16 of the Act on Temporary Employment Businesses.

Employment of foreign posted workers without permit is a crime pursuant to section 15 of the Act on Temporary Employment Businesses. This offence is committed by anyone who, as a temporary employment business, supplies a foreigner who does not possess the required residence title, permission to remain pending the asylum decision or a suspension of deportation which entitle to economic activity or who does not possess the required work permit pending the transitional period of a Member State joining the EU (section 284(1) Book Three of the Social Code) to a third person without the required permission (section 1 of the Act on Temporary Employment Businesses). The offender is liable to imprisonment up to three years or to a fine. In especially serious cases the penalty is imprisonment from six months to five years. An especially serious case typically occurs if the offender acts on a commercial basis or out of gross self-seeking.

Hiring of foreigners without permit under serious conditions is a punishable crime pursuant to section 15a of the Act on Temporary Employment Businesses. This crime is committed by anyone who, as the hirer to which a foreigner is posted, lets the foreigner become active under working conditions of the posted workers relationship which are in clear discrepancy to those of German posted workers performing the same or a similar activity if the foreigner does not possess the required residence title, permission to remain pending the asylum decision or a suspension of deportation which entitle to economic activity or does not possess a required work permit pending the transitional period of a Member State joining the EU (section 284(1) Book Three of the Social Code). The offender is liable to imprisonment up to three years or to a fine. In especially serious cases the penalty is imprisonment from six months to five years. An especially serious case typically occurs if the offender acts on a commercial basis or out of gross self-seeking (section 15a(1) of the Act on Temporary Employment Businesses).

Whosoever as a hirer simultaneously lets more than five foreigners become active, who do not possess the required residence title, permission to remain pending the asylum decision or a suspension of deportation which entitle to economic activity or do not possess a required work permit pending the transitional period of a Member State joining the EU (section 284(1) Book Three of the Social Code) is liable to imprisonment of up to one year or a fine. The same applies if the hirer persistently repeats a wilful act of letting the foreigner become active under working conditions of the posted workers relationship which are in clear discrepancy to those of German posted workers performing the same or a similar activity. In both cases, the penalty is imprisonment up to three years or a fine if the offender acts out of gross self-seeking (section 15a(2) of the Act on Temporary Employment Businesses).

IV. Exclusion from Public Subsidies and Contracts

1361. In cases of illegal employment of foreigners, the employer can be excluded from public subsidies, as stipulated in section 98b AufenthG. The authority competent to grant subsidies may reject applications for subsidies (section 264 of the Criminal Code) in full or in part if the applicant or the applicant's representative authorised by statute or law has been subject to an incontestable fine of at least EUR 2,500 under section 404(2), No. 3 of Book Three of the Social Code or has been sentenced to an incontestable prison term of more than three months or a fine in excess of ninety daily rates under sections 10, 10a or 11 of the Act to Combat Clandestine Employment. Fines in German criminal law are calculated in the form of daily rates that take account of the economic situation of the convicted person; thus rich people pay more than poorer people for the equivalent crime.

Such rejections may be issued within a period of up to five years after the incontestable imposition of the fine or prison sentence depending on the severity of the offence for which the fine or prison sentence was imposed.

However, rejection cannot be imposed if a legal entitlement to the subsidy, which is applied for exists. It can also not be imposed if the applicant is a natural person and the employment that caused the offence was for this person's private purposes. The same applies if the offence consisted in the unlawful employment of an EU citizen.

Furthermore, public contracting entities (section 99 of the Act Against Restraints of Competition, *Gesetz gegen Wettbewerbsbeschränkungen*) may exclude a candidate or tenderer from competing for a supply, construction or service contract, if the candidate or tenderer or its representative authorised by statute or law has been subject to an incontestable fine of at least EUR 2,500 under section 404(2), No. 3 of Book Three of the Social Code or has been sentenced to an incontestable prison term of more than three months or a fine in excess of ninety daily rates under section 10, 10a or 11 of the Act to Combat Clandestine Employment (section 98c AufenthG). Until there is proof of restoration of reliability, the candidate or tenderer may be excluded within a period of up to five years after the incontestable imposition of the fine or prison sentence depending on the severity of the offence for which the fine or prison sentence was imposed.

These sanctions do not apply if the offence consisted of the unlawful employment of an EU citizen.

Section 21(2)–(5) of the Posted Workers Act on procedural rules applies accordingly, where a public contracting entity makes use of the possibility of such sanctions.

V. Liability for Costs

1362. Pursuant to section 66(4) AufenthG, anyone who has employed a foreigner who was not permitted to pursue an economic activity under the provisions of the AufenthG is liable for the costs of the foreigner's deportation or removal. The same applies to a contractor for whom an employer has performed services as a direct sub-contractor, if the contractor was aware or should have been aware, if the contractor had exercised due diligence, that the employer has hired a foreigner, who was not permitted to pursue the economic activity under the provisions of the AufenthG as an employee, to perform that service. Equally liable is the prime contractor or intermediate contractor without a direct contractual relationship with the employer who is aware of the employment of a foreigner who was not permitted to pursue that economic activity under the provisions of the AufenthG.

Liability of the employer (section 66(4) No. 1 AufenthG) is to be waived if the employer has fulfilled his or her obligations of verification and notification (section 4a(5) AufenthG), section 28a of Book Four of the Social Code in conjunction with sections 6, 7 and 13 of the Data Collection and Transfer Ordinance or pursuant to section 18 of the Posted Workers Act, unless the employer was aware that the foreigner's residence title or the certificate confirming permission to remain pending the asylum decision or confirming suspension of deportation was forged.

§2. SANCTIONS AGAINST WORKERS

I. Administrative Offences

1363. Foreigners engaging in employment without the required permission may be liable to an administrative fine under Book Three of the Social Code.

Anyone who wilfully or negligently pursues an economic activity as a worker whilst not possessing the necessary work permit pending the transitional period of a Member State joining the EU or a residence title, which entitles its holder to engage in economic activity commits an administrative offence. The administrative fine may be up to EUR 5,000 (section 404(2), No. 4, and (3), and section 284(1) of Book Three of the Social Code, and specified in section 4a(3), sentence 4 and (4), section 6(2a), section 7(1), sentence 4, first half sentence, section 16a(3), sentence 1, section 16b(3), also in conjunction with (7), sentence 3, section 16b(5), sentence 3, second half sentence, section 16c(2), sentence 3, section 16d(1), sentence 4, (3), sentence 2 and (4), sentence 3, section 16f(3), sentence 4, section 17(3), sentence 1, section 20(1), sentence 4, also in conjunction with (2), sentence 2, section 23(1), sentence 4, first half sentence and section 25(4), sentence 3, first half sentence, (4a), sentence 4 first half sentence and (4b), sentence 4, first half sentence AufenthG).

II. Criminal Offences

A. Residence Act

1364. Foreign workers may be liable to criminal punishment if they engage in economic activities without the required permission.

Whoever wilfully engages in employment without the necessary work permit pending the transitional period of a Member State joining the EU or the necessary residence title which entitles to engage in economic activity, who requires a residence title in order to reside in Germany and only possesses a residence title in the form of a Schengen visa is liable to imprisonment up to one year or a fine (section 95(1a) AufenthG, sections 284(1) and 404(2), No. 4 Book Three of the Social Code, and specified in section 4a(3), sentence 4 and (4), section 6(2a), section 7(1), sentence 4, first half sentence, section 16a(3), sentence 1, section 16b(3), also in conjunction with (7), sentence 3, section 16b(5), sentence 3, second half sentence, section 16c(2), sentence 3, section 16d(1), sentence 4, (3), sentence 2 and (4), sentence 3, section 16f(3), sentence 4, section 17(3), sentence 1, section 20(1), sentence 4, also in conjunction with (2), sentence 2, section 23(1), sentence 4, first half sentence and section 25(4), sentence 3, first half sentence, (4a), sentence 4 first half sentence and (4b), sentence 4, first half sentence AufenthG).

B. Act to Combat Clandestine Employment

1365. The Act to Combat Clandestine Employment contains criminal law provisions that apply to foreigners pursuing an employment without a permit or without residence title on a larger scale in section 11.

Whoever persistently repeats a wilful act of pursuing employment not possessing the necessary work permit pending the transitional period of a Member State joining the EU or the necessary residence title which entitles to engage in economic activity is liable to imprisonment of up to one year or a fine (section 11(1), No. 2 of the Act to Combat Clandestine Employment, section 404(2), No. 4, and (3), and section 284(1) of Book Three of the Social Code, section 98(2a), No. 1, and (3), No. 1, and specified in section 4a(3), sentence 4 and (4), section 6(2a), section 7(1), sentence 4, first half sentence, section 16a(3), sentence 1, section 16b(3), also in conjunction with (7), sentence 3, section 16b(5), sentence 3, second half sentence, section 16c(2), sentence 3, section 16d(1), sentence 4, (3), sentence 2 and (4), sentence 3, section 16f(3), sentence 4, section 17(3), sentence 1, section 20(1), sentence 4, also in conjunction with (2), sentence 2, section 23(1), sentence 4, first half sentence and section 25(4), sentence 3, first half sentence, (4a), sentence 4 first half sentence and (4b), sentence 4, first half sentence AufenthG).

Chapter 4. Legal Remedies and Procedural Safeguards

1366. The same legal remedies and procedural safeguards apply in the context of employment of foreigners as do to foreigners in general and Germans in this matter.

Part VIII. Access to Self-Employed Activities

Chapter 1. Overview of Applicable Legislation

1367. Various provisions in the AufenthG provide general rules on self-employment of foreigners. These provisions are complemented by provisions in the Act to Combat Clandestine Employment. The Ordinance on Employment also contains provisions relevant for self-employed foreigners.

Chapter 2. Conditions for Entitlement to Work in the Country as a Self-Employed

§1. GENERAL CONDITIONS

1368. The conditions for economic activities as a self-employed person have already been dealt with in the chapter on independent economic activities.[119]

§2. ADMINISTRATIVE RULES AND PROCEDURES

1369. The relevant administrative rules and procedures for economic activities as a self-employed person have already been dealt with in the chapter on independent economic activities.[120]

§3. CONDITIONS FOR SPECIAL CATEGORIES OF SELF-EMPLOYED

1370. The conditions for engaging in special categories of self-employment have already been dealt with in the chapter on independent economic activities.[121]

---

119. *See* Part III, Ch. 4, §3 and §4.
120. *See* Part III, Ch. 4, §3.
121. *See* Part III, Ch. 4, §3.

Chapter 3. Sanctions Against Illegal Exercise of Self-Employment

§1. Administrative Offences

1371. Anyone is deemed to have committed an administrative offence who wilfully or negligently pursues a self-employed activity not possessing the necessary residence title, which entitles to engage in economic activity. The fine may be up to EUR 5,000 (section 98(3), and specified in section 4a(3), sentence 4 and (4), section 6(2a), section 7(1), sentence 4, first half sentence, section 16a(3), sentence 1, section 16b(3), also in conjunction with (7), sentence 3, section 16b(5), sentence 3, second half sentence, section 16c(2), sentence 3, section 16d(1), sentence 4, (3), sentence 2 and (4), sentence 3, section 16f(3), sentence 4, section 17(3), sentence 1, section 20(1), sentence 4, also in conjunction with (2), sentence 2, section 23(1), sentence 4, first half sentence and section 25(4), sentence 3, first half sentence, (4a), sentence 4 first half sentence and (4b), sentence 4, first half sentence AufenthG).

§2. Criminal Offences

I. Residence Act

1372. Illegal self-employment of foreigners can qualify as a criminal offence pursuant to the AufenthG.

Whosoever wilfully pursues a self-employed activity not possessing the necessary residence title which entitles to engage in economic activity who requires a residence title in order to reside in Germany and only possesses a residence title in the form of a Schengen visa is liable to imprisonment up to one year or a fine (sections 95(1a), 98(3), No. 1, and as specified in section 4a(3), sentence 4 and (4), section 6(2a), section 7(1), sentence 4, first half sentence, section 16a(3), sentence 1, section 16b(3), also in conjunction with (7), sentence 3, section 16b(5), sentence 3, second half sentence, section 16c(2), sentence 3, section 16d(1), sentence 4, (3), sentence 2 and (4), sentence 3, section 16f(3), sentence 4, section 17(3), sentence 1, section 20(1), sentence 4, also in conjunction with (2), sentence 2, section 23(1), sentence 4, first half sentence and section 25(4), sentence 3, first half sentence, (4a), sentence 4 first half sentence and (4b), sentence 4, first half sentence AufenthG).

II. Act to Combat Clandestine Employment

1373. The Act to Combat Clandestine Employment also contains criminal law provisions foreigners pursuing a self-employed activity without the required residence title on a larger scale.

Whosoever persistently repeats a wilful act of pursuing a self-employed activity not possessing the necessary residence title which entitles to engage in economic activity is liable to imprisonment up to one year or a fine (section 11(1), No. 2 of the Act to Combat Clandestine Employment, section 98(3), No. 1 and specified in section 4a(3), sentence 4 and (4), section 6(2a), section 7(1), sentence 4, first half sentence, section 16a(3), sentence 1, section 16b(3), also in conjunction with (7), sentence 3, section 16b(5), sentence 3, second half sentence, section 16c(2), sentence 3, section 16d(1), sentence 4, (3), sentence 2 and (4), sentence 3, section 16f(3), sentence 4, section 17(3), sentence 1, section 20(1), sentence 4, also in conjunction with (2), sentence 2, section 23(1), sentence 4, first half sentence and section 25(4), sentence 3, first half sentence, (4a), sentence 4 first half sentence and (4b), sentence 4, first half sentence AufenthG).

Chapter 4. Legal Remedies and Procedural Safeguards

1374. There are no special provisions on legal remedies and procedural safeguards that apply to independent economic activities of foreigners. They are subject to the same remedies and safeguards that apply to foreigners in general and Germans in relation to self-employment.

Selected Bibliography

Jan Bergmann & Klaus Dienelt, Ausländerrecht: Aufenthaltsgesetz, Freizügigkeitsgesetz/EU und ARB 1/80 (Auszug), Grundrechtecharta und Artikel 16a GG, Asylgesetz, 13th ed., 2020.

Harald Dörig (ed.), Handbuch Migrations- und Integrationsrecht, 2nd ed., 2020.

Roland Fritz & Jürgen Vollmeier, Gemeinschaftskommentar zum Asylgesetz und Gemeinschaftskommentar zum Aufenthaltsgesetz, 2013 et seq.

Kay Hailbronner, Asyl- und Ausländerrecht, 4th ed., 2016.

Bertold Huber, Johannes Eichenhofer & Pauline Endres de Oliveira, Aufenthaltsrecht, 2017.

Winfried Kluth & Andreas Heusch (eds), Ausländerrecht, 2nd ed., 2021.

Reinhard Marx, Aufenthalts-, Asyl- und Flüchtlingsrecht: Handbuch, 7th ed., 2020.

Hubert Meyer, Klaus Ritgen & Roland Schäfer, Handbuch Flüchtlingsrecht und Integration, 2nd ed., 2018.

Rudolf Schiedermair & Michael Wollenschläger, Handbuch des Ausländerrechts der Bundesrepublik Deutschland, 2019 et seq.

Selected Bibliography

Index

Index

Index

Index